RADIO FREE EUROPE AND THE PURSUIT OF DEMOCRACY

GEORGE R. URBAN

Radio Free Europe and the Pursuit of Democracy

My War Within the Cold War

Yale University Press
New Haven & London

Published with assistance from the Louis Stern Memorial Fund.

Designed by James J. Johnson and set in Aster Roman and Syntax types by Tseng Information Systems, Durham, North Carolina.
Printed in the United States of America by Vail-Ballou Press, Binghamton, New York.

Library of Congress Cataloging-in-Publication Data

Urban, George R., 1921–
Radio Free Europe and the pursuit of democracy : My war within the cold war /
George R. Urban.
p.   cm.
Includes bibliographical references and index.
ISBN 0-300-06921-9 (cloth: alk. paper)

1. Radio in propaganda—History—20th century.   2. Radio Free Europe—History—20th century.   3. International broadcasting—History—20th century.   4. Cold War—History.
I. Title.
HE8697.8.U73   1997
384.54'094—dc21   97-20926

A catalogue record for this book is available from the British Library.

10   9   8   7   6   5   4   3   2   1

This volume is dedicated to those of my friends and former colleagues in Radio Free Europe, Radio Liberty, and the European Service of the British Broadcasting Corporation whose names do not appear here but who spent their working lives—largely unknown to the Western public—in the pursuit of a more just and humane order in Central Europe and on the territories of the former Soviet Union during the Cold War.

Contents

Preface

Before inviting the reader to delve into the unquiet waters of international broadcasting during the Cold War, I must say a word about the structure of Western foreign broadcasting between the end of World War II and 1994, when Radio Free Europe, the flagship of the Western effort, began to be drastically reduced in preparation for being eliminated altogether.

Two kinds of broadcasting in the national languages of Eastern Europe and the former Soviet Union existed and to some extent still exist in the Western world. The first sort comprised stations representing the national interests and cultures of Western governments and societies: the British Broadcasting Corporation's European Service, the Voice of America, and at different times, French Radio, Vatican Radio, Deutsche Welle, and various smaller stations. Their purpose was to pursue national diplomacy by other means, and their brief was to "project" their nations. Naturally, their broadcasters took a sympathetic interest in the fortunes of the people they were addressing, but their mission was essentially confined to capturing the respect and goodwill of their audiences on behalf of French, American, British, or German national interests in foreign policy, trade, and culture.

The second sort, which had an entirely different purpose, included Radio Free Europe and Radio Liberty. These were American-sponsored but distinctly Polish, Czech, Hungarian, Russian, Romanian, Bulgarian, or Ukrainian national radio stations—"surrogate" in the sense that their broadcasters identified fully with the interests, culture, history, and religion of the nations under Soviet or Soviet-inspired rule. Speaking in the first person plural, they articulated the kind of opinions that free media would have done had a free press, radio, and television existed under the Soviet dispensation and were in effect national "home" services speaking from abroad.

The two "surrogate Radios"—Radio Free Europe and Radio Liberty —began broadcasting in 1951–52 from Munich, with U.S. government funding but without editorial supervision by any government department, despite their connection with the Central Intelligence Agency up until 1971.

My own association with Radio Free Europe falls into four phases. Between 1960 and 1965 I was a middle-ranking executive in one of the research departments and then head of the Radio University programmes; between 1970 and 1982 I served as a political writer and consultant with my base in Britain; between 1983 and 1986 I was the director of Radio Free Europe; and between 1986 and 1991, I resumed working as a consultant from my retirement in Britain. Several of my publications originated in Radio Free Europe broadcasts during the period between 1970 and 1993. Interspersed with these activities were visiting fellowships in Soviet and East European Studies at Harvard University, Indiana University, and the University of Southern California.

This book does not purport to be a history of Radio Free Europe, much less a history of Western foreign broadcasting since World War II. It is confined to the story and issues connected with my work for the Radio, and especially the climate in which my colleagues and I operated on the eve of the demise of the Soviet system and empire.

Acknowledgements

For invaluable practical assistance I am indebted to Richard H. Cummings, A. Russell Poole, Karel Kasparek, and Petronella Gaal, formerly of Radio Free Europe/Radio Liberty. My manuscript editor, Susan Abel, and Jonathan Brent, director of the series Annals of Communism, both of Yale University Press, were most helpful in subjecting my text to a meticulously detailed scrutiny.

I have incurred a debt to Devon Gaffney Cross for solidarity and advice.

My particular thanks are due to Frank Shakespeare for friendship and encouragement.

RADIO FREE EUROPE AND THE PURSUIT OF DEMOCRACY

Introduction

This volume is about a war that did not happen—not on land, not at sea, not in the air. It has come to be known as the Cold War but it has a better claim to be remembered as World War III, for it flowed organically from the twin disasters of World Wars I and II and the fundamental reorganisation of the European power structure that followed the second. But it was a real war in another sense, too. The magnitude of the resources committed; the ferocity of the enmities and the subversion generated; the casualties and dislocations exacted in Korea, East Germany, Poland, Hungary, and Czechoslovakia; and the sheer length of the ideological polarisation which gripped our entire planet were unmistakable signs of a bitter conflict that was a war in all senses except for the shooting.

The results of the conflict, too, were unmistakably characteristic of a great conflagration, for at the end of it, in 1989 through 1991, the Soviet sociopolitical system lay in ruins, the Soviet economy had been rendered impotent, and the Soviet empire had disintegrated. All the objectives of a shooting war had been achieved without—on our side—major human sacrifices. Carl von Clausewitz never asked for more; nor could we have done better.

What was most astonishing about this war was its wholly unconventional character: words, ideas, perceptions, papal visits, foreign travel; arguments about "shopping baskets," economic pressures, the correct interpretation of the Marxist canons, and other "soft" means in our repertoire sufficed to accelerate the erosion, and then to play a material part in bringing about the self-destruction, of an outwardly confident, ideologically arrogant, and nuclear-armed superpower. And the men in command of these tools were neither generals nor admirals but historians and economists, Kremlin watchers and intelligence ana-

1

lysts, writers and poets, songwriters and fashion designers, diplomats and the scholarly creators of the threat—though not of the operational reality—of the American Strategic Defense Initiative. For the first time in history, the power of ideas and perceptions was being systematically deployed over a long period, not as an adjunct to military action but as a weapon in its own right—a weapon that proved effective enough to decide the outcome of the war when skilfully brought to bear on the domestic contradictions and miscalculations that were tearing the heart out of the Soviet system.

Within the unconventional confines of this war, however, another and even more unconventional factor was working for its success. Although financed from the public purse, the most telling and cost-effective instruments of this war were in the hands of semiprivate agencies only loosely or nominally controlled by Western governments. This "privatisation" of much of the Cold War had striking advantages. It enabled the Western democracies to pit flexible institutions of great as well as subtle intellectual and political power against the rigid, totalitarian information and disinformation organs of the Soviet (and Chinese) side. Among those flexible Western institutions were Radio Free Europe, Radio Liberation—later called Radio Liberty, certain international trade union organisations (in a different category), the foreign-language services of the BBC, with their own brand of sophistication and very considerable editorial freedom, and the Congress for Cultural Freedom, with its worldwide network of influential journals.

That a number of these were, for a time, funded by appropriations from the budget of the U.S. Central Intelligence Agency reduced but did not undermine their authenticity. Indeed, in some cases the suspicion and then the certain knowledge of CIA support added to the force of their message, for many in the Soviet domains liked to feel that the "private" voices heard on Western airwaves were expressing more than the nostalgia of exiles or undisclosed factional interests.

Of course, the privatisation of Western political warfare carried its own penalties, as we know from the disturbing story of the 1956 Hungarian Revolution, examined in this volume. But the overall merit of putting the Cold War predominantly into unofficial hands, and more particularly of encouraging "surrogate" broadcasters to speak to Russians *as* Russians, Poles *as* Poles, Czechs *as* Czechs, greatly outweighed the risks of privatisation. In no other way would it have been possible to undermine self-confidence within the dictatorial communist nomenklaturas or support ordinary citizens in their persuasion that they were being unjustly and unfairly governed. State Department prose and Foreign Office handouts would just not have filled the bill. The unimpressive record, throughout the Cold War, of the European language services of the Voice of America is proof enough of the unsuitability of bureaucratic micromanagement in cases where elusive factors such as political allegiance, private ethics, rules of public conduct, educational preferences, faith, national identity, and the like, have to be weighed and addressed in diverse cultural environments.

Even the privately organised surrogate broadcasters of Radio Free Europe and Radio Liberty did not always find it easy to stay in phase with East and Central European national sentiments or to guide them constructively. The complicated process of speaking to twenty nations (in as many languages), each with its proud traditions and aspirations, was strewn with natural pitfalls. Only complete editorial freedom, painstaking background research, and thoughtful leadership, away from the politicking of Western capitals and émigré politics, could ensure a kind of broadcasting in which the national interests both of those addressed in the East and of the funding nations in the West could be kept in tolerable harmony.

Such thoughtfulness and such leadership, however, were hard to come by—partly because the process for selecting leading personnel was weighted in favour of run-of-the-mill members of the American bureaucratic establishment, and partly because Western, and especially American, national sentiments were no easier to gauge than those in the Soviet Union and its glacis. American public opinion—to the extent any existed about obscure issues of foreign policy in faraway Eastern Europe—was, in fact, the opinion of members of the East Coast intelligentsia, and many of these, unlike the average citizen, were nursing long cultural and historical memories, most of them hostile to European conceptions of national identity and nationhood.

Radio Liberty's identification with the interests and feelings of the Russian nation drew fire from American intellectuals and journalists much more readily than Radio Free Europe did for *its* identification with Poles, Czechs, and Hungarians. Russian national sentiment was suspect in the eyes of these American critics because Russian history was suspect. Steeped as they thought Russian history was in the spirit of autocracy and orthodoxy, with few democratic episodes to make it palatable to the modern Western mind, numerous members of the American intellectual establishment looked upon the Russian legacy as something Radio Liberty should scrupulously avoid embracing. Whatever the rights and wrongs of that judgement, it did have an impact and made it exceptionally difficult for Radio Liberty to perform its mission as a Russian "home service."

The successful pursuit of the Cold War and certain American domestic preferences were now in conflict—something the KGB was not slow to exploit. Indeed, as will appear from these pages, the KGB played a significant role both in inventing and then in fanning the flames of the conflict. Radio Liberty's plea that it was building on the democratic elements in Russian culture and history fell on deaf ears among its critics. Whenever it was hewing to what were thought to be anticommunist Russian feelings and perceptions, Radio Liberty stood accused of promoting the case of Russian traditionalists and antidemocrats and even of anti-Semites. If and when it stuck to the dissemination of news and press comment, it was jeopardising its raison d'être as unofficial surrogate radio. Here was a dilemma never resolved and, arguably, incapable of resolution.

If the American purpose was—as it was—to turn the Russian public against the communist dictatorship by appealing to national sentiment, then it was a sign of considerable immaturity for the U.S. political class to argue that no such appeal should be financed with American tax dollars, because Russian national sentiment and the spirit of Russian history were not in line with liberal thinking at American universities. To maintain consistency in such matters is commendable in an academic vacuum, but it does not win wars—not even Cold Wars. If Stalin was an acceptable ally in America's war against Hitler, Americans had no moral justification to balk at cautiously exploiting Russian national consciousness in their long and lethal conflict with the Soviet system.

Another debilitating factor, too, was gnawing away at the roots of Radio Liberty's mission: the Radio was under orders to pursue what amounted to incompatible policies. In 1951–52 the founding fathers recognised that the character of unofficial radio addressed to countries under imported communist rule and Soviet control in the middle of Europe had to be very different from the kind of broadcasting transmitted to the people of a victorious great power whose institutions were enjoying fairly broad, if grudging, public support. Wisely, they established two separate broadcasting organisations—Radio Free Europe (the senior service) for the satellite countries, and Radio Liberation (later Liberty) for the Soviet Union.

But the same founding fathers failed to make another distinction.

They did not openly acknowledge that the Soviet Union was a colonial empire and that the sort of message addressed to the union's non-Russian nations and nationalities would have to be different from—indeed antithetical to—that broadcast to the Russian nation. Had they done so, they would have had to go one step further and recognise the need for one surrogate broadcasting authority for Russia and another for Ukraine and the other non-Russian republics, nations, and nationalities, including the Baltic states. But they did not. Perhaps, in the first stages of the Cold War, setting up a separate broadcasting authority for Russia's colonial possessions would have seemed too provocative to American public opinion or too damaging to American-Soviet relations, for it would have implied that the long-term strategy of the United States was the disruption of the territorial integrity, if not the actual dismemberment, of the Soviet Union. This was a topic barred at the time from public discussion. Indeed, throughout the Cold War, and more specifically after 1976, both Radio Liberty and Radio Free Liberty were under orders neither to encourage separatist or secessional movements nor to raise territorial issues within the USSR,[1] and the policy was strictly adhered to. At the same time, the two Radios' guidelines laid it down that Radio Liberty should sympathise "with the right of all national groups to thrive, to be able to display pride in their historical and cultural achievements, and to express themselves in their own language. RL [Radio Liberty] also supports the right of individuals freely to assert their national origins as well as their religious and political convictions and to be secure against discrimination on these accounts."[2] But the rule book did not say how all this could be amicably achieved in the teeth of a relentlessly despotic and Russo-centric superstate.

In the event, the policy problems posed by Russia-versus-the-rest-of-the-empire were conveniently ignored and kept out of public view. Radio Liberty's fourteen (originally nineteen, then eighteen) language services were subsumed under a single heading and subjected to a single broadcasting ethos as well as a single management. Radio Liberty, though staffed by Americans, employed, astonishingly, Russian as its working language.

Worse, in 1976 under unenlightened congressional pressure and the exigencies of détente, Radio Free Europe and Radio Liberty were administratively amalgamated and subjected to joint policy guidelines. A grotesque state of affairs now arose at the two Radios' headquarters in Munich: both the Central European victims of Soviet control and political tutelage and the Soviet beneficiaries of that control and tutelage were addressed by "RFE/RL" *tout court*, from the same premises, under a single board, a consolidated management, and a joint president, even though the political identity of the two Radios was preserved. Détente and arms control were the "exciting" issues in Washington in those days; offending the Kremlin had to be kept within strict limits. There was a premium on smoothing away moral distinctions.

Despite valiant efforts to overcome it by successive teams of executives, the conceptual confusion at the heart of Radio Liberty's mandate jeopardised its execution to the end of the Cold War. The United States did, of course, want to weaken the Soviet empire, but it did so slowly, hesitantly, away from the public gaze, and with a characteristically guilty conscience. That the Radio nevertheless performed as well as it did was owing to the dedication of some of its directors (notably the unflinching George Bailey, at the time of my tenure) and their flexible interpretation of their brief. But compared with the penetrating influence Radio Free Europe attained in Eastern and Central Europe, Radio Liberty's performance was disappointing. The multiplicity of purposes it was called upon to serve was a true reflection of the changing moods of members of the American political class and of their wavering resolve about whether—and to what extent and in what way—they wanted to see the power and influence of the Soviet system and the Soviet Union globally eliminated.

Radio Free Europe was free from such inner conflicts and thus easier to handle. All nations within its radius of operation had been independent before the Soviet takeover, and every one of them was eager to regain its national sovereignty as well as its freedom of choice in the domestic area. In clear distinction to the dominant tradition in Russia and Ukraine, the indigenous roots of authoritarianism and dictatorship were not uniformly strong in the nations addressed by Radio Free Europe, and some—notably the Czechs, Hungarians, Poles, and Estonians—seemed likely to be able to reactivate the spirit of democratic traditions and decency in public life.

The Cold War had not one but two objectives: promoting the self-destruction of the Soviet system without war and preventing the revival of intolerant nationalisms and thus the return of instability in Europe. Looking back at this trial of strength from a postcommunist vantage point, we can, I believe, safely claim that the first of these objectives has been fully, and it is to be hoped lastingly, achieved. The second, however, only partly so. Readers of this volume will note how desperately the men and women in charge of Cold War broadcasting were trying to achieve the second objective as well—some because they were fervent supporters of European unification, as I was, others because after the ravages of communist rule the spirit of reconstruction demanded no less.

In hinting at partial failure, I do not, of course, have in mind that of surrogate broadcasting but rather the failure of Western, and especially West European, statesmanship to deal with the war in former Yugoslavia. A look at the map of Eastern and Central Europe shows that the countries Radio Free Europe was addressing have, so far at least, escaped civil strife and war in the aftermath of the collapse of the Soviet empire.

Radio Free Europe's founders had kept Yugoslavia out of our catchment area on the argument that, after its expulsion from the Cominform in 1948, Tito's realm was, in effect, on the Western side of the power equation and thus no appropriate target for surrogate broadcasting. This was a power-political stand of consummate cynicism, for the early Titoist record on human rights was especially nauseating; but it was possible to make that stand so long as Stalinism was riding high in the Soviet Union and any fissure in the ranks of the world communist movement was greatly to the Western advantage. But as tensions gradually built up in Yugoslavia after the death of Tito, it was no longer justifiable to prevent Radio Free Europe from addressing the South Slavic nations—or the Albanians, either in Kosovo or in Albania itself. Yet Radio Free Europe was kept out of the area, regardless, as though the world had stood still since Tito's funeral.

Hypothetical questions are hard to answer: Would the Serbian aggression and the genocidal civil war have taken a different course had Radio Free Europe been empowered, in good time, to use its pacifying influence among the South Slavs in much the same way as it had in defusing the potential for conflict between Czechs and Slovaks, Hungarians and Romanians throughout the Cold War? We cannot tell, but I like to believe that our mere presence on the airwaves would have brought the power of the United States and the weight of the European Community close to the minds of all South Slavs and acted, to put it no higher, as a moderating influence.

Here, certain metahistorical questions confront the communicator. Are nations and societies "teachable"? Do they profit from their experiences? Under what conditions are collective memories aroused or

dissipated? How do national stereotypes arise and how are they overcome? At what point do national culture and national identity threaten
to turn into national exclusiveness and xenophobia? At what level of
escalation do words become deeds?

These are questions of burning relevance in the light of the postcommunist state of the former Yugoslavia and the former Soviet empire—and scholars have no good answers to them, any more than do
the nations and societies most affected. Between 1990 and 1996, in
almost every successor state, communists, neocommunists, and members of the old nomenklaturas retained positions of power or rose to
power in free elections. In Russia itself, freely elected communists and
extreme nationalists dominate the state duma; in March 1996, they
voted overwhelmingly to renounce the dissolution of the Soviet Union
and to re-create it.

How do these astonishing developments square with our libertarian
expectations during the Cold War? They do not; we are puzzled. If decades of oppression and mismanagement have not immunised the majority of Russians and East and Central Europeans against "socialism"
and the men who ruled them in its name—what will? Could the elec-
torate's apparent preference for a qualified sort of authoritarianism be
ascribed exclusively to the poor performance of the free market? To the
ugly face of capitalism? To the nonarrival in short order of the good
society? Would a fat Russian be more supportive of liberal democracy
than a lean Russian? Such, if endorsed by evidence, would be our most
hopeful (if slightly marxisant) explanations, for they would imply that
prosperity is a universal solvent of conflicts and a key to moderating
extremism and folly. But there is no such evidence.

Our perplexity does not end there. How do we explain the return of
a deeper malaise: the spectacular revival of the superior force of race
and religion over reason and compromise—of national short-termism
over investment in the larger good of the area and of Europe? In the
Balkans, and over large swathes of ex-Soviet territory, old prejudices
and enmities have robustly survived under the permafrost of totalitarian rule. The thirst for revenge for (real or imagined) wrongs suffered
has been quietly transmitted from generation to generation. A high lit-
eracy rate and long schooling (I purposely avoid the word *education*)
have done nothing to civilise those who would not be civilised; and in
this vile brew there also survives in a rather fitting combination the
spirit of Lenin's call for "the logic of the axe"—for a state of affairs
"totally unlimited by any laws, absolutely unrestrained by any regula-

tions, and based directly on the use of force."[3] Sarajevo, genocide, and Zhirinovsky are more likely to be remembered as the true symbols of the postcommunist era than any new world order or the preposterous notion that in 1989 through 1991 history "came to an end."

But this sobering state of affairs is balanced by significant lessons of a more hopeful character. Aldous Huxley's, Yevgeny Zamyatin's, and George Orwell's forecasts of a uniform and brainwashed totalitarian society have been extremely wide of the mark. Brainwashing by indoctrination did not work. Orwell's Big Brother did his best, but his best was not good enough. He failed, it is true, at a huge price in lives and the values of culture, but his failure has been so spectacular that the nonmaterialisation of *Nineteen Eighty-Four* constitutes, in my judgement, the single most important psychopolitical event of our century. After decades of Soviet or Soviet-inspired rule, the man in the street in Prague, Budapest, or St. Petersburg is no more depersonalised or regimented than are his democracy-bred counterparts in Paris or New York, and probably less so. His brain has not been washed—it is rather the work of his mentors and minders that has been flushed away by the rapid reassertion of plain common sense. Agitprop has proved to be a more profound vaccination against propaganda than anything Madison Avenue has yet managed to inflict on Americans.

We may now tentatively predict that ideological dictatorships still active or yet to come will not have to be toppled by war, as some had to be in the past. Exposed to the impact of instantaneous electronic communications—especially radio, the Internet, and television—and to the more undetectable influence of economic contamination, they are more likely to implode than to explode—more likely to suffer from their inability to retreat into intellectual and political isolation than to seek stability at home by taking strong-arm action abroad.

A sample of three or four is, of course, too small to extrapolate from; yet I would hazard the forecast that in the more distant future, too, ideologically based totalitarian systems, once put under appropriate pressure, are more likely to be eroded by their own absurdities than to challenge us to war. If true, this is an inference of some importance. It may, of course, not apply to authoritarian nation states driven by the traditional goals of expansionism and empire building or, it hardly needs saying, to totalitarian and command societies deliberately kept afloat with Western assistance in order to satisfy this or that economic interest or power calculus. Communist China may yet survive with Western connivance; so might a revamped Russian national empire.

But I am confident that the key to the rise and demise of ideologically based totalitarian societies in their pure form is now in our possession.

I end these prefatory observations on a personal note. *Propaganda*, in contemporary usage, has acquired deeply pejorative connotations. In part, the word has been brought low by the spurious claims and intrusive presentation of commercial advertising; but the principal causes of the odium attaching to it are Stalin, Zhdanov, Mussolini, the fascist *Balilla* youth organisation, Hitler, Goebbels, and the Maoist disseminators of ideological misrepresentation. Under their semantic hegemony, the word *propaganda* became synonymous with the deliberate manipulation of people, facts, and ideas. In many cases propaganda resulted in the rule of fanaticism, in the *Gleichschaltung* of the individual and his institutions, and even in the physical consumption of the bodies of the class enemy, as during the Chinese Cultural Revolution. The seventeenth-century Catholic conception of propaganda as the supervision of Christian teaching abroad has all but vanished.

I like to think that the work my colleagues and I were performing in international broadcasting during "World War III" was of an entirely different—indeed of an antithetical—kind, and that the notion of propaganda is wholly inadequate to describe it. We sought to impart a sense of the "right measure of things" to the communist world across the whole range of human activities; we hoped to make it easier for our audiences to distinguish reality from illusion, facts from fabrications, ideas consonant with a dignified and life-enhancing conception of man and the human environment from ideas neutral or hostile to them. In so doing, we never shrank from criticising our own side where criticism was due.

Long before Pope John Paul II magisterially restated an old verity in *Veritatis Splendor* in 1993, many of us had deeply believed that certain forms of evil—killing, mutilation, physical and mental torture, humiliation, coercion, deportation, the instigation and cultivation of hatred—were wrongs so great and so obviously in conflict with human nature that they could not and should not be relativised, much less excused, by any reference to historical necessity, social deprivation, or orders from above. Such abuses were intrinsically evil and had to be rejected in war as in peace. So, with very rare exceptions, had the notion that ends, "in an imperfect world," justify means. My support of the Nuremberg war crimes tribunal followed from such considerations, despite the Nuremberg procedure's flawed legal basis and the even more questionable participation of the Soviet judiciary. It was on those same principles that I opposed the Soviet system and made "propaganda" in the hope of bringing about its fall.

All statements about man and his place in society and history are, in the last analysis, moral statements. The Soviet system and the Soviet state were, in my judgement, evil from their inception because they were institutionalised expressions of the spirit of hatred writ large in the theory of the class struggle, in the name of which an astonishingly crude but deadly ethical relativism was decreed, promoted, and enforced. "Revolutionary morality," "socialist legality," and "revolutionary justice" were but some of its more awesome manifestations. If the system was to work, any and all means to promote it were permissible. "We do not believe in eternal morality," Lenin said in a speech to the Young Communists in 1919, "and we are exposing the deception of all the fairy tales about morality."[4] The resulting corruption of meanings and feelings, and the suspension of our innate sense of justice and equity, constituted in their joint effect a form of barbarism that was new to the human experience.

Rerum cognoscere causas[5]—to understand the causes of things—is important but not enough. Every now and then, as Karl Marx famously observed, we also have to do something about those causes. Marx did and won through Lenin one victory. But we in the West, too, did something about those causes, in the Cold War, and won another victory—over Marx and Lenin. I was fortunate to be part of that Western effort, on a limited front, but fully stretched. My regret is that my colleagues and I had to spend so much of our time and energy fighting off the mischief of those who seemed, formally at least, to be on our side of the conflict but had in reality come under the spell of the Soviet system and who became its apologists. The moral neutrality, and often direct hostility, of an opinion-making segment of the American intelligentsia was a more serious hindrance to our work than anything the Soviet side was able to do to thwart us. We had in effect to do battle on two fronts, and we won two separate contests—it remains to be seen how lastingly.

CHAPTER ONE

Preparations

M y eyes remained dry when the Soviet system finally imploded; yet I felt a curious pang of loss. A sparring partner who had in some ways served me well had fallen by the wayside. A predictable foe beyond the hills, often heard but seldom seen, had paradoxically been a source of reassurance. Having a great enemy had been almost as good as having a great friend and—at times of disaffection within our own ranks—arguably better. A friend was a friend, but a good adversary was a vocation. Or was it, I sometimes wondered, that my long preoccupation with the "dialectic" had so thoroughly infected me that I could imagine no life beyond an adversarial one? The reader will judge.

It was not that my contrapuntal relationship with communism responded to some deeply felt need in my character. The compulsion to argue, fence, and fight, almost regardless of the objectives, was not the force that drove me—although it was, all too clearly, the motivation that fuelled some of my friends and colleagues in the Cold War. But even I was taken aback when the ground began to shake around the Soviet system and empire. Would they be swallowed up by their own incompetence without a final knock-out blow from us? Would history in my lifetime pit us against another worthwhile challenge? Would it bestow on Europe another unifying enemy of the stature of Stalin—anyone as ruthless, cunning, and worthy of our blade? True, the ideology of communism was unlikely to desert us—ideologies seldom do; but it was the practical embodiment of that ideology—Soviet power and the Soviet organisation of human lives—that had absorbed most of my energies and given meaning to my life; and it was the self-destruction of that outwardly indestructible colossus that made me, in 1989, rejoice and feel deprived at the same time.

If it sounds as though I spent the Cold War pursuing intellectually enjoyable activities, that was not always the case. Tangling with the Leninist utopia was mostly tedious. Like a repeating groove on a gramophone record, the polemics were confined to a smallish number of themes of increasing absurdity. With a few exceptions, they strained my patience without stimulating my imagination or intellect.

In contrast to the remarkable Soviet achievements in the craft of subversion and global image building, much Soviet and all Chinese broadcast propaganda was parochial, simple-minded, and misdirected. (And I said so, to the astonishment of my Chinese hosts, when I was given a tour, as a "friendly" visitor, of the Chinese foreign broadcasting establishment in Peking in 1979.) There were no audiences for "positive heroes" in Western Europe; the show elements of the show trials were blindingly obvious; and the Colorado beetles allegedly dropped by American aircraft to destroy the North Korean potato crop could destroy no potatoes because there were none to destroy. Poles, Czechs, and Hungarians found it a little difficult to believe, especially after the oppressive applications of Soviet power in 1956 and 1968, that imperialism and colonialism were exclusively capitalist devices; and to the proletariat of East Germany it was not immediately obvious that the West German workers under capitalist management were getting progressively impoverished while they in the German Democratic Republic were marching forward to an ever more radiant future.

The surrogate component[1] in communist propaganda was just too inept, the incitement too crude, and the vocabulary too transparent to carry credibility. Only Western intellectuals bent on self-delusion would be deceived. We in the West had an easier time of it with the words we were addressing to the East. In the electronic age, the facts spoke for themselves. All Western public diplomacy had to do was to provide the echo chambers and voice the sentiments of those who could not speak for themselves.

Grappling with the theory of communism was a different matter. There existed a higher sort of hermeneutics of the sacred texts. Such criticism could be intriguing and deployed to some purpose; but the demand for it was minimal, and what demand there was came principally from Western universities where Marxism was riding high and the taste for public jousting was widespread. Tilting lances with academic communists, whether of the orthodox or deviationist school, was always worth a visit to Cambridge or Columbia University. In the communist countries themselves, however, the canons of Marx and

Lenin were, outside the official coteries, treated with contempt and had become socially unacceptable.

It was only towards the end of the Soviet system and after its collapse that the Cold War gave me a modicum of satisfaction. It was then that I had my first encounters with people who had read me or listened to me over the years behind the Curtain and who told me how some of us, and the institutions we represented, had, apparently, contributed to keeping the spirit of resistance alive and brought a measure of light into their universe. This was good to know. It was a reward for the rather puritanical work ethic I had imposed on myself to obliterate the pain of having to wrestle, day after day, with the repetitive falsehoods and empty triumphalism of Soviet propaganda.

One of the most remarkable pieces of feedback came my way on my very first visit to post-Soviet Kiev in November 1991.

While I was waiting for my guide, Oxana, at the Café Dnieper, someone unexpectedly tapped me on the shoulder and asked in fair English:

"You are George Urban, aren't you?"

"And who are you, and how do you know my name?"

"Ah," a squat-looking middle-aged man replied, taking off his fur hat, "thereby hangs a long tale, which I haven't got time to tell you right now because a party of German businessmen I'm escorting to Simferopol is waiting in a car downstairs. Let me just say this: I had heard from your interpreter, Oxana Taranenko, a former colleague of mine, that she was meeting the Austrian Airlines flight from Vienna, with you on board. My German guests were on the same plane, so I decided to try to make myself known to George Urban."

"But why did you? And how is it that my name means anything to you?"

"Well," he went on, speaking at great speed, partly in English, partly in German, "This may surprise you. I had been an officer in the KGB, ending up with the rank of colonel. As we can now talk about these things quite freely, I want you to know that for many years I was a spy and had to learn German and English, and other languages. At one time I was the head of the USSR's entire spy network in the Middle East. But then the Israelis got me—and eventually I fell from grace . . ."

"This is all highly interesting, but how do I come into your story?"

"Oh, that's very simple. When I was being trained for intelligence work as a young officer, one of the Western journals we had to study as part of our syllabus was *Encounter* magazine, because that, we were told, would give us an insight into the enemy's thinking and ideological machinations at the most sophisticated level. Now, your name and your writings figured prominently in *Encounter* for many years. I had to study you," he said with great emphasis, "*study you!* How could I forget your name?"

"And did you find our writings in *Encounter* useful as a clue to what the 'enemy' was plotting?"

"Useful, useful—I found it so fascinating that gradually you and your colleagues weaned me away from my oath and my ideology and made me into a dissident. You see, the *Encounter* syllabus was too persuasive. It spawned doubt, then occasional insubordination, and finally open dissent in the mind of a master spy! I read you first as a threat and then as a source of inspiration. Can you beat that?" he said with a broad grin. "I was arrested and given a prison sentence, and when things began to change under Gorbachev, I was released and took up a post as professor of German literature at Kiev University, where your guide, Oxana, too, is a lecturer. In any case, I have to rush; let me just thank you and *Encounter* for having done what you have for us."[2]

The story of the ex-KGB colonel (Yuri Linov was the name he gave me) was the highlight of my trip and an extraordinary recognition of the *Encounter* group's work in the contest of ideas. But in the 1950s and 1960s, any prospect that we could turn the tables on communism had been distant in the extreme and not, as I then saw it, worth a lifetime's investment of intellectual energy.

I found the Soviet system not only cruel and oppressive but also crude and vulgar. There was a grubbiness, a meanness and degradation about organised communism that offended my sensibilities. Even to argue against it struck me as implying complicity. Should I allow myself to be distracted from my other and, as I liked to believe, more worthwhile, pursuits in philosophy and literature? And could one challenge an ideology from liberal democracy's uncertain platform, "light denied"?

Clearly, I was suffering from the half-truth syndrome that troubled Arthur Koestler. My will, my instincts, my youth were all lined up to do battle with the false creed, but what exactly the true creed was, was harder to decide. I saw European unification, in the early 1950s, as the only new and deeply encouraging initiative. It was a fitting though much belated response to the 1914–45 European civil war. But in Britain, despite Churchill's 1946 Zurich address, the idea of a united Europe was being treated with condescension, if not contempt. A nation that had won World War II on paper but had in reality lost it could not muster the humility or the vision to fit in with the other losers. The grave consequences of that postwar British hubris are still with us. Britain's self-imposed satellite status vis-à-vis the United States is by now a fact of life, even though Britain is, formally at least, part of the European Union. For a nation supposedly as realistic as the English (the Irish, the Welsh, and the Scots are a different matter) to be deluded by a myth of superiority for so long and with such self-damaging effect is one of the sad marvels of the modern world.

In the event, I managed to gather a certain amount of assurance from the anxious man's customary belief that so much wickedness cannot go unpunished. But that was more of a prayer than a programme. I drew strength, more seriously, from the spirit of the Stefan George Circle,[3] which was the subject of my slowly evolving doctoral dissertation and, in a different sense, from my very private interpretation of Christianity. But these were abstract, philosophical, and aesthetic sources of inspiration. To apply them to international communications would have been a hopeless and perhaps even ridiculous enterprise. "A private radio station broadcasting esoteric verse to select East European audiences in the small hours," should have been my chosen medium—as an irreverent George Mikes[4] (then a BBC colleague) once quipped in the mid-1950s. He may have been right.

The decision was made for me by the way the Soviet Union was run and Soviet power was exercised. I found myself a belligerent the day I joined the BBC in late 1947, and I went on being profoundly involved in the global engagement to the end. I never doubted that what I was doing was right and important. I was putting my shoulder to the wheel with an enthusiasm that some of my friends thought was worthy of a better cause. I myself did frequently wonder whether creating some good, no matter how humble, in one's private environment might not leave a more positive mark, and give more satisfaction, than polemicising with a dated, and even then clearly ailing, tyranny. A book, a strong spiritual commitment, even two stanzas of verse, might survive, give a modicum of pleasure, or induce reflection; but who would remember the rank and file who contributed in one way or another to the demise of bolshevism—if indeed it ever occurred? For in the 1950s, 1960s, and 1970s the Soviet system was on the march, and it was not wholly beneficial for one's career or intellectual reputation to be known as an anticommunist.

Least of all was it easy to oppose the Soviet system from the right or even, as I did, from the liberal right. My long preoccupation with Stefan George, my defence, at various meetings in London, of Cardinal Mindszenty after his show trial in 1949, the "reactionary" and, I might add, very mediocre poetry I had published in Hungary (duly banned by the authorities) had made me suspect in the eyes of various socialists and fellow-travellers at many British universities, in some sections of the BBC, and of the British press. My first application for a job in Britain was turned down by the BBC Monitoring Service on the argument (openly stated) that I was too hostile to the new facts of life in Eastern Europe. Significantly, the post I eventually obtained in the European Service had just been vacated by a writer who had gone back to Hungary to support the same Soviet-sponsored regime that had caused me to leave. Within two years he was in prison, and his case was not exceptional. In those early postwar years, Stalin, Tito, Mátyás Rákosi, Anna Pauker, and other Stalinist leaders had many admirers in the British establishment. For them, World War II had not quite ended and wartime allies remained friends.

There was, I readily concede, a large piece of truth in the BBC's contention that I was hostile to "the new facts of life" in Central Europe. I had never been a communist, a social democrat or indeed a member of any political party in Eastern Europe or elsewhere. This set me apart from many of my co-belligerents, whose confrontation with communism began with a confrontation with their earlier convictions and consciences as members of Marxist, and mostly also Leninist-Stalinist, congregations. The advantages of having these fallen communists on our side as colleagues were many. They spoke with the eloquence and fervour of the convert and were therefore indispensable to undermining the rationale of communism. I respected them for the thoroughness of their heresy. Most of them were still fuelled by the search for social justice; that motivation was helpful, but they were also overwhelmingly driven by the desire to get even with their past delusions and to warn the world against imitating their folly. Above all, they were sharpening their knives for their former comrades. Although I admired these people for being what they were, I could never quite feel at ease in their company, nor, I suspect, could they in mine. Their protestations were too intense, their cynicism too stark, and their analyses too reflective of the world they thought they had left behind. They marched in negative step, but in step all the same. I was marching to a different drummer.

My dispute with communism, however, was not merely something history had imposed on me, much less just an intriguing way of making friendships and alliances with people with whom, in the absence of a common enemy, I would probably have forged no such friendships. My critique of communism had powerful roots in what, from my late teens on, I thought was the right way of judging and doing things. To say that I was a born reactionary would be to miss the point, for the implication would be that the far Left was pursuing "action," whereas all holistic schemes for the betterment of the human condition can surely be regarded as the truly retrograde (and, alas, only too common) element in history. But it is certainly true that I had been spiritually committed even before I fully understood what Marxism and Leninism were about.

From an early age I believed that all mechanistic explanations of man and history stemmed from a naive conception of human affairs.[5] Henri Bergson and Karl Popper, when I eventually read them, came as recognitions, not revelations. My profound belief in the autonomy and irreducible worth of the individual and of work was as strong in my youth as it is now. To explain them through the categories of background, race, nationality, religion, or even culture struck me as factually mistaken and morally demeaning. Reductionism was, for me, the great intellectual crime of our century.

More important, I saw reductionism and deterministic views as ignoble. Nobility mattered. Could anyone choose to look for his ancestors in the zoo when they could be found instead on Olympus? The Hungarian élite would spill little ink in arguing whether Darwinism or religion was the true way of seeing the world, for "truth," though constantly invoked, was not all-important for them. Honourable conduct was. The truth was forever contingent, elusive, and open to human error, but we *could* tell noble behaviour from base behaviour, a good Samaritan from a Cain. It followed that whatever the "scientific" truth about man and history, the Judeo-Christian view of it was nobler and more life-enhancing than anything we could read in the works of Marx and Darwin.[6] This did not mean that members of the Magyar élite were profoundly Christian. They were usually Christian in name only, but they did have an exalted, spiritual, resigned yet hopeful, sweet-sour view of themselves and their nation. It sustained them as scholars, bohemians, and nation builders—for then as now, they tried to be all three.

I opposed communism not only because the Soviet system was a ruthless and totalitarian dictatorship (though that would have been reason enough), but because it encapsulated in particularly objectionable form everything I felt was repulsive about the reshaping of our civilisation after two fratricidal world wars: the cult of "scientific" materialism and pragmatism, with the attendant enfeeblement of the spiritual dimension in our lives; the mindless application of Cartesian categories to the humane sciences; the destruction of the environment; the population drift from small communities to megatowns, the massification of society; the meaninglessness of work; the alienation of labour; the depersonalisation of the individual and the destruction of his or her dignity. I may have been fighting modernity itself, as some unfriendly critics suggested, but I like to think I was opposing only a thoroughly debased and debasing form of it—a travesty of the values of the Enlightenment from which communism claimed to have descended. This misapplication of rationalism and the progressivist view of history upset me as much as the Soviet incorporation of the Baltic states or Stalin's show trials.

In short, my slowly evolving participation in the Cold War was driven by principle rather than by any prospect of a career-promoting international conflagration. For me the Cold War was to remain just that; I never conceived the contest of ideas as a prelude to a shooting war. At the age of thirty-seven, while a staff member of the BBC, I joined the Inns of Court Regiment of the British Territorial Army because I felt I was in need of toughening, but I did so on William James's principle that young (and not so young) men needed to embrace the "moral equivalent of war." I would have hated to fire a shot in anger. My father and three of my uncles had served in the Austro-Hungarian army in World War I, and their stories haunted me into adulthood. The ravages of that senseless slaughter were everywhere around me in Hungary in the form of armless and legless veterans with begging bowls on their knees and the fear of the future in their eyes. My vaccination against violence came early in life and has stayed with me to this day. The Hungarian conservative establishment's revisionist braggadocio left me cold, although I was well aware of the historical injustice and political folly of the Treaty of Trianon which had given rise to it. In November 1938, my father took his family to Kassa (Košice) to attend the reintegration of his ancestral home into Hungary. My own enthusiasm was small.

Years later, the British inclination to glorify wartime achievement, the jingoism of the gutter press, the use of the expression *to have had a good war* (could there be such a thing?), and the award of knighthoods and peerages for warlike pursuits struck me as uncivilised, wholly inconsistent with what Continentals had been led to believe was British "culture," and singularly ill suited to promote European reconciliation and unification. A sense of contrition would have done the British, the Germans, the French, the Americans—all of us—a power of good, but it was nowhere to be found, not even, with rare exceptions, in the Church. Everything in me rebelled against the notion that serving the "national interest" could relieve a nation of moral responsibility, and now in 1996, in the light of the barbaric war in the former Yugoslavia, appeals to the national interest—as though the national interest represented some self-evidently superior good—strike me as especially reprehensible. Nor, for the same reason, could I subscribe to the philosophy of "my country, right or wrong." Indeed, in 1959 my forlorn attempt to use a single moral yardstick on my own small patch in foreign broadcasting brought about the termination of my contract with the BBC.

As deputy programme organiser in the BBC's European Service, I had the temerity to suggest that Britain's repressive policies in the crown colony of Cyprus vis-à-vis the rebellious Archbishop Makarios and his supporters were incompatible with our libertarian message to Soviet-occupied Hungary in the aftermath of the 1956 revolution and therefore counterproductive on the international scene. My refusal to participate in one particularly offensive broadcast earned me a reprimand for insubordination. I was downgraded in status, my earnings were reduced, and I was eventually eased out of the organisation, but not before British policy had performed a volte-face on Cyprus, the colony had gained independence, and yesterday's political wisdoms had suddenly been repudiated. I was then told that, yes, historically I had been vindicated and could, if I so wished, be rehabilitated; but BBC broadcasters were paid to do as they were told—not to have historical foresight or moral scruples. I declined rehabilitation and within a few weeks accepted a generous offer from Erik Hazelhoff, then director of Radio Free Europe (and a famous hero of the Dutch Resistance), to join his organisation. Little did I suspect that one day I would be occupying his post.

I have never regretted my protest. It provided me, in retrospect, with fresh strength for the struggles that lay ahead, with the Soviet system and with the numerous members of Western establishments who—whether out of cowardice, conformism, or opportunism—seldom hesitated to give the Soviets and their agents of influence the benefit of the doubt. I was now in the possession of a single yardstick for all seasons—a rare gift in political life. But the consciousness of having been penalised for speaking the truth before it was opportune to do so has stayed with me.

Among the more distant influences that shaped my attitude towards communism of the Soviet type, the idiosyncratic culture of Hungary was an important one. I will say little about it because it is all but inaccessible to those who do not command the language. Let me simply state that from the beginning of the eighteenth century to the middle of our own, Hungarian life and letters gave us dozens of poets possessing the highest powers of thought and feeling. They speak to us in phrases that linger and haunt the mind. Their intoxication with the music of words puts them on a par with the best we can read in the literature of the more widely spoken European languages. To say that the Hungarian sensibility brought forth in the verbal arts geniuses of the stature of Béla Bartók and Zoltán Kodály in the musical world is to understate their achievement. A great literature laced with universal sympathies but housed in a small nation's language—could there be a more poignant tragedy for writers and potential readers alike?

For many years, I was caught up in the cadences of Hungarian verse. It is poetry in the sense in which poets are seers and legislators and the rhythm of their words is a portent of destiny. To condense feelings in verse struck me as not only the most economical but also the most sui generis Hungarian way of being. But the Hungarian communion with the perennial topics of poetry—childhood, love, disillusion, disloyalty, old age, death—was a communion with a difference. Much of the best Hungarian verse was deeply anchored in history and intensely patriotic. Hungary's poets of the eighteenth and nineteenth centuries conjure up the sounds and images of Magyar battles with the Turks, the Austrians, and the tsar's army; they speak to us about the loneliness of political exile and the pain of national oppression. Yet beyond the suffering there is a fund of perpetual life; we hear of a Hungarian God in Heaven and a protective Hungarian providence. We sense a nationalism more intent on the preservation of a dwindling race than on conquest or aggression.

I dwell on these peculiarities of the Hungarian collective experience because they made the nation especially resistant to communism. It is not that Hungarian literature is entirely without a social message, even though much of the message was peasant-socialist and wholly untheoretical. There are egalitarian and radical currents in Sándor

Petőfi, Endre Ady, and Attila József, and especially in the village-exploring populist prose writers of the 1920s and 1930s. But these voices, although widely heard and discussed, had little practical political impact on precommunist society. The nation deserved better, for the Hungary I knew was ripe for radical change. An impoverished and partly landless peasantry, almost serflike in its deference to the gentry and nobility, was crying out for rights and land reform, while industrial labour was trying to escape from self-perpetuating poverty, social stigmatisation, and working conditions reminiscent of the "satanic mills" of mid-nineteenth-century England. Alongside this vast underclass there lived, in a state of guilt-ridden but not unhappy symbiosis, a highly educated, vibrant, and ultrasensitive intelligentsia.

It was this cruel nexus between deprivation in the ranks and a creative but powerless compassion in the intellectual élite that made Hungary fertile ground for the highest achievements in music, literature, the visual arts, mathematics, and the natural sciences. *Felix culpa?* I would shun so callous an attribution. Yet undeniably, many of these achievements occurred under the mostly illiberal regency of Miklós Horthy. A fully liberal Western-style government might have achieved less—a fully illiberal Muscovite regime did achieve less—in point of fact, almost nothing at all. In Hungary as elsewhere, Stalinism proved the death of a genuinely national culture.[7]

Why the wretched state of the Magyars did not upset me more than it did I cannot easily explain. My slightly privileged status based on a little family wealth—and pride—cannot account for it, because some of my friends with similar backgrounds were deeply disturbed by the same conditions and sided with the Social Democrats or the peasant Left and in a few cases even with the then completely isolated small band of underground communists. Looking back over a distance of fifty years, I can only surmise that my mental makeup would just not have allowed me to go along with the idea that greater social justice—of which I was otherwise passionately in favour—would make for greater human happiness, if, indeed, I could have brought myself to concede in the first place that happiness was a goal of human existence. Christianity certainly supported no such view. I was conscious of the need for the tragic sense of life long before I read Unamuno.[8]

There was something unworthy, even indecent, about making the satisfaction of creature needs and comforts the central concern of great political parties and governments, I felt on arriving in Labour-dominated Britain in 1947, and the resulting public debate struck me as thin and demeaning. These needs did, of course, have to be met, and met quickly, for the state of Britain in those early postwar years was appalling even by the standards of war-ravaged Hungary. But the improvement of the social condition of society could not be an end in itself. It had to be subordinated to ideas that pointed beyond the mundane round of housing, feeding, and breeding. Yet the promotion, with full state support, of the welfare and education of all did not seem to me to be in conflict with a higher dispensation. A decent and civilised standard of living was, indeed, its precondition. Without fully realising it, I was a one-nation conservative and an advocate of the social teaching of the Roman Catholic Church.

Politicians whose programme and rhetoric were confined to problem solving upset me, and I felt sorry for the audiences they attracted. For one brought up to see Britain through idealistic Hungarian eyes, it was hard to believe that such disadvantaged audiences still existed. But they did, and it didn't take me long to discover that subtle British wartime propaganda as well as my own self-delusions during the war had left me with a more lasting legacy than I had been ready to admit.

Socialisms of Marxist inspiration ran counter to what I fondly imagined was the unstoppable spiritualisation of our self-understanding. I had been, to be sure, equally outraged by the violence, the nationalistic phrase-mongering and rabble-rousing propaganda of the various fascist movements that mushroomed in Central Europe before and during the war, but those were for me beneath contempt: it was any self-respecting person's manifest duty to thwart them. I tried to do my bit in that direction too as a member of a short-lived and not very effective resistance movement in 1944–45.

My revulsion against communists, pragmatists, do-gooders, scissors-and-paste historians, easy-profit makers, and the newly rich and vulgar persuaded me to deepen, whilst already in Britain, my study of Stefan George and his circle. I spent seven years doing so, working simultaneously at the BBC, and produced a mediocre volume under the less than popular title of *Kinesis and Stasis*.[9] This was my doctoral dissertation and a labour of love, but it was a firebreak against the devastating triviality of the modern world and a reaction to that particularly barbaric form of rationalism and muddy populism that poured into Europe in the wake of the Red Army in 1944–45.

In spirit, but to some extent in practice too, I became a belated associate of the George Circle. I met some of its members and dedicated myself to that solemn *Hauch*[10] of an esoteric existence which made it easier to bear the depressing realities of an impoverished and downgraded postwar England. At the time, I did not think I was trying to escape from the real world. I was convinced that the poetry of George and the writings of Friedrich Gundolf and other scholarly disciples were the only world fit to be embraced by a man of common sense. That one of George's early followers—Ludwig Klages, the turn-of-the-century feminist "cosmic" philosopher—unwittingly provided fuel for the subsequent ideological fantasies of certain nazi thinkers (many of George's favourite disciples were German Jews later active and famous in the United States and New Zealand) did not dampen my enthusiasm, although I realised that my choice of subject caused eyebrows to be raised by one or two unknowledgeable left-oriented British intellectuals. Like all men and women of great stature, George was liable to be used and abused by all sides.

Stefan George died in December 1933. He resisted Nazism in all its forms and chose to be buried in Minusio in Switzerland with his head turned away from nazi Germany. One of his disciples, as a schoolboy and a young man, was Count Klaus Schenk von Stauffenberg—the staff officer who led the plot to kill Hitler on July 20, 1944, and paid for its failure with his life.[11]

For me, George was the consummate symbol of the individual's refusal to be depersonalised, to be subsumed under the categories of a progressivist history, to be treated as raw material for social engineering. Also, and not least, George was a king among poets and a composer of words which did, indeed, communicate before they were understood. "A spark of that holy fire"[12] of which the twentieth century had emptied itself, he stood for the prophetic strain in human thinking and for unshakeable integrity. His world was a self-enclosed whole in which harmony prevailed—a house was a house, a vase was a vase, everyone knew his office and performed his duty. The euphony of his words seemed to reach me from some nonterrestrial source and to point to a fulfilment beyond the human adventure. At times, in my arrogance, I had visions of having been "sent" to mediate George's legacy to the less inspired and, I am ashamed to admit, I treated things and people in the workaday world with a touch of condescension. But it was the workaday world in which I had myself to pull my weight, and to which, after periodic excursions into other and sweeter realms, I had to return. The particular approach and tenor of my critique of Marxism-Leninism and the Soviet system probably bore some of the marks of my long and exhilarating immersion in the sounds and ideas of Stefan George and his extraordinary circle.

CHAPTER TWO

The Contest of Ideas

Precisely because ideology in the Soviet scheme of things had in effect little to do with improving the life of the man or woman in the street, I took the ideological appeal of communism seriously. Although its adherents were supposedly pursuing the millennium in the name of ordinary citizens, communism was in fact a secular religion attempting to shape those citizens' minds and secure their loyalties. It gave me some wry satisfaction to observe it in action, for here was proof positive that even the most materialistic political philosophy yet known could not get its message across without making use of the despised paraphernalia of "church," dogma, and ritual—and that after having spent seven decades in uncontested power. I found the pseudo-sacred verse celebrating Stalin, Mao, and the other would-be saints of historical materialism bizarre—and thoroughly engrossing. The grotesque cult of Lenin and his fanatical credo was a bonus.

Here, too, ironically enough, was a fine case of "voluntarism" as understood, and derided, in the Marxist vocabulary—official thinking and triumphalistic rhetoric colliding with the sombre facts of everyday life under "socialism." The truth, to the concealment of which Soviet propaganda was so fervently dedicated, was simple: societies of the Soviet type were technologically backward, socially inequitable, and abysmally poor; yet the opposite was claimed and widely believed—on both sides. We on the inside track of Soviet studies knew perfectly well that beyond the Curtain lay a slum-empire, but our transmitters did not cover the free world. For Western public opinion, unversed as it was in the curious ways of the "dialectic," the discovery that the powerful USSR in fact resembled the Third World came as a shock, and only after the demise of the system. The world-weary observation, widely heard during the Cold War, that our information policy should have

25

covered the West as well as the lands under Soviet control had more than a soupçon of truth in it. The Western nations needed to be told the unvarnished facts about the state of the Soviet side as much as the Soviet public needed to be told what we were thinking.

From the high ground we occupy close to the turn of the century, I may have ascribed undue importance to ideology, but in the 1950s and 1960s it was far less clear than it became in the 1980s that ideology was all "superstructure," with little "base" to support it. The ideological tenets of communism, while crucial as a framework within which the system was seeking to establish, and time and again to re-establish, its legitimacy, had in reality few genuine takers. Our opponents were almost exclusively select members of the communist élites, and we at the commanding posts of intellectual warfare were virtually their only sparring partners. The interminable Marxist-Leninist expostulations, which Western scholars spent so much of their time analysing, remained private to the universe of the "new class"—Agitprop ideologues, their servitors in journalism, and gluttons for punishment in our own ranks. I was one of them.

Nevertheless, ideological engagement was of crucial importance. The élites *were* the communist system. They were running the Soviet bloc and shaping its language. The decisions they took had to be justified within the framework of Leninism. Their rule and their personal interests were tied to the stability of the official creed. Their self-replenishing caste stood above the will of the people. "We can no more have free elections now [1984] than we could ten or twenty years ago, even less so, because we'd lose. There's no doubt of that. So what's the point of such an election?" the Stalinist Jakub Berman observed from retirement.[1] Even a man of the stature and scepticism of General Dmitri Volkogonov believed for a while with the Russian muzhik's disarming naivety that Lenin was a "creator," a "prophet," an "earthly god," a "saint."[2]

Undermining the communist élite's faith and shattering their self-confidence was, therefore, indispensable to the destruction of the totalitarian system. Initially, at least, there was no other way of doing it.

Voluntarism had its piquancies. While West European unity was proceeding apace on the marxisant assumption that economic interdependence must precede any effective political supranationalism, the Soviet Union, belying its philosophy, was acting in reverse order. Throughout the USSR and its glacis in Eastern Europe, societies were

remade and economies recast (and ruined) on Moscow-inspired utopian *political* models. Power was, indeed, growing out of the barrel of a
gun. That this Leninist tactic fell foul of the true spirit of Marx and was
likely to lead to economic disaster even faster than command methods and collectivisation along orthodox Marxist lines would have done
was not allowed to interfere with the agenda of the Soviet leaders. We
in Radio Free Europe did our bit to remind them.

This state of affairs tended to make life simple for us. For a time,
it made the ideological and political conflict supreme and relegated
the more exacting but unexciting economic fencing to a humble place,
without of course eliminating it altogether. But for men and women
under "socialism," the economic facts of life were far from unexciting.
Comparisons in terms of living standards and shopping baskets were
what they understood best and were eager to be offered. And offered
it they were, frequently with such misplaced fervour that when self-
liberation eventually arrived, the "West" had come to mean little more
in East European eyes than privatisation, a well-stocked supermarket,
and moral licence, to boot. Accurately reflecting our own (flawed) priorities, we had "sold" the East a strong sense of Rights and Demands to
the virtual exclusion of any consciousness of Duties and Obligations.
The "idea" of the West that reached Eastern and Central Europe in the
formative 1989–94 period had been shorn of most of the substantive
characteristics of a free and responsible society.

For me, this was bitterly disappointing, and the reader will allow
me a digression to explain why. Instant gratification and the "culture"
of intellectual relativism were not the things I had spent some forty
years of my life to promote. Indeed, I like to think I had fought both
with the same resolve as I had opposed Sovietism in all its variants.
That our struggle against a great wrong should have ended in the apparent triumph of untrammelled greed, permissiveness, and a meretricious society reaffirmed my pessimistic reading of the human adventure. History was not only cunning, as Hegel thought; it was steeped
in the spirit of absurdity. But worse was to come.

We had, in our unofficial articulations to the peoples of the Soviet
Union and Eastern and Central Europe, assured them over the years
of our sympathy and assistance should they find a way of shedding
(peacefully, as we insisted) the communist system and Soviet tutelage.
We did this in guarded language over the airwaves of the BBC, Deutsche
Welle, Radio Free Europe, Radio Liberty, the Voice of America, and

through the articulations of countless Western representatives, both official and unofficial, and our domestic media. No one advocated the violent overthrow of the system, or, indeed, its overthrow at all. After the Hungarian debacle in 1956, Radio Free Europe made no promises and bandied about no inducements. Communism was to be liberalised from within, by "convergence," small steps, gradual improvements, the effects of détente, Left talking to Left, or Eurocommunism's (as it was believed in the 1970s) taking the sting out of Stalinism. Nevertheless, the very act of deploying, over four decades, a great psychological apparatus to address the hopes and grievances of more than three hundred million people carried the silent subtext that the Western nations would not be mere bystanders if and when the East had to be rehabilitated. "Loosen your reliance on Soviet power and instal a democratic order," we appeared to be saying, "and we will help you to build up your prosperity and regain your independence."

Almost a decade has now passed since the peoples of the former USSR and Eastern and Central Europe achieved all that and much else. They undermined and then overthrew the communist system, subverted the Soviet empire, destroyed the Warsaw Pact, and changed, to our immense advantage, the world balance of power. They won a war for us as well as for themselves without a single NATO soldier having had to lay down his life. Yet, with the exception of Germany, the Western world did little to honour its tacit but unmistakable pledges of assistance. As a communicator who had been deeply involved in conveying the spirit of solidarity and hope to the then captive nations, I felt betrayed; and so—more important—did the peoples of the former Soviet Union and Eastern and Central Europe.

Their spectacular and on the whole bloodless act of self-liberation marked the birth or rebirth of democracy and national sovereignty. Seldom has so much history been written into so short a period. Yet, not many years after those seismic events, the multiparty system and the unregulated free market economy are increasingly discredited. They have not been able to satisfy elementary needs; indeed, they have, in the majority view of postcommunist society,[3] conspired to reduce the already miserable living standards prevalent under egalitarian communism. Having raised expectations in the euphoria of liberation, Western-style liberal democracy is widely seen to have been the cause of company closures, unemployment, poverty, and humiliation for the many, and to have bestowed wealth and privilege on the few. There is much truth in such perceptions. "Socialism with a human face" has not been followed by capitalism with a human face, but by a Mafia economy, a Mafia-controlled society, and the return of members of the old nomenklatura in capitalist guise. In Russia, a new form of autocracy is demanding readmission, offering—as the German communists and then Hitler did in the Weimar Republic—demagogic answers to the frustrations of a humiliated national society. Will history judge that what the Versailles treaty did for the rise of Nazism, our indifference to Russia after the fall of the Soviet system will have done for its aftermath—the rise of that uninviting mixture of "socialism," personal rule and Slavic nativism to which a precise name has yet to be appended?

Between 1993 and 1996, in almost every state in the area, communists, ex-communists and formerly communist-sponsored forces were brought back to power through the free will of the people. Next to the "soft" fall of the communist ruling establishments in 1989–90 (Romania was the partial exception), the soft return of the communist ruling establishments in the immediate aftermath of their collapse is the most remarkable development in the history of the period. That members of these establishments were just *arrivistes* both when they were first installed in power and when they were subsequently returned to power, may or may not be true; but in 1993–96 they were certainly freely elected as symbols of an economically and socially more equitable life experienced under communist rule. Who would have thought that the name of Brezhnev would strike a chord of nostalgia in so many Russian hearts so soon after the collapse of the hated system, or the name of Ceauşescu in the hearts of Romanians? The failure of the West could not have been greater. "For two years," Jeffrey Sachs observed, "reformers in Moscow struggled for power while Western governments promised them large-scale aid. . . . The reformers could not win without outside help, but help never arrived, and the reformers paid the price. . . . Of the roughly $18 billion that the IMF and the World Bank were to lend to Russia in 1993, only $2 billion was handed over. . . . This was . . . disastrous foreign-assistance policy—and worse foreign policy."[4]

Explanations have, of course, been offered for why the Western world did not do more to help, and not all of them deserve to be described as mere attempts to camouflage expediency. General unpreparedness and disunity prevailed in the Western ranks, and a long recession was weakening our economies. But the fact, now stubbornly

inscribed in the minds both of those who had given and of those who
had received our encouragement over the years, is that a moral tres-
pass was committed—and a great opportunity missed.

But moral factors apart, our reluctant and miserly contribution to
the rehabilitation of the former East Bloc countries is also a danger to
ourselves. Poverty, disaffection, disorder, internecine wars, left-wing
and right-wing dictatorships may destabilise the whole of Europe, not
just the ex-communist part of it. This is so elementary a truth that I
would hesitate to commit it to paper had we not already mentally written off several of the East and Central European countries—and certainly Russia—as candidates for a full-fledged democratic order. We
increasingly accept that they have chosen, or are fated, to live under
authoritarian, semi-authoritarian, or paternalistic rule of one kind or
another, hoping against hope that an economic recovery will turn the
tables and do for them and the free world what Western governments
were too shortsighted to do immediately after the fall of the empire,
when assistance was most needed and Eastern friendship and loyalties
were there for the taking.

Much as I enjoyed the cut and thrust of intellectual warfare, even
that was flawed in many avoidable ways. It handed us a weapon our
governments did not know how to wield to best advantage if, indeed,
they chose to wield it at all. In our opponents' camp, the concern
with "hearts and minds" was an integral part of political planning;
on our own side of the conflict, however, it was relegated to journalists and frequently brushed aside or even repudiated as unworthy of
great nations and democratic institutions. The U.S. Congress, in particular, and some members of the administration (even under Reagan
and Bush) tended to be shamefaced about "propaganda." This was
puzzling, for neither America nor Britain had been afflicted with such
inhibitions during World Wars I or II. But were we at war? The realisation that the Cold War, too, was a war, albeit a war-by-other-means,
never penetrated Western public consciousness, and our leaders, until
the election of Ronald Reagan, chose not to say so, for fear of interfer-
ing with the complacency and self-indulgence of their electorates.

In Britain, a group of members of the Centre for Policy Studies attempted in 1981 and 1982 to induce Margaret Thatcher as prime minister to broaden her policy base at No. 10 Downing Street to make
it easier to tailor government articulations to the needs of our con-

flict with the Soviet Union.[5] We were turned down—not because the prime minister was unaware of the need (she was extremely conscious of it and distrusted a great deal of Foreign Office advice) but because important government departments were reluctant to allow outside academics to second-guess their judgements. It spoke for Margaret Thatcher's broad-mindedness that the advice we were occasionally asked to tender was nevertheless carefully considered, albeit outside the institutional framework.[6]

But the disability on our side that dismayed me most had virtually incurable educational and cultural roots. The minds of many of our political leaders had developed in an environment of vacuous pragmatism. Their contempt for principle in politics matched their ignorance or belittlement of the rationale that governed the politics of their opponents in the communist countries. Our economists, for their part, suffered from a chip they had put on their own shoulders. They were anxious to demonstrate that their craft was no less deserving of respect, because of no smaller predictive value, than the natural sciences, to the status of which they fervently aspired. And as it was impossible to indulge in prognostications without a data base, they relied overwhelmingly on communist statistics and got things unreasonably wrong.

Also, our politicians and diplomats alike suffered from a familiar *déformation professionnelle*. They found it hard to think away from Western models and political experience. The ability to make an imaginative leap from one culture to another was not their forte. They did have a sound appreciation of what economic rivalry, power struggles, and infighting were about, but that was only a necessary, not a sufficient, tool for understanding and dealing with the international machinations of the Soviet élites. Their insight was weak—their will to gain access to the inner states of their opponents nonexistent. These were considerable handicaps in a world in which disinformation had to be dispelled and human loyalties won on a global scale. So it happened that our leaders and diplomats found the Stalinists' and Maoists' appeals to the irrational mind not only alien but incomprehensible and hateful. Our governments' understanding of what was actually happening in the East, and how communist weaknesses might best be exploited, suffered accordingly.

This was, of course, not uniformly so. In Britain, as I say, Margaret Thatcher, driven by intellectual curiosity, repeatedly called for outside expertise in the form of seminars and written studies to deepen her understanding of the Soviet modus operandi and to assist her with her public articulations. But Margaret Thatcher's temper and intellect were highly untypical of the British way of doing things and at odds with the ethos of the bureaucracy.

Until 1960, to take one example, the Sino-Soviet conflict was almost entirely ignored by Western policy makers; and when they could no longer avert their eyes from it, they tended to look upon it as a gigantic deception designed to trap us into believing that the communist world was falling apart and that it was safe for us to lower our guard. Analysts versed in the history of religious schisms would have known better—did know better—but our political class found it hard to transcend the mentality in our foreign ministries and assimilate the arcane arguments and oriental feuds rife at the courts of Mao Tse-tung and the Soviet oligarchs. The inside story escaped them. The international implications of whether "Mao Tse-tung's Thought" or "Mao Tse-tung Thought" was to rule the Chinese people was considered unworthy of their attention, and by the time they were not, we were close to a Sino-Soviet military conflict. Some acquaintance with the fourth-century Nicene controversy about *homoousion* as distinct from *homoeousion* would have been helpful.

Up to 1969, Chinese ideology was guided by Mao Tse-tung's Thought. The use of the possessive seemed to limit its origin and authority to Mao's person. In April 1969, however, at the Ninth Congress of the Chinese Communist Party, Mao Tse-tung Thought was enshrined in the party's constitution, and thereafter generally used, as a generic term, on a par with Marxism-Leninism. The adjectival phrase was meant to assert the consubstantiality of Maoism with the words of Marx and Lenin. It was a call for a fresh interpretation of the creed and a realignment of "socialist" loyalties. The challenge to Moscow was unmistakable; the Cultural Revolution had begun.

Even scholars of great distinction found it hard to get a purchase on what precisely was happening. I remember the observation by Zbigniew Brzezinski (who seldom got things wrong) in Munich in 1960 that Moscow's conflict with Peking was nothing more remarkable than a family squabble, a manifestation, as he put it, of "divergent unity"; and the brilliant William E. Griffith's ascription of the Cultural Revolution to an outbreak of "Chinese madness."

The most common Western view was that the conflict was a skirmish between traditional Russian and Chinese territorial ambitions and economic interests. The doctrinal clash was said to be mere camouflage; its extravagant language was intended for the hierocracy and could be ignored.

National interest and especially the struggle for supremacy in Asia did, of course, play a significant part; and so did the withdrawal of Soviet technicians and Soviet aid at a critical time (the "Great Leap Forward" movement) in China's development. But these explanations did not manage to convey either the true spirit or the true scale of the conflict between a virulent and a declining form of messianism for the soul of the world communist movement and, as the Chinese leaders fondly expected, the soul of mankind. In Chinese eyes, the lines were being drawn between a renegade, sated, Americanising Soviet giant which was betraying its Leninist heritage and a poor but pure and militant socialist China with the underprivileged and dispossessed of the world as its natural constituency.

The Western proclivity to misread the signals of totalitarian thinking and behaviour flawed the judgements of all our chancelleries. One would have thought that scholars and foreign ministry officials who had studied Lenin and Mussolini would project their findings onto Stalin, Hitler, Mao, and Pol Pot, and provide early warnings of what the world might expect. Not so. Every dictator came as a surprise and was misjudged—sometimes gratuitously, but more often in order to satisfy the preconceptions or suit the convenience of this or that government or pressure group. The incremental growth of wisdom in human affairs was, once again, conspicuous by its absence.

None of this, however, need have happened the way it did. Although many of our policy makers were steeped in a mundane utilitarianism, they also carried another item in their cultural baggage. Before specialisation or institutional bias about what constitutes the "national interest" distorted their outlook, they had access in their schools to that humanistic general education which Sir Isaiah Berlin so persuasively described in one of his finest pieces of writing[7] and were then sent to our ancient universities to deepen their knowledge and broaden their horizons.

Perhaps it is preposterous in our time to posit a connection between education and political maturity, but for me it was certainly surprising that when practical judgements had to be made, the classics helped our civil servants and politicians as little as the reading of Dante, Gibbon, Goethe, or Montesquieu. Once firmly ensconced, they

seemed impervious to the lessons of the past and could neither see beyond the next general election nor offer leadership to others less fortunate in their education. One always knew how ill equipped they were
to feel at home in the world of science, but their inability to take the
measure of contemporary human events was astonishing.

Here was the Sino-Soviet conflict—a schism of historic proportions, with a dual papacy and a clash of dogmas and interests staring
them in the face; yet their sympathies were too narrow, their imagination too thin, and their vocabulary too pedestrian to make sense of
it and shape it. Henry Kissinger, though himself no stranger to misjudgements, had an historian's feel for the fears and hopes of princes
and knew how to infuse a sense of history into, and exploit, Moscow's
bitter struggle with Peking.

Outside the mainstream Western bureaucracies, it is true, certain
centres of serious analysis did tend to get things more often right
than wrong, although the impact of those centres on domestic public opinion was almost nil. In Radio Free Europe, for example, many
years before my appointment as director, the significance of the Sino-
Soviet conflict was at once recognised. Under the shrewd guidance of
Richard V. Burks, an historian from Detroit and a dab hand at exegesis
and the ferreting out of heresy, the Radio mounted nightly transmissions in all its broadcast languages, putting comparable Soviet and Chinese official statements and editorials side by side without comment.

The seriousness of the schism was already known to us but not
to the communist élites in the Soviet Union and Eastern and Central
Europe. To inform them was essential to our policy of disturbing their
confidence in Sino-Soviet unity and the solidarity of the international
working class. Our broadcasts did just that. Years later we discovered
that our transmissions had been given priority treatment by the various communist monitoring services and circulated to senior officials.
The myth of a single centre began to crumble. National deviations,
polycentrism, the Prague Spring, Eurocommunism, and eventually
the loss of Moscow's control of the world communist movement followed. I am, of course, not claiming that we were the sole, or even the
main, promoters of these fissiparous developments. Tito's challenge in
1948, the 1956 Hungarian uprising, the disruptive presence of Palmiro
Togliatti in the wings as one of the progenitors of "national" roads to
socialism, Khrushchev's initial heresy, and principally, of course, the
unbending heritage of Stalinism were the true sources of disintegra-

tion. But our early recognition of the contending popes and of the conflicting interpretations of the holy texts did accelerate the process.

Just how hermetically the Soviet élite had been sealed off from undesirable truths struck me dramatically in the summer of 1969 in California. I was at the time working at the Soviet affairs Research Institute of the University of Southern California.[8] From time to time I entertained visiting scholars from the Soviet Union, usually at the request of the State Department or the National Security Council.

One day I was sent the then head of the Institute of Far Eastern Studies of the Soviet Academy of Sciences. I was wondering aloud to him what course the Sino-Soviet border hostilities (then at their most virulent) might take along the Amur and Ussuri rivers and asked what he made of the vitriolic accusations and counteraccusations flying across the border. To my astonishment, my visitor, a Sinologist, knew nothing about the Chinese side of the argument, nor did he have the slightest idea of what his own country was saying to China in its broadcasts in Mandarin, much less how Moscow's clandestine Radio Peace and Progress was handling the border issue in French, English, and other languages. Whether he was insufficiently trusted or not high enough in the communist hierarchy (or both) to receive confidential materials I could not determine, but his intellectual isolation was manifest.

"How do *you* know about these things?" he asked. I pointed to a mound of galley proofs on my desk waiting to be edited. "The coming issue of our journal here will carry elaborate documentation of what your side and the Chinese are saying about the border conflict," I said. "We receive these materials from the press and various American and British monitoring services. The quarrel is now out in the open; everything about it is public knowledge here."

This put my visitor into a state of great agitation. "I had to come to California to find out what is going on between the Soviet Union and China—in my own field!" he exclaimed. "Could I possibly borrow your proofs overnight?" Next day, my visitor looked much the worse for wear. What I had given him were the proofs of Leonard Schapiro's article "Communists in Collision," Peter Berton's "Background to the Territorial Issue," and documentation from both Mao's China and the USSR running to 233 closely printed pages. "Could I possibly have photocopies of all this and take it back to Moscow?" I readily agreed and supplied the photocopies.[9]

I am dwelling on the Sino-Soviet issue at length merely as an illustration of the kind of challenge we came up against when dealing with communism as a politico-intellectual phenomenon on a world scale. This was a field I enjoyed being drawn into. I felt I was doing something useful at the psychological roots of human activity, transcending that humdrum sequence of politicking and power brokering that passed for politics in most Western countries.

CHAPTER THREE

High Communism

The more conventional impediments to our proper understanding of the communist system and to the forging of appropriate policies to counter it came from Soviet-friendly members of the Western intelligentsia and Western businessmen who felt threatened by any sign of instability in their Eastern markets.

Businessmen had a profound interest in blunting the cutting edge of the Coordinating Committee for Multilateral Export Control (CO-COM) list of proscribed Western high-technology exports. Their criticisms of the enforcement of COCOM's operating rules invariably went hand in hand with attempts to whitewash the Soviet system. They spoke well of the peaceful exertions of the Soviet and Soviet-controlled governments, playing down or ignoring their violations of human rights and trying to show that "capitalism" and "socialism" were, in any case, rapidly converging.

Frequently, this stratagem worked well, especially when coordinated with Soviet disinformation. The leaders of industry and commerce in all Western countries tried their hand at it, often with the secret or tacit connivance of their governments. And where the COCOM rules could not be bent, the Soviet authorities made use of certain Far Eastern and neutral states as their conduits for contraband equipment.

But of the two groups, the intellectual appeasers were the more dangerous. There were more of them, and they were infinitely more sophisticated than the wheelers and dealers in military hardware or trade secrets. A small but vocal segment of the American political class singled out Radio Free Europe and Radio Liberty as targets for ceaseless sniping (I will have more to say about this in the following chapter). No charge was too absurd to be levelled at them by assorted

Congressmen, the "liberal" American press and American supporters of détente. Even within the two Radios' management, policies of near-appeasement were from time to time laid down and enforced in the 1970s on the grounds that they would forestall confrontation and lower the temperature. Distinguished international authorities such as Lord Chalfont, Bernard Levin, Carl Gustav Ströhm and even Alexander Solzhenitsyn were frequently barred from the two Radios' airwaves or were allowed to be heard in doctored form only. Eurocommunism, too, had some influential advocates in the Radios' councils; so had the idea that there was not much to choose between the "shortcomings" of communism and those of American capitalism.

Certain guidelines imposed in the late 1970s by the Board for International Broadcasting ruled out any advocacy of the independence of the USSR's constituent republics, even though, ironically, the 1977 Soviet constitution clearly provided for their right to secede.[1] The United States wanted us to be more solicitous on behalf of the integrity of the Soviet Union than the Soviets themselves demanded. Other guidelines were equally absurd. One stated that the two Radios had no mandate to advocate "the establishment or disestablishment of any particular system, form of state organization, or ideology"[2]—a rule which struck at the heart of what foreign broadcasting and indeed Western democracy stood for. Our very raison d'être was the disestablishment of the one-party state and the totalitarian dictatorship. Strictly interpreted, this stipulation of the Policy Guidelines would have emptied our mandate of all meaning.

One chairman of the board[3] was so anxious to underline the Radios' commitment to "balance" in their output that in 1977–78 he proposed to invite Soviet and East European communist officials to the two Radios' studios to challenge us whenever the communist side judged that the Radios had been unfair to the Soviet system or particular communist policies. Congress countermanded this folly, but it had come very close to realisation.[4]

We could have wished for a more supportive home base to enable us at the sharp end of the Cold War to confront the Soviet challenge, for the Soviet challenge was not merely one of power and subversion, although it was that, too; nor merely a question of social and economic competition, although that, too, was a (minor) part of it; but communism's stated purpose to remake human beings and society in its own image. From that claim sprang all the evils in the practical application of Marxism-Leninism. A New Man, homo sovieticus, and a new society could not be created on the foundations of the old; they had to be force-bred, and doing that required violence. It required terror, brainwashing, and menticide, the laundering or erasure of the past, the redefinition of words and ideas, and, in extreme cases, the destruction of everything and everyone liable to remind the citizen that an order different from the communist order was imaginable or had ever existed. Mao's Cultural Revolution and Pol Pot's genocidal civil war were only the most appalling manifestations of this utopian intoxication, but it had its first run in Europe under Lenin and Stalin and was latent in all communist rule, and arguably in all communist thinking.

It was, as I say, this intellectual-spiritual dimension that fascinated me most about communism. Oppression, racism, human beastliness, the suppression of minorities, unjust government, corrupt law enforcement were as old as history. I deplored and opposed them, but they did not generate in me that white heat of indignation without which nothing worthwhile can be attempted. Lenin's absolutist blueprint for a New Beginning did. Its sources lay deep in the follies as well as the idealistic aspirations of man.

I write about my own views, but I believe my attitude towards the Leninist utopia was typical of many like-minded conservatives of the European Christian Democratic persuasion. If Lenin's grand design so upset me, it was not because I was in any way anxious to preserve the old Adam. Who could doubt in our blood-soaked century that he was in need of reform if not, indeed, of redemption, perhaps even through the rigours of some "cultural revolution"? I had an idiosyncratic sense of Original Sin and tended to equate it with myopia and our inability to learn from the crimes and delusions of the past. Hence a radical shake-up of our education system and a reassertion of discipline and respect in our daily commerce with one another held no terrors for me. But it was one thing to improve the imperfect human creature and quite another to create a lobotomised, pliant monster. To oppose this prospect of a communist *Gleichschaltung* was a task I embraced with enthusiasm.

We can now see with the benefit of hindsight that our fear that under communism Orwell's *Nineteen Eighty-Four* would become a reality was greatly exaggerated. Neither Orwell nor before him Zamyatin, Campanella, More, or Huxley had an adequate appreciation of the resilience of the human mind. *Nineteen Eighty-Four* never happened (though a one-dimensional society did) and was probably at no time even close to happening. When the walls came down in 1989, no one in

the USSR or Eastern Europe had the slightest doubt that he could recognise a lie or a misrepresentation when he saw one. The blinkers may
have been heavy, but the eyes remained unaffected. The whole mon-
strous fabric of mendacity peeled off faster than parliaments could
rewrite the laws or historians the textbooks.

But while the struggle lasted, it would have been unsafe to assume
that a skilled combination of terror and collective brainwashing would
be having so little long-term effect, even though one had reason to distrust the then fashionable findings of behaviourism. What we could
see was that the communist side—China every bit as much as the USSR
and its satellites—was lavishing lives, brainpower, and treasure on a
global programme to redesign *homo sapiens* and to instil a code of behaviour which was crude, base, and lethal to the survival of man as a
civilised and civiliseable being.

Moreover, evidence was at hand (although it was not overwhelming) that, under extreme conditions, brainwashing did work. After the
Korean war, many American prisoners of war found it hard to shed
the effects of communist indoctrination, despite the fact that their rehabilitation was greatly assisted by their families and a supportive U.S.
environment. Until well into the Brezhnev era, visiting Soviet dele-
gations did not cease to astonish us with their perverse reading of
the outside world and indeed of their own culture and history. Their
conditioning appeared faultless. When NKVD and then KGB pressure
was at its peak, Orwell's "newspeak" did indeed become the language
of the system. Words and ideas were gutted and then invested with
new—or no—meaning; heretical thought became unutterable and certainly most dangerous. All thinking in the media, the armed forces, the
bureaucracy, in secondary and tertiary education was homogenised.
A bogus image of the West as the archetypal enemy was implanted
and the cult of war making and war winning carefully nurtured from
the cradle to the grave. The threat, foreseen by Alexander Herzen, of
"Genghis Khan with a telegraph" was, in the 1950s, 1960s, and 1970s,
by no means an intriguing prophecy or a piece of science fiction—and
would have proved to be very real indeed had the conflict between the
Soviet Union and the West ended up in a shooting war, for example, at
the time of the great communist imperial leap forward in the 1970s.

What made communism so difficult to handle was its appeal, with
such deceptive plausibility, to so many people. Had the wickedness of
communism alone stood out as its defining characteristic—as it abundantly did for those who experienced it in the shape of the terror, the
Gulag, or the marauding Red Army—it would have been easier to deal

with, but it also enlisted much misplaced idealism and sacrifice. In
the minds of the communists themselves, there was often only a thin
line separating truth from mendacity, genuine faith from self-delusion,
selfless dedication from criminal folly, radicalism from violence, the
promise of national liberation from Moscow's colonialism. They deceived us because they deceived themselves. To tangle with this complex and elusive creed seemed to me worth a lifetime's work.

But our effort to get the better of the creed and its practice was also
jeopardised by a self-inflicted weakness—if that is what it really was—
in our attitude towards the Soviet system. We tended to upgrade what
ought not to have been upgraded to make it worthy of our labours.
Conceiving of communism as a timeless utopia seeking to be translated into reality—"high communism"—was infinitely more challenging, and intellectually more respectable, than thinking of it as a gigantic deception to cover up the machinations of old-fashioned merchants
of power and influence. Those of us who took the millennial appeal of
communism seriously and were looking for analogies delved into the
rich texture of earlier utopias, religions of all kinds, and cognate phenomena in a wide field of learning. This was stimulating, but it did, as
I say, make communism seem a more sophisticated and nobler thing
than it was. Nazi studies never gained academic respectability in the
Western world outside Hitler's Germany—why should Soviet studies?
It was hard for students of Soviet affairs to participate in erudite Sovietological conferences at renowned seats of Western learning without
at the same time tacitly conceding that the Soviet system was legitimate
and here to stay. And to insinuate that implication was, of course, the
unacknowledged objective of some academic conference organisers.

Undoubtedly, our escape into sophistication did confer on communism a spurious respectability, but the same sophistication and respectability also attracted brains and produced analysis of high quality.
Both were essential to Western preparedness. Some of our ablest practitioners might not have been drawn to the study of Sovietism had
they had reason to believe that Soviet communism was, in reality, only
another instalment in the long saga of human corruption and national
aggrandisement. The Soviets, who knew better, were amused by our
self-delusion and the funds it attracted from earnest capitalist foundations.

Those of us who had a foot in both history and philosophy were
facing a special problem. As a chronicler, I had more than a passing suspicion that an understanding of crude national interest, per-

sonal power, and privilege might turn out to be the true key to undermining the Soviet system. Yet, such were the attractions of inhabiting
the world of ideas that without neglecting the power factor in Soviet
society during my stewardship of Radio Free Europe, I stuck to the
intellectual/moral conception of communism to the very end. It was
an allurement I had no reason to regret. In 1989–90, I found to my satisfaction that the fall of the Soviet Union and the Moscow papacy was
indeed due to the exhaustion and irrelevance of Marxism-Leninism
rather than to the fallibility or wickedness of its representatives, substantial though both fallibility and wickedness had been throughout
the course of Soviet history.

Now the struggle appears to be over. Did *we* win the Cold War?

Only a qualified answer can do justice to that question. In one sense,
communism of the Soviet Russian type succumbed to its own vices
and absurdities and to the unnatural, indeed criminal, methods it employed to enforce their acceptance. It claimed that ends in a political
struggle justified means, but the means struck back and brought the
ends down with them. By the mid-1980s, some of the Soviet leaders,
headed by Mikhail Gorbachev, had gradually reached the fatal condition of no longer believing that in them still resided the right to rule
in the name of the proletarian revolution, or indeed that the proletarian revolution as handed down to them was worth preserving. The
regime was going under because trust in its legitimacy had evaporated.
"Gorbachev's historic role . . . was not so much that he destroyed the
totalitarian system, but rather that he did not prevent its self-destruction."[5]

Soviet communism, moreover, frontally challenged man's fundamental beliefs and institutions—the autonomy of the individual, private property, the inviolability of the family, transcendental faith, the
worth of nationhood, the dignity of tradition—and lost.

In my more fanciful moments I conjure up an imaginary scene in
which a mischievous godhead deplores, tongue in cheek, the defeat of
Soviet communism on the grounds that there is so much wrong with
the record of human history that a little social engineering and genetic
manipulation can hardly be thought not worth the experiment.

In the real world, however, such experiments are paid for with defeat and ignominy. By the late 1980s it would have been impossible to
salvage the Soviet system, short of reactivating the savage discipline of
Stalinism. Communism's bizarre skyscraper was rotten at its foundations and came crashing down when the time was right.

It is in preparing and bringing forward that rightness of time that the Western world's contribution to the self-defeat of the Soviet system has to be seen. The defeat happened in many ways and over a long period.

The Western embrace of Alexander Solzhenitsyn and the promotion of his *Gulag Archipelago* meant underwriting the ideas of a man who had, in the words of Leonid Brezhnev, "encroached on the holiest of holies, on Lenin, on our Soviet system, on the Soviet regime."[6] The Helsinki round of agreements made nonsense of the Soviet siege-mentality and legitimised the quest for human rights. The provisions of "Basket Three" of the Helsinki Final Act in particular broke the communist stranglehold on information and travel policy. American support of the Afghan fighters opened deep wounds in the side of the Soviet regime and the Russian people. Western "differentiation" in favour of the reforming communist states weakened Moscow's control over its satellites. Western refusal to bail out the bankrupt Soviet economy accelerated the rise of a group of heretical Soviet economists. Our deployment of intermediate-range nuclear weapons in Western Europe deprived Moscow of the myth of nuclear invulnerability. And, to cap it all, the American-induced belief among Soviet leaders that the Strategic Defense Initiative (SDI) was an accomplished operational fact (which it was not) brought with it the prospect of fresh and unsustainable economic burdens.

And yet, and yet—the reader would be misguided to believe that our governments had shrewdly coordinated these individual policies or had been hatching any overall plan to destroy the Soviet Union. Nothing so sophisticated had been thought of. Liberal democracies are peaceable polities—slow to anger, quick to forget and to forgive. The Western leaders' delight, in 1989–90, at seeing the walls come down was matched only by their surprise and by their unpreparedness to deal with the resulting disorder. They had made no provision whatever for a postcommunist world because they never believed Soviet power would suddenly collapse—and perhaps never wanted it fully to collapse.

The American-Soviet duopoly was not an uncomfortable state to be in. The balance of power was at times a little unsafe, but familiar. Backward-looking nationalist politicians in England and to a somewhat smaller extent in France saw the Soviet Union as welcome insurance against any extension of German influence. Generals had their jobs, nuclear rockets their targets, propagandists their enemy-image.

The rules of engagement were clear-cut on both sides, the tills never stopped ringing in Silicon Valley, and the misfortunes of the oppressed seemed a small price to pay for world stability. Such was the state of our civilisation until the autumn of 1989.

But with the collapse of Soviet power, this Cold War idyll, too, came to a sudden end, and so did Europe's hopes for a deeper union. Speaking as a confirmed European federalist, I feel the Soviet Union expired a trifle too soon and was not, while it lasted, menacing enough to hammer Europe into an unbreakable whole. Another decade or two of the flexing of Soviet Russian muscle might have knocked sense enough into Europe's restless tribes to put their fratricidal instincts unalterably behind them. As things stand at the end of the millennium, Sarajevo, symbol of a fearful past and present, may be on its way to becoming a symbol of the future. If the house of Europe is not rapidly completed, we shall be revisited by many more ghosts of our inglorious European history.

I regard my own intellectual engagement with communist affairs as a thing of the past. It is not that I cannot see those special problems with which the postcommunist world has to grapple. In a tug-of-war, when one side is defeated, both sides fall down. The awesome crimes committed in the name of "ethnic cleansing" in Bosnia, the genocidal civil war in Nagorno-Karabakh, the destruction of Chechnya, the revival of nationalistic and racist extremism in some of the other ex-Soviet republics and Russia itself, and the spreading cultural void in the East and the West alike are so many warnings that the stable instability of the bipolar world has been replaced by a wholly unstable instability, which our governments have hardly begun to understand and are therefore in a poor position to cope with.

But all these developments, deplorable as they are, are variations on themes well known to us from history. They do not engage my passions (though they enlist my compassion) and do not unduly excite my intellect. After the deep freeze come renewals, and with the renewals dislocation, turbulence, extremism, anarchy. Such has always been the rhythm of history. Can there be anything drearier and less instructive for the future than rehearsing the wrongs of Russian imperialism, the grievances of Romanians against Hungarians, of Bulgars against Turks, of Poles against Lithuanians, of the Irish against the English, or the fluxes and refluxes of poverty and privilege? I find it more pleasurable to study the crimes and follies of mankind vicariously by reading Polybius, Vico, or Gibbon than by following the daily savageries of

Serbian thugs or getting exasperated by the articulations of unreconstructed English, Russian, French, or German nationalists.

The one fundamental intellectual and political challenge of our
time—communism of the totalitarian brand—has suffered defeat. That
is no small event to enter in the annals of our century. I am content to
leave it to the judgement of the reader how much Western psychological warfare had to do with it.

CHAPTER FOUR

Second Conductors

The questions I most frequently encountered on my travels in Russia and other parts of Eastern and Central Europe after the collapse of the Soviet system (earlier I had been debarred from going there) tended to boil down to these: Who had been in charge during the Cold War of Western "propaganda"? More particularly: Who had determined "the line" in those three influential organisations, Radio Free Europe, Radio Liberty, and the BBC? Had there been—as many suspected—two "conductors" rather than one; and if so, who had been wielding the second baton?

Behind these questions it was easy enough to detect an informed surmise that there must have been a second conductor—or a single conductor of either schizophrenic inclinations or uncommon sophistication, for in no other way could it be explained that, while official Western policy vis-à-vis the East had been cautious, accommodating, unimaginative, and fragmented, Western propaganda had been robust, target-oriented, consistent, empathetic, and, as it happened, remarkably successful. Little did my questioners appreciate the power of chance and confusion in the conduct of Western affairs, or the flexibility of Western institutions.

Their suspicion did, of course, reflect the old East European inclination to see conspiracies where none existed, but the assumption that a hidden hand had guided international broadcasting was given a measure of plausibility by the unfortunate circumstance that for two decades certain areas of American "public diplomacy,"[1] including the work of the two Munich Radios, had been funded in one way or another by the Central Intelligence Agency. Western public diplomacy has never been able to live down this particular, and quite avoidable, American folly. It was a self-inflicted wound which wrought havoc for some years with the two Radios' reputation. But damaging though it was, it had no lasting impact on our ability to bring the intellectual contest with the Soviet system to a successful conclusion. I will try to throw light on these vexed questions because they are still surrounded by ignorance and hypocrisy.

The Central Intelligence Agency's precise role in the life of Radio Free Europe and Radio Liberty will not be known until the files have been released and a definitive history is on hand. In my own limited experience, Radio Free Europe's connection with the Central Intelligence Agency was, up to 1971, when the links were severed, of a subtly consultative and mutually enriching rather than of an order-taking kind. What do I mean by "mutually enriching"?

In the period between 1961 and 1965, while a middle-rank executive in charge of the Radio's "Third Programme" (so named after the BBC's but very different in content), I found to my surprise that my choice of ex-communist outside contributors was not questioned, much less opposed, by senior executives. My policy at the time was to provide a platform for well-known former exponents of the faith, because I felt they stood a better chance of appealing to the interests of some of the already dithering Soviet and East European communist élites than any other type of broadcaster. Richard V. Burks, the policy director, and I launched a long series of talks and discussions by men and women of the stature of John Strachey, Ignazio Silone, Richard Löwenthal, Margarete Buber-Neumann, Manès Sperber, Arthur Koestler, and others, each running to as many as a dozen programmes and addressing communist intellectuals where it hurt most—in the area of moral conflict which we knew existed between their erstwhile idealism and their slavish yes-manship.

I believed at the time that had our broadcasts been under CIA control, there would probably have emerged at least some opposition to such transmissions, for in the existing climate of opinion in the United States it could not be taken for granted that the CIA would agree without demur that former communists—even renegades or heretics—were acceptable instruments for the public promotion of American policies. But there was no such demur. On the contrary, the policy director—whose earlier links with the CIA became known to me only after I had resigned from the Radio in 1965—supported my operation with enthusiasm. He felt as I did that tackling the system's "soft underbelly," and using famous apostates to do it, was an intelligent way of subverting the system. I had to assume that the Radio was either under no (or only very lax) CIA supervision or that the CIA, or some part of it, had become uncharacteristically sophisticated. It was only many years later, in 1995, that light was indirectly thrown on the Agency's—and probably only part of the Agency's—policy preferences at the time.

The point needs stressing because much of official America in the 1950s and the early 1960s was still in the thrall of McCarthyism, and the intellectual environment in which it operated was crude in the extreme. Cohn and Shine had just finished purging American government libraries. "Godless communism" was not meant to be fought in the company of communists—not even ex-communist anticommunists.

Two fine personifications of this unsubtle American mentality were right in our midst in Radio Free Europe in the shape of General Rodney C. Smith, director of the Radio, and his deputy, Colonel Chester W. Ott. Both were profoundly uncomfortable with what Burks and I were doing. General Smith, a competent enough administrator, with his background in U.S. Army engineering, believed in using firepower and not mincing words. Intellectuals and intellectual radio were not for him. He felt that the use of unfamiliar compounds and longish quotations from communist literature was a flaw in our anti-Soviet credentials. Couldn't the unsuspecting listener take us for a Communist station through the jamming? Couldn't we, he asked, design broadcasts without quoting so many communists? This was grotesque. Had Burks and I been guided by such fears, we could hardly have entered into polemics with the Soviet system. But political illiteracy of this kind was not rare among influential Americans. With my resignation in 1965, Smith allowed the Third Programme to lapse, and my post remained unfilled.

This episode has a curious background. In the late 1960s, while teaching in California, I was given to understand that during the 1950s and part of the 1960s, the CIA had harboured a number of outstanding Soviet and East European specialists whose political views were, under the prevailing conditions, insufficiently conservative to assure their holders adequate (or perhaps any) professional employment in the academic market but whose knowledge and experience were nevertheless invaluable for the Agency's self-understanding and the accuracy of its analyses in the Cold War. Some of our senior people in Munich had apparently come from such "internal émigré" quarters. This circumstance would, if true, explain the ready reception in the 1960s of my ideas as well as other unorthodox policies the Radio was pursuing. Not many were inclined to think of the CIA in those days as a safe haven for innovative liberals.[2]

Yet, this explanation fails to convince. An article in 1995 in the CIA's own journal,[3] revealing Agency support given to the "Congress for Cultural Freedom" in the 1950s and 1960s, shows that from June 1950—when the "Congress" was launched in Berlin—elements within the Agency, and then the Agency itself, gave long-term covert backing to democratic socialists, including former communists, as a means of generating unrest in Stalin's empire and neutralising the then rapidly unfolding Soviet peace campaign. We are told that the Congress had set itself the mission of pitting liberal and socialist opinion against Stalinism, using the same sort of principals as Radio Free Europe was to deploy on its airwaves in the early 1960s—Strachey, Koestler, Silone, and others. Although the idea of outflanking Stalinism from the left had originated outside the CIA—Sidney Hook, James Burnham, Ruth Fischer, Melvin J. Lasky, Michael Josselson, James T. Farrell, Arthur Koestler, Manès Sperber, and Franz Borkenau were the progenitors of the idea—the staff of the Agency's fledgling Office of Policy Coordination under Frank Wisner soon embraced the idea, took matters into their own hands, and began providing financial support as well as orchestration.

Great secrecy surrounded the CIA's sponsorship, and when it came to light in the late 1960s, the Congress was fatally weakened and eventually collapsed all but in name, even though some of its journals, notably *Encounter* under the indomitable Melvin J. Lasky, survived and even grew in importance for the duration of the Cold War.

In retrospect, one is tempted to assume that if the CIA so liberally supported, via the Congress for Cultural Freedom, the anti-Soviet Left in order to undermine the Soviet system, then it was most likely to have initiated similar policies through Radio Free Europe, too, especially in the shape of programmes deployed by the Radio's intellectual bureau, of which I was in charge in the early 1960s.

This may well have been among the CIA's intentions; but if so, news of it failed to reach me. The initiative for such policies had come exclusively from a very small group within the Radio. True, that initiative eventually received the support of the policy director, but at my level we certainly had no operational relationship whatever with the

Agency. I, for one, had no knowledge of what the CIA's position would be on any of the questions I was handling, or even whether there *was* a CIA position to consider.

Nor can it be said that by giving pride of place to the views of leading heretics, the staff at the Radio—or at the CIA—were particularly innovative in terms of psychological warfare. Using apostates and defectors from the "enemy" camp to turn the tables on it was a tactic as old as human conflict. It required no original thinking. "Selling" the policy to official America did.

The truth is straightforward: the policies my colleagues and I were eager to promote in the early 1960s coincided with the thinking of many Americans well versed in the affairs of the communist East, including, as it would now appear, certain policy-making members of the CIA. The policies coincided not because there was a conspiracy to make them coincide, but because any intelligent analysis of the state of the Cold War resulted in similar conclusions. Employing the democratic Left to subvert the totalitarian Left was the most promising approach under the circumstances. Soon, the 1968 Prague Spring was to prove the policy right.

What stands out is the Radio's autonomy. Even when financed out of CIA appropriations, the Radio's policy decisions were neither dictated nor in any way guided by the Agency. This aloofness of the CIA was, I hasten to add, not always a pure blessing. Looking at the Radio's chequered record during the 1956 Hungarian Revolution (see Chapter 14), one could wish that the Agency or the State Department *had*, from time to time, exerted a modicum of operational influence. Had they done so, they might have prevented some of the blunders of Munich's programme makers.

Later on, certainly under my tenure as director (1983–86), we had no contact whatever with the CIA. Naturally, our local protective security arrangements were and always had been coordinated with American and German intelligence, and there was liaison between the two Radios and the U.S. consulate general in Munich. But as far as policy formation and tactics were concerned, we were our own masters, subject only to the invited and uninvited comments and influences which came our way in the context of normal, democratic opinion formation. I shall discuss these presently.

The most remarkable overall feature of the two Radios' association with the CIA both before and after 1971 can be framed in the question, Who influenced whom? It was, in my judgement, the two Radios that left their imprint on Agency thinking rather than the Agency on the policies of the two Radios, and that for perfectly natural and respectable reasons: the specialised personnel of Radio Free Europe and Radio Liberty had wider knowledge, were endowed with finer political instincts, were closer to the scene, and produced more penetrating analyses of all aspects of the communist world than members of the CIA.

The Radios' extensive and sophisticated audience evaluation, with its elaborate information intake at various points along the Iron Curtain, assisted the authenticity and accuracy of their broadcasts, but it was also available to outside scholars and journalists. Radio Liberty's political and sociological reports—distinct from the two Radios' political and economic research—were regularly published.[4] Through a variety of political, cultural, and economic research bulletins (available by subscription to the general public), the two Radios were in a position to shape thinking in American and European military, political, and journalistic quarters—including the Central Intelligence Agency. And through the gradual and entirely normal transfer and eventual promotion of their young research men and women to senior positions in the State Department, Congress, the National Security Council, various think tanks, and the CIA itself, the two Radios developed friendly contacts in virtually all sections of the American political, military, diplomatic, and security communities.

As time went on, Radio Free Europe became a school for the brightest and the most dedicated. Various departments of the American government, the White House, foundations, and the universities regularly sent us their young men and women for total immersion in the affairs of the East. In the United States, where the free movement of people and ideas between universities, think tanks, government agencies, industry, and the military was and is a well-accepted and, indeed, cherished way of life, the two Radios' contacts in Washington, and Washington's in Munich, were looked upon as a perfectly legitimate and desirable state of affairs. And so they were. When all is said and done, that web of informal relationships constitutes, to my knowledge, the bulk of the CIA's role in the affairs of Radio Free Europe and, I should imagine, of Radio Liberty too. Everything in that relationship was more relaxed, improvised, and informal than the American progressivist press suspected or the KGB feared.

My sole personal contact with the Agency also occurred through

this friendly network of "alumni" in the late 1960s, well after I had resigned from my first post with the Radio. Three of our former interns
were, at the time, holding down significant positions in the CIA, headed
by Fritz Ermarth, then (if my memory serves me) principal desk officer
for Soviet affairs. It was this group that invited me to conduct, while
on a visit to Washington, an informal *tour d'horizon* for staff researchers at Langley, Virginia. My tour turned out to be a bland enough affair, not unlike any seminar I had attended at American universities,
and less sharp than some. It ran true to that pattern of disputatious
opinion sharing that I suspect must have been the story of the Radios'
entire connection with the CIA in the 1960s. My first and last foray into
CIA territory ended on a note of resounding banality.

But Central Intelligence Agency apart, were my Eastern interlocutors right in assuming that American foreign broadcasting of the Radio
Free Europe type had been directed by unseen hands? My short answer
to that question is a qualified yes: there had been second, though not
invisible, "conductors."

Between 1945 and the collapse of communism, the Western world
was, officially at least, at peace with the communist states. Full diplomatic relations were maintained, and despite periodic tensions, official visits were exchanged at the highest levels. Fraternisation, détente,
trade and aid, the recognition of East Germany as a sovereign state—
these, and much else in the genre of peaceful coexistence as Western
public opinion was induced to understand it, took place. Even after the
Soviet intervention in Afghanistan in 1979, some Western leaders took
the view that détente should be upheld regardless, and until Ronald
Reagan's election in November 1980, the curve of "normal" East-West
activities went on growing.

But in the real world, a non-shooting war was being waged for
global power and influence. Although widely seen by the Western public as a symbol of mutual tolerance, even peace, détente excluded, in
the Soviet definition, any idea of peaceful coexistence between "antago-
nistic" political systems and ideologies.[5] It was in this second, unconventional area that government ministers and diplomats found it hard
to make useful contributions. They knew well enough what the ideological contest and subversion were about and how the Soviet side was
pursuing them, but in a liberal democracy it was extremely difficult
to muster the political will and find people with the right experience
to meet this unorthodox challenge within the existing institutions. The

contest was just too theoretical and outlandish to attract civil servants. It called for intellectual and linguistic qualifications that proved slow and laborious to acquire and difficult to deploy outside the Soviet context. For most career men and women, it was a cul-de-sac.

Serious gaps were opening up in our defences. Agitation and propaganda (Agitprop) in the Soviet sense had, of course, no Western counterparts; so how were the gaps to be filled? A breed of unofficial policy makers began to emerge—some, such as the "surrogate broadcasters" of Radio Free Europe under American auspices, by design; others, such as the BBC's foreign broadcasting personnel, by default, because government ministers and members of the foreign service did not have the mandate, the foresight, or the inclination to fashion "close-to-the-citizen" approaches to the communist lands and, with rare exceptions, did not regard it as their business to identify with the cultures of Eastern Europe. This was a confused and confusing way of pursuing the Cold War, but it worked. Looking back at the record, I believe I am right in saying that many of the successes of Western psychological warfare are more properly ascribed to good luck and the fortuitous interplay of improvisation and muddle than to intelligent planning. But it is not a formula I would recommend for future application.

Who, then, were the second conductors? The European Service of the BBC and Radio Free Europe were the two principal sources of historically effective public diplomacy, and as I played a minor part in the first and (I like to think) a major one in the second, I will examine whether these conductors had, in fact, a policy-making role of their own.

The brief of the European Service of the BBC was to "project Britain"—and not to provide alternative "home services" for audiences in the USSR and Eastern Europe. But projecting Britain was subject to many interpretations. Could the BBC remain aloof when Soviet occupation and communist rule were provoking unrest in Eastern Europe and British public opinion, Parliament, and the British political class were showing concern? Did projecting Britain not imply the need, indeed the duty, to project that concern?

Thus it happened that in the late 1940s, under the title of "projection," the BBC's European Service gradually developed a forceful role of its own; its approach was in many respects indistinguishable from what was to become, in the early 1950s, the Radio Free Europe type of "surrogate" broadcasting. The BBC spoke for Britain, but precisely because it spoke for Britain, it also spoke for the people of the Czech lands, of Poland, Romania, and Hungary. For once, the interests as well as the sentiments of the British coincided with those of the people of Central and Eastern Europe. There was a common enemy.

I was a member of the BBC European Service from late 1947 to 1960. Taking this wide-angle view of what constituted British interests, I wrote and read many a comment for East European and world consumption. True, our voice was civil, and we never indulged in incitement, but we made it crystal clear that we saw the communist system as evil, the suppression of Eastern Europe as temporary, and the Soviet empire as a threat to Western civilisation. Unlike the Voice of America, which was in effect the voice of the U.S. State Department, we never broadcast government-inspired editorials or trimmed our sails to the prevailing winds in Westminster.

Day after day, week after week, batteries of BBC commentators, both British and nationals or former nationals of the communist states, addressed Poles, Czechs, Slovaks, Hungarians, Russians, East Germans, and others in their own languages and on their own cultural terms with messages that would have astonished British parliamentarians and the press had they taken the trouble to gain access to the files of the BBC.

No such approach would have been tolerated at the Voice of America under the U.S. regimen of spoon-feeding. But in Britain, there existed a hallowed tradition of self-righteous hypocrisy tempered by self-mockery; a penchant for speaking the truth but not the whole truth; and an aura of arrogant infallibility inherited from the BBC's successes during World War II which made all this possible. Britain was at the time so wrapped in virtue—at least in its own estimation—that even lapses of judgement and veracity were exempt from internal criticism. Could there have been a better foundation for "propaganda"?

But the word *propaganda* was banned from all internal discussion, and when it was used by outsiders in reference to BBC programming, the BBC management felt profoundly offended. Prime Minister Margaret Thatcher once complimented the BBC on its excellent record in international propaganda, not realising that members of the BBC's external broadcasting staff had quite genuinely managed to convince themselves that what they were producing was not propaganda. At once, the managing editor of the BBC External Services protested in the "Letters" column of the *Times* that the BBC had nothing to do with propaganda. On the contrary, he said, it was providing only objective news and fair comment.[6]

The BBC, as it happened, could and did have the best of both worlds: its wartime record lent it respectability, while its stoical handling of Britain's postwar loss of influence gave it credibility. Truthful reporting of the rapid disintegration of the British Empire and of other British postwar calamities endowed the BBC's news bulletins with so many items massively unfavourable to Britain's image in the world ("credibility items," in Radio Free Europe parlance) that few in the USSR and Eastern Europe were inclined to question the truth of the BBC's daily criticisms of the Soviet system and empire. Nothing in public diplomacy succeeds like defeat clearly and rapidly admitted. Could a source so exceptionally willing to depict its own misfortunes be suspected of misrepresenting the truth in areas less central to its interests?

I am not implying that the BBC, like Radio Free Europe, directly addressed its Soviet and East European audiences *in the name* of those audiences, but it certainly provided formidable echo chambers for dissent, and encouragement for the disadvantaged and disaffected. By re-enacting in the summer of 1956, for example, in the BBC's studios, a stormy all-night session of the Hungarian Petőfi Circle (June 27, 1956),[7] transcripts of which had reached us through confidential channels, we gave the rebellious proceedings nationwide publicity. We promoted the spirit of dissent in the communist ranks, probably advancing, albeit indirectly, the day of reckoning (October 23, 1956). Was this subversive of a government with which Britain was maintaining normal diplomatic relations? It certainly was. Was it in consonance with the British commitment to democracy and freedom? It was that, too. We were stretching our brief, but that was what the ideological conflict demanded and what unofficial Britain tacitly accepted.

Broadcasts of this sort abounded in all our "Cold War" languages. The BBC followed the Kostov, Rajk, Mindszenty, Slansky, and Nagy trials, and then those of Sinyavsky and Daniel, blow by blow, with full legal and forensic apparatus, sparing neither communist jurisdiction nor communist law enforcement. We questioned the legality and the results of communist elections; we scorned the legitimacy of communist governments and poured irony on their leaders. We sustained the voices of the independent farmers and of the freely elected trade unions after they had been silenced, and kept the spirit of Christianity alive with religious broadcasts and services in the vernacular. Dramatised versions of Orwell's *Animal Farm* were put on air to underline the absurdities of Stalinism, and excerpts from Pasternak's *Doctor Zhivago* were broadcast in the Russian language in almost nightly instalments when the book was proscribed in the Soviet Union.

All this and much else was done over the years in the name of "projecting Britain," and it gives me a certain quiet satisfaction that I was allowed to play a small part in the BBC's effort. My idealism, I felt, was harnessed to a worthwhile enterprise, and it did not much matter to me whether we called it projecting Britain or preventing the spread of an odious despotism.

Projecting Britain in the narrow sense—promoting British exports or boosting the image of the Edinburgh Festival—was certainly one of the things we were doing, but our major and (as we now know) historically decisive work flourished under the batons of the BBC's second conductors and as a result of the alternative scores from which we were reading. Who were these men? Most of them were "conviction broadcasters" of clear purpose and considerable courage—Gregory Macdonald, Maurice Latey, David Graham, George Tarján, Malcolm Mackintosh, Walter Kolarz, Hugh Lunghi, [Sir] Robert Bruce Lockhart, László Veress, Janis Sapiets, Anton Logoreci, Martin Esslin, Andrew Martin, László Cs. Szabó, and Jan Novak and Noel Bernard (later also of Radio Free Europe fame)—to name only a few of those who were active in my own field. Their story remains to be written, as does indeed the Cold War history of the BBC's European Service as a whole.

How much did official Britain know about these activities? A double-track approach prevailed. The truth was sacrosanct but not the whole truth had to be told; ends did not justify means, but some means were more acceptable than others; the rules were to be respected, but they could be bent if some superior consideration so required. What government ministers could not say openly was left to be told by those not directly answerable to Parliament. The Foreign Office ran in those days (albeit with a somewhat guilty conscience and with minimal publicity) a very effective Information and Research Department (IRD), which did sterling work in countering communist disinformation, supporting publications it deemed tactically useful, and supplying the BBC, too, with confidential material at a time when the USSR and Eastern Europe were almost hermetically sealed off. Also, we at the BBC had access to and were free to use some of the cables from the British embassies behind the Curtain, although we were not supposed to be aware of their origin. Knowledge came our way through other channels too. In sum, Whitehall knew what we knew, but it was not always fully aware, and perhaps did not want to be fully aware, of what exactly the BBC was saying in its non-English broadcasts. The British government had control over the choice of languages in which we broadcast and the airtime devoted to addressing different countries, but it had, and aspired to have, no hands-on control over how we shaped the minds and influenced the actions of people in the countries under communist control.

It was the BBC's second conductors who defined the context and set the tone for the critique of communism and decided how much, or how little, solidarity Russians, Poles, Czechs, Hungarians, and East Germans could expect from the Western world at various times in their bruising relationship with the Soviet-imposed system. It was in their gift to emphasise or de-emphasise the place of the Catholic or the Orthodox Church in the lives of our audiences, and it was they who created legendary BBC radio personalities, with usually devastating impact on the communist regimes, for almost every Eastern country. In the English language, the BBC European and Overseas Services may well have sounded cool and impartial, but there could be no mistaking the BBC's commitment in its foreign-language broadcasts.

I do not want it to be thought that these unofficial powers were lightly exercised. Consultations were held, although they were informal and based more on personal trust than on written directives. There were no guidelines; there did not have to be any. The people heading the various teams were, with rare exceptions, men and women of profound responsibility as well as remarkable learning. They knew each other well. Most of them had been brought up in the spirit of the BBC's Reithian tradition of intellectual excellence and moral probity.[8] Some had firm roots in Christianity, others drew special authority from work done and fame acquired outside the precincts of the Corporation. I witnessed the birth of many a famous book and play over the coffee tables of the BBC canteen in Bush House. George Orwell, too, had penned some of his work in BBC canteens, as a member of the Overseas Service. His model in *Nineteen Eighty-Four* for the Ministry of Truth's uninviting feeding place was the BBC's dilapidated canteen at 100 Oxford Street in London.

The BBC's senior "language staff" supplied that element of foresight, depth, and cultural identification which the politicians and civil servants could not. It was their counterpoint to the official voices of Britain that made listeners in the USSR and Eastern and Central Europe feel that there were forces in the West pursuing an agenda larger, wiser, and more helpful than that articulated by the politicians.

Not everything was, of course, rosy in the gardens of the BBC. Salaries were miserable. In 1948 my pay ran to the princely sum of £410 per annum, about $1,600. Foreigners, even naturalised foreigners, were rather suspect and seldom promoted outside their language areas until after the mid-1960s. An old-fashioned and exceptionally buttoned-up bureaucracy resented the presence of so many highly educated and highly motivated broadcasters, and it felt especially uncomfortable in the company of the BBC's many Continental intellectuals. If those foreigners would only stop broadcasting in their outlandish languages! English nationalism and anti-Europeanism were already raising their unsightly head, and we had more than our share of trouble with the philistinism of retired naval commanders who were holding down jobs as administrative officers. They had the power to annoy but not to thwart our purpose. In almost every case I can remember, the intellectual leadership carried the day.

During my years with the BBC I was far too junior and inexperienced to play any part in that leadership, but I am eager to record and pay tribute to the character and services of the men and women who did. They were my guides and teachers in the European Service's unique genre of broadcasting. Their names are unknown to the public, and the honours conferred on them are nil or derisory; yet I feel they should be remembered on a par with Britain's great military commanders, for their contribution to winning a long and bitter war—the Cold War—was comparable only to what generals might achieve, with luck on their side, after much bitter fighting.

The rehearsal of these facts seems essential if future historians are not to be misled by the conventional opinion that the BBC was always a model of dispassionate objectivity—that it would stoop to nothing so vulgar as dispensing "propaganda." The truth is that for many years after the World War II the European Service of the BBC was an almost self-contained power in the land, a foreign office within the Foreign Office, with a corpus of knowledge and experience at its disposal on which government departments could and did draw, and with something like an agenda of its own. It acted in what the BBC's "conductors" considered to be the broad interests of Britain, European civilisation, and human decency. Policy was not "made"—it emerged, in time-honoured British fashion, over lunch and on the tennis courts. I caught the tail end of that civilised and effective tradition, and I grieve that it no longer exists.

CHAPTER FIVE

Reluctant Americans

Radio Free Europe was, on paper at least, a very different enterprise from the BBC, and one of great complexity. It stood for a new genre of psychological and political warfare. Sponsored by the U.S. government, it yet remained substantially outside its immediate control. Incorporated as "an independent broadcast media [sic] operating in a manner not inconsistent with the broad foreign policy objectives of the United States," it served, in effect, the long-term, historical interests of the captive nations. Supervised by a board appointed by the American president, the Radio had, nevertheless, sovereign rights of policy making in conjunction with the board. Yet, because it was reliant on Congress for its budgetary allocations, it was in some ways answerable to Congress in the manner of any government department. As several of the Radio's transmitters were on Portuguese and Spanish soil, Portuguese and Spanish sensitivities put some restraint on certain of its foreign affairs broadcasts; and because the Radio's headquarters were in Germany, it operated under not American but German labour law, with its generous (and expensive) provisions for the employee, including the virtual impossibility of removal on grounds of poor performance or political unsuitability. Our employees' frequent lawsuits against the Radio for "wrongful dismissal" and the like were a permanent and costly result of its location in Munich; for the German labour courts almost invariably found against Radio Free Europe.

Not only that, but in its first formative years the Radio was in reality not a single entity, much less a single American entity, but a sort of American-European confederal communications enterprise composed of several national radios, certainly under American funding and administrative management, and enjoying the advantages of an American infrastructure, but politically sovereign—or nearly so. "As director of the Radio Free Europe Polish programmes," Jan Novak wrote in 1996, "I had considerable autonomy within a very broad framework of policy rules, which were discussed and agreed upon between the American management and the head of the Polish Service. The Basic Guidelines of 1952 established that there was not one Radio Free Europe but there were five separate radio stations broadcasting to five countries in East Central Europe."[1]

This dispensation ended in the late 1950s—following the Radio's unsatisfactory performance at the time of the 1956 Hungarian Revolution, more rigorous controls were introduced—but while it lasted, it was taken seriously. The key man in Radio Free Europe in those early years was William E. Griffith, the American policy adviser, but his functions were consultative and his word carried, on paper at least, no executive authority. The Radio probably took the Free French of World War II for its model: General de Gaulle had broadcast from the BBC's London studios under British auspices but had pursued entirely (and for the British Foreign Office often irritatingly) French national policies.

It would be difficult to think of a more complicated formula and one less likely to allow an answer to the question whether there were second conductors. The confusion in the Radio's structure was only partly built into its original blueprint. It developed, as these things do in pragmatically inclined democracies, in the course of time, through a process of muddle and tinkering. There were initiatives to put surrogate broadcasting under stricter, and then under looser "control"; to cut back and then to increase funding; to appease or not to appease (or to what extent to appease) the American progressivist media establishment; to merge or not to merge Radio Free Europe with Radio Liberty—and other policies more closely related to infighting in Washington than to the needs of broadcasting on site. The American inclination to muddle through rather than plan or employ foresight was every bit as impressive and depressing as were similar inclinations governing the political process in Britain. A like impulse to trim and adjust regardless of principle was once considered a colourful peculiarity of the Habsburg empire.

Public confusion about the true character of Radio Free Europe, both outside and within the United States, stemmed from a psychological factor which has seldom been openly acknowledged. The American political class and the American public in general felt extremely uneasy about "propaganda" and were deeply disturbed to be told that the size and power of the United States thrust "imperial" responsibilities on American shoulders. How could a former colony born in a revolution against empire be expected to assume the mantle of empire? It was a monstrously un-American thought, and the idea of "propaganda" as a tool of empire, or even just of the Western community of nations, was considered offensive. In all discussions of the work of Radio Free Europe the word *propaganda* was scrupulously avoided, and *empire* was unmentionable in any discussion of America's role in the world.

Even within the Radio, great opprobrium attached to the word *propaganda*—exactly as it did in the BBC. Our large, mainly U.S.- and Commonwealth-staffed News Division worked hard over the years to dissociate itself from the "propaganda" activities of the editorial "language" departments, until it achieved separate divisional status and bureaucratic independence. From then on, its support of the Radio's political mission was half-hearted or nonexistent. Early in his chairmanship of the board, Frank Shakespeare summoned the entire News Division and read them the riot act but, within a few weeks, the effect of his words evaporated.

A sense of unease, even guilt, about the Radio's mission affected our research departments too. Mindful of the left-leaning character of most American scholarship and of their career prospects at American universities, many of our researchers were keen to put clear water between their own work and the "compromised and compromising" ethos of the Radio. These doubts and reservations greatly complicated the self-understanding of our frontline national broadcasters and undermined their morale. How could they do their work with conviction and a clear conscience when U.S. and Commonwealth colleagues in management, the News Division, and research treated them with condescension if not contempt? That making propaganda was looked upon as unclean and even culpable led to a state of affairs in which personal grievances could be dressed up as protests against propaganda for presentation to sympathetic members of the American Congress or the American press. Repeatedly, both groups were mobilised.

Hence, Radio Free Europe was under continual suspicion and the target of countless investigations—by congressional committees, the Library of Congress, inspectors from auditing authorities and individual members of both houses of Congress. The Radio was presumed guilty of transgressions seldom clearly stated, and it had to demonstrate its "innocence" again and again. Its real guilt lay in its very existence.

Why, apart from the historical reasons I have mentioned, a nation proud of its freedom and openness, and of the persuasive techniques of Madison Avenue, should have shied away, at a time of great peril for the United States, from embracing an activity infinitely more truthful and honourable than any in commercial advertising has never been adequately explained. It may have had something to do with that curious combination of "infantilism passing directly into senility, with the stage of maturity entirely missed" that Leopold Labedz[2] bitingly identified as one of the characteristics of American public life in our time. If so, it may have been the early recognition of that handicap, and of the related volatility of American public opinion, that had persuaded the Radio's founding fathers not to expose the Radio's oversight to Congressional caprice but rather to create for it a politically safe haven under the umbrella of the Central Intelligence Agency. A charity campaign—the "Crusade for Freedom"—was put up to hoodwink the public.

My own exasperation at the unworldliness of American public opinion moved me to write in 1984:

> That touch of subtle self-righteousness and civilised hypocrisy that has made the British and French into persuasive disseminators of the values of their civilization is utterly lacking in American political culture. Americans of our time no longer believe that they have a compact with "manifest destiny." Much less that it might be in the public interest to propagate American premises with anything smacking of pride of achievement or a sense of leadership. . . .
>
> The custodians of the US image on the world's air waves have, therefore, their work cut out for them. They have to represent the interests of a world-power that is reluctant to be a world-power, that distrusts any balance-of-power politics, and has the notion of supra-national morality so deeply embedded in its national psyche that it frequently cannot decide whether it is really involved, as it says it is, in some international conflict, or is standing on the sidelines to adjudicate the quarrels of less-enlightened breeds.
>
> This referee-complex is the despair of America's allies and makes the lives of those who have to represent and interpret the US abroad exceptionally difficult. Sceptical Europeans remark jokingly, but with only slight exaggeration, that the US has never quite made up its mind whether it is a church or a country—that Americans enjoy their power sadly because, for a moral person, that is the only way in which power can be enjoyed. They chide Americans for paying no heed to Machiavelli's warning that it is wiser for the Prince, if a choice has to be made, to be feared than to be loved.

These are, in many ways, engaging characteristics, for they depict a society that lacks any sense of braggadocio, has no taste for imperialism and does not even like to tell the world about its virtues; and when it does, tends to do it with so many reservations that it does it badly.

The ugly American, the footloose American, the uncultured American, the aggressive American do not, as stereotypes, correspond to anything in real life, but they are images of great power in the world because the reputation of Americans, like some superior French wines, does not travel well. It is marred at base by an exceptionally quarrelsome political class, a lack of self-confidence in dealing with foreigners, an iconoclastic intelligentsia, and a media establishment whose ruling passion is the destruction of the reputation of America's elected leaders.

Have compassion, then, for the men and women who run the United States Information Agency, Radio Free Europe, Radio Liberty and the Voice of America. Soviet propaganda and disinformation are only one of their headaches; the inhibitions of US political culture are another and almost as powerful. Their mandates are accident-prone and the ground under their feet responds only too readily to the tremors of the political landscape.

As so often in US political life, the domestic tail tends to wag the American dog, and, with its body out of balance, the dog tends to whimper when it ought to bark.[3]

I ascribe the American reluctance to don the arms and regalia of a superpower and pick up the threads of a balance-of-power politics to the morally attractive American puritanical tendency to belittle the virtues and exaggerate the vices of American society. George Kennan speaks for many Americans when he insists that America is mired in the sins of drink, drugs, crime, miseducation, ignorance, and vulgarity. Who are we (he asks) to teach the world decency in public affairs? How do we know whether the idea of socialism does not, at its core, harbour some incipient hope for a better future? The world outside the United States may or may not be a wicked place, but American guilt and decadence are manifest. And although dictatorships such as the Soviet system may have sinned against humanity more radically than we have, it is not for Americans to police the globe. The business of America is to improve its own conduct and not to bestride the stage of the world preaching virtues it is not prepared to practise. "Wouldn't we be better advised," Kennan said to me in 1976, "if we put our main effort into making ourselves worth protecting?"[4] And in 1993 Kennan added: "I should make it clear that I'm wholly and emphatically reject-

ing any and all messianic concepts of America's role in the world: rejecting, that is, an image of ourselves as teachers and redeemers to the
rest of humanity, rejecting the illusions of unique and superior virtue
on our part, the prattle about Manifest Destiny or the 'American Century.'"[5]

This breast-beating puritanism—a Jewish as well as a Protestant
trait in American thinking—is reinforced by the masochism of the
American Left. Enjoyable self-flagellation, never distant from the
minds of East Coast intellectuals, was much in vogue in the late 1960s
and the 1970s. Direct approval of socialism of the Soviet type was, by
the mid-1960s, mildly frowned upon, but anticommunism was intolerable. Many American "liberals" equated America's moral failures in
Vietnam with the depredations of the Soviet system, and wore their
anti-anticommunism with pride. Two rival imperialisms were abroad
in the world (they said), and there was little to choose between them.
They looked upon émigré Polish Catholics and self-exiled fighters of
the 1956 Hungarian uprising with suspicion. Surely they had axes to
grind; surely their witness could not be trusted; surely capitalism and
communism would eventually converge; surely détente was, in the
meantime, a constructive way forward. Men and women of liberal intent should respect the idealistic core of socialism (we were told) and
not be misled by its Soviet variant. Socialism was on the march, and
the best we could do was to "manage" Western decline. Meanwhile,
Eurocommunism was worth taking a look at.

Such, in imperfect outline, was the progressivist attitude to things
Soviet and East European in our field of activity. It dominated, with
honourable exceptions, the American media landscape, though it could
not always be openly articulated. Radio Free Europe was a natural
whipping boy and an easy one, for it had no popular domestic constituency. "You don't want to create trouble in Czechoslovakia!" I was
warned by a testy Senator Claiborne Pell in 1978. That the Radio was
profoundly critical of communism, not to say, *horribile dictu*, anticommunist, was enough to undermine its credentials in liberal eyes.
And who, it was asked, were the men and women we were employing?
Weren't they people who had fled the Red Army? And weren't such men
and women fascists or reactionaries (to whatever degree) almost by
definition? Wasn't it more honourable for a person of democratic convictions to exert himself behind the Curtain to improve socialism from
within, rather than try to undermine from the outside—and on CIA pay

to boot—misguided but basically progressive governments? And how could one be sure that surrogate broadcasters were not spreading the spirit of anti-Semitism under the cover of promoting the national consciousness of "traditionally racist" countries such as Russia, Poland, Ukraine, and Romania?

Anti-Semitism was an especially lethal charge, likely to ruin reputations[6] and undermine support. It was regularly levelled against Radio Liberty (though not against Radio Free Europe) by "politically correct" critics and even certain centrist thinkers in the Reagan administration. I can recall no such accusations being made against either Radio under earlier presidencies—Republican or Democratic.

Reagan was, of course, the bête noire of the progressives, though not as cordially loathed as Nixon had been. The belief that Radio Liberty was a conspicuous symbol of Reaganite Cold War politics and that Reaganism itself would be dealt a blow if Radio Liberty could be shown to be promoting racist broadcasts was a much-favoured theme in the thinking of the East Coast intelligentsia. That such racist broadcasts had not been made was well known to all who were fully informed, but for those with axes to grind (of whom there were many both at American universities and in the government bureaucracy), hearsay was enough of a basis on which to raise a great hue and cry and damage Radio Liberty—to the considerable benefit of Soviet information policy and the KGB. The truth was less colourful but rich in irony.

Of Radio Liberty's overall Russian staff, 32 percent were Soviet Jews, many of them occupying senior positions, and the proportion rose steeply to about 50 percent in the early 1990s among Russian Service newsmen and programme makers. So favourable indeed to Soviet-Jewish interests (especially Jewish emigration policy) were Radio Liberty's broadcasts judged to be by the Soviet side that Moscow regularly castigated the Radio as "Zionist-inspired" and staffed and paid for by the "American-Israeli Jewish community," confidently expecting that this would gravely damage it in the eyes of non-Jewish Russian listeners.[7] On one occasion I was myself asked by the board to register an opinion ex post facto about a certain Radio Liberty broadcast then under indictment for anti-Semitism. I found the text unexceptionable. The author himself—an outside contributor—turned out to be a Jew who was devastated by the charge of insensitivity to Jewish feelings.

One personal tale that reveals the grotesqueries of those years is Frank Shakespeare's account (in a verbal statement to the author in

December 1993) of how, in one instance, in 1984, the charge of anti-
Semitism came to be levelled against Radio Liberty.

> Senator Charles Percy, who was running for re-election in Chicago [in
> 1984], felt he was in trouble,[8] and perhaps because he was trying to in-
> fluence the Jewish vote in Illinois, his office put out a statement to the
> effect that the senator had heard that there was some anti-Semitism
> evident in the operations of Radio Liberty and that he was going to hold
> hearings on the matter. This was, of course, a great story in the coun-
> try and especially Illinois, and it may be that it helped the senator. At
> the board, we were *horrified*. We were very close to the operation, and
> we knew that there wasn't any truth at all to the senator's charge. Ben
> Wattenberg and I got into the matter right away—Ben at the time was
> vice-chairman of the board to myself as chairman. Ben and I found
> that someone from B'Nai Brith had provided materials for the sena-
> tor's staff. So Ben and I made an appointment with the president of the
> B'Nai Brith, and we went over to see him.
>   We told him that we were appalled by the accusation; no one had
> talked to us or checked with us. We pointed out the story was totally
> untrue and had gravely damaged the Radios. Ben who is (thank God)
> Jewish, took over after he had told me earlier, "Frank, let *me* handle this
> matter after you've said what you were going to say." So Ben Watten-
> berg then proceeded to tell the president of B'Nai Brith that his grand-
> father kept a brick stained with brains and blood as a souvenir in his
> study in Odessa, which he had brought back from Kishinev after a ter-
> rible pogrom there. So (Ben said) he knew what anti-Semitism was,
> and he knew that it did not exist in the Radios. Wattenberg was very,
> very tough with this fellow.
>   We took the strongest action we could because the story released by
> the senator's office was dreadfully untrue and damaging . . . ; the tar
> brush of anti-Semitism can have awful effects. . . . We asked for a pub-
> lic apology. We said flatly that there was not a scintilla of truth in the
> accusation—and of course coming from Wattenberg, our message was
> much more forceful that it could otherwise have been. We pointed out
> all the obvious things: that the director of Radio Liberty was George
> Bailey, whose wife came from a German-Jewish family, that the head of
> Radio Liberty News Division was Eduard Kuznetsov, a former Israeli
> hero, and so on. The irony was that having gone to all this trouble,
> Senator Percy lost his seat.

To what extent the various campaigns against the two Radios in the
1970s and early 1980s were the work of the Eastern security services
remains to be fully examined. What can be said with certainty is that

had a section of the American intelligentsia not been deeply suspicious of the Radios and responsive to Eastern innuendos in the first place, Moscow could have achieved little. But it *was* suspicious of the first and responsive to the second. Also, the openings created by détente and the aftereffects of Vietnam and Watergate were waiting to be exploited. Moscow, Warsaw, Prague, and East Berlin—for these were the principal centres of disinformation—went to work with determination and skill. Their undisguised aim was to discredit the two stations (together with RIAS in Berlin) as "spy radios" controlled by the CIA and thus destructive of the whole architecture of East-West reconciliation.

West Germany and the United States were the most susceptible to such charges. *Ostpolitik* and détente saw to that. In both countries there was growing reluctance to confront the Soviet system, or even to maintain the contest of ideas at existing levels. Turning to West Germany, the Soviets now argued that the presence of American broadcasting stations on German soil was an infringement of German sovereignty and a special threat to the Federal Republic's freedom to forge closer ties, under Ostpolitik, with its Eastern neighbours and the Soviet Union. Willy Brandt was regularly quoted in support of the view that twenty-five years after the war it was absurd that foreign radio stations should still be carrying on propaganda against third parties from German territory. (Brandt did, in fact, make such an observation, and in 1983 in Brussels, even the level-headed Helmut Schmidt uttered a similar opinion, albeit privately, within my earshot.)

In the United States, public figures critical of the existence of Radio Free Europe and Radio Liberty for ideological reasons of their own were the main targets of Eastern disinformation. They included Senators William Fulbright, Clifford Case, and later Claiborne Pell, as well as certain Soviet-friendly or gullible members of the journalistic and academic communities. Soviet propaganda homed in on the disclosure that up to 1971 the Radios had indeed been funded from CIA appropriations. Moscow banked on a storm in Congress which it expected would jeopardise the two Radios' future—as it very nearly did. A number of Polish and other communist agents, who had worked in the Radios for years under cover as "sleepers," were paraded on the international stage and induced to "unmask" Radio Free Europe. Their stories, though too abstruse to have an impact on the general public, were nevertheless grist to the mill of a portion of American and German opinion.

Among the more spectacular escapades in this campaign was a

break-in, in 1972, by a Polish secret service commando unit, into the Chicago home of the editor of the largest Polish-language American newspaper. Two letters by Jan Novak were stolen and tampered with so that the resulting forgeries could be used to compromise Novak and the Polish Department of Radio Free Europe in the eyes of Senators Fulbright and Case and other dovish members of Congress.

Side by side with these clandestine machinations, the communist governments were also extremely active in open diplomacy, pursuing the identical objective of trying to silence Radio Free Europe. In May 1971 Walter Scheel, then West German foreign minister, received a note from the Polish communist leadership, and President Nixon received another. In the note to Nixon, the Polish communists voiced their expectation that in its effort to remove sources of tension from American-Polish relations, the U.S. government would terminate the activities of Radio Free Europe.[9]

A few years ago I wondered whether the original charge that Radio Liberty was anti-Semitic had also been the work of the Eastern secret services, especially the KGB. I had at the time no hard evidence that it had, but I had a strong suspicion that somewhere along the line the KGB must have been involved—or else it would not have been doing its job. I knew that the "Reaganite" management of Radio Liberty was particularly feared by the Soviet leaders, for it was not difficult to gauge from the way in which we were reforming the Radios that we had a clear appreciation of the mushrooming vulnerabilities of the Soviet system and were hoping to accelerate its self-destruction.[10] At the same time, however, I was also aware that starting with the early 1970s, serious infighting at Radio Liberty between a growing number of newly recruited Soviet Jewish employees and their non-Jewish Russian colleagues had generated its own heat, which had reached the German courts and the U.S. Congress. Could this earlier package of problems, too, with its attendant reverberations in the press, be ascribed to the machinations of the KGB? In 1992, there was no way of making a safe judgement. But it would have been surprising if the communist secret services had not done their bit to exploit what must have seemed to them a great windfall and an excellent opportunity to damage the two Radios' new leadership.

Since then, former KGB general Oleg Kalugin's revelations have supplied the evidence I was looking for. In his book *SpyMaster* (1994) he put it on display:

My job was to attack Radio Liberty at the source—at its European headquarters in Munich—by placing agents on its staff. If we could not control what Radio Liberty was broadcasting, at least we could know what it was up to. . . . In meetings with his [Radio Liberty editor Oleg Tumanov's] KGB case officers in Germany, he kept us well informed about activities in Radio Liberty and the CIA's involvement with the station. He subtly helped us spread rumours and disinformation, and did what he could to create conflict among the staff. Among other things, he wrote anonymous anti-Semitic letters which caused rift among some station employees. He also told us which of his colleagues might be ripe for recruitment.[11]

Earlier in his book Kalugin discloses that at the KGB station in Washington, he and his men invented and then continually spread the smear of *American* anti-Semitism as a "counter to anti-Soviet propaganda emanating from the United States."

While I was in Washington, the Soviet Union was under increasing attack for its discrimination against Jews and refusal to allow some Jews to emigrate. Our bosses in Moscow branded these attacks as an 'ideological diversion' and ordered us to fight them. We did so by once again flooding American Jewish organisations with anonymous rabidly anti-Semitic materials, as well as by hiring people to desecrate Jewish graves and paint swastikas on synagogues. Then, of course, the Soviet media faithfully reported on the wave of anti-Semitic activity sweeping America.[12]

Kalugin's tribute to Oleg Tumanov warrants a detour from my argument, for here was an agent who had attained senior rank in Radio Liberty and was directly linked to the KGB's daily operations to undermine the Radio. In February 1986, Tumanov disappeared from Radio Liberty and then from Munich. With KGB assistance he secretly returned to the Soviet Union, where he was given a hero's welcome and portrayed by the KGB as a fighter who had penetrated "that nest of foul imperialist propaganda." His unhindered rise, over a period of twenty years, to the top post of deputy editor-in-chief of the Russian Service of Radio Liberty, with full policy-interpreting powers, was Radio Liberty's most spectacular and damaging security failure. At Radio Free Europe, Vladimir Kusin, another agent of importance, never quite attained a hands-on function in the policy area (see Chapter 7). At Radio Liberty, Tumanov did.

Neither Tumanov's American debriefer in Frankfurt after Tumanov's spectacular "defection" in 1966 nor any of his directors at Radio

Liberty under various managements suspected a spy in him. Even the
Frankfurt lie detector failed to pick up his unreliability. On the contrary, Tumanov was extremely well thought of as genuinely fresh blood
from Russia, and to his surprise, he was repeatedly promoted. To the
Americans, he seemed straightforward (as these things went among
émigré Russians)—not openly anti-Semitic, uninvolved with émigré
politics, and suitably undereducated to make a good radio bureaucrat.
That Russian was his only language was quickly forgiven him. He remained homo sovieticus to the end. Reminiscing from Moscow in 1993,
he tells us: "I saw everything collapse with my own eyes . . . ideology,
party, faith, the economy. . . . In the end, the union, too, destroyed itself.
The formerly mighty state, once respected by all, cut itself off from
communism. And the result? Chaos, armed conflicts, crime, poverty,
inflation. . . . If this is what the opponents of communism wanted to
achieve, then I am not at all sorry that for twenty years I fought them
as an agent of Soviet intelligence."[13]

That Oleg Tumanov's original American debriefer might himself
have been an undercover Soviet agent, and thus in a position to clear
and put other KGB men into sensitive Western positions, has been rumoured but, to my best knowledge, never confirmed.

It was in 1982–83 that James Buckley, George Bailey, and I took over
the two Radios' management in Munich under Frank Shakespeare's
chairmanship of the board in Washington. For me, Ronald Reagan's
speech to the joint houses of the British Parliament at Windsor Castle
(June 8, 1982) had been an inestimable encouragement. Announcing,
in effect, the end of the West's retreat in the Cold War, the president
undertook to confront Moscow's worldwide ideological offensive with
an offensive of our own. He said it was not the West that found itself
in the throes of a great revolutionary crisis, as the Kremlin was telling
us, but the Soviet system and empire. And he predicted that the march
of democracy and freedom "will leave Marxism-Leninism on the ash
heap of history." This came like a breath of fresh air.[14]

Reagan's ideas, and the language in which they were couched, were
in stark contrast to the apologetic and defensive guidelines Radio Free
Europe was meant to follow. They were the American riposte to Khrushchev's forecast, "We will bury you," and to the Politburo's, including
Gorbachev's, still unreconstructed Leninism. I certainly looked upon
the president's words as the best justification yet of the ideas my com-

bat historian–friends and I had been advocating in London. Some of us at the Centre for Policy Studies had, indeed, written to Reagan on his inauguration (in January 1981), suggesting certain policies to counter Soviet might and militancy. They were not dissimilar to those he spelt out at Windsor, though I have no evidence that the two were in any way connected. Here, I felt, was higher authorisation for second conductorship, if one were still needed. It soon transpired that it was.

Surprising things started happening. Within eighteen months of my arrival in October 1983, Radio Free Europe and Radio Liberty were subjected to a barrage of fault-finding missions from the congressional establishment. Outwardly amicable, our investigators were bristling with ill-will. The charge for which they sought confirmation was simple: Radio Free Europe and Radio Liberty had become "anticommunist" under our stewardship, and the guidelines laid down by the Board for International Broadcasting were either too lax, insufficiently observed, or purposely violated. Radio Liberty was also accused of anti-Semitism. Congressman Lawrence (Larry) Smith, an unremarkable but opinionated legislator from Florida, having spent two days in February 1985 at the Radios (accompanied by a staff director, a staff consultant, and a minority staff consultant), observed in his "Trip Report" to Dan A. Mica, chairman of the Congressional Subcommittee on International Operations (March 8, 1985):

> Rumors of politicization of the radios first surfaced last year in an article of the *Washington Post*. At the time, it inferred that Messrs. George Bailey and George Urban were attempting to promote a much less subtle uniform anti-communist line throughout the Radios. Complaints since then have been received. . . . Discussions with both Directors revealed that they are motivated by a drastically more ominous view of events in the East. The situation in Eastern Europe and the Soviet Union is so tenuous that the Soviet Union could be on the verge of collapse [they said].[15] Their views regarding the situation were almost too dramatic. However, their purpose in painting such a dark picture was to imply that we should push harder so that we can precipitate the fall of the Soviet Union.

The promotion of such "ideological views over others," Smith stressed in his conclusions, was wrong and detrimental to the Radios' credibility and mission.[16] He charged that the Radios were run by Shakespeare, Bailey, and me, sidelining Buckley and loosening the established structure of controls. "The BIB can no longer objectively oversee, as directed by law, the radios as a result of its active involvement in daily operations." He struck a high moral tone. Eight years later, on August 2, 1993, Congressman Smith was convicted on charges of tax evasion and false campaign reporting and sent to prison in Miami. He announced that he would not seek re-election.

Almost immediately after Smith's lightning visit, two very young Congressional investigators appeared in Munich at the behest of Senator Claiborne Pell to conduct another enquiry, this time for the U.S. General Accounting Office. Without linguistic qualifications and boasting barely a schoolboy's knowledge of East and Central European history and geography, they recommended increased control of our broadcasts both inside the Radios and by the federal authorities, more stringent "coordination" with the State Department, and the presence of State Department personnel at the meetings of our board.[17]

As if all this were not enough, in the same period one Geryld B. Christianson, minority staff director of the Senate Foreign Relations Committee, also sat in (slightly more benevolent) judgement over us, also at the instigation of Claiborne Pell, in order, as Pell put it, to assure compliance with the policy guidelines. Christianson dutifully stated that "the changes made by RFE/RL's new management suggest that the *potential* for an increase in broadcast violations exists," and like the visitors who had come before him, he recommended tighter guidelines and more censorship.[18]

This was the inauspicious environment in which American-sponsored surrogate broadcasting had to operate even under a robustly Republican administration. After the collapse of the Soviet system, my friends in the East found it hard to believe that Radio Free Europe and Radio Liberty's main problem throughout their existence had been neither the sophistication of Soviet propaganda (which had been highly manageable) nor the effectiveness of Soviet jamming (although the latter had been intense) but the ceaseless sneering, jeering, and outright hostility of progressivist American opinion makers. Of the two battlefronts the Radios had to cover—the Soviet communist and the American left-liberal—it was the latter, with its influential arm in Congress and the State Department, that gave us by far the most trouble. It looked as though a section of the American political class were having second thoughts about the powerful broadcasting organisation influential Americans had created in the aftermath of World War II but did not quite know how to kill it without embarrassment. Appeasement was in the air under the name of détente. Radio Free Europe and Radio Liberty, like the countries they represented, stood in the way of what threatened to become a retreat in all but name—a retreat, moreover, at a time when the Soviet system was, as some of us strongly suspected, close to expiring.

CHAPTER SIX

The Soft Approach to Communism

B ut I have run ahead of my story. With the election of Ronald Reagan and the eventual (and much delayed) appointment, in January 1982, of a revamped Board for International Broadcasting, some of the confused brief of the Radio was clarified. Frank Shakespeare, a former director of the U.S. Information Service and a leading supporter of Nixon, became chairman. This was decisive. Not only was Shakespeare a dedicated opponent of communism and Soviet power, but he was also a born leader, a devout Catholic, and an accomplished strategist. He eventually gathered round him a board which included James A. Michener, Ben Wattenberg, Lane Kirkland, Michael Novak, Malcolm S. Forbes, Jr., and other men of influence and distinction from both Republican and Democratic quarters. With former senator James Buckley as joint president of Radio Free Europe and Radio Liberty, Shakespeare set about finding the key men to run the two organisations—the directors of Radio Free Europe and Radio Liberty.

I will not go into the intrigues surrounding my own appointment. Several months elapsed between the first indications that I would be asked to head the Radio and the making of the offer. James Buckley himself would have been, as it soon transpired, more comfortable with a trusted representative of the establishment and was hoping to attract a particular foreign service officer of ambassadorial rank awaiting (vainly, as it turned out) accreditation to Poland.

I had, apparently, a reputation for not suffering communists, appeasers, and fools gladly. "A fine chap"—so I heard it said—"as an intellectual driving force and a 'resource,' but not to be quite entrusted with managing a large and intricate organisation." The cult of "management skills" was running high in the United States. Dedication to the organisation came first, substantive knowledge second. One of my predecessors had been (as I related) a U.S. Army general; two others had come from the American Civil Service. Bureaucrats usually feel more at home with their own sort than with men and women driven by the bizarre desire actually to achieve stated ends and achieve them quickly. Jeane Kirkpatrick once told me (and she was in a good position to know) that whatever administration was in power in the United States and however many committed outsiders had been brought in to pursue a particular policy, the business of government usually ended up with lawyers and bureaucrats talking to lawyers and bureaucrats, and often the same lawyers and bureaucrats.

I don't know whether this is a law of nature; it certainly appeared to be the dominant practice in American politics in the 1980s. I found it irritating, but neither new nor shocking. Civil servants in Britain tend to show a similar reluctance to be associated with people of ideas and other unreliables. It later turned out that some of my supporters fought hard for my appointment precisely because they felt that the Reagan administration provided a golden opportunity for revitalising Radio Free Europe and putting fresh pressure on the Soviet system. It was a skirmish they eventually won, but only because Frank Shakespeare's distrust of career diplomats (or anyone, for that matter, who had held down a senior post in the U.S. Information Service or the Voice of America) was, if anything, even more profound than mine. Even my British citizenship was not allowed to stand in the way. Shakespeare had no use for people who had been trained to take orders, because he felt such people were not cut out to respond creatively to the changing challenges of our great psychological confrontation with the Soviet system. Having headed USIS, he knew what he was talking about. My political and, I might say, spiritual understanding with Shakespeare was to remain at the very heart of our policies.

In the event, the board did break with tradition and took the unorthodox step of appointing a couple of "gnostic" outsiders—George Bailey and me—to head the Radios. Bailey was a great fighter, a well-known journalist, and a respected student of Soviet affairs with whom I was to forge a profound friendship. He was closely associated with the idea of rehabilitating the Russian people on the lines advocated by Alexander Solzhenitsyn. That intention, in the United States, meant taking a risk with one's career, for the bulk of American intellectuals had as little sympathy with Solzhenitsyn as they had with the two Munich Radios.

Initially, at least, we were a happy team. We were guided by the single purpose of returning the Radios to their original inspiration and expediting, to the extent that could then be imagined, the disintegration of the Soviet system. I use the word *system* purposely because it was clear to us that the cancer in international relations was not Soviet power alone, but the Marxist-Leninist organisation of society, with its long reach into all compartments of life within and outside the communist world.

All was not well in Munich. In 1975 and 1976 the two Radios had been put under joint administrative management, to the detriment and dissatisfaction of both. The distinction between the Soviet aggressor — addressed by Radio Liberty, and the victims of aggression — addressed by Radio Free Europe, was being blurred. For congressional consumption it was, of course, more convenient, and cheaper, to put the two under a common roof as networks "addressing communist nations." The offence implicit in so cavalier a simplification ought to have given pause to the American legislators; but it did not. They failed to realise that even if the Soviet Union could perhaps be thought of as a communist nation (there was, in reality, no such nation), the East and Central European countries could not.

RFE/RL — as the two stations came to be known after the administrative merger — was also suffering from the effects of détente and a loss of purpose and direction. There was growing doubt within senior management whether the conflict with the Soviet system could be won and whether winning it unconditionally was desirable. A thirty-year organisational fatigue was taking its toll. Bureaucrats were replacing men of political commitment; mediocrity and a willingness not to rock the boat were increasingly reckoned as virtues and passports to promotion.

Washington did not help. Time and again funds had been cut, staff reduced, and the legitimacy of the two Radios' mission put in doubt. Outspoken members of staff — among them Jan Novak of the Polish Service, war hero and a powerful second conductor in his own right — retired or were retired.[1] Radio Free Europe's message was toned down, the spirit of liberalisation replacing liberation, and the presence of Soviet troops in Poland and Hungary was de-emphasised or ignored. Certain Western sources of news and opinion were censored or kept out of programming altogether if they were judged to be unduly critical of Soviet interests. The two Radios' new guidelines placed no restrictions on the criticism of Western policies and Western politicians, but the leaders of the East European communist parties and governments were protected. There was open season on the failings of Ronald Reagan but not of Leonid Brezhnev. One point stipulated "avoidance of any material which could be characterised as petty gossip, slander, spiteful reference to or attack on the personal lives or families of government or party leaders."[2] Leonid Brezhnev, Nicolai Ceauşescu,[3] and Todor Zhivkov,[4] whose own and whose families' personal lives epitomised much that was wrong, indeed criminal, in the communist system, could hardly have hoped for more chivalrous treatment. Another point proscribed the use of "obsolete" terminology "such as 'the Communist bloc,' 'Communist satellite countries,' and 'capitalism vs. Communism.'"

Frank Shakespeare's appointment gave rise to particularly unsavoury comments. "The fascists have arrived," it was darkly hinted by soft-line sophisticates in Munich; "the garage mechanics are taking over." There was a time in the 1970s when the evaporation of the American political will, disguised as a funding crisis, brought the two Radios to the brink of closure.

In fairness to the advocates of détente, I will say that their case was neither incomprehensible nor out of tune with the then dominant strain in Western opinion. It was simply erroneous. It amounted to perceiving communism itself as an agent of reform—a creed in flux, capable, it was thought, of rehabilitating its heretics and taking off in a fresh and liberal direction. For détente to be successful, it was argued, the governments in the East had to be helped to attain a modicum of legitimacy. Legitimacy building, however, required supporting any initiative within the ruling communist parties that promised to smooth away the hard edges of the party-state dictatorship. With a domesticated form of communism assimilated by the peoples of Eastern and Central Europe, Western public opinion would more easily accept the reformed regimes as partners in détente. Helmut Sonnenfeldt's ill-fated and amoral "doctrine" was rooted in considerations of this kind. The idea that the rule of communism could be fully terminated was quietly set aside.

Seeing that both the Hungarian uprising of 1956 and the Czechoslovak reform movement of 1968 had started with disaffection within the communist hierarchies—and that the West, when the crunch came, did nothing to support either—it was not unreasonable to argue that our encouragement of self-generated, piecemeal reforms, assisted by a judicious deployment of Western sticks and carrots, was a realistic alternative to both confrontation and inactivity. Also, a policy bestowing a human face on the communist system would, it was hoped, help to soothe Western consciences: if an "organic relationship" (Sonnenfeldt's term) between the rulers and the ruled could be brought about, détente might go ahead without arousing a sense of betrayal in Western public opinion.

These were, as I say, not specifically Radio Free Europe–Radio Liberty policies. The Radios merely reflected, with restraint in some of their languages—with enthusiasm in others—that hotchpotch of improvisations that passed for policy in the 1970s in all Western chancelleries. They were all built on the assumption that the Soviet system was here to stay and that the Soviet Union was a coherent and purposefully led "superpower." It would, therefore, be historically inaccurate to suggest that Radio Free Europe "went soft" on communism. The entire Western world had gone soft on communism and was willing to make its peace with the USSR if the terms could be presented to the public as vaguely acceptable. In the world of practical action, Henry Kissinger's complex détente strategy—the combination of deterrence and coexistence—proved too hard to handle.

I am choosing my words carefully because no black-and-white analysis can do justice to this distressing chapter in the Radio's record. It was one thing to exploit weaknesses within the ruling communist parties as a step on the road to their destruction (many of us used that tactic on suitable occasions) and quite another to believe or to imply that all we needed to aim for was a reformed sort of communism or "socialism." The Italian and Spanish Communist Parties became favourites in some of the Radio's councils because their liberalised version of the creed—Eurocommunism—was thought to offer a dispensation under which both sides could live.

This was politically naive as well as mischievous. Ordinary citizens in the East were resisting or ignoring communism as best they could, yet Radio "Free" Europe was attempting to make a case in some of its broadcasts for communism à la Carrillo or Berlinguer. But even this attempt was not all of a piece. A long series of colloquies addressed mainly to intellectuals in the East, which I had been asked to design as an outside consultant in 1977–78, came to the conclusion that Eurocommunism was a name without substance, that it was only under capitalism that communism could change and prosper, and that in an international crisis, Western Eurocommunists would return to their Stalinist loyalties and betray NATO.[5] This, too, was broadcast, even though the hope at the Radio appeared to be that my project would depict Eurocommunism as a friendly and useable alternative to the ruling variety. Some of my critics on the right felt that the acceptance of my hawkish contributions was the détente-minded management's preemptive alibi for a change of course in Washington.

Fortunately, the Radio's uncertain flirtation with Eurocommunism in the 1970s, which so agreeably amused the imagination[6] of a sector of senior management, was not always given play in broadcasts to Central and Eastern Europe. Each national station within the Radio used its remaining independence to play or not to play the Eurocommunist card. What the listener heard in this period was, nevertheless, a Radio dedicated, in theory at least, to a robust critique of the Soviet system but practising a diluted form of it. This discrepancy was confusing and demoralising for staff and the public alike. How could the two Radios exert pressure on the Soviet system if the integrity of the Soviet state—with its extensive colonial acquisitions—could not be questioned, despite the clear provisions contained in the 1975 Helsinki Final Act (under Principle VIII) for national self-determination, and elsewhere for the peaceful change of frontiers?

I make these criticisms with a heavy heart, for I had many friends in the Radios' management and on their research staff throughout the 1970s and early 1980s. They had their own grave differences with Congress and the State Department and had to overcome innumerable obstacles to secure the smooth functioning and at times even the survival of the Radios. Some were widely respected as scholars of Eastern and Central Europe with books and academic recognition to their names, while others, in management, displayed a loyalty to the Radio that bears comparison with that of naval captains to their ships. Some feared for their positions in the Radios' hierarchy. This led them to unquestioning obedience to whatever was thought politically right in the "front office." Others had become the victims of fashionable but flawed analyses of the Soviet scene. Only a small minority—but an influential one—were genuinely persuaded that communism was capable of root-and-branch reform, and that it was for us to encourage and embrace it.

The intellectual case for a "soft" approach to communism was, to my knowledge, never put into writing, but in its main elements it was akin to the American liberal critique of the two Radios' general role in East-West relations. Its aim was a third road between capitalism and socialism: qualified pluralism, a mixed economy, and human rights within the confines of a broadly radical system. Two arguments were tacitly enlisted in its favour: first, that the communist establishments' long experience of cooperation with the Western bourgeois ruling classes and capitalist culture were gains which should not be wantonly abandoned once communism had been stripped of its Stalinist and typically Russian accretions; and second, that the world balance of social forces should not be weakened in favour of an exploitative transnational capitalism. Communism, however unsavoury in its Soviet forms, did provide (it was argued) an "iron reserve," a focus of resistance, and an intellectual inhibition to injustice and inhumanity worldwide. Little was it foreseen that the failure of the Soviet system would make a genuinely radical (social democratic) critique of Western capitalism easier rather than more difficult, for any guilt by association with Soviet models of economic management and Soviet ways of thinking would fall away. The liberal Left would prosper because it would no longer be embarrassed by awkward relatives in Moscow. And so it proved to be in much of Western Europe after the collapse of the Soviet Union.

It would be erroneous to think that Americans who entertained such ideas were procommunist or pro-Soviet. Their real motivation was domestic: they hated American conservatives and "Cold Warriors" with an incandescent passion and found it easy enough to identify with their enemies' enemy. Most of their arguments were not openly stated and could not be, but they were there as assumptions informing some of the policies of the State Department and (as I say) even the Radio's own councils in the 1970s. They were difficult to pin down because they could be explained (and explained away) as requirements for achieving détente, slowing the arms race, and preventing a nuclear conflagration. But in the field of policy making, a nudge and a nod are as good as stated objectives—and nudges and nods were not in short supply.

Other psychological factors also promoted Radio Free Europe's (and Radio Liberty's) agenda of accommodation. Many among the Radios' American and Commonwealth staff harboured ill-concealed suspicions of "émigré broadcasters" whom they had to service and in theory to serve. The Americans made great show of stressing their professionalism and jealously maintained their status vis-à-vis "amateurish," "unwashed" Bulgars or Uzbeks. The more stringently the Radios' Bulgars or Uzbeks criticised Bulgar or Uzbek communist policies, the more likely it was that English-speaking management would react by quietly intimating that there must after all be some good in those Bulgar and Uzbek communist policies. Such, in many cases, was the pre-vailing spirit of collaboration in our ranks.

The "stain" of the original CIA connection left members of the Radios' management and intellectual leadership with fundamental in-hibitions and an unadmitted but abiding sense of guilt. Emigré broad-casters, with their periodic insistence on sticking to their original mis-sion (their consciences tended to stir unpredictably), stood in the way of removing that stain and rehabilitating the Radio's policy-making intellectuals in the eyes of their peers in America. But as émigré broad-casting happened to be the Radio's whole raison d'être, the conflict between respectability (as defined by the progressives) and effective-ness (as demanded by the Radio's mission) was beyond resolution. The board's vague intention, in the late 1970s, to fashion the Radios' sur-rogate functions into a bland "international radio"—the phrase first found its way into the 1976 mission statement—did not get very far, but the intention was enough to induce staff to believe that the Radio's days in the vanguard of Western information policy were numbered. The contrast with the pre-détente definition of the Radios' role as offer-ing a domestic or home service was stark.

Among the more pedestrian factors that made for left conformism in the 1970s was intellectual boredom with anticommunism. Intellec-tuals tend to be neophiliacs. Ours felt it to be simply too tedious, after so many years, to go on harping on the vices and shortcomings of the communist regimes and their leaders when saying something shock-ingly favourable about communism could make their reputations. The device of claiming—regardless of the facts—that the Soviet system was "in reality" neither totalitarian nor unstable, much less subver-sive or aggressive, was a wonderful way of attracting attention and putting mediocre academics on the map. The Radio was not exempt from that influence. Jerry F. Hough found supporters in Munich even before he famously revised Merle Fainsod's work on *Smolensk Under Soviet Rule*.[7]

But this retouching of the image of the Soviet system was (par-enthetically) by no means restricted to the Radio's larger intellectual environment, or to the 1970s. In 1968, while serving as one of the two founding editors of the academic journal *Studies in Comparative Com-munism* at the University of Southern California, I was asked by Ross Berkes, head of the School of Politics, to mix into our studies of the communist world articles favourable to the Soviet system, on the rea-soning that inclusion of too many critical examinations might cause

the journal to be branded as anticommunist and jeopardise its respectability in the United States. Naturally, I ignored the request and, in a
long and heated correspondence, fought the mentality it expressed. I
received valuable support from Bertram D. Wolfe and Sidney Hook,
among others. Wolfe's eloquent assistance was especially to the point
because it was the appearance in the journal of one of his articles
("Dress Rehearsals for the Great Terror") that had given offence to the
progressivist political science department of this otherwise conservative university. In 1968 to 1970, the first swell of political correctness
was already breaking the surface.

An even more pedestrian factor that made for a measure of left conformism in the 1970s was the pleasant life and good remuneration of
staff in Bavaria. The tennis courts were in front of our building and
the skiing grounds within an hour's drive. Munich's two opera houses
were cheap and accessible. The dollar was a great equaliser; in large
quantities it was a great homogeniser. Generous salaries, almost complete job security, free housing and services, long annual vacations
topped off by home leave in the United States, a well-tolerated absen-
teeism, free medical insurance, and a noncontributory pension plan
ensured that most members of the broadcasting staff would toe the
line, even if the line ran counter to their original convictions. For many
of them, writing for or against an idea created no lasting crisis of conscience. Institutionalisation was setting in; broadcasters of conviction
were stepping down to make way for administrators. Rebellions were
rare, almost nonexistent. Title was all: directors, associate directors,
deputy directors, assistant directors, supervising editors, and editors
of all kinds proliferated—they could be counted in their hundreds—
but foot soldiers were thin on the ground. Staff were obeisant to the
Radio as a generous and exploitable patron, but they were no longer
persuaded that they were expected to work for the defeat of the Soviet
system, or that such a defeat was possible.

Ultimately, the American openness to new ideas—good and bad—
worked in the West's favour, for on balance the new alternative policy
makers' interpretations of the Soviet–East European scene turned out
to be emphatically more right than wrong. It gives me some satisfaction to note that when it was politically safe for them to do so—though
not a moment before—even some of our most vocal American critics gave us credit for the sophistication we had brought to surrogate
broadcasting.

That is more than can be said about the British political establishment, which treated British talent at the universities, in the think tanks,

and in journalism with calculated detachment and deeply resented (and usually frustrated) their attempts to contribute to the making of foreign policy. Margaret Thatcher's thirst for knowledge was the exception. But even under her stewardship, men of the distinction of Robert Conquest, Hugh Seton-Watson, Peter Wiles, Leonard Schapiro, Ronald Hingley, Peter Reddaway, H. T. Willetts, Hugh Lunghi, Max Hayward, Brian Crozier, and Leopold Labedz (to name but a few) did not receive due recognition, much less opportunities for consistent participation in the policy-shaping process. I was myself working in an official vacuum. When my advice was periodically sought by Margaret Thatcher as prime minister, no official papers crossed my desk, and my contacts with members of the foreign policy establishment were limited to the luncheons and seminars we ran for them at the Centre for Policy Studies, never the other way around. The French knew better. They had the good sense, earlier in the century, to send men of the calibre of Paul Claudel, Jacques Maritain, and other writers and thinkers abroad as their ambassadors. No such rival talents were allowed to interfere with the complacency and career prospects of British civil servants.

But freedom of the spirit in the American sense also had its drawbacks. Principal and most disturbing among them was our inability to establish some form of homogeneity in our ranks. Our American friends willed the ends but were frequently reluctant to will the means to achieve them—an all too familiar dilemma in human affairs. We were, as I have related, never in a position to limit staff to men and women with the right intellectual qualities, the political will, and also the stomach to confront the Soviet system. Some possessed the first but not the second; others had the second but not the third. Never in my experience of the Cold War did defeatism in our ranks not have the best tunes or the most persuasive journalistic backing. Here is a warning for the future.

I like to remember my own work in Munich in the 1980s in terms of the successes we achieved in hurrying our conflict with the Soviet system to a satisfactory conclusion. After four decades of pressure, the system imploded. But I will not forget that long and bitter domestic opposition which dogged our activities almost every inch of the way, nor how close the West had come, through complacency, inattention, and incomprehension, to appeasing the modern world's most complete and most tenacious despotism.

I cannot end this account without giving the reader a postcard-size description of the physical home of the two Radios, Bavaria. But

I must declare an interest—I'm a lover of the Alps and a dedicated mountaineer. For me, after two spells of residence, Bavaria gradually became a second home. Of all the lands I have lived in or visited, no other offered that serene sense of timelessness and closeness to the earth experienced on the upland meadows and peaks of this extraordinary country. Here individual men and women were still the measure of all things; the seasons were distinct; a farmer was a farmer, a family a family; every village fire brigade boasted a brass band; and the celebrations of grief and joy, of the saints and the harvest responded to an ancient order. Christianity was still a daily experience because it drew its metaphors from local music and imagery. My sophisticated local bank manager partook of every Ascension Day parade and Easter procession, and so did many of our German staff at the Radio.

To say that Bavaria is a land of exquisite natural beauty, steeped in the tradition of the baroque, and a matrix of much music and music making, is restating the obvious. But the real connoisseur of Bavaria knows something else, too. He is aware that this "free-state" within the German Federation is a fine blend of tradition and modernity, of technological efficiency and an exceptionally relaxed life-style, of high culture and down-to-earth wealth creation, of North German self-discipline and the more permissive ethic of Latin Europe. I marvelled at the affluent burgher's willingness to uphold, indeed to promote, the ways and values of the *Bauer* (peasant farmer).

For the burgher as for the farmer, the protection of the natural environment was not just a peripheral issue, much less a left-of-centre extravagance to annoy governments, but a symbol of the realisation that living off our ecological capital is a bankrupt economic strategy. One would be hard put to think of a more appealing model for environmental balance under modern conditions than this land of pellucid lakes—and high technology. For a radio that had to do justice to both the traditional values of Eastern and Central Europe and its technological progress, Bavaria was not a bad place to broadcast from.

But this rather romantic view of Bavaria was very much my own. It was not shared by most of the Radio's language staff, who looked upon their soft landing in Bavarian "exile" as a fate much to be deplored. True, we had appreciative foreigners on our staff too—Americans and émigrés with German wives or husbands and children in German schools; Fulbright scholars practising their music on German stages and platforms; skiers, mountaineers, and opera lovers for whom Munich, Salzburg, Bayreuth, Bamberg, Oberammergau, Hohenems, and their surroundings meant the fulfilment of a dream. But the run-of-the-mill émigré journalists would turn up their noses at all things Bavarian. Their lack of curiosity to explore what was right on their doorstep never ceased to amaze me. Some of our staff members seldom ventured beyond the walls of their service apartments or the city of Munich and spent their lives in self-created seclusion. This was the more curious because the Radios were playing host to a seemingly endless stream of American visitors whose real reason for coming to Munich was not so much to inspect or to consult us as to enjoy the sights and sounds (and beer) of Bavaria.

Some of our Romanians, for example, could not wait to get "back" to the sophisticated milieu of Paris, which they claimed as their spiritual homeland; our Poles were so estranged from all things German that many of them would deny, after a lifetime spent on German soil, that they commanded any knowledge of the German language and would refuse to work from German-language press materials, even though these were part and parcel of the Radio's information input. Members of Radio Liberty's Russian and minority language services did genuinely have no "foreign" languages except Russian, and Radio Liberty management's attempt to induce them to learn English was minimal seeing that the business of Radio Liberty itself was, foolishly enough, conducted in Russian.

There was, furthermore, the pull of the South—mainly of Italy—on the argument that Bavaria was too wet, too dry, or too much exposed to the allegedly disabling Föhn winds and, most frequently, because Germany in general and agricultural Bavaria in particular were "too square" to meet the advanced tastes and standards of our Magyars, Bulgars, Slovaks, and Byelorussians. There were even those on our American staff who resented Bavaria (and much of Europe for that matter) because it was too scenic, too much like a dream, corrupting, "unreal," and un-American. The real world for them began with Detroit and Chicago.

Thus it happened, much to the surprise of our Bavarian partners and employees, that Radio Free Europe and Radio Liberty became alien enclosures in the land, with virtually no social contacts linking them to the German population and few to Bavarian culture. The CIA connection during the period between 1951 and 1971 did not help. Even within the two Radios, the various language groups inhabited incestuous communities of their own making and sat at separate tables in our common canteen. Our Russians were the poor relations.

This narrow-minded ethnocentrism (to give it a charitable name) was sometimes defended on seemingly plausible grounds. It was argued, for example, that the authenticity of the Radio's message could be guaranteed only by encouraging such small, isolated hothouses, because in them alone could the spirit of national identity survive uncontaminated by the surrounding culture. The deracinated nature of the Voice of America was usually cited as a warning about what happens to foreign-language radio when the host culture is allowed to dominate.

It was, of course, true enough that the Voice of America turned out to be a poor source of inspiration whenever it tried to perform surrogate functions in Eastern and Central Europe; but from that it did not follow that the enjoyment and exploitation of the Radio's Bavarian location would prejudice the authentic tenor of these national microcosms. In any case, a significant part of our mandate was to project the pluralism and variety of the West, and that very much included projecting the country in which we were so agreeably housed and hosted.

Fortunately, Bavarian and South German culture inevitably broke through and coloured Radio Free Europe's message in the same way as did the American, French, English, and Italian cultures. The exceptions were our Polish- and Russian-language broadcasts. Here the fear that any undue emphasis on our German location would diminish or confuse our identity as surrogate Radios (the "Munich stations") predominated, and the fear, though distasteful, was well founded: one of Moscow's standard charges against us was that our broadcasts were biassed because they had to reflect the national ambitions of our host nation—"revanche-seeking" (or indeed nazi) West Germany. That this charge was in conflict with the accusation that we were the hirelings of American-Israeli Jewish interests and international Zionism did not lessen the ardour of our accusers.

My affection for Bavaria was, of course, an entirely private matter. I made no attempt to insinuate it into the thinking of our staff members or the output of Radio Free Europe. But I felt it was a pity that our reporters and commentators did not take a more generous and productive view of their new, but after forty-odd years near-permanent, home.

Their alienation surprised me, even though I should not have been surprised. During my twelve years with the BBC I had found members of the BBC European Service just as critical of the British surroundings as were our émigré staff of Bavaria. When among themselves, the BBC's broadcasters had spoken about English sloth, English disorganisation, English perfidy—and the English weather—with the same mocking contempt as inspired the attitude of many of Radio Free Europe's men and women to whatever shortcomings they chose to discover in Bavaria. In London at least, poor pay and generally low standards of living may have explained émigré alienation; but what was there to explain it in wealthy Bavaria—unless it was high pay and too much comfort, lavished on our broadcasters by both their American sponsors and their Bavarian hosts? Affluence as a cause of alienation? The truth was simple: exiled or self-exiled intellectuals were not cast out to be happy. Satisfaction and assimilation in their new environment would have been an insult to their pride and integrity and a sign of the betrayal of their stated purpose that one day they would return to their liberated homelands.

CHAPTER SEVEN

Before the Implosion

With my appointment as director of Radio Free Europe, thirteen years of thinking and writing in the relative tranquillity of my study in Brighton came to an end. The shock of being surrounded not by books but by a disputatious breed of bureaucrats and journalists from the United States and all parts of Western and Eastern Europe was profound. I found my first few months in the saddle utterly bewildering. An escape clause was written into my contract at my request, for experience in the 1960s had taught me that Munich was a destroyer of health and reputations. Yet I was not quite prepared for what was to hit me. Signs of disaffection, accumulated over a long period, began arriving on my desk in large numbers. The frustrations of the détente period were now clamouring for redress in the form of demands and unsubtle hints for rewards or punishment. Never before had I experienced, under conditions of material plenty, so uninhibited a display of greed, envy, and ill will—or so much sycophancy. Requests for promotion, job titles, transfers, superior living quarters, foreign assignments, and indeed almost any advantage that might upstage a rival were presented to me, frequently as elements essential to the pursuit of what were thought to be my policies. The elbowing for pedestrian gain bemused but did not surprise me—the jockeying for favours in political disguise did, or would have done had long experience not drained me of the last vestiges of credulity.

Some of the resulting exhaustion was my own fault. I had let it be known that my doors were open to all comers—in a building that was home to the activities of more than a thousand staff, albeit not all of them were directly responsible to Radio Free Europe, and we had hundreds more abroad. Frequently I had to put in twelve-hour days and worked weekends. In the early hours of every morning I had to digest a massive collection of overnight reports. Many of my notes and guidances were written at home well before office hours, with my wife doing duty as typist. But this forced march was essential to the new team's strategy. With détente firmly behind us and a new board in charge in Washington, I wanted to ensure that the arrival of the new leadership and the resolve to suffuse the Radio's mandate with fresh purpose were fully and quickly appreciated. That my openness occasionally cut across bureaucratic lines of command was regrettable, but a price well worth paying.

Even while I was still in England, my mail underwent an ominous increase. The very rumour of my appointment was enough to call forth often book-size documentations and indictments of the alleged sins of members of the existing policy management, with suggestions for their removal. There were denunciations, attempts to rewrite the record, and some very transparent grovelling. I found these unsavoury, but it would have been irresponsible to close my mind to the complaints, even though I was aware that some were the work of congenital malcontents and troublemakers. After my arrival in Munich, I acted directly on none of them, but I was now sensitised to the mood of things at the Radio, and that put me ahead in a game to which I was an almost total stranger.

This is not the place to recount in detail the changes Frank Shakespeare, James Buckley, George Bailey, and I carried out between 1983 and 1986, but a thumbnail sketch of my own reforms in Radio Free Europe should shed some light on our second-conductorship.

Within a week of my arrival, I abolished the Radio's daily short list of articles and reports "recommended" to our various broadcasting services for use or exclusion. The list, in fact, represented the Radio Free Europe director's political policies—a choice of approved, deselected, or partly censored news and views from the world media, in the light of which the Radio's commentators and editors were expected to formulate their broadcasts and against which they were later checked, by way of postbroadcast audits, by our control (Broadcast Analysis) department. Originally, the list was meant to be a time-saving device, a check on accuracy, and a belated reaction to the chaos that had prevailed in the Radio's political management at the time of the 1956 Hungarian Revolution (see Chapter 14).

In practice, however, it meant censorship. In the détente period, the list had become especially one-sided, reflecting almost exclusively the mentality within the American East Coast liberal press—a curtailment of freedom of speech, freedom of opinion, and thus also of our mission.

My abolition of the list in its existing form came as a shock for a few but a relief for many. The majority of complaints that had reached me while I was still in England, and indeed the majority of complaints received by all and sundry throughout the late 1970s and early 1980s, had concerned the Radio's censorship practices as demonstrated at their clearest by the character of these daily selections. Something had to be done and done promptly after my installation. In our new daily list we confined ourselves to directing our editors' attention to items most likely to be relevant to our listeners' interests—without prejudging whether they were in line with this or that group's political preferences in Washington or elsewhere. The director's office still retained control over the factual accuracy of the materials offered to our language services, but preemptive political selection and suppression were no more. Soon after my retirement in 1986, however, the daily censorship list was reintroduced, in attenuated form, by Gene Pell, the new president.

Why did I act so swiftly?

In 1981–83 alone, the suppression of articles in whole or in part (through blacklisting or blue-pencilling) affected an amazing spread of news agencies, newspapers, periodicals, and radio stations.[1] Among those whose articles or interviews had been censored were Milovan Djilas, Vladimir Bukovsky, Victor Meier, Carl Gustav Ströhm, David Binder, George F. Will, Joseph Kraft, Paul Lendvai, Rowland Evans, Jr., and Robert Novak, Patrick Buchanan, John Vinocur, Bernard Margueritte, John Goshko, Henry Stanhope, and numerous other prominent writers.

The ostensible reasons for mutilation or suppression were expressed in cautionary tags pinned on the offending items in the Radio's daily recommended list, such as: *oversimplified; inaccurate; unconfirmed; exaggerated; unconfirmed rumours; confused; overwritten; unbalanced; overdramatised; overspeculative; erroneous; irresponsible.* But the real reason for deselection was our selectors' fear that this or that view in the world press might offend the Radio's political line as interpreted by our predecessors.

Milovan Djilas, for example, was censored because he forecast the spread effect of the 1981 crisis in the Polish communist system (*Die Welt,* October 23, 1981), and Patrick Buchanan because he wondered why the United States and Radio Free Europe in particular were not doing more to assist the Polish strikers and dissidents (*Philadelphia Inquirer,* August 28, 1980). Our selectors' deletions in Djilas's article were coyly described as for "background information only," and Buchanan's piece was totally proscribed as "irresponsible." Both were thought to be liable to promote instability in the East, and that was judged to be incompatible with détente and thus undesirable.

The result of my abolition of the daily recommended list in its old form was the radical enlargement of the pool from which our services could draw information and inspiration for comment. Our editorial writers were no longer constrained by the feeling that they were constantly watched and nannied. We were injecting freedom into the editorial life of Radio Free Europe. Guidance emerged from the give-and-take of our seminar-like, and often highly sophisticated, daily staff meetings (freely attended by visitors) and from notes periodically issued by my office. The remnants of the mentality which had given tacit preference to the progressivist approach to the Soviet system and tried to keep certain alternative voices out of our score were finally re-moved—removed, that is, as far as the central guidance of Radio Free Europe was concerned. The human factor in our ranks was a very different matter.

The personnel I inherited was by and large well qualified and politically reliable, but I also had handed down to me a number of editors and researchers with communist and left-socialist backgrounds and leanings. Some had come on board in the wake of the Prague Spring (1968) as a result of the Radio's support of reform communism and were so punctiliously protected by our unions and German labour law that they were virtually irremovable. Most of them had ceased to be communists in the narrow sense, but their loyalty was suspect and they were quietly doing what they could to trip up the policies of the new management. They included, as I had reason to believe (and my suspicion was amply borne out after the fall of the communist system), members of various Eastern intelligence networks whom our minute security apparatus was in many cases incapable of identifying, or identifying in time. The signs of subversion had been there for a long time. Even a condensed account of it makes instructive reading.

On February 21, 1981, the Czechoslovak wing of the Radio's Munich headquarters was wrecked by an explosion that caused four serious injuries and considerable material damage. According to the German Gauck Authority's STASI files (see Appendix A), the bombing had been planned and financed by the Romanian Security Service. Ceauşescu himself was said to have contributed one million dollars, with the support of other East European secret services, to cause panic in the Radio's Romanian Department. The attack was the work of one Johannes Weinrich, a German member of the pan-European terrorist network Prima Linea (or ETA), under the guidance of the Venezuelan terrorist "Carlos" (Ilich Ramirez Sanchez); an originally cooperative communist Hungary served as their base. Thirteen years on, in August 1994, Carlos was run to earth in Sudan and handed over to the French authorities for investigation and trial. In June 1995, Weinrich was arrested in Yemen under a warrant of the German federal prosecutor. The charges against both included the bombing of Radio Free Europe.

In 1970–73, several years before that bombing, the Czechoslovak Security Service (StB) had made preparations to set off another explosion. Pavel Minarik, an enthusiastic StB agent employed by Radio Free Europe between 1968 and 1976, when he re-defected, was to plant the explosives, but for reasons unclarified, and to the dismay of Minarik, the plan was eventually abandoned. After the collapse of the communist regimes, Minarik was charged on September 14, 1993, by the new Czech authorities and sentenced by the Prague municipal court to four years' imprisonment for his part in planning the attack. No link has been reliably established between the bombing plots of Carlos and Minarik. At the time of the termination of his service at the Ministry of the Interior in 1990, Minarik carried the rank of lieutenant colonel of the police.

In 1994, however, within a year of Minarik's conviction, credit for the 1981 bomb attack was publicly claimed by the unrepentant KGB general Oleg Kalugin. In his book *SpyMaster* he states with satisfaction that the bombing was his initiative. He had it carried out, he relates, by an East German agent with the assistance of Oleg Tumanov, the principal undercover KGB agent at Radio Liberty. "The explosion was my idea, and my aim was not to hurt anyone but rather to stir up sentiment to move the rabble-rousing station out of Munich and Germany."[2] Kalugin's alleged operative may have been the same Johannes Weinrich whom the STASI files refer to as Heinrich Schneider. Tumanov in his own memoirs does not admit complicity, but given the character of the work and its author, that amounts to evidence neither for nor against his participation.

The Carlos group's activities deserve more than a passing mention.

The bombing of Radio Free Europe was embarrassing for Carlos's Hungarian hosts and eventually undermined the group's safe haven in most of Eastern Europe. But for a long time the Hungarian communists were fearful and dithering. Documents in the possession of the

Hungarian public prosecutor's office show that Carlos and his associates started their bombing mission from Hungary and returned from it directly to Hungary. They could have been charged for attempted murder under Hungarian law, but no such charge was brought. The group's activities had been under surveillance for some time, but it was only after the Munich bombing that the Hungarians, on Kádár's personal authority, cautiously decided to advise Carlos to leave.

The STASI files bristle with evidence that the whole Eastern secret service community was systematically involved with the work of Carlos and his terrorist clan—something communist governments and their Western apologists indignantly denied in the 1970s and 1980s. The gang worked closely with the KGB, the STASI, the StB in Prague, and above all with the Romanian Securitate, from which it took orders and received assistance and rewards. For a considerable period of time, Hungarian security officials, too, were aware but tolerant of the terrorist acts Carlos was plotting from his hotel rooms in Budapest. Radio Free Europe was only one of his targets.

The STASI documentation also affords lighter moments, in the form, for example, of the occasional splendid euphemism. At one point Hungarian security suggests that the Cuban comrades should be asked to provide a "secure place of residence" for Carlos and his people so that their energies may be deflected from Central Europe to "a new field of activities in Latin America." Not to alienate the gang too much or provoke it into some defiant reaction (such as joining the enemy camp), the Hungarians decided that, even after the Carlos team's departure from Hungary (they were to be allowed to take their "materials" with them), its members would go on enjoying short-stay and transit facilities. Angering them was much to be avoided, and this was a prudent precaution, for in August 1979, the gang unceremoniously opened fire on a carload of Hungarian security police who were tailing them. Carlos was not to be trifled with.

In the event, despite the Hungarian government's decision to ease them out of Hungary in 1981, Carlos and his group could not be induced to leave until 1985.

Just how intimately communist policy and contract terrorism were at times linked to one another is apparent from a comic incident in Prague in 1979. Agents of the Romanian security service had been instructed to try to persuade Carlos to liquidate Ceauşescu's former security chief, General Ion Pacepa—a much hated defector under sentence of death in Bucharest but safely ensconced in the United States. Having, however, caught a glimpse of Carlos's lavish life-style, they judged that the ten-thousand-dollar reward they were going to offer him in cash was too small to induce him "to help in carrying out the sentence." Yet, more money they were not authorized to put on the table. Pacepa stayed alive.[3]

The 1981 bombing was not the last of Ceauşescu's attempts to destabilise Radio Free Europe. In October 1983 preparations were made, this time by the Romanian Foreign Intelligence Service (CIE), for another bomb attack. Three senior diplomats from the Romanian Embassy in Bonn were caught in the act of planning and expelled from Germany. Assassination attempts were made on the lives of the Radio's senior Romanian staff in Munich and Paris. Other Romanian broadcasters received parcel bombs and death threats in Munich, Cologne, and Washington.

A letter dated December 10, 1990, addressed to Emil Georgescu, an editor in the Radio's Romanian department, was typical of several.[4] Signed by the "Legion" of the Iron Guard, it was probably the work of the Romanian Communist Security Service.

> Oh, Deformed One,
> We have heard that you have begun to bark at us, you mangy Judas. While you were on the other side of the Iron Curtain you devoured all you could; you imprisoned many Iron Guardists and other true Romanians. Here you are howling against us; you have sold out to the Masons and the Jewish Mafia at RFE. . . .
> If you don't shut your Jewish trap, we'll see to it that you will be gripping clay underground along with other contaminated monsters.
> Be careful, viper, we'll be cutting off your venomous tongue.
> Tell the Jews to prepare a crown for you, and you yourself should make your Jewish last will and testament.
> Long Live the Legion and the Captain!

After the collapse of the Romanian communist system more light was thrown on how exactly the Securitate had been trying to operate against Radio Free Europe—and on how it frequently failed.

"In order to intimidate RFE freelancers and other adversaries of the former [Romanian] regime, some explosive postal devices were used which, through detonation, produced the known effects," Virgil Magureanu, director of the postcommunist Romanian intelligence service, wrote in response to a Radio Free Europe enquiry on July 16, 1992.

We learn from him, however, that much of the planned sabotage could not be carried out. Magureanu tells us on a melancholy note that

some of the would-be saboteurs went over to the Radio's way of thinking and refused to follow orders. "The Securitate, despite its intentions,
could not put into effect 'classic infiltrations' within RFE. . . . Officers
meant to carry out such operations became dependent on RFE ideology which caused them to cross over to the other side. These types of
occurrences were 'far from few,' as is well known."[5]

But there were also other and more open obstacles to be overcome,
most of them of the Radio's own making. Our New York–based Guild
of Journalists was fiercely hostile to the new team, especially to Bailey
and me. The News Division as a whole, aided by some of the two
Radios' former executives, was on the warpath against the "Reagan
people" from the day we set foot in the building. In December 1985, the
guild launched its own journal (*By-line*). In its first issue it gave pride
of place to a long and acid critique of the two Radios' political line
in the period between 1982 and 1985, that is, under the management
of Buckley, Bailey, and me. The author of the critique was Ralph E.
Walter, the two Radios' former executive vice president. Some of the
denunciations which periodically surfaced in the American press and
in Congress had been inspired by members of this unfriendly neigh-
bourhood force.

As a small example: on Saturday, August 11, 1984, President Reagan
quipped while preparing for a radio address in California that he had
"just signed legislation which outlaws Russia forever. We will begin
bombing in five minutes." Reagan thought the microphones had been
disconnected, but they had not. His words were recorded and reported.
At our daily policy meeting the following Monday, the head of our
News Division proposed that we report Reagan's joke as an ordinary
news item. I refused on the grounds that the Soviets, deeply suspicious
as they were of Reagan and the Republican administration, would mis-
interpret the joke and take it to be an American threat to Soviet security. The Soviet public, too, unable to receive accurate signals from us
through the jamming, might run away with the idea that nuclear war
was imminent and panic. None of these conceivable results were in the
interest of peace or consistent with our mandate. I said we would treat
the president's joke in one or several of our feature programmes, the
scope of which allowed for painting in the background and offering
proper explanation. George Bailey agreed, and that is how Reagan's
jocular voice test was treated by both Radios.

But neither the News Division nor our local Journalists' Guild (the two consisted of largely the same people) were satisfied. Supporters as they were of the progressivist agenda, they saw here a welcome opportunity for presenting Reagan as both a fool and a warmonger. Although they represented less than 10 percent of our staff, they managed to mobilise against us some of the American liberal media, including the *New York Times*,[6] contacted Congressmen, and wrote a number of unpleasant letters, not least to and about me. But Bailey and I stuck to our decision; our broadcasters were behind us. A letter carrying the signatures of 164 of our senior journalists was sent to the board on September 11, 1984, in support of our action.

A few days later, my fear that Reagan's joke might be misread in the USSR was confirmed by a Reuters despatch from Tokyo: "A leading Japanese newspaper said today [October 1, 1984] that the Soviet Far Eastern Army issued a coded signal on August 15, saying it was going into a state of war with the United States, but withdrew it 30 minutes later. . . . The reported signal followed a joke by President Reagan on August 11. Reagan said during a voice test for a weekend radio broadcast that he had signed legislation outlawing Russia and added: 'We begin bombing in five minutes'. . . . [The paper] said US forces in Japan and Japanese authorities went into a state of high alert. . . . Prime Minister Yasuhiro Nakasone immediately ordered checks on Soviet troop movements."[7]

In my own office too, the cards had been stacked against me. Robert Hutchings, the deputy I had inherited, was a man of progressivist inclinations. His expertise and administrative competence were impeccable, but he was unreconciled to the change of the guard in Washington and tried to frustrate or slow down our reforms. Consideration of his family circumstances (a very sick child) prevented us from moving him back to Washington for the best part of a year.

Hutchings had put his wrong foot forward by sending me, shortly before my arrival in Munich (October 18, 1983), a recommendation for the urgent promotion of Czech-born Vladimir Kusin, one of the Radio's research analysts, to a sensitive post in the policy-oriented Research Department. Kusin, he told me, had in fact already been informally installed in his new position and, pending my approval, was familiarising himself with the operation. Kusin possessed, I was told, "an ideally unique combination of substantive knowledge, analytical skills, languages, administrative talent, and proven reliability and loyalty. . . . I have no doubt that he would make a superb deputy director." I had superficially known Kusin in Britain and had serious though unprovable doubts about his political reliability. Was he on our side in the contest of ideas? An extra (though in retrospect flawed) security check in London under my tenure in 1984 produced no results. Indeed Indeed it appeared to give him a clean bill of health which I reluctantly endorsed. It proved administratively impossible not to confirm him in his post as deputy, but to ensure that we would have no loose cannon on board, in July 1985 I also appointed William Murphy, a man of out-standing intelligence and long experience in security affairs, to head the Research Department and thus to be Kusin's immediate supervi-sor. Nevertheless, before my retirement in the summer of 1986, I left warnings behind for Gene Pell, the incoming president. I urged him to appoint Kusin to no policy-making or policy-supervising position. His background as a former instructor in Communism made him in-eligible, although he had at one point paid a price for dissenting from the party line. That was as far as I could go without hard proof in hand to back up my suspicion. By the end of 1986, however, Kusin was acting head of the Research Department and had considerable though indirect influence on the formation of Radio Free Europe policy.

Five years after my departure and two years after the collapse of the Soviet system in Central Europe, Kusin was found to have been a long-standing Czechoslovak secret agent, and probably at times a "resident," of the Czechoslovak security services.[8] On July 9, 1991, Pell abruptly retired him. For several months after this discovery, however, Kusin went on supplying studies on post-Soviet affairs for the office of the NATO secretary general. These were circulated to a select list of scholars and government officials and marked as "particularly worthy" of Western attention. Clearly, Munich and Brussels did not communi-cate—a tribute to the Radio's independence though not to the wisdom of its political management.

Kusin proved a highly public embarrassment for Radio Free Eu-rope. On May 24, 1990, the Radio opened its news bureau in Prague. At the inaugural ceremony in the great hall of the Valdstejn Palace, Kusin served as the Radio's interpreter between Vaclav Havel, presi-dent of Czechoslovakia, and Gene Pell, president of the two Radios. Photographs in the Radio's house journal capture the proud moment.[9] Kusin's dismissal followed only fourteen months later, upon a warn-ing by Jan Ruml, the Czechoslovak deputy minister of the interior. The Radios then carried out yet another investigation, under A. Ross Johnson, whose report confirmed Ruml: Kusin had, partly by his own admission, indeed worked for the Czechoslovak secret service. Pell did not ask the German authorities to prosecute. Johnson suffered an even greater embarrassment. In May 1991 Kusin accompanied him on a

tour of Czechoslovak public institutions, including the Foreign Ministry, and counseled him (!) on the effort these institutions were making
to overcome the communist past and expel communist functionaries
and secret-police collaborators.

Richard Cummings, director of the Radio's Security Office, observed on July 8, 1991, in a note for the record: "After a senior staff
meeting, Pell asked Gregg Prillaman [personnel director] and me to
remain behind. He wanted to make sure I was in the picture about
Kusin. He stated that if Gregg or I got any enquiries about Kusin, we
were to have no comment. He wanted Kusin to leave with 'his dignity.'
Gregg said Kusin would be out of the building by the end of the month.
The meeting ended, I went to Pell's office to retrieve my file on Kusin,
which turned out to be incomplete. Pell has removed his own memo-
randa and notes."

According to Cummings's testimony, both he and, later and sepa-
rately, the German authorities, demanded prosecution. The German
investigators proposed to serve a subpoena, but Pell refused the Radio's
cooperation. Kusin was allowed to stay on the Radio's payroll until
December 31, 1991, and then granted a severance pay of DM 103,792
(twenty-six weeks of salary). His company pension and health care
rights were safeguarded. His letter of termination carried the title of
"Mutually Agreed Separation Agreement"—unusual language for dis-
missing a spy.

My own enquiry to Gene Pell (May 8, 1994), who had in the meantime left the Radios, wondering why Kusin had been allowed to go
quietly, remained unanswered. Did he try to avoid exposing the Radios
to adverse publicity at a time of dwindling support in the United
States?

Kusin's infiltration was the most serious but by no means the only
example of Prague's keen interest in the Radio's affairs. Our Czechoslovak Service was especially well endowed with agents. After the collapse of the communist system, and in some cases before it, several
Czechoslovak editors, analysts, and announcers in addition to Kusin
and Minarik were found to have worked with communist intelligence.
The former Czech security officer Josef Frolik's revelations at a Senate hearing on November 18, 1975, had been the first authentic and
detailed indication of how the Prague government was trying to undermine Radio Free Europe.

There was also, although on a different plane altogether, the small
matter of whether the Radio should go on employing former commu-

nists as permanent members of the staff. Before I took up my post in Munich, Shakespeare and I had an informal understanding that, barring exceptional circumstances, we would restrict recruiting to applicants who had not been members of the East or Central European communist parties and had not held leading positions in the party or government establishments. A pool of qualified or trainable noncommunists was available for the jobs we had to offer. I could see no reason for giving former communists access to our councils or our microphones. Those we inherited and could not decently cast off were burden enough. I was especially determined not to allow the libertarian ideas we stood for to be mocked by people who had made names for themselves as propagandists for the regime and were notorious as such to our audiences. Nothing could have done greater damage to our credibility than allowing former propagators of Marxism-Leninism to be heard on our airwaves enlarging on the virtues of the market economy, liberal parliamentary democracy, and individual freedom.

But this commonsensical rule would cease to apply if pressing reasons existed for a different course of action. I let it be known that if, for example, former communists of the standing of an Arthur Koestler or a Milovan Djilas applied for employment, we would always find jobs for them. The new rule did not, of course, apply to free-lance contributors, of whom we had hundreds on our books in all parts of the world. Our eventual promotion of the confessions of András Hegedüs, a deeply Stalinist former Hungarian prime minister, shows how liberally the rule was interpreted.

Most of our staff supported my policy with enthusiasm. For several years before our team's arrival, many of them had been agitating for precisely this kind of a reform. But there was a minor outcry in our small but vocal liberal lobby. Otto Pick, head of our Czechoslovak Service (his tenure proved short), accused me of embracing the notion of collective guilt. "Once a communist, always a communist?" I was asked.[10] Zdzislaw Najder, head of our Polish Service, launched a campaign against me on the Washington power circuit because I had refused his request to appoint as his deputy Jacek Kalabiński, a former Polish communist broadcaster of high visibility (a kingpin of the Jedynka [One] series). Some of Kalabiński's tendentious reporting, especially about Israeli-Arab relations, had been used in Polish prisons as closed-circuit communist propaganda, and we had immediate proof of it from former Solidarity prisoners we were in touch with. The Works Council, under its chairman, Karel Kasparek, protested. Kalabiński's appointment would have caused a rebellion at our Polish station. I did not allow it to happen. But the pressure from Washington continued to the day of my retirement. "Networking" in Congress on behalf of this former leading communist broadcaster proved so powerful and persistent that for almost a year we were put on the defensive— but did not give way.[11]

The rationale of my policy was straightforward. No one was born into the Communist Party; nor was anyone forced to join the Communist Party. Any talk about collective guilt was, therefore, nonsensical. Despite the pressures, joining or not joining the party was ultimately a decision for the individual. "The righteousness of the righteous shall be upon himself, and the wickedness of the wicked shall be upon himself" (Ezek. 18:20).

Those who joined must have been guided by one of two considerations: either they were genuinely convinced Marxist-Leninists, or they were opportunists who signed up for reasons of power and advantage. If they were genuine Marxist-Leninists, how could we be sure that they ceased to be communists the day they joined our Radio? If they were turncoats and opportunists, how could we entrust our message to them? In either case, we would have been buying trouble—men and women vulnerable to blackmail, whose loyalties were divided and therefore questionable. The beguiling but too obviously self-serving justification that one had to become a party member before one could subvert the party was not, as yet, in the whitewashers' tool kit. After the demise of the system, however, it was to be deployed without a blush by members of the *apparat* in search of democratic credentials and a new career throughout the formerly communist lands. Astonishingly, in most cases they succeeded.

There was nothing arbitrary about my personnel policy. It rested on the conviction, well supported by evidence, that we were, except for the shooting, at war with the Soviet system and could afford to entrust our future only to the most loyal and the most effective. On September 4, 1985, I wrote to Frank Shakespeare:

> The present, non-shooting war is the only war we are likely to have to fight in the foreseeable future. It is a war of words, ideas, and symbols. It is a war which the nature of the Soviet system has forced upon us and we do not always fight well because we do not, as peaceful democratic polities, clearly realise that it *is* a war, or dare not say so for a variety of domestic reasons.
>
> But, speaking amongst ourselves as part of the Western 'high command' on information policy, we must be clear that RFE/RL is one of the prime instruments in this war of ideas and values which we dare

not lose lest the Soviet Union garner the *fruits* of war without having fired a shot in anger. That is why we cannot afford to take any but the most qualified, the most dedicated and the most clear-headed of men, whether in the position of President or humble news sub-editor.

Despite many obstructions, robust support from the board enabled me to make swift changes both in policy and personnel. The directors of four out of six of our principal departments were retired, transferred, or (in Pick's case) released from service. A new sense of purpose was quickly imparted to the organisation. For once, a large part of the American administration, though not Congress,[12] stood four-square behind the Radios. Our independence and intellectual freedom were guaranteed. Frank Shakespeare proved a decisive chairman of the board with the ability and the will to use the levers of Washington power to maximum effect. Even our finances took a huge turn for the better—or nearly so, because after the heady promises of 1983–84, our Washington-inspired wish list for more staff, new field offices, additional transmitters, and other facilities had to be drastically scaled down, under the pressures of the growing U.S. national budget deficit.

Signs of a great wind of change were, nevertheless, quite unmistakable. Buckley and I arranged a series of visits and public discussions for Jeane Kirkpatrick (then U.S. ambassador to the U.N.); Max Kampelman (the chief U.S. delegate for the arms control negotiations with the USSR); Richard Schifter (the American human rights ambassador); Edward Teller (the distinguished Hungarian-born U.S. physicist); Otto von Habsburg at the head of a group of European parliamentarians; the historians Lord Thomas of Swynnerton, Robert Conquest, Adam B. Ulam, and others. Some of their visits were of significant intrinsic political and intellectual benefit to staff, but they also demonstrated, in the case of the American visitors, the U.S. administration's solidarity with our work.

Kirkpatrick, Kampelman, Schifter, and Teller were all in close touch with the White House and were leading the Reagan administration's offensive against the Soviet system in their different fields. Their appearance in Munich, their endorsement of the new team and of me personally were signals to the East that a new chapter was about to be written in our contest of ideas with the Soviet system and empire. But they were also signals to our American critics and ill-wishers, including those within the Radios, that our two stations' orphan-status had come to an end.

Upon my appointment I had received a warm telegram of con-

gratulations from Secretary of State George Shultz.[13] Although some
members of our administrative staff thought this was a back-handed
reminder of our continuing dependency on the State Department (a
dependency of which they were in favour), Shakespeare and I preferred to read it as a straightforward sign of goodwill and support. We
were, after all, soldiering on the same side and representing a shared
set of values and ideas. There was no need to suspect ulterior motives.

But it was in policy formation that the most important changes
came to be enacted under my stewardship. Radio Free Europe's general mandate had been well thought out, but I did see a need to deepen
and sharpen existing programme approaches in two areas.

One was to increase the seriousness and expertise of our analysis of
the communist system within the framework of the system. We were
aware that each of the ruling communist parties, although monolithic
in name, consisted in fact of several often irreconcilable factions. We
tried to show how sanity, the requirements of the modern world, and
many of the tenets of communist ideology that antedated Lenin militated for a thorough reform of existing socialism. We offered sophisticated arguments for thinking that real life, as well as the moral inspiration of the young Marx and of later idealistic socialists, called for
liberty as much as for workers' power and workers' welfare. A better
deal for the working man and woman could not be had, we suggested,
without the freedoms of civil society.

We were, in other words, giving unobtrusive support to de-Stalinis-
ers and de-Leninisers. We spoke sotto voce, but as participants in the
communists' debates—not as spectators. The time devoted to such programmes was small, but they represented the sharp edge of our thinking. Elite audiences within the state-party establishment were our targets, for we knew well enough that the only peaceful way of ridding
the world of Soviet rule was to encourage dissenting elements within
the system to undermine its legitimacy step by step. We worked, in
effect, for Gorbachevism much before Mikhail Gorbachev, and when
Gorbachev was elected general secretary, we supported and heavily
cross-reported his reforms, even though the first two years of Gorbachev's perestroika were but a pale reflection of what the Hungarian
communists had already achieved (with, as I like to think, Radio Free
Europe's significant encouragement).

Our decision to put András Hegedüs, the former Stalinist prime
minister of Hungary, on air with a book-length series of broadcasts,

aroused particular interest. Hegedüs had been knocking on our gates for some time with an offer to "spill the beans" about the communist system in a series of autobiographical interviews. We had at the time a highly sophisticated political correspondent in Vienna in the person of the sociologist Zoltán Zsille, himself a former communist, who had known Hegedüs both as prime minister and later as a reform socialist. Like Hegedüs in 1973, Zsille had been expelled from the party for "revisionism." Here was the ideal man to conduct a series of colloquies in a language the apparat and party élite would understand.

Our Hungarian editorial staff was split. Should Radio Free Europe confer a star role on this notorious puppet of Stalin and Rákosi—the man who had signed the communist government's request for Soviet military intervention in 1956 and was seen by the Hungarian nation as a traitor par excellence? Could we implicate ourselves in his rehabilitation?

Giving or not giving the green light for the series to go ahead was, of course, ultimately my responsibility, and I shared some of the misgivings. But I also well remembered my first meeting with András Hegedüs in Budapest, soon after the Soviet occupation of Czechoslovakia, in 1968. Hegedüs was already well advanced on the road to apostasy and was making life uncomfortable for János Kádár and especially the hard-liners in the party. Like György Lukács, whom I saw on the same visit,[14] Hegedüs was publicly opposing the suppression of the Prague Spring and would soon lose his job as director of the Institute of Sociology for his pains. His expulsion from the party in 1973 made his dissent even more outspoken and his theoretical writings of rapidly increasing significance both in Hungary and among communists and socialists worldwide. He began to appear on the international (especially Eurocommunist) conference circuit.

Hegedüs was, of course, not a figure of the intellectual power of an Arthur Koestler, a John Strachey, or an Ignazio Silone—all of whom I had known well and put on air at great length during my first stint in Munich in the 1960s[15]—but his knowledge of the mechanics and psychology of Stalinism was first-hand, his recall excellent, his intelligence outstanding, and his eagerness to "confess" disarming. This was a formidable combination. Yet was András Hegedüs the same man in the soothing environment of late Kádárism, in 1985, as he had been in the prime of his heresy in 1968? Would the Radio not be trapped into airing the views of a sly dialectician—an apologist, as we had reason to fear, for the Kádár regime? Would he be willing accurately to describe and apologise for his own disgraceful part in the events of 1956? And again: Was it for us to promote him?

My friends and colleagues in the Hungarian Department—László Ribánszky, its director, Péter Halász, his deputy, and Levente Kasza, a senior editor—were divided. I decided to talk to Hegedüs myself. We met for lunch in the Sacher Hotel in Vienna, and I left convinced that this unprepossessing and visibly sick man was simply trying to bestride the world's stage once again, but now as an inside critic of the system he had once stood for. For us, that reversal was crucial. It augured well for our ability to make an impact on wavering communists in Eastern Europe and the Soviet Union. And so we did. The series was broadcast in many instalments in Hungarian and in all our languages. Out of it came a book,[16] first in Hungarian and then in German, and several articles, including one by me.[17]

The significance of the Hegedüs confession was simply the authenticity of the penitent. Zsille had a fine cutting edge to his mind—his questioning and comments were remorseless, but he could also be a patient listener. Not since the heresy of Milovan Djilas had we had a senior communist politician describing the psychology and techniques of communist rule, blow by blow, lie by lie, crime by crime; and even Djilas could not speak to us as a former chief executive. My grave reservations about the personality and record of András Hegedüs were overcome by the need to provide the heresiarch with a sounding board and so to shatter the self-confidence of the ruling élites throughout the communist lands. The year was 1985. We were both revising and making a piece of history:

> HEGEDÜS: The Politburo session [of October 23, 1956] began with a discussion of the MEFESZ[18] demonstration. . . . We were informed that the students were planning a large solidarity demonstration with Poland for the afternoon. The majority of Politburo members present took the view that the demonstration should be banned. So we banned it.
>
> But it soon transpired that our decision was not to be final, for protests started coming in almost at once. The editorial staff of *Szabad Nép*[19] protested . . . with Márton Horváth at their head. . . . The trade unions, too, protested, led by Sándor Gáspár, surrogate member of the Politburo. . . .
>
> That our decision was soon changed was due, however, not so much to these protests, as to what László Piros[20] told us, namely that he would not be able to stop the demonstration without a major conflict. He said that our decision to ban the demonstration could be

enforced only at the price of a very brutal clash between the police and the students.

Naturally, the Politburo wasn't keen on a showdown either. After a long period of indecision, around three in the afternoon, it was decided that we would, after all, allow the demonstration to go ahead.

ZSILLE: Looking back on this from where we are today, do you feel that decision was the right one?

HEGEDÜS: I believe it was. On that day, October 23, the national uprising could no longer be thwarted. The demonstration would have gone ahead even if we had banned it. The police could either have intervened or not intervened. Had it intervened, then the explosive character of the uprising would have assumed an even sharper form than it actually did, because it would have been challenging the law . . . ; the Politburo at that moment was no longer able to play any part in controlling events.

ZSILLE: How did members of the Politburo react to this new situation?

HEGEDÜS: Gerő was extremely tough. He was neither nervous nor demoralised—he was tough. . . . My own thought was, "Now nothing matters any more." I realised that whatever we decided would prove to be the wrong decision. I was gripped by paralysis and passivity. . . .

Around five o'clock, Gerő phoned to say that the demonstration had taken on massive proportions and would probably get out of hand. He asked me [to go] over to the Party Centre.

I put the receiver down, stood up, and looking out the window, I could see that the head of the demonstration had reached the middle of the Margaret Bridge. But from where I stood—the window of the prime minister's office—I could see no sign at all that the demonstration was getting out of hand. I walked over to the Party Centre—and was to stay there until October 27.

ZSILLE: What did you feel, as prime minister, when you saw a demonstration in Hungary—surely the first for a great many years—that had not been ordered by you, that was neither a May 1 demonstration nor one to celebrate April 4 [21] but a spontaneous demonstration?

HEGEDÜS: It was a frightening spectacle. Even if I had not realised it earlier, now would have been the time for me to realise that what was unfolding here was the challenge of national resistance to the central leadership and a personal one to the policies of the old leaders—including, of course, myself—and that this resistance would simply sweep us away, *will* sweep us away. I could see: now the people were coming! [Láttam: most jön a nép!] [22]

In putting this kind of material on air, we had, of course, to be careful not to appear to be supporting reform communism as an end; but I believe we managed to avoid giving any such impression. The echo chambers we provided for underground literature covered the whole range of dissent, from revisionist communism to religious protest. Our surrogate advocacy of reform communism did not stand on its own. It was one element in our major preoccupation—that of keeping the spirit of national identity, tradition, culture, and religion alive along the whole front of our almost twenty-four-hour broadcasting.

Most of my reforms were concentrated in this second area of keeping national cultures and identities in good working condition. I did not change the nature of these "national" transmissions, but I did shift their foci and their emphases. Under the previous management, the independence of our national language services had been curtailed. They had lost their original right to broadcast their own editorials on issues other than those dealing with the domestic affairs of their own lands. Such had been the erosion of their independence and integrity that on international topics they were obliged to take their cue (as I have already related) from a central list of approved articles. No respectable newspaper in the United States or Western Europe would have tolerated such interference. I saw to it that our national services' right to editorial opinion in all fields was restored. I wanted to maximise our credibility by making it crystal clear that Czechs, Hungarians, Poles, Romanians, Bulgarians, and later on Latvians, Lithuanians, and Estonians could look to us as the authentic keepers of their national interests and untrammelled free speech. The events of 1989 showed this policy to have been right. On a memorable visit to Bucharest as a guest of the Eminescu Trust early in 1990, I saw evidence that the process of identification had succeeded beyond our wildest hopes.

We *were* being looked upon as the Romanian nation in exile—custodians, at a time of national disempowerment, of Romania's cultural and historical continuity. How had we done it? I was repeatedly asked. Surprise and admiration were expressed that despite Ceauşescu and the Iron Curtain, our identification had been so close and our knowledge of Romanian home affairs so precise—better, I was given to understand, than the Romanian people's own. Every now and then it was meaningfully suggested (we were, after all, in the Balkans) that the Radio could not have achieved all that without a decent network of agents on the ground—and why not?—I was patronisingly told, as though spawning spies were the most natural thing for a radio station to do. But my assurance that we had planted no spies but had instead developed a much more potent and distinctly *un*secret weapon—intelligent "surrogate broadcasting" based on elaborate research—clearly strained my questioners' credulity.

Seven years after Romanian self-liberation, President Emil Constantinescu visited Radio Free Europe's Prague headquarters (March 11, 1997) and eloquently restated the Radio's role in the erosion of the totalitarian system: "Communism could exist only through lies and lack of information. Communism could not be defeated by the power of arms, but only by the power of words and profound convictions. That is why Radio Free Europe was much more important for us than armies, rockets, or even the most sophisticated equipment. The 'rockets' that destroyed communism were launched by Radio Free Europe. This was America's most important investment in the Cold War.

"I don't know whether the Americans themselves realise this now, seven years after the event, but we understand it well. . . . The trial of communism still is not finished."

Our identification with inside knowledge was no less intense in other parts of Eastern and Central Europe. On a visit to Hungary in the summer of 1988, I was trying to get in touch with the dissident Catholic priest György Bulányi, but all my enquiries ended in failure. Remembering that Budapest taxi drivers were the eyes and ears of the nation (and frequently of the communist police) I took a chance with one of them. "Do you happen to know where Father Bulányi may be living? I have already tried every source of information I can think of, but to no effect."

My driver reflected for a moment. "No, I'm afraid I can't help you; I know his name but that's all I know about him. But—do you know what? I'll stop at the phone box over there and you ring Radio Free Europe in Munich. *They* know everything!" His chuckle was one of the most pleasing sounds I can remember from my career as an international broadcaster.

It did not, however, take me entirely by surprise. Early in 1985, listeners in Central Europe began phoning in with their questions and comments. They were doing so defiantly, in most cases at government expense, for they were calling from their workshops and offices, where detection was less likely. Their cup was overflowing—clearly, they were no longer afraid. Soon, under our broadcast encouragement, a veritable avalanche of telephone calls descended, mainly in Czech, Hungarian, and Bulgarian. Having satisfied myself that we would not be adding unreasonably to the risks listeners were willing to take with their security, Buckley and I authorised special lines and recording equipment to be installed to cope with the telephone calls. Here was feedback on an undreamt-of scale—positive, negative, thoughtful as well as frivolous. My overall impression was that the callers' knowledge was meticulous, their criticisms were sober and to the point, and their trust in us as keepers of their consciences and honour was nothing if not amazing. Our broadcasters were buzzing with excitement. For the first time in the Radio's existence, they were in live contact with the men and women they had hitherto had to address "blind." Listening to many hours of the tape recordings we were continually making of these telephone calls was one of my most moving experiences as a broadcaster, and a prodigious confirmation of my feeling that our guidance was indispensable and the Soviet empire nearing its end.

In Poland our feedback was, if anything, even more gratifying. Jan Novak—a longtime thorn in the flesh of certain members of the U.S. State Department because of his highly successful but unorthodox leadership of our Polish station—was celebrated as a national hero upon his return to his liberated country in 1989. He addressed an extraordinary session of the Sejm specially called to honour him for his work at Radio Free Europe. The Estonians were equally appreciative. In February 1991 President (earlier Foreign Minister) Lennart Meri of Estonia, a dedicated listener of many years' standing, recommended Radio Free Europe for the Nobel Peace Prize. In Hungary, on October 23, 1991 (thirty-fifth anniversary of the 1956 Hungarian Revolution), László Ribánszky was awarded a cross of the Order of the Hungarian Republic by Árpád Göncz, president of the Repubic, and József Antall, prime minister, in recognition of Ribánszky's work as head of the Radio's Hungarian Service. There were many other examples.

The transfer of the Baltic services (October 8, 1984) from Radio Liberty to Radio Free Europe was a red letter day in our calendar. Due to Frank Shakespeare's personal pressure, the transfer was a fresh signal from the U.S. administration that the Soviet incorporation of Estonia, Latvia, and Lithuania, which had never been recognised de jure by the United States or several other Western governments, might soon be de-recognised in fact as well. Already in November 1983 the creation of a separate Baltic Service, still under Radio Liberty, had pointed the way. "The establishment of the Baltic Radio Division reaffirms United States policy of not recognising the forcible and unlawful incorporation of Estonia, Latvia, and Lithuania in the Soviet Union," President Reagan said in a statement on November 18, 1983. "The new call signal, 'the Baltic Service of Radio Liberty,' will reinforce the distinct identities of the Baltic states and separate them from the rest of the Soviet Union." The transfer a year later of the three services to Radio Free Europe made Reagan's meaning unmistakably clear.

I had always taken great personal interest in the fortunes of our Baltic neighbours. I was overjoyed to be able to welcome their representatives in our ranks. We received about thirty Baltic staff members, many of them outstandingly capable and keen to underline, through their identification with Radio Free Europe, their European—non-Soviet— credentials. Kestutis Girnius for Lithuania, Janis Trapans for Latvia, and Tomas Ilves for Estonia, who at different times headed our three Baltic broadcasting stations, played significant roles in preparing the restoration of independence in their countries and then promoting it amidst the hazards of the post-Soviet world. Tomas Ilves was eventually appointed Estonian ambassador to the United States and in 1996 foreign minister, and Janis Trapans became for a time Latvian defence minister.

My own involvement with the Baltic leaders, both before and after liberation, was fairly close. I met Lennart Meri, Vytautis Landsbergis, Anatoliys Gorbunovs, Stasys Lozoraitis, Marju Lauristin, Andrej Krastyns, Janis Jurkans, Algirdas Saudargas, Georgs Andrejevs, Pater Vaclovas Aliulis, Gunars Meierovics, Andrejs Pantelejevs, and others, some of them repeatedly. A large part of European learning, music, and literature had its origins or home in Riga, Kaunas, Vilnius, Tartu, and Tallinn. They were oases in the Soviet desert. I worked for Baltic self-liberation with conviction and was moved when it was accomplished.

Yet the Radio's identification with "Europa," strong though it was, needed even more explicit articulation. European unification was a hallowed notion in our target area, but our reliance on American sponsorship made our European credentials less than fully persuasive in the eyes of some of our listeners. This was especially so after the slow erosion of the once robust backing of European unification by successive American administrations. The days when George Ball had reinforced the commitment of Jean Monnet were long behind us.

Here, too, I was able to pave the way for policies which went beyond our explicit mandate, for in the Radios' guidelines no thought had been given to Eastern Europe's place in a united Europe. I established friendly rapport and political understanding with Otto von Habsburg and a group of European parliamentarians under his leadership. They repeatedly visited our headquarters. Discussions were started to make the future of the East and Central European nations central to the concerns of the European Parliament and the European Community, and our Radio's extensive data base on Eastern and Central Europe supportive of their work. Otto von Habsburg wrote to me in 1984:

> Fortunately, the European Parliament is now definitely engaged in following a course for a 'greater Europe'"; I suggest a permanent representative of Radio Free Europe be appointed [in Strasbourg]. His task would be . . . to gather from the European Parliament information about those many activities that are being carried out in the field of politics and human rights in support of the Soviet-occupied nations. At the same time he could establish personal contacts with members of the European Parliament . . . and provide them with information at your disposal. All this might help to encourage the nations of Central Europe [to feel] that they are not forgotten in the free world, while we would be receiving ammunition from your side.[23]

Financial cutbacks under the restrictive Gramm-Rudman legislation prevented us from putting this plan into effect. Cooperation nevertheless continued at both the formal and informal levels. I developed a personal admiration for Otto von Habsburg. I found him an individual of scintillating wit and a politician of outstanding intellect and wisdom. But for his name and the Austrian Constitution, he would have made an excellent president of the Republic of Austria, I once told him in the 1960s, only half in jest. Under his dynastic title, as archduke and heir to the empire, he did not aspire to the throne of any of his former lands;[24] but I kept wondering whether Otto the European parliamentarian might not consider holding down the first presidency of the United States of Europe—if such were to be created—as an ironic but fitting climax to his life and career. Stranger things have happened in history. The European Community was, after all, the notional legatee of the Holy Roman Empire which the Habsburgs had headed since the thirteenth century. Could there be any harm in underlining the connection?

Otto von Habsburg did not think so; he himself made the connection. "'The man who first offered us an intellectual bridge, as a matter of conscious policy, between the Holy Roman Empire and the European present was Count Richard Coudenhove-Kalergy . . . ; he was the first to realise that after the fratricidal mess of the First World War, Europe had to be rebuilt as a single civilisation on pan-European lines. I merely follow in his footsteps.'"[25]

We at the Radio were of course not in the business of making European policy, but as we were talking to millions of enthusiastic Europeans in Eastern and Central Europe, I felt our credibility would be enhanced if our freshly forged association with Otto von Habsburg and the ideas he stood for could be clearly and consistently articulated. Our listeners expected the resolution of many of their problems—spiritual as well as material—from their eventual return to Europe. In Strasbourg and in Brussels, Otto von Habsburg and his group of Euro-M.P.'s were the principal, and frequently the only, people who regularly spoke up, and spoke up with knowledge and empathy, for the nations under Soviet rule. They did not, in the mid-1980s, represent power or the practical future any more than the U.S. State Department or the Quai d'Orsay represented spirituality; but the work of Otto von Habsburg's group was rich in symbolism and suggestive of hope at a time of seeming hopelessness. They stood for a conception of Europe close to the hearts of most educated Europeans, and succinctly put by Colin Welch in a famous *Encounter* symposium: "This little peninsula at the west end of the Asiatic land mass—how precious, how vulnerable it seemed and seems to me! Its woods and fields and rivers, its cities and cathedrals, its splendours and castles, its mountains, inns and valleys have always appeared to me not alien but my own; its peoples not strangers but brothers. I weep to think of what is already lost: Poland, East Germany, Czechoslovakia and Hungary and other points east, not forgetting holy Russia herself. Who could contemplate without horror the loss of a single acre more, still less the subjection of all that remains, to an eastern tyranny?"[26]

CHAPTER EIGHT

The National Interest

U nder the two Radios' preceding board and management it was unstated policy that if and when a conflict arose between the American national interest, as interpreted by the executive arm of the U.S. government, and the long-term interests of the nations of Eastern and Central Europe, as interpreted by the surrogate radios, the American interest would prevail, although it was always assumed that such conflicts would be rare and could be kept from public view. But when Frank Shakespeare took over as chairman of the board, fresh priorities were laid down. The board decided that in any such conflict our first responsibility was to speak for the people we as surrogate broadcasters represented, even if their interests seemed to be in disharmony with those of the United States. This was perhaps straining the Radio's mission, but our mandate was, as I have tried to show, vague enough to make a flexible interpretation legitimate.

I was wholly in agreement with the board's revised reading of our mandate and had it carried out in Munich at the operational level, even though I had reason to fear that we would run into a welter of difficulties. Were we the rightful custodians of the national interests of Czechs, Slovaks, Poles, Hungarians, Bulgarians, and Romanians? We had no institutional connections with the East and Central European émigré organisations in the West and deliberately excluded their advice from our counsels for fear of becoming enmeshed in émigré politics. Our interpretation of what constituted the national interest had to be made on the run. We took the temperature of the nations we were addressing as best we could through wide-ranging audience research and by consulting independent authorities at Western universities. The composition of our staff was of intrinsic value, for staff had been so selected from the very birth of Radio Free Europe that it represented all shades of political opinion, barring only fascism and communism.

Radio Free Europe was facing an easier task than Radio Liberty. We could count on the spirit of national independence as well as the spirit of national rejection of the imported, though domesticated, communist system. The countries we were addressing wanted to be both sovereign and democratic. The Soviet case was different. Lenin's years of exile and the sealed train through Germany notwithstanding, bolshevism had been born and bred in Russia. There was evidence at all levels of Soviet life that in the USSR the Stalinist organisation of society had been well assimilated and that the Russian people, despite prolonged suffering, relished the respect and fear Soviet power was inspiring throughout the world. "Russia has at long last achieved its rendezvous with history—never mind the hammer and sickle under which this has happened"—this was (and still is) a popular theme in Russian thinking.

Radio Liberty had an almost impossible task to accomplish: How could it humour the nationalist spirit of the Russian people while trying at the same time to wean it away from bolshevism, to which most Russians felt they owed their status as a superpower? Also, the Radio's very attempt to identify itself with Russian national consciousness immediately evoked, as I have related, unfounded charges in the American liberal press that Radio Liberty was trying to reinstate the values of the ancien régime and was advocating undemocratic, even anti-Semitic ideas. Yet some identification with Russian national consciousness was indispensable to the Radio's mission, as our board well recognised. Only by appealing to the national-democratic and religious elements in the Russian past and in the Russian psyche could Radio Liberty hope to encourage the spirit of resistance to totalitarianism and to ingrained habits of conformity.

Fortunately, my own responsibilities were, formally at least, limited to Radio Free Europe and its "catchment area" in Eastern and Central Europe. The pursuit of the various Central and East European national interests was seldom at odds with the pursuit of the U.S. national interest. It was clearly in the American national interest to contain Soviet expansionism, enlarge the area of freedom within the Soviet client states, promote political and economic pluralism, and keep the peace. These were eminently East and Central European ambitions, too. If and when conflict did occur, we invariably spoke up on behalf of the peoples whose historical legatees we considered ourselves to be.

Here lay the crucial difference between the work of the Voice of America and Radio Free Europe, and the novelty of our special kind of broadcasting. The Voice of America spoke for official America; we represented the conscience of all Western democratic nations as well as the interests of the Eastern nations we were addressing. That we could do both, using American funds, is a tribute to the independence and farsightedness of the new board under Frank Shakespeare, and of the men and women who supported him in the White House and elsewhere in the U.S. government. In some ways Radio Free Europe was a strangely idealistic enterprise. I would not go so far as claiming that it was run in the spirit of undiluted altruism; but it did make it possible for us to argue from certain moral principles which, in the aftermath of World War II, key American policy makers had embraced and were prepared to make sacrifices for. This was certainly more than could be said about the context in which Eastern affairs were being conducted in the corridors of power in France and Britain. The Americans, having identified the adversary, were willing to put power behind their principles. Britain and France were not because, sadly, they possessed neither, except in their rhetoric.

In the last analysis, our nonconformism *did*, of course, serve American interests, too, but mainly by promoting "interests" far wider in scope: the universal human interest that justice and the rule of law should prevail in international affairs and decency in man's everyday commerce with man. Much of the satisfaction I was able to derive from broadcasting to the captive nations stemmed from this aspect of our work, even though I knew well enough that neither the first nor the second of these desirable objectives could be realised without a radical change in human nature.

My personal attitude to the nationalisms and national interests of Eastern Europe flowed directly from my own brand of supranational, slightly left-of-centre conservatism. I was and am a conservative in the spirit of the West European Christian Democracy which ministered at the birth of what has become the European Union. Narrow ideologies of "national destiny"—of the primacy, the superiority, or the primogeniture, of this or that nation over others—had been the curse of European civilisation. Hardly a state or a nation in Europe had not, at one time or another, staked out a claim that in *it* resided some unique collective virtue—the true idea of Civilisation, the true fount of Democracy, the true defence of Christianity, or some other unmatchable excellence of mind or military valour. The history books of the

European countries had accordingly wrapped themselves in national colours, poisoning the minds of generations. This spirit of national hubris threatened to revive in our target areas in the aftermath of communism.

Such infantilism could have no place in the Radio's stock of ideas or in its vocabulary. In Western Europe, under the impact of unification, national prejudice was on its way out. It could not be allowed to jeopardise any postcommunist reconciliation in the East. I make no apologies for having stepped on it if (very rarely) it raised its head at the Radio. I stepped on it even at the risk of exposing myself to accusations of élitism. I was indeed an élitist, in the sense of being cool to any display of tribal muscle and opposed to any conception of the postcommunist world as a zero-sum game in which one nation's advantage could be purchased only by inflicting a corresponding disadvantage on another. I was much helped in this assertion of a single yardstick by our American partners' weak sense of history, and especially their indifference to the pull of irrational, ethnocentric European nationalisms. While fighting with might and main against the communist attempt to homogenise the East European nations' historical consciousness, I also felt, looking to the postcommunist future, that a dash of historical amnesia would, from time to time, serve these nations well. Regrettably, from the mid-1980s, Margaret Thatcher's nationalistic, anti-European rhetoric set a harmful example far beyond the shores of England.[1]

There were times, however, when conflicts of a minor kind between official American policy and the Radio's preferred options had to be dealt with. It had been State Department policy, for example, to cosy up to Nicolai Ceaușescu because the Romanian dictator was thought to be an agent of disunity in the communist camp. From time to time we were gingerly asked by the State Department to pull our punches, mainly on various human rights issues, so that U.S. policy makers could obtain or maintain Ceaușescu's goodwill. We knew that human rights and living standards were foremost on the Romanian people's agenda and that we could not be mild or silent about them without alienating our audiences, betraying our mandate, and causing long-term damage to the reputation of the United States. Under my stewardship of the Radio, such requests were politely refused after civilised discussion. At times, the staff at the State Department objected; but realising the influence and determination of our new board and the close understanding that existed between its chairman and the new director of Radio Free Europe, the diplomats desisted, and our dispute usually ended there. U.S. Ambassador David B. Funderburk was not so fortunate. His opposition to the State Department's appeasement of Ceauşescu caused him to step down from his post in protest.[2]

But attempts to influence our policy were not confined to the State Department. On a visit to the White House in 1984, at the invitation of Walt Raymond, Jr., of the National Security Council (NSC), I had a session with Jack Matlock, then Soviet affairs adviser to President Reagan. He asked why we had retired the head of our Hungarian Service. He was fully aware, he said, that Radio Free Europe was not accountable to the NSC, but he was personally curious to know our reasons.

I told him that we were indeed not accountable to any department of the U.S. administration, but I would give him a private answer to what I took to be a private question. And I proceeded to tell him that, in recent years, until my arrival in Munich, the Hungarian Service had observed a spectacular silence about the presence of Soviet forces on Hungarian territory. Some senior members of the service explained this to me as deliberate policy. They saw János Kádár as a force for the good, deserving of our support. It would not help the growth of Hungarian liberalisation, I was given to understand, if we drew attention to a topic which, like any discussion of the 1956 revolution, was off the Hungarian public agenda. Why stir up trouble between Moscow and Budapest when things were running sweetly?

I could not accept that reasoning, I told Matlock. Our mandate and credibility made it inescapable for us to question the presence of foreign troops on Hungarian soil and the resulting curtailment of Hungarian sovereignty, and I had directed the service to discuss the matter in measured terms whenever circumstances so required. The withdrawal of Soviet forces had been the key demand of the 1956 revolution—we could not ignore it without being untrue to our mission. Whereupon the head of the service, rightly sensing that he did not have my full confidence, asked for his early retirement.

To my astonishment, Matlock proceeded to embrace the view I had rejected in Munich. He said things were going so well in Hungary that if the Kádár regime decided to keep silent about the matter of Soviet troops, so should the Radio. If so much liberalisation could be achieved in the presence of Soviet forces, why cause ructions by asking for their departure? In any case, he said, the question of Soviet troops in Hungary was a function of a larger international equation. We could and should try to do nothing about it unless Kádár or the West put it on their own agenda.

My answer was simple. This was a cogent view which I took very seriously, but I held a different one. The retirement of the service head was an accomplished fact and so was our change of policy. We left it at that.[3] I knew I had the board fully behind me.

On the same visit to Washington I was put under similar pressure by Mark Palmer and his senior colleagues in the State Department. Once again, the Hungarian issue was raised, and so were others concerning the now fully asserted independence of Radio Free Europe under the new board. I budged on neither, proceeding on the principle of *fortiter in re suaviter in modo*. This old tag served me well throughout my tenure. I maintained amicable relations in U.S. government quarters, even though the bureaucrats' unease at my radicalism was as manifest as my resentment of their short-termism and readiness to compromise their own American principles.

Palmer was a young, shrewd, and personally charming deputy assistant secretary. He respected my views as I respected his. He thought he had at least a residual right to influence our output. I thought (in unison with the board) that he had none except the right to be heard. Later on, in 1987 and 1988, as U.S. ambassador to Hungary, he attained fame and extraordinary popularity through his skilful support of dissident forces and personalities; and he stood to become a kind of latter-day Palatine had financial misjudgement not suddenly dislodged him from his post and indeed the State Department. He was Lawrence Eagleburger's man and could, but for this mishap, have advanced to the top ranks of the department when Eagleburger became Secretary of State. In June 1989, while attending the spectacular reburial of Imre Nagy and his associates, I saw Palmer again and congratulated him on his achievement. He seemed no longer worried about American interference in communist Hungary's domestic affairs. He was carrying out the interference himself and doing it extremely well.

From time to time unofficial pressures took a more discreet and personal form. While on a visit to Brussels in April 1985, Edward Teller told me that at a conference he was attending in town he had encountered Nicholas M. Salgó, President Reagan's then ambassador to Hungary, who had expressed the wish to talk to me. I readily agreed, although I knew well enough that Salgó's credit was not high among my Republican friends in the United States and that he was also under a cloud in Budapest on account of his closeness to the communist authorities and dealings he was alleged to have had in the art market. We met at the American ambassador's residence, where he was a house guest. Salgó, like me, is of Hungarian birth; yet he insisted on speaking to me in his somewhat rudimentary English. He probably felt that using the language of his office would add weight to what he had to tell me. Not so. I thought he was a political appointee who, as had been repeatedly suggested, owed his embassy to the contributions he had made to Ronald Reagan's campaign funds. My patience with worthy amateurs who were dabbling in serious matters of state was limited.

Salgó's complaint concerned Radio Free Europe's negative attitude to the Kádár regime, and especially to the forthcoming, not entirely monolithic but still communist-controlled Hungarian elections. Why did we not embrace these as positive signs of the Communist Party's evolution towards a multiparty system? Why such purism and scepticism? Did we have a better choice to head liberalisation than Kádár and his team?[4] I listened to his reasoning carefully but disagreed. A few concessions within the system did not amount to pluralism, I said. The reforms had not been institutionalised. We had appreciated in our broadcasts Kádár's merits on a great many (too many) occasions and would do so again if developments warranted, but we would be weakening the more robust forces of dissent within the party and outside it if we now gave high marks to a feeble and party-directed gesture. Hungarian public opinion, I said, recognised the preparations for the elections for what they were—a mini-improvement, no more.[5] So did Radio Free Europe.

I was not sure whether Salgó liked what he heard from me. We had a courteous if somewhat strained conversation. I admired his self-confidence (of which he had a generous supply). Later on, his criticisms of the Radio and of me personally continued. We answered these patiently whenever an answer was called for, but our policy remained unchanged.

On other occasions, the U.S. government welcomed the distance that existed between it and Radio Free Europe, and gave our unorthodox second-conductorship its seal of indirect approval. This fine dichotomy had a great many uses, as the communist side well recognised. It made it possible for the State Department, especially under the Reagan presidency, to encourage and benefit from certain types of message to the East without being identified with the messenger. We were deniable.

In July 1985, for example, encouraged by the brilliant William McGurn of the *Wall Street Journal*, I wrote an ad hominem comment about Jerzy Urban, my namesake in Poland. He was one of the most infamous but accomplished and entertaining propagandists on the other side—a star of ministerial rank among the dull, grey men in charge of the public presentation of policy in the communist world. I felt Jerzy Urban had been telling just too many lies for comfort, and that he had played a particularly distasteful role in preparing the climate in which Father Jerzy Popiełuszko's foul murder became possible. The minister was ripe for exposure. He was, of course, getting it in fair measure from all our language services, but I felt a little chastisement in a large English-language newspaper could do no harm.

It has been so ordered by an unkindly fate that I should share a name with Jerzy (George) Urban: spokesman for the Polish authorities, scourge of Western governments, a man of vitriolic tongue and temper and—at least in his own estimation—a gallant and a wit, to boot. Never a man to mince his words about the depredations of bourgeois society or to use one adjective where three will do, Mr. Urban is a public entertainer in the world where official humour is rare. There are few jokes in Marx or Lenin. Mr. Urban (communist) supplies them and has the Warsaw government laughing all the way to the Western banks.

His principal venue for doing so is the unusual (for communist countries) device of the press conference, where facts and fiction, hearsay, surmise and straightforward mendacity mix and mingle to the bewilderment of Western correspondents and the Polish public alike. But he also uses a pen name (Jan Rem) in the official press to give himself more room for invective than his official position as a government minister and spokesman would allow. Where Jerzy whispers Jan can roar.

But I must not overtax my metaphor, because Mr. Urban is in the serious business of justifying the existence and spinning yarns on behalf of an unelected Soviet-sponsored government. The activities of elected governments are, goodness knows, difficult enough to justify. Unelected ones require special talent. Mr. Urban has it.

To say that he is on uncertain terms with the truth would be doing an injustice to his intelligence. He is, rather, the product of that strange Alice-in-Wonderland kind of universe known as Leninism, in which the truth is precisely what Mr. Urban and his masters say it is. Not that Mr. Urban is a communist. He says he is not a party member. It just so happens that he is in hearty agreement with the policies that the cabal around Polish leader Wojciech Jaruzelski pursues and Moscow supports.

A few weeks before the murder of the Rev. Jerzy Popiełuszko, Mr. Urban observed in the restrained language characteristic of his articulations that the priest had been guilty of inciting the public to violence.

"Seances of hatred are organized in Father Popiełuszko's church," he said. "He presides over sessions of political rabies. He conducts black masses."

Yet when the same priest was brutally murdered by police agents brought up on the philosophy and vocabulary of Mr. Urban and his colleagues, the target of Mr. Urban's indignation was a long way from the murderers sitting in the dock in Torun. He announced to a startled audience: "Public opinion in Poland is watching with disapproval the brutal US police repression of churchmen and worshippers from the Holy Trinity Church in Clairton, Pennsylvania, whose only offense was their charitable support of a few thousand laid-off steelworkers." . . .

How do I, the other George Urban, relate to all this? The answer is "not very much," even though Jerzy and I were recently depicted in the *Detroit Free Press* as "two identically named men, warriors in the East-West confrontation in command of the most important weapons system there is: words." If there is such a personal contest it leaves me singularly cold. Who could equal the resourceful Dr. Goebbels? Who would want to?

I came to head Radio Free Europe long after the other Mr. Urban had been dispensing comment (and policy) from Warsaw. I shall probably leave the scene long before he does. In the meantime, I never cease wondering what my indefatigable namesake might invent next, and how we might chip away at his fabrications. We may not always succeed; indeed, we have chalked up some failures. But I suspect that though Mr. Urban speaks only for General Jaruzelski's self-appointed government, we at Radio Free Europe speak—and are seen to be speaking—for the Polish people. The Mr. Urban sitting in Warsaw knows this and doesn't like it, and I take courage from the fact that he doesn't. In the popular language of those disclaimers that run before American films, I cordially submit that any similarity between the two George Urbans is strictly coincidental.

Observers of Jerzy Urban who know him better than I have remarked that there is something diabolic about his demeanor. This is unkind. I prefer to think that the vignette once appended to Dr. Edward Aveling, the wayward son-in-law of Karl Marx, also applies to Mr. Urban: "Nobody can be as bad as Dr. Aveling looks."[6]

Jerzy Urban took my comments in very bad part, and so did his government. My namesake was Poland's official spokesman and a member of General Jaruzelski's cabinet. He felt my observations were "insulting and defamatory," and he was especially upset by my claim that while he spoke only for General Jaruzelski's self-appointed government, Radio Free Europe spoke for the Polish people.

One day after my article had appeared, the U.S. chargé d'affaires in Warsaw was summoned to the Foreign Ministry and handed a "verbal *démarche*" with a demand for "an appropriate explanation."

> There is no doubt that George Urban of Munich speaks for Radio Free Europe, which is an agency of the United States Government. It confirms once more that Radio Free Europe is an instrument of the United States Government for interfering in the internal affairs of Poland. The United States Government cannot avoid responsibility for the activities of the broadcasting station it funds and supports, which are directed against Poland. Radio Free Europe has nothing in common with the Polish people or state. By its broadcasts in Polish it has been trying for years to destabilize the situation in Poland, to incite tension, to divide Polish society and to slander Poland's constitutional authorities. It should be stressed that this highly insulting article by George Urban was also broadcast by the United States Government broadcasting station Voice of America on July 25.[7]

Truthfully and wisely, the American chargé d'affaires dissociated the U.S. government from Radio Free Europe and its director, undertaking, however, to "review the substance of the article" and to convey to the Polish government any response. To my best knowledge the démarche was left unanswered.[8]

Two years later, in February 1987, Jerzy Urban gave a talk at the Royal Institute of International Affairs in London, where, for the first time, we met. Surrounded by journalists, we were introduced to each other by Christopher Cviic of Chatham House: "George Urban — George Urban."

"You will recall," I said, by way of an opening gambit, "that some eighteen months ago, when I was in charge of Radio Free Europe, I made a number of unflattering comments about you in the *Wall Street Journal* which I understood you did not much enjoy reading."

"Oh, not at all," Jerzy answered with a genial smile, "you gave me greater publicity in the Western world than I'd ever had before. I'd like to thank you."

But the mask dropped as soon as Jerzy Urban mounted the rostrum. He accused the West of inciting unrest in Poland and thus being co-responsible for the imposition of martial law in December 1981. He observed that Radio Free Europe was in reality not a radio station at all but a subversive agency which violated international law and which it was thus legitimate to jam.

Those familiar with Jerzy Urban's past pronouncements were not surprised. Only fourteen months earlier he had told the *Washington Post* that the imposition of martial law by General Jaruzelski's communist government had been the work of no other person than President Reagan. Reagan, he claimed, could have forestalled the suppression of Solidarity had he acted on secret information in his possession and warned the world of what the Polish communists were planning. But, said Jerzy Urban, Reagan was more interested in a "bloody upheaval than the peaceful solution of the Polish crisis."

After the fall of the system, Jerzy Urban, now a bourgeois, free-market publisher and listed as one of Poland's one hundred richest men, found himself at the centre of a pornography scandal and was taken to court in 1991. "My trial," he said after his acquittal, "had nothing to do with . . . pornography. . . . It transformed me from an oppressor into a fighter for freedom of speech."[9] And following the unexpected victory of Aleksandr Kwásniewski's ex-communist Democratic Left Alliance at the September 1993 Polish general elections, Jerzy Urban was shown on the front pages of Polish newspapers holding a magnum of champagne, his tongue stuck out in defiance of his critics: "The victors of 1989 are the vanquished of today," he was quoted as saying.[10]

I have few regrets about the unkind words I wrote about my namesake in communist Poland.

CHAPTER NINE

Jealousies in the Region

Another group of problems that gave us cause for concern was the uneven affection in which some of the East and Central European nations held one another. We had to take careful account of their prejudices—old and new—not only because these could weaken the collective force of their resistance to Soviet hegemony but also because they threatened to undermine peace in the area if and when their sovereignty was restored. The Polish underground's forward role in the mid-1980s was a case in point.

Poland was then in the vanguard of self-liberation. The massive Polish underground, which expressed itself in an amazing array of publications and privately run publishing companies, was the marvel of the communist world. In Czechoslovakia and Hungary, however, the Polish example created more resentment than support. Many Hungarians felt the Poles were misdirecting their energies—they should work harder and upgrade the Polish economy rather than indulge their national passion for libertarian heroics and buying salami off the Hungarian shelves. The Czechs simply disliked being increasingly left behind in the self-liberation stakes, without, however, having formulated any clear idea of how they might advance beyond the modest programme of Charta 77.

Here was a problem that demanded my immediate attention. It was absurd, and would have proved self-defeating for all nations concerned, if the country showing the greatest courage and sophistication in chipping away at the communist system were to be ignored or stigmatised by its neighbours for doing what it was doing in effect on behalf of all of them. I decided to mount systematic cross-reporting in all our languages to inform our non-Polish audiences of what exactly the Poles were advocating and how they were proposing to go about it—

for the Polish underground was not merely making nonsense of the communist system but pointing the way to a whole alternative way of thinking and being. Polish samizdat was now reaching floodlike proportions, with more than six hundred titles coming our way at regular intervals. A major effort was needed to test, edit, and translate the most telling items. We did all that, and the results were not long in coming.[1]

Naturally, it was not the first time Radio Free Europe had made use of this type of broadcasting. Amplifying the impact of unofficial publications of small circulation but attested authenticity was one of the Radio's standard techniques. Indeed, our mandate as surrogate communicators for the nonexisting free media demanded it. What was new was the sheer size of the Polish underground and the concentrated manner in which we promoted the ideas it represented for the benefit of millions of people all over Eastern and Central Europe. A new, centrifugal force now boosted our influence.

But even this seemingly straightforward operation was in danger of being misrepresented. Our critics in Poland and in the United States put it about that some of the Polish underground literature was our invention. We had, they claimed, commissioned it to suit our own political goals and then broadcast it nationwide as genuine samizdat. This was wholly untrue, but exceptionally hard to refute. Our Polish Service was, in fact, in daily contact with the Polish underground, as was its journalistic duty. We did have a tradition of making royalty payments for the broadcasting rights of all outside contributions, including of course the texts we were receiving from Polish sources. Outside Poland, we were *the* natural outlet for samizdat. It was also true that Zdzislaw Najder, our hyperactive, sophisticated, and shrewd Polish Service director, had a web of intimate contacts with a wide range of people in Poland, including, as it later transpired, the secret police,[2] the Polish underground, and especially Solidarity. At one time, under the code name of Zapalniczka, he appears to have received payments from the secret police for services rendered.

Under sentence of death for high treason, Najder appeared to be a man of patriotism and courage, but also one of great arrogance and deviousness. He could neither deal peacefully with his staff nor accept guidance from his superiors. Why he had been appointed by the previous management has never been adequately explained. Although my support of Solidarity and of the rest of the Polish underground was second to none, I had to ensure that our pursuit of Polish interests did not expose the Radio as a whole to avoidable attacks in the

United States. If evidence had emerged that we had been commissioning our own underground literature or funding the underground in other ways, the consequences in Congress and the American media would have been severe. I had to and did make doubly sure that all broadcast Polish samizdat texts were of a genuinely indigenous inspiration and that they had appeared in Poland in reasonable print runs before we used them. In other areas, too, I had to enforce discipline in our Polish Service in ways I would have preferred to avoid, Najder himself being the cause of much unpleasantness. At one time he and certain members of his staff would not talk to one another in the absence of witnesses. This was intolerable. Time and again, Buckley and I had to still the voices of rebellion in the department. Najder's job hung by a thread to the day of my retirement.[3]

It was equally difficult to deal with the related problem of nationalism (as distinct from national consciousness) as a tool in our workshop. It was especially hard for me personally. From childhood on, I had been (as the reader will by now be well aware) an admirer and supporter of European unification. I believed in the oneness of European culture, and I was convinced that we could tolerate no more European wars. I was, therefore, opposed to rekindling any form of modern—ethnocentric, xenophobic, myth-making—nationalism. But could we make the most of our leverage against Soviet domination without supporting *some* form of it? If the elimination of the Soviet system was our overriding objective, wasn't a more robust sense of national consciousness the handiest means of achieving it? Would nationalism necessarily backfire on us once liberation was attained, or need it undermine the Central and East European nations' chances of joining a unifying Europe if they stuck to the *original*, nineteenth-century conception of a *liberal* national emancipation?

In the mid-1980s, these were entirely hypothetical questions. The Soviet system seemed stable and the empire cast in concrete. The problem preoccupying most policy makers was not how to prepare for an equitable *peace* after the Soviet world had gone, but how to cause the Soviet empire to reach the point of self-destruction. Worse, to the minds of many in the establishment the demise of the Soviet empire did not seem a desirable objective in the first place. The balance of power seemed more important.

I was, in reality, debating with myself—not an uncomfortable position to be in if there is a dearth of more desirable partners for conversation. By the time I reached Munich, it was clear to me that the

Radios' brief on the national question was broadly right (national consciousness, yes; militant nationalism, no); but it had to be applied more widely to be effective. Radio Free Europe never countenanced the forces of nationalism in the various states of Eastern and Central Europe. It consistently condemned and heavily discouraged any idea of the revision of frontiers, the reallocation of territories, the transfer of populations, or the prejudicial treatment of minority populations by the majority, and vice versa. We broadcast programmes criticising the postwar Czechoslovak deportation of the Sudeten Germans (under Allied auspices) many years before the Czechoslovak reform communists began, to their honour, to do so in 1967–68.

The Radios' managers, I hasten to add, pursued these policies of moderation not because they were guided by perspicacious considerations about a united Europe, but because, like the American political class as a whole, they were unable to see beyond the status quo created by two world wars and were especially reluctant to rock what was popularly but wrongly thought to be the Yalta settlement. The Yalta documents had not, in fact, surrendered Eastern and Central Europe to Soviet tutelage. It was the Soviet advance to the heart of Europe (uncountered by the Western allies) that had created the status quo.

But whether for good reasons or poor ones, a policy had emerged to which I was happy to subscribe. Neither before my directorship nor under it did we give quarter to national revisionism, irredentism, or separatisms of any kind. This was not always easy. We were, for example, brought under serious pressure by influential members of the Slovak emigration, the Roman Catholic Church, and especially Slovak prelates in Rome, to underline the distinct nationhood of Slovakia by splitting our Czechoslovak Service into a Czech and Slovak one. We did not do so because no one in the West was at the time prepared to question the results of World Wars I and II but also because we knew that the bisection of the service would give encouragement to separatist aspirations elsewhere.

In Romanian-Hungarian relations, we were facing a particularly delicate dilemma. The large Hungarian minority population in Transylvania was being increasingly squeezed out of its human rights under the tyrannical rule of Ceauşescu. So, of course, was the entire Romanian population, but the Hungarians attracted the Romanian dictator's special wrath. He nursed an unconcealed hatred for Hungarians and Jews, and tended to equate the first with the second. Under normal conditions we would have been well justified in embracing Hungary's rumbling unofficial concern—and would have been acting within the letter of the Helsinki Final Act had we done so. But because any such move would have fanned the dormant passions of nationalism on both sides, we scrupulously abstained from doing so until, in January 1978, Ceauşescu's discriminatory policies against the Transylvanian Hungarian minority became international front-page news. As a result of our moderation, we periodically incurred the disapproval of sections of the émigré communities and of some of our audiences in both countries, but we accepted that as a penalty well worth paying in the service of what we thought was a superior good—keeping the peace between the two communities. Concern had been expressed before my appointment by leading members of the Romanian, Czech, Slovak, and even the Polish émigré communities that a Hungarian-born director might not be as evenhanded an advocate of their national aspirations as one born and bred in the United States or Western Europe. I believe I am right in saying that our handling of the Romanian-Hungarian discord laid that anxiety to rest. To the end of my work with Radio Free Europe, I heard no more about it.

I was greatly assisted in steering a cautious course in Hungarian-Romanian affairs by two service directors of exceptional moderation and wisdom: László Ribánszky and Vladimir Georgescu. The issue of national minorities created no problem between us and—more important—none between the Romanian and Hungarian Services either. I was shocked when, two years after my retirement, in November 1988, Vladimir Georgescu died after a short illness—the third Romanian Service director in a row to suffer the same fate under Ceauşescu as Romanian President. Two of them, Noel Bernard and Vladimir Georgescu, were among my close friends and collaborators. The third, Mihai Cismarescu, died after a one-year tenure, in February 1983. Georgescu and especially Bernard, who had been brought low by a galloping lung cancer in December 1983, became national figures in Romania and left their mark on East European history. I had basked in Bernard's reflected glory when visiting Romania in 1969 as a private scholar. Ceauşescu was in power—Bernard's name had become a byword for liberation. Whether some common thread connected these premature deaths and the work of Ceauşescu's Securitate has not been established. They seemed the more suspicious because the Radio had suffered no comparable loss in any of its other national services. When questioned by the Radios' management, the postcommunist Romanian security authorities denied any knowledge of foul play; but according to General Ion Pacepa's controversial testimony, Radio Free Europe and its Romanian personnel were high on the target list of Ceauşescu's secret services: "Ceauşescu finally broke the silence, his voice exceedingly soft. 'I would rather neutralize "chatterbox" [Radio Free Europe] from inside than jam it on this end. . . . I want to get rid of Bernard.' . . . Ceauşescu paused, reached for one of my buttons and started twisting it. Very, very softly he said, 'I want to put "Radu" [cancer inducing radioactive material] in Bernard's office.'"[4]

Earlier in his book, Pacepa reports Ceauşescu's decision to silence *Emil* Georgescu, an editor in the Radio's Romanian Service in the 1970s and early 1980s: "'Emil Georgescu must be silenced for ever,' Ceauşescu ordered. 'He should have his jaw, teeth, and arms broken, so that he will never be able to speak or write again.' He added that the job should be done by foreign criminal mercenaries."[5]

In January 1976, Emil Georgescu was, in fact, seriously injured in what appeared to be a car accident; and in July 1981 a vicious attack by a Frenchman in the staircase of his home in Munich left twenty-two stab wounds on his body. Miraculously, Emil Georgescu survived and was still active during my tenure. I consulted him occasionally. In January 1985, however, he succumbed to the aftereffects of his injuries.[6] Broadcasting to Eastern Europe had its risks.

The cause célèbre of these violent proceedings was the "poison umbrella case"—the assassination of Georgi Markov at Waterloo Bridge in London in 1978. Markov was a BBC man, but he was regularly heard on Radio Free Europe, too, as an outside contributor. Former KGB General Oleg Kalugin provides a description (how accurate remains to be examined) of the Bulgarian authorities', the KGB's, and his own part in the killing.

There was one significant premonitory link between Markov's assassination and the Bulgarian Service of Radio Free Europe: a ricin pellet similar to the one found in Markov's leg after his exhumation had been injected into the body of Vladimir Kostov, a Radio Free Europe freelancer and former Bulgarian state security officer, in Paris, presumably also by an umbrella. In Kalugin's account:

A few weeks before Markov's death, a Bulgarian defector in Paris, Vladimir Kostov, had felt a sting while riding the Metro and seen a man with an umbrella standing close to him. After hearing of Markov's death, Kostov alerted officials in London that Markov might have been the victim of an assassination attempt. A month after the attack on Kostov, French doctors extracted a still-intact ricin pellet from his body; he had been saved either because the poison had been old and ineffective or had not been released. Officials in London then exhumed Markov's body, and an autopsy showed a tiny pellet lodged in a small wound in his right thigh. By the time of the autopsy, the ricin had decomposed.[7]

The approach to the Russian people of Radio Free Europe, as distinct from that of Radio Liberty, was of special concern to me. In the heat of our long conflict with the Soviet Russian system we nevertheless tried hard—and I believe we managed—to be fair to the Russian people. We went to great lengths to draw a line between what was Soviet and what was Russian, even though it was tricky in the extreme to do so. One of my three long broadcast colloquies with Adam B. Ulam was dedicated to showing just how hard it was not to use *Russian* and *Soviet* as interchangeable adjectives.[8] Soviet indoctrination saw to it that even the average Russian was not sure where one ended and the other began. But we, of course, knew that there was a difference, we knew how to get a purchase on it, and we were determined to make it clear in our broadcasts that although we were opposed to the Soviet system, we were in no way hostile to the Russian nation. This was, on my part at least, not just a matter of expediency but a restatement of the belief that despite its great historical weaknesses and economic backwardness, the Russian nation deserved better than what had been imposed on it since 1917 and that that recognition was essential to any future peace between Russia and Eastern and Central Europe.

Our policy at Radio Free Europe consisted of two related elements: to try to harness the power of our audiences' national consciousness to the aspiration to attain freedom from Soviet rule, and to counteract Moscow's policy of Russification. Both aims called for broadcasts of a kind in which the anti-Soviet argument was not always as distinct from the anti-Russian as would have been fair to the Russian nation. This lopsidedness was regrettable but almost entirely unavoidable. We were not operating under laboratory conditions.[9]

In all Central and East European countries, the communist system had arrived on the point of Russian bayonets and in the shape of a communism entirely Russian made. Under Stalin's rule and for many years after, the Soviet Russian model was applied with fanatical force across the whole field of human endeavour. Eastern and Central Europe became a Russian colony. Some of it was, indeed, incorporated into the USSR. Polish, Czech, and Hungarian military uniforms were exchanged for models taken from the Russian national wardrobe; national history was recast along pro-Russian lines; and even the history of science was corrupted and given a Russian slant.

In the popular imagination, communism was inextricably bound up with the daily experience of the least appealing features of Russian life—indiscipline, disorganisation, drunkenness, rape, repulsive habits of hygiene, disrespect for the individual and individual property—and the oppressive presence of Russian troops. This perception made it rather difficult for us, too, to achieve complete fairness to the Russians as a people. It would have been impossible to endorse the Poles', Romanians', Latvians', or Hungarians' desire for independence without at the same time endorsing their feeling that their tribulations were due to the Russian as much as to the Soviet factor. Here, then, despite our intentions, our second conductorship assumed at times a slightly anti-Russian character. We were, of course, neither racist nor xenophobic, but we did, as we had to, reflect to some extent our listeners' conviction that their culture and civilisation were superior to those of the invading East and that they had little to gain from the Russian connection. Could they have played Greeks to the Russians' Romans? The public in Eastern and Central Europe did not want it and the totalitarian system did not permit it.

I was, to repeat, deeply conscious of the need to avoid generalisations and stereotypes. We drew a clear line of separation in our transmissions between the Russian people and the Soviet system of which the Russian nation was, after all, the principal victim. Privately, however, I was not so sure. Custine's reading of Russia in 1839 explains too much about *Soviet* Russia as well for the distinction to be easily tenable,[10] and Richard Pipes's superbly documented view that a fundamental continuity exists between the tsarist past and the Soviet present was persuasive.[11] But I kept this reading to myself. In my work for the Radio I insisted on an unambiguous differentiation. The wartime example of the Nazis' hate-inspired enemy-image of the Russian people and then Ilya Ehrenburg's racist harangues against the Germans as a people[12] were constantly in the forefront of my mind as horrible warnings, and I was determined to allow no such thing to occur on our airwaves. In any case, our sister station, Radio Liberty, was embracing *Russian* national consciousness as its passport to credibility. It would have been absurd and wrong had we spoken with two different voices.

The citizens of Eastern and Central Europe themselves had a finely honed ability to distinguish Russian from bolshevik characteristics.

They may have thought about the Russians with a certain condescension, but they did not treat them with hatred. During the first (though not the second) phase of the bloody events of the 1956 Hungarian Revolution, and twelve years later in Prague, few Russian soldiers came to harm—indeed, in Hungary some joined the uprising before the Red Army reinvaded Budapest on November 4, 1956. Similarly, the 1956 upheavals in Poland and then the 1981 crackdown passed off without Russian casualties, although the cry "Russians Go Home!" was widely heard throughout the Western glacis of the colonial empire. "Soviets Go Home!" was a rarity.

It is unclear whether this remarkable display of self-discipline by the captive nations was due to our Radio's moderating influence, but we could see evidence of it on more than one occasion. In 1989, too, when the communist system finally expired, the popular desire to settle scores with domestic oppressors (an easier task than tackling disciplined forces of an occupying power) was absent. "Velvet" revolutions carried the day. Except in Ceauşescu's Romania, the war with the Soviet Russian system was won without domestic bloodshed or any outbreak of violence between Romanians and Hungarians or Czechs and Slovaks. Yugoslavia alone turned out to be a very different case, but then—we never broadcast to that country. We should have done.

In Eastern and Central Europe two forces were quietly beginning to compete for recognition. The general public was yearning for the unheroic ordinariness of civil society, the retreat of the Eastern colossus, and a return to "Europe." The average Pole's or Estonian's idealisation of the European dimension and enthusiasm to become part of it was almost boundless. For the worker, Europe promised prosperity; for the white-collar classes, a remarriage of cultures and values which a cruel half-century had put asunder; for Christians, a reabsorption into some vaguely imagined Christendom.

At the same time, however, in the undergrowth of the national psyche, schools of thinking began to take shape which—while not always directly hostile to the European idea—championed nativistic models lifted or imagined from the national past. Paradoxically, such unsocialist ideas had been protected and even promoted by the populist rhetoric of communism. In the name of recovering the origins and pristine values of the people, a kind of archaising populist "national" socialism was born (reborn, in some cases). Side by side with folkloristic studies, the refurbishment of old castles and tombs, the preservation of the purity of the language, and the restoration of churches and monasteries, there developed an approved sort of socialist nationalism, ready to come out into the open as straightforward nationalism, or indeed "national socialism," when the time was right. Stalin's "indigenisation of socialism" (for that is how it all started) produced some strange fruit.[13]

I was watching both streams of the struggle for national emancipation with interest. The enthusiasm for Europe and the desire to join it were so universal that they needed little encouragement. Atavistic nationalism was a different matter. In many respects it too was our natural ally, for without it, our attempt to preserve East European national identities would have been more difficult to achieve. I was, therefore, trying to see to it that our contacts with the East and Central European underground were not confined to heretical groups within the communist establishments. These were articulate enough and keen to be in touch, but unrepresentative. We also had to embrace what was best in the "national" resistance and give it the publicity it deserved.

This was more easily said than done. Western liberal opinion, including most of the American press and specialists at the universities, favoured the repentant communists. Their mental background and vocabulary were close to those of our own opinion-making left-of-centre intellectuals. A disillusioned communist was a safe bet; he was intellectually "exciting" and could be taken for a man from Stanford or Harvard. The nativistic nationalists were suspect. Recent West European experience provided few keys to understanding them, and the American experience none. Radio Free Europe, however, had to play on both instruments; for it was clear enough that although our opening chords would have to be sounded on communist keyboards, the main themes to follow would have to represent the genuine, long-term will and interests of our various national communities.

In the event, we managed to do both. We were, in effect, conducting a foreign policy which was complementary to but also distinct from official American and other Western policies. The official policy boiled down to the simple and undemanding formula of "differentiation": reward the liberalising regimes in Eastern Europe; punish or keep aloof from the conservative ones. The distinction was naturally incorporated in all our work, but it did not take in enough of the landscape. We represented in our transmissions the views and interests of the whole panorama of forces in the East and Central European national communities. In a manner of speaking, we were both understudies of Western governments—especially of the U.S. government—and surrogate governments-in-exile of the nations we were addressing, a state of affairs neither bureaucrats nor legislators could be expected to understand or to endorse publicly.

Not all our initiatives were successful. My own attempt to mount a Radio Free Europe Albanian service never got off the ground. From the day I set foot in Munich in 1983, I felt that Radio Free Europe's coverage was incomplete without a Balkan—and more specifically an Albanian—dimension. Tito's Yugoslavia was a friendly state in American eyes because it appeared to be a troublemaker for Moscow and a valued pillar in the Balkan power game—never mind its unsavoury domestic record, such as the horrible fate meted out to "Cominformists" on a prison island in the Adriatic, or earlier the mass slaughter of tens of thousands of prisoners of war forcibly returned to Yugoslavia by British forces in 1945. Hence Radio Free Europe's mandate omitted covering Yugoslav territory. Albania, for its part, was too small to matter in the eyes of American policy makers, even though the Chinese presence there in the 1960s and 1970s should have given them pause. I sampled Enver Hoxha's despotic rule, as well as the behaviour of the Chinese "advisers," during an unnerving visit in August 1969.

After the withdrawal of the Chinese in 1978 and the installation of Hoxha's "go-it-alone" policy, a power vacuum developed on the Eastern Adriatic, which it was not unreasonable to expect that Moscow might try to fill. Albanian-language broadcasts by Radio Free Europe, I was persuaded, would reduce the isolation of the Albanians and assure them that in Western eyes Albania was not irretrievably identified with Hoxha's government. I wanted to expedite the removal of an anachronistic and aggressive outpost of Stalinism (Tirana boasted the most powerful medium-wave transmitter in Europe, with a multilingual programme that covered the whole continent). We could open the way for Albania's return to Europe and to a semblance of domestic normality.

The board, with Shakespeare still heading it, was undecided—was Albania worth the expenditure? But after a working lunch with Eagleburger and Palmer, my idea was accepted in general terms, and I set to work to draw up a plan. On April 15, 1985, shortly after Enver Hoxha's death, I reminded the board that "our presence on the international airwaves in Albanian is an essential U.S. interest." We got as far as looking for staff in Italy and preparing a budget and a schedule. The board, however, would not budge, and I heard rumours to the effect that opposition was being encountered in the White House.

Eventually, at a conference in 1985 marking the tenth anniversary of the Helsinki Final Act, I saw Jack Matlock briefly in Helsinki and asked him whether, in fact, the White House had objections, and if so, what they were. The objections, he said, were his own. He looked upon Yugoslav stability as a prime American objective and could not see how we could address the people of Albania without stirring up unrest among the Albanians in the neighbouring Kosovo province of Yugoslavia.

I told Matlock that we had carefully thought about that possible objection and were satisfied that we could handle the problem of dual listenership in exactly the same way as we were handling all the other delicate minority problems in Eastern Europe—by thoughtful analysis, moderation, and dissemination of the values of liberal democracy. Matlock did not quite believe that we could. The board, now weakened by Shakespeare's resignation, pursued the matter no further and did not give us the power to go ahead. In theory, we could have started the service without White House or State Department agreement but, in the absence of Frank Shakespeare, the board lacked the willpower to make full use of its independence.

Matlock's reasoning was inspired by uncertainty and fear. I cannot say these were entirely irrational, but they throttled that feel for history which differentiates the statesman from the civil servant. "Feel for history," however, is an elusive quality which government officials are not paid to have. In Munich, my colleagues and I could sense that sooner or later there would be trouble in the Albanian-speaking areas of the Balkans, and we were keen to transmit a voice of reason and renewal with which the Albanian people could identify.

It was only a decade later, after three years of war and civil war, and the breakup of Yugoslavia, that the board and the U.S. government came to the same conclusion and agreed, under the Radios' pressure (in 1993), to instal a Radio Free Europe South Slavic Service. But it was not installed (and then only with a Serbian, Croatian, and, later, Bosnian emphasis) until 1994–96, by which time the original multinational character of Radio Free Europe had been effectively destroyed by the same U.S. Government.[14] In the meantime, the situation in the Balkans had changed. Albania proper had freed itself from the tyranny of the communist regime, and the autonomous Kosovo province of Yugoslavia had been reduced to an area of Serbia under the jackboots of Slobodan Milošević's forces and of marauding Serb nationalist gangs such as those headed by Željko Raznjatović ("Arkan") and Vojislav Šešelj. At the time of Albania's fresh wave of unrest, under the presidency of Sali Berisha (February to March 1997), Radio Free Europe was still lacking funds and authorisation to address its Balkan audiences in Albania. Fourteen years had elapsed since the Radio's original initiative.

In trying to rehearse what I may have got wrong in the course of my long association with surrogate broadcasting, I am led to acknowledge at least one important misjudgement. My sustained disapproval of signing human rights accords with the Soviet side proved ill-founded. By the time of my appointment in the autumn of 1983, it was becoming more and more evident that I had been wrong because official support for human rights—as initiated by Carter and Brzezinski—was weakening the Soviet system and empire beyond anyone's expectations.

One of the first leading Americans I invited to visit the Radio after my appointment was Max Kampelman, the man responsible for widening the application of the human rights provisions of the Helsinki Final Act and the uncrowned head of the Western negotiating teams at the 1980–1983 Madrid conference. Earlier, he had insisted at a long colloquium[15] that if properly implemented, the stipulations of the Helsinki and Madrid documents would redound markedly more to our benefit than to that of the Soviet side. I was gradually won over. Once in Munich, I reinforced the work of my predecessors to ensure that the Helsinki provisions were widely known and fully exploited. We gave all possible support to the Helsinki monitoring groups in the East which were then springing up everywhere in direct response to the Helsinki and Madrid agreements.

Up to 1983, I had believed that sitting down to negotiate with the Soviets—and on human rights, of all things—after their continuing aggression in Afghanistan and the suppression of Solidarity, would bestow an added legitimacy on the Soviet leaders and help them to polish up their image. And so it would have done, had a Lenin or a Stalin been running the affairs of the USSR. But as Kampelman rightly suspected, the sensibilities and reactions of the citizen under latter-day communist governance were very different from reactions during the rigours of the 1920s and 1930s. Several factors played a role in the transformation: the unravelling fabric of Sovietism, the power we were ready to put behind our concern with moral issues, the all-pervasive reach of shortwave radio and television, the great difficulty the Soviet leaders experienced in trying to fly in the face of their own rhetoric about human rights, and, above all, the "Basket Three" provisions of the Final Act. At long last, the idea of *pacta sunt servanda* was penetrating the popular consciousness. Words and agreements began to matter even in a society as thoroughly conditioned by double-talk and double vision as the Soviet.

In the event, it was those on the Soviet side—and especially the already unorthodox Polish and Hungarian communists—who found themselves forced to make increasingly far-reaching concessions, trapped as they were by the words they had subscribed to at the negotiating table. The quid pro quo the Soviet leaders were hoping to secure—the recognition, in lieu of a peace treaty, of the postwar borders of their empire, along with the economic help to sustain it— simply eluded them. Nor did the Western public come to be persuaded, as I had feared it might, that negotiating with the Russians in Madrid amounted to granting them a clean bill of health. To the extent it paid the negotiations any heed, the West remained sceptical.

My predecessors at the Radio sized up the human rights factor earlier than I did, although I had reason to believe that some of them had embraced the Helsinki accords mainly because they allowed for an improving but still "socialist" system—not a change of system. But by the time I arrived in Munich, I was aware of the power of the weapons I was inheriting. My colleagues and I went in hot pursuit of Helsinki violators in all the countries we were addressing. We devoted tremendous time and energy to making the Helsinki monitors' articulations and ordeal (many were put in prison) generally known, and as we now know, these courageous people played a vital part in accelerating the implosion of the Soviet system.

So thorough was my conversion to human rights as a point of leverage that in the spring of 1986 I gladly agreed to be a public delegate on U.S. ambassador Michael Novak's delegation to the Helsinki "Experts' Conference" in Bern. With Mikhail Gorbachev in charge of the Soviet Union, Western diplomacy was granted fresh and unexpected opportunities to wear down the dictatorship of the proletariat. They ran parallel with the opportunities I had some experience of exploiting at Radio Free Europe. Michael Novak's eloquent and militant diplomacy and the sort of radio we stood for in Munich were not far apart.

CHAPTER TEN

Draining the Poison out of the System

I am returning to a point I have already touched upon—the company I had to keep. Some of my fellow combatants were of an intolerant, obstructionist, even anarchistic disposition—outside the confines of Radio Free Europe as much as within. For novelists and playwrights, such characters will undoubtedly provide colourful material for the imaginative re-creation of the period. Some were larger than life, with ambitions that far exceeded their talents; others, deprived of the cosy integument of their communist "collectives," were suffering the torments of insignificance and of not being understood. I marvelled at their refusal to make the slightest concession to a society they had chosen to live in and watched their antics with a mixture of amusement and exasperation. But in "real life," they were a hindrance. Undertaking "propaganda by the deed," in the unsubtle phrase of Mikhail Bakunin, had a far greater attraction for them than designing ways of dealing with the aftermath of "the deed."

It was disconcertingly easy to attract collaborators for work in which they thought they could "kill," "hit," "force into unconditional surrender," "unmask," "expose," "show up," or "undermine" things and people, and correspondingly hard to agree on what precisely should be done once the unmasking and destruction had attained their purpose. Destruction was all. For *enragé* ex-communists, commie-bashing—like Jew-baiting for the Nazis—was a satisfying end in itself. "Liquidation" and "annihilation" occupied privileged places in their thinking and, under only the thinnest of covers, in their vocabulary. George Kennan points scathingly to the professional military mind's obsession with the concept of destruction—destruction for its own sake—as the central aim of warfare.[1] We were suffering from a similar blight. It was not my way of conducting the Cold War.

137

Soviet and East European studies attracted many who, for one reason or another, had been badly wounded in their personal lives, were brimming with resentment, or were temperamentally just plain bloody-minded. They struck me as a psychological type Carl Jung would have enjoyed appending a name to. Some had a quarrel with themselves or the world. This turned them against the communists, for want of a better target, but they could have been anti-anything. Often (as I have tried to show) they were brilliant analysts and became indispensable collaborators because they commanded inside knowledge of the Soviet system; but they made uncomfortable bedfellows. Their specialty was character assassination and intellectual overkill; the sinews of their reasoning, however, were identical with their opponents'. Far from showing tolerance as an antidote to the intolerance which they were meant to counter, they flaunted their intolerance. Their ill-disguised fear was that our confrontation with communism would suddenly come to an end, for their hearts were more in keeping the conflict alive than in any final victory.[2] Sometimes I wondered whether fighting the Soviet system in the company of such men was not an excessive price to pay for our convictions. I managed, on the whole, to keep them at arm's length in my private life, but I was frequently appalled to find myself sharing antennae with them. I found converts from the extreme right no less displeasing than those who had come from the far left.

In one ironic instance, soon after my arrival in Munich for my first assignment in 1960, Emil Csonka, the erstwhile fascist youth leader of Hungary's short-lived but bloodthirsty Arrow-Cross regime (1944–45), tried to befriend me on the argument that now we were on the same side of the fence. And he proceeded, without visible embarrassment, to offer me a life insurance policy on behalf of an American company for which he was the local stringer. Communism, he claimed, had brought us together — and he was anxious to insure my life. Fifteen years earlier, he would have had me strung up as a resistance man, from the nearest Budapest lamppost. I was amused but decided to insure my life elsewhere. Csonka, to do him justice, was only twenty when he became a youth leader, and he underwent, while working for the Radio, what looked like a genuine conversion to democracy. He wrote a couple of excellent books and became one of his department's most effective analysts.

I saw genuine conversions on the left too. One of the Radio's most knowledgeable commentators in the 1960s was Sándor Kőrösi-Krizsán, an elderly gentleman with silvery hair, courtly and expansive manners, distinguished speech, and a liberal sense of self-mockery—a specimen, to all intents and purposes, of the old land-owning upper class. Surprisingly, his expertise was communism, for the simple reason that in his youth he had been an underground Communist Party organiser in Transylvania after World War I and had met Lenin.[3] In the 1920s he broke with the Bolsheviks, retaining, however, a remarkable inner compass for communist affairs which served our understanding of the communist mind extremely well. He, like Csonka on the right, had said his *mea culpas* in public. No one could ask for more. Men of his record tempered my aversion to the less contrite and less forgiveable former extremists in our ranks of whom we had a sprinkling—a sprinkling too many, to be sure, but a sprinkling without influence.

Shakespeare, Buckley, Bailey, and I had brought along with us a general emphasis on "conservative" principles; but how were these to be converted into the currency of our special kind of broadcasting? Could we, should we, appoint ourselves as guides to a deeper sort of change than reforming the communist system? Could such work be pressed into our mandate? Would we not be accused of making Christian—more precisely Roman Catholic—or just plain reactionary propaganda? Did we have the understanding, the human resources, and the dedication to offer such guidance?

I had no doubt that we did. From the beginning of my work in Munich, I wished to promote a climate, and in some ways even a code, of decency in public affairs as the necessary basis for any postcommunist reconstruction. Eastern Europe was bleeding from countless wounds. These had to be healed by the power of mind and spirit as much as by re-engineering the economy. At the risk of acquiring a reputation for do-goodism and an unmodern concern with firm values, some friends and I set out to try to do so. Little did I suspect that in just over two years, our splendid Reaganite foursome would be reduced to one— myself.

"Of the original leadership team appointed by President Reagan," ran an article in the *New York Post* on November 29, 1985, "only the distinguished scholar, Dr. George Urban, is still in place, as the director of Radio Free Europe. It is very much in the US interest that the more vigorous, critical and independent course plotted by the Radios under the Shakespeare regime be continued." Our time was to be brief.

Communism had spawned a great combination of evils and disabili-

ties: a climate of thoroughgoing cynicism; a "culture" of almost obligatory mendacity; a loss of any sense of guilt; a blindness to squalor; contempt for the environment; and a deep dichotomy between what was
acceptable to the private person in his private life and what the same
person would tolerate and promote in his public activities. The utopian
targets, and the surreal language employed to pursue them, set official
thinking so far apart from a reasonable citizen's private code of conduct that duplicity and make-believe became defensive virtues in the
service of sanity. I knew of countless examples of the devastating effect
this communist-induced schizophrenia was having on the moral fibre
of society. The sickness varied in intensity from Ceauşescu's physical
and psychological terror to the kind of subtle self-censorship and self-
deception that were rife in Poland and Hungary. But the absence of
trust between citizen and citizen, and between citizen and public authority, was universal. I was hoping against hope that we could do
something to drain the poison out of the system.

Looking back at this rather Reithian exercise from a distance, I can
see why we must have looked naive to many hard-nosed fellow combatants. We were not naive; but unless we assumed that something, no
matter how little, could be achieved by the combined powers of the
mind and the microphone, nothing at all would be achieved. In the
East, mind and idealism still mattered and could be addressed in a way
in which they no longer could be in the jaded West. Paradoxically, the
cynical methods of communism had shaken up the human psyche and
laid bare reserves of innocence and thoughtfulness in the consciousness of East Europeans which we felt we could turn to good account.

It was worrying, though, that we were advocating ethical behaviour and a more contemplative order of things from a platform which
was itself intellectually shaky and morally flawed. But this assessment
too has to be qualified. No equivalence existed between the piecemeal
moral degeneration of Western societies and the bloodbaths carried
out under the Soviet system in the name of utopia. Nothing would
induce *me* to gloss over the vulgarisation and general debasement of
Western culture—but to say that we had no right to condemn the executioners of the KGB because of unsavoury homosexual behaviour in
San Francisco, violence in the Hollywood film studios, or hooliganism
on British football terraces was absurd. That was, of course, a favourite
theme of Soviet propaganda, but it was conventional wisdom in the
West, too, not least in progressivist American circles. Had Western appeasers cast the deciding vote on our future, Radio Free Europe would

have been fatally weakened or taken off the air altogether, many years before the historic culmination of its usefulness in 1989.

Usage and vocabulary were two of our principal problems. The lure of adopting the semantic conventions of the other side was enormous. Human consciousness and the meaning of words were being corrupted under the communist system; the very grammar of honest accountability had been rewritten. Newspeak had made unexpected inroads, even though the overall brainwashing of society had failed. The creeping growth of socialist usage had to be neutralised, and unvarnished meaning restored to words and ideas. As wordsmiths and keepers of the veracity of words, we were Orwellians to a man and in a unique position to help.

But language and content were inseparable from our political policies. Early in my tenure (February 1984), I warned against any undue preoccupation with the fortunes of the Western communist parties. Our audiences were, of course, considerably interested in how the Western reform communists were faring—especially those in Italy and Spain—and we were providing them with ample information. Excessive coverage, however, would have implied that our preferred alternative to Soviet-style rule was an improved form of communism (Eurocommunism), rather than no communism. I knew I was treading on sensitive ground within the Radio itself, for some of our broadcasters (as I have related) were keen to hold up models of Eurocommunism as alternatives worthy of emulation; but it was important not to mince words from the start.

Western media reporting was another problem. Even at its most evenhanded, it gave pride of place to our own shortcomings, scandals, and disasters, on the time-honoured principle that "bad news sells the paper." This journalistic tradition tended to result in an imbalance in our output, for we were, of course, receiving no comparable accounts of "bad" news of a domestic character from Soviet or satellite sources. I therefore asked our journalists to make sure that we were not painting ourselves blacker than we were and not lending authority to the Soviet contention that the capitalist West was indeed permanently teetering on the edge of disaster.[4]

This was a fairly tall order. In the West, journalistic hyperbole, especially in our working language, English, was well understood to represent only part of—and sometimes no great part of—the truth. But such exaggerations, when put into Polish, Hungarian, or Russian, carried

meanings much heightened from those they conveyed to the minds
of sceptical Western audiences in an open intellectual climate. Words
such as *triumph, defeat, shock, disaster, collapse*—devalued in English
under the strain of frivolous usage—retained in translation their pristine and hence misleading meanings. *Opposition defeated*, for example,
had a rather different ring to parliamentary British ears than it had
for citizens brought up in the Soviet Union. It was up to us to strike a
truthful balance.

In a fast-moving journalistic environment, where deadlines had to
be met several times a day, it was almost inevitable that convenience
should take precedence over substance, but I was resolved to do what I
could to counteract the distortion. I reminded our commentators that,
unfettered by any ideology or the physical and psychological pressures
of communist society, they were their own men and women, free to
play from their own scores.

For those never involved in the dialectics of the Cold War, it will
seem surprising that a reminder of this sort should have been necessary in the first place. But in the Cold War's particular contest of ideas,
those speaking for an all-encompassing and, it was claimed, "scientific" ideology had a natural, if short-lived, advantage over our own
journalists. It was for our men and women to pose the difficult questions—but the snappy, self-confident, seemingly plausible, but usually
false, answers came from the nomenklaturas in the East. Our staff had
to be constantly reassured that projecting a wide range of opinions
was their task and that they should be unafraid to do so. The temptation to walk in negative step with the communists was great. But our
whole raison d'être was not to pit a counterideology against the Soviet
way of thinking (free speech, for the dyed-in-the-wool Soviet citizen,
was counterideology enough), but simply to encourage the habit of
untrammelled enquiry. This can be too much to ask for even in liberal
parliamentary democracies, at all but the highest levels of public dis-
course. But we asked for it regardless.

An even longer-term engagement, however, had to be envisaged—
the one to maintain, and indeed frequently to attain, standards. I observed in a circular: "The right to serious thought is a human right too.
We stand for what is rich in reflection and experience. We discourage
what is thin, meretricious and ephemeral. Try to preserve the dignity
of the spoken word and the purity of your native language. . . . Do not
mock the values serious men cherish, either on our side or that of our
opponents. Not everything that is new is worthy of our attention; nor

is everything that is of Western provenance. . . . Speak a free man's language." (See Appendix B, "On Language and Context.")

Ultimately, a thoroughgoing cultural change was called for to free the population of the mental crutches of Marxism-Leninism. There was a need to purge East European thinking of inert facts and received ideas, to encourage a sense of intellectual adventure, to curtail the appeal of undue specialisation, to stimulate a demand for the disinterested study of history and philosophy, to remove the "embarrassment factor" from the impulse for religious experience, and to institute other reforms of a metacultural character. Many of these were, of course, sorely needed in the West as well, and we never hesitated to say so (*"don't* go by our example" was a noteworthy feature of some of our university broadcasts). But whereas in Western Europe our culture seemed, at the time, strong enough to survive the impact of television, commercialisation, and trivialisation, in the East, under communist rule, European culture seemed to be in danger of extinction.

To generate reform on so broad a scale was perhaps overambitious; but if we were to get anywhere at all, our reach had to exceed our grasp. I cannot say that we managed to make more than a modest beginning. But we did, I believe, sensitise the public to forms of experience which communism ignored or discouraged. What sort of experiences were these?

Restoring the true facts of national history always figured high on Radio Free Europe's agenda. This was no mean ambition, for even in the West, where historiography is free, how easy is it for the unprejudiced reader to get at the "true facts" of national history, given the unscientific nature of historical writing and the jealousies of historians? But an effort had to be made. Much before my tenure, the Radio offered what amounted to remedial courses in all its broadcast languages, by respected historians from diverse schools of thinking; and in some languages radio universities balanced the general distortion of knowledge under Marxism-Leninism. I gave these approaches a new emphasis, having at an earlier stage of my work for the Radio (1962–65) founded RFE Third Programme.[5]

On November 5, 1984, I launched our Czechoslovak Service's Radio University series with an introduction in which I told our audiences that we were setting out to offer, week after week, a corrective to the warped perspectives of communist historiography. Distinguished scholars from Western universities would give them the history of the first Czechoslovak Republic from its foundation in 1918 to its destruction in 1938. Of course, I observed, the independent study of history could offer no infallible compass to guide us in our current situation, but it could generate certain moral qualities which might help us to find worthy answers to the basic question of human existence: "How do I behave towards my neighbour so that I can live at peace with my conscience?" And I pointed out that the proof of education was not a book, but a man. It was to the formation of that independent individual that we hoped, through our Radio University series, to make a contribution. (See Appendix B, "History in 1984.")

Not all my initiatives were so elevated. The historical compass I had in mind was meant to serve at least some practical purposes. I saw an urgent need to weaken certain historical memories, and especially to try to erase the psychological legacy of World Wars I and II from the minds of victors and vanquished alike. The nationalistic habit of revisiting the military glories and disasters of the past was a menace to our future. European unification was bound to be inhibited if nothing was being learnt and nothing forgotten.

More particularly, it was important to neutralise Soviet attempts to sow discord within NATO. The Kremlin exploited every opportunity to lead Western public opinion to relive the wartime alliance, as if nothing had happened since 1945. The German Federal Republic, it was ceaselessly repeated, was a revanchist power led by former Nazis and members of the former military establishment. The room for Soviet mischief was great, for Soviet propaganda could rely on the support of our own far Left as well as on the goodwill of frequently well-meaning but naive nuclear disarmers and peace campaigners. The fortieth anniversary of the conclusion of World War II in Europe (May 10, 1985) threatened to become a special boon for Soviet propaganda. Exploiting the remnants of anti-German sentiment was an opportunity the Soviets could not be expected to miss—*anti-German* meaning anti–*West* German in the Soviet vocabulary, for socialist East Germany had redeemed itself by definition, in Soviet eyes, from the sins of the past, when membership in the socialist camp was foisted upon it.

To counteract these Soviet machinations to the extent we could, I noted in a circular (February 3, 1985) that, although Moscow's game plan was far from unintelligent, it was flawed and self-serving. The Russians were stressing the common war effort by the USSR and the Western Allies and rehearsing the crimes of the common wartime enemy. But then followed the wholly unsubstantiated claim that Nazism and revanchism were reviving in West Germany—indeed that the

German Federal Republic was "objectively speaking" the successor to nazi Germany. Moscow had three aims: to undermine the democratic credentials of the Federal Republic in the public perceptions of Germany's allies, to discredit NATO itself as a force of aggression by playing up the alleged nazi-German connection, and to claim that the true guarantor of peace and progress in the world was thus the socialist fraternity, with the Soviet Union at its head.

The Soviet case rested on a deeply flawed reading of the Western world, as it did in so many other cases: no one at official levels and few in the general public were inclined to identify the Federal Republic with Hitler's Germany; the Federal Republic had no territorial claims on its neighbours; NATO had guaranteed forty years of peace, not threatened it; and the Soviet Union, then in its fifth year of war in Afghanistan, could hardly claim to be a force for world peace. I asked our commentators to stress that the Western allies were determined that the commemoration of the dead and of the victims of one totalitarian tyranny would not benefit another totalitarian tyranny. "Hitler's hubris has been duly punished. Stalin's has not. It would be an odd sense of historical justice that demanded that the free world should celebrate the nemesis of modern barbarism in Soviet company."

Another danger we had to guard against was the mirage of an economic new deal within the existing social order. To concentrate almost exclusively on the economic critique of the communist system was a temptation many of our broadcasters found hard to resist. They saw it as an easy, handy, and rational way of dealing with a larger and, as it then seemed, intractable problem. Their professionalism led them to rely on statistics, and those had to come from sources within the Soviet bloc. The scales were being tipped against independent analyses. Also, we were suffering from a plague of economists. What poets and pamphleteers had been to the 1848–49 revolutions, economists were to the Central European reform movements in the 1970s and 1980s. Airtime had to be filled and they were keen to fill it. I recognised their usefulness but could seldom warm to them; the "dismal science" attracted too many dismal scientists.

In a note of July 18, 1984, I reminded my colleagues that we had to be aware of the political, military, and ideological provenance of the Soviet and Soviet-sponsored systems and guard against allowing ourselves to be trapped into "economicising" what was essentially political. If the shortcomings of communism could be shown to be overwhelmingly economic in nature, then the lack of freedom and human rights, the inequities of the single-party state, Soviet occupation, and other crucial issues could be minimised or conveniently ignored. We had to be careful not to lend credence to that process. Creating a society of serfs comfortable enough to accept their serfdom could not be our objective; and we had to be just as careful not to endorse the findings of certain Western observers who chose to make light of the totalitarian and expansionistic character of the Soviet system and insisted on describing it as a "modernising economy."

To be sure, I welcomed economic reform, decentralisation, and indicative planning to the extent that these promised to offer better ways of satisfying human needs and might enlarge the area of human liberty. Universal want and penury, we emphasised, made any resistance to despotism all but impossible. But such reforms within the system were unlikely to provide acceptable models of communism, and I could see no reason we should be offering arguments to make the communist reforms work better. It was not for us to teach the East European regimes Marxism. "We do nothing to sustain the idea that the command economies, reformed or unreformed, offer a model of national housekeeping, yet to be proven right or wrong, and essentially neither better nor worse than our own mixed economies. We do not do so because the testimony of experience tells a different story." (See Appendix B, "We Do Not Teach Them Marxism.")

This guidance caused some muffled unhappiness among left-inclined economists on our staff but no further objection.

We had, moreover, the novel task of recognising and supporting the liberties which the citizens themselves were gradually gaining under the weakening communist regimes, especially in Poland and Hungary. To cross-report these to the more dogmatic communist states had always been one of the Radio's favoured methods of operation. My policy was to point to their implications on wider ground and to larger audiences. The ripple effect had proved strong on earlier occasions; there was reason to believe that, in the liquefied condition of "existing socialism," it should prove stronger still. Naturally, our recognition of concessions already obtained should not amount to any recognition of the wisdom or leniency of the system; rather Radio Free Europe's broadcasts would pay tribute to the population's increasing self-confidence, demonstrated so clearly that the system could no longer resist it.

By 1984–85, fear as an agent of obedience and self-censorship had evaporated from the hearts of Poles and Hungarians. Stalin, Beria, and the Gulag were distant memories. I pointed to the lessons of the trial of four leading Polish dissidents—Jacek Kuron, Adam Michnik, Zbigniew Bujak, and Zbigniew Romaszewski—for the benefit of the rest of the Soviet-controlled world:[6]

> The trial of the four members of the Workers' Defence Committee (KOR) by a military court in Poland is in stark contrast with earlier trials we have known in Eastern Europe. The defendants are being genuinely defended by lawyers of their own choosing. Friends and former critics of the accused show their support in the full glare of world publicity. Wałęsa, former head of a suppressed nationwide trade union, appears at the court and demands admission. He is refused and survives to tell the tale. The defendants themselves are unrepentant. They challenge the legitimacy of their trial and that of the government. Their defiance is public and reaches the world press. The government is embarrassed and in search of an escape from its dilemma. Residence abroad is on offer. The accused refuse it.
>
> No such things could have occurred at earlier stages of Soviet and East European history. Military courts then sat in secret. The verdicts were a foregone conclusion and usually ended with the hangman's rope. Public abuse was heaped on the victims.
>
> The change is due to the new self-confidence of the Polish nation and its open solidarity with the men on trial. The fear that gripped the Soviet Union and Eastern Europe under Stalin is gone. Despite martial law and the suppression of Poland's elected trade unions, the Polish people are uncowed and unrepentant. They inhabit a universe that is not of the government's and party's making. They have opted out from an intolerable culture and created their own.
>
> KOR cannot be 'tried' any more than the whole Polish nation.
>
> This is the background to the trial of Kuron, Michnik, Bujak and Romaszewski. This is their, and the Polish people's, message to the rest of Eastern Europe.

This guidance drew a message of warm recognition from senior staff in the State Department who were receiving courtesy copies of our policy guidances, albeit only well after they had been circulated. My note happened to be in harmony with the department's preference for an entirely home-generated kind of self-liberation in Eastern Europe. Whilst we too were, of course, greatly in favour of self-liberation, we were also doing a little more than that, not least in Poland. Throughout the 1980s, Radio Free Europe was an inalienable part of Polish political life, of Polish culture, and especially of the life of the Polish trades unions. Asked about Radio Free Europe's impact on the growth of the Solidarity movement and his own political rise under communism, Lech Wałeşa observed on November 15, 1989, in Washington: "Would there be earth without the sun?"

In the Western world, however, the rapid demise of communist control was either not fully appreciated or not trusted. Even well after the KOR trial, the disappearance of fear as an agent of self-coercion and self-censorship was treated with scepticism. In the summer of 1989, having just returned from Hungary, where I had attended the ceremonious reburial of Imre Nagy and his associates as national martyrs, I spoke at a lunch given by *Encounter* magazine about the extraordinary openness I had experienced in Central Europe. (Sir) Peregrine Worsthorne, whose political instincts, though sometimes wrong, were always worthy of respect, questioned me closely. How could fear have evaporated from the lives of Hungarians, Poles, Russians, seeing that the communist dictatorships were still in place and the means of coercion and opinion making still in the hands of closely knit oligarchies? Was this not a deception on the order of "Let a Hundred Flowers Bloom," he asked, intended to help ferret out dissidents and punish them all the more severely when the time was right? My reply was that although no relapse could be entirely ruled out, only a successful hard-line putsch against Gorbachev could now arrest the slow disintegration of the communist regimes in Central Europe. A year later, my impression was to be borne out by the facts.

In 1983–86, however, no such disintegration could be detected. Yet it was already clear to close observers that Moscow's control over its client states was slipping and was undergoing review. By early 1985, well before Gorbachev's election as general secretary, the Soviet party was less able and less inclined to impose its will on the satellites than the general public in Russia or Eastern Europe was allowed to know; and the satellite leaders had much more room to distance themselves from Soviet models than they would admit or were prepared to use. They were satraps fearful of any weakening of the imperial authority on which their survival depended. From the high ground we were occupying in Munich, we could clearly detect great fissures in the monolith. They were not quite so visible from Prague, Budapest, and Warsaw. Our purpose was to make the public and governments alike fully conscious of the opportunities which were now beckoning as a result of the power struggle and disorientation in Moscow. Things were "falling apart," and I, for one, was convinced that, barring military intervention, out of the debris of the Soviet-controlled system in Eastern and Central Europe a freer dispensation could arise, if only the East and

Central Europeans played their cards wisely and with courage. We had to assume that even satraps were anxious to save their skins. On September 2, 1985, I communicated these views to the Radio's staff in a circular. (See Appendix B, "Openings in Moscow.")

China in the mid-1980s proved another source from which Eastern and Central Europe could draw encouragement for reform. In 1979 I had visited China and seen the devastating effects of Mao's Cultural Revolution. By the post-Mao communists' own admission, a hundred million Chinese had been victimised—killed, imprisoned, or deported. Under Deng Xiaoping, however, China was beginning to jettison some of the old ideology and abandon the Stalinist principles of economic management. The lessons for Eastern Europe were important, even though, ironically, it was from revisionist models in Eastern Europe that the Chinese had received their original inspiration for reform. I saw an opportunity here for enlarging the area of ideological uncertainty among our audiences and putting fresh ammunition into the hands of "national" communists. If the hidebound Chinese comrades could see their way clear to abandoning the sacred texts, what was there to hold back sceptical Poles, Czechs, and Hungarians?

China's blueprint for the radical reform of its economy was the most significant repudiation we had yet seen of the entire philosophy and practice of Soviet-style command economies. The framers of the Chinese reform plan recognised the importance of market forces, the inefficiency and insufficiency of central planning, the infeasibility of a bureaucratically controlled pricing system, the drawbacks of enforced egalitarianism, and the penalties for withholding material incentives from individual workers.

Industry was to be decentralised and subjected to the laws of supply and demand. Wages were to be pegged to productivity. The acquisition of wealth was depicted as an inspiration to those less well off. China was taking down the whole Maoist-Stalinist edifice and putting a good deal of "capitalist practices painted yellow" in its place. China must show, proclaimed the Chinese Central Committee, that "socialism does not have to be pauperism."

This was strong stuff, but for us the Chinese reforms carried an even more compelling message. They implied a belated rehabilitation of the economic philosophy of the 1968 Prague Spring, and especially of the men assembled at the time around Ota Sik and his Economics Institute. They drew inspiration also from the Yugoslav model of self-management and, more important, from the liberalisation of the command economy as practised in Hungary. Sik and his friends had visited Peking. The Chinese had visited Eastern Europe and looked at the Yugoslav and Hungarian models under working conditions.

All this had to be brought home—and was brought home—to the power holders in East-Central Europe. Public opinion had to be mobilised. On October 22, 1984, I wrote to RFE staff: "The lessons of the Chinese moves will not be lost on Eastern Europe. Never has a large communist power so blatantly declared that Marxist-Leninist society is flawed at its economic foundations. If the foundations are shaky, can the rest hold up?" And on December 10, 1984, I added in another guidance that the Chinese experiment demonstrated a remarkable outbreak of sanity. It showed communist leaders to be capable of taking a cool look at the real world and deciding in the best interests of their country to part company with what was most damaging in the doctrines of Marx and Lenin.

The Chinese reforms carried a special message for those East European leaders who were unable or unwilling to put nation before dogma, the good of the people before the good of the oligarchy.

Here was a special message for the Soviet Union, in particular; for the Chinese challenge made the anachronisms of the Soviet system more glaring and any thought of a Sino-Soviet reconciliation more remote. (See Appendix B, "China Questions the Faith.")

In the noncommunist world, it was neighbouring Austria, with its smoothly running democracy and considerable prosperity, that seemed to offer lessons of immediate relevance to the Central and East Europeans. In the world press and in world diplomacy, the Austrian example was much neglected because Austria itself was neglected. But from Prague, Warsaw, and Budapest, Vienna was seen as an example by which they were keen to be guided. The ordinary Pole, Hungarian, Slovene, or Czech harboured no suspicions of modern Austria—despite the warped view of the Habsburg Empire which was being foisted on him in his history lessons, and despite the genuine divisiveness of Central Europe's troubled history.

Austrian visitors were among the most popular, Austrian know-how and investment the most sought after, and Austrian standards in wealth creation, social welfare, and housing the most admired. Moreover, Austria was a small country which, like some of its "socialist" neighbours, had suffered (partial) Soviet occupation but had marched to prosperity with remarkable speed after Soviet withdrawal in 1955.

Still more important, the Austrians were at the time, together with the Bavarians, the only noncommunist legatees of the shared cultural heritage of Central Europe and of a whole Central European array of perceptions, tastes, and habits (to say nothing about that intangible but still quite unmistakable "imperial belt" of cooking and pastry making, which included Zagreb but excluded Belgrade, included Kraków but excluded Warsaw, and so on). These attributes secured for Vienna a special place in the hearts of once hostile Slavs and Magyars. Hence, the East and Central Europeans' identification with Austria, and their aspiration to the status of Austria, were strong. So was the Austrians' readiness, in both 1956 and 1968, to help their Hungarian and Czech neighbours in their confrontation with Moscow. Austrian courage and solidarity in the shadow of the Soviet superpower were a happy augury of how things might develop in Central Europe if and when Soviet hegemony retreated from the region.

We made the most of this advantageous playing field in a way no foreign ministry could. I was especially keen to convey that for a few years in the aftermath of World War II, Hungary and Czechoslovakia had been—like Austria—well on the way to becoming liberal democracies—and that they could yet become liberal democracies if the Soviet presence were removed. On May 28, 1985, I said in a note to our editors: "Those brief years between 1945 and 1948 gave testimony to the world that the nations of Central and East Europe had the will, the vitality, and the application to contribute their bit to the reconstruction of a free Europe and to rebuild their own self-respect and identity.

History may have temporarily cheated them out of their inheritance but not of their spirit of *reculer pour mieux sauter.*

From time to time, I also had to build up the waning self-confidence of our own troops. In the second half of the 1980s, Gorbachev's phenomenal popularity in Western Europe and America, his triumphant march through our capitals, and especially Margaret Thatcher's ill-chosen words at Chequers in December 1984 ("We can do business with him"), had a chilling effect on the Radio's staff. Questions about the political and intellectual legitimacy of what we were doing began to be asked by our broadcasters. What was our justification for refusing to accept the facts facing us in Eastern and Central Europe when our governments did accept them? If the West had virtually given up, shouldn't we? Poles, Lithuanians, Czechs, and Bulgarians (it was argued) knew well enough that they were living in poverty and under an unjust system; what was the point of our reminding them again and again if we could do nothing about their situation? Weren't we rubbing salt into their wounds? And what was our title to credibility, when we were addressing them from affluent Bavaria and sharing none of their fears and privations? Could men and women with American salaries, generous pension schemes, free housing, and other perquisites demand self-denial, even heroism, from people living in dire conditions under communist rule?

I had a good deal of sympathy with this quest for self-examination. It was always a commendable thing to step outside the whirl of events for a period of reflection. Soul searching by usually cynical journalists was uncommon and could do nothing but good. But I had no sympathy with the conclusions they tended to reach. On March 9, 1986, I wrote to our staff:

> The heroism of the individual in Eastern Europe is . . . . not of our making. Some of it is imposed on him by a system he has not chosen but from which he cannot escape. Some of it . . . . *is* the heroism of choice, an expression of Luther's perennial cry: "Hier steh ich, ich kann nicht anders." But outside influence has very little to do with either. It is the Marxist/Leninist system that creates the martyrs and the heroes. We merely help to lift them into the consciousness of the nations we address.
>
> There is, then, little reason for our broadcasters to be inhibited by the notion that they are preaching to their countrymen what they themselves do not seem to practice. We have, of course, men and women in our midst whose authenticity is made the more formidable by the record of their own heroism and suffering—men and women who spent years in the Gulag because they would not surrender their faith, or acknowledge the right of the totalitarian system to restrict their right to think and speak freely. Some opposed Stalin, some Brezhnev, some Ceauşescu, some Tito. Some stood up in the name of the Cross, some in the name of Judaism, some in the name of a pluralistic humane society. But even those of our broadcasters who have no such records have every right to speak to the East Europeans with authority, because in them are vested the conscience and identity of their nations.
>
> How do we know that? We know it from countless personal testimonies, letters and telephone calls which impress it upon our broadcasters every day of the week never to weary of speaking in the name of those millions who cannot put their views freely and would go under without the solidarity they receive from us.
>
> Our listeners have been sobered by history. So have we. We do not hold up the image of some promised land to them, but we keep faith with them. We cannot do more—we dare not do less.

CHAPTER ELEVEN

Misapprehensions

When agreeing to head Radio Free Europe in 1983, I was, of course, aware that the moral regeneration of Eastern and Central Europe was too ambitious an aspiration to be named as a practical goal of our broadcasting, even though Shakespeare, Buckley, Bailey, and I were unanimous in thinking that that had to be our more distant objective. The Radio's mandate called, first and foremost, for an evenhanded dispensation of untainted information and the presentation of conflicting opinions and life-styles. Thoughtful listeners were keen to receive those from us, and did, as György Konrád, former president of International PEN, personally confirmed to me in Munich in 1986.

"If we yearn for the West," Konrád wrote subsequently in a long letter of January 5, 1986, "it is for the West's variety; and even if diametrically opposed viewpoints appear in the Western press, this presents the West not in a grotesque but in a highly desirable light. As the process of social pluralisation gets under way in Hungary, it is precisely the values of disparateness, of differing personalities, of pluralism that are most highly cherished; more than majority rule, it is the freedom of the minority to express itself without victimisation that makes democracy so attractive for us. It is uniform greyness we don't like. We don't want the West to present a united front to us. That would simply remind us of the cult of unity which is so much part and parcel of Soviet rhetoric. Here, indeed, the medium is the message: the message of the West is its pluralism." But within pluralism, choices still had to be made, and although shortwave radio was ill-equipped to produce root-and-branch change, it could, by its tone and selection of topics, nevertheless point the way. If the electronic media could be so easily misused to spread false values and smother our instincts for outrage, it was hard to see why they could not be more honourably used to propagate decency, sanity, and self-restraint. The mere recital of facts and views was not enough. We would show our audiences a larger map of life, on which the transcendental statements of the higher religions as well as the wisdom and vision of isolated thinkers would be the principal landmarks.

This sounds more eclectic and more high-falutin than it turned out to be. On that imaginary map, the Judeo-Christian inspiration predominated, as it naturally had to, but the readings we presented under my stewardship were drawn from several cultures, and I was hoping that they would, in one way or another, counteract the materialism and moral relativism of the socialist way of life without, however, seeming to foist counterpropaganda on people who had had their fill of propaganda under the Soviet system. Our selections included Lao-tzu, Plutarch, Marcus Aurelius, the Buddhist scriptures, the early Christian writers, Saint Anselm, Thomas à Kempis, Pascal, Pastor Bonhoeffer, and others. We broadcast short, self-contained extracts from these sources as "thoughts for the day" in addition to our religious services on Sundays and holy days.

Looking at those transmissions with the wisdom of hindsight, I concede that they were probably lone and slightly recondite calls for more cultivated sensibilities and more discerning judgements in an inhospitable environment. They were also unrepresentative of the public mood and majority culture of Western Europe and the United States and perhaps failed to make an impression on any but a small segment of the population. But that minority mattered and still matters. If we deterred a single camp guard from using his fists on a single prisoner, we could claim to have done something to protect human life and dignity.

But even so modest an objective was not easily attained under our self-punishing guidelines. In June 1984, I had one of several spats with James L. Buckley, then joint president of the two Radios, over a programme in which our Polish Service had named some particularly brutal Polish prison guards and listed their sadistic activities. Buckley, a decent man of great charm but averse to confrontation, objected. He felt that "uncorroborated attacks on individuals" would discredit us.

He wrote (June 13, 1984), "When misdeeds and crimes against innocent persons or the general public are a matter of public record, [only] then should these be reported in a responsible manner."

This stance betrayed a very innocent attitude to crime and punishment in totalitarian societies. The misdeeds of government thugs were never a matter of "public record" under either Nazism or communism. So elaborate indeed was the cover-up under Soviet rule that several years after the disintegration of the Soviet and Soviet-inspired systems, we still cannot say with certainty how and under whose blows millions of innocent people perished. Who was called upon to point to the coercion and violence, if not we? I understood Buckley's dilemma to be that of a man of goodwill from New England suddenly catapulted into a world of which he had no experience and which he did not fully understand. I said in my reply (June 28, 1984):

> The men named had, according to the samizdat document from which we quoted, committed brutalities against defenceless prisoners. One prisoner tried to commit suicide because he could bear the beatings no longer. Clearly, we would have done less than our duty had we omitted to name the men in question once they had been listed in samizdat and we were reasonably satisfied that the charges laid at their doorstep were correct. . . . What we are facing in the USSR and Eastern Europe is terrorism-by-the-state under the guise of the law. Evidence of terrorism-by-the-state can never (or exceedingly seldom) be obtained in a totalitarian country. No one returned from Hitler's gas chambers to point a finger at the men who had turned on the gas-taps. Such of the slave labourers as survived the construction of the White Sea Canal in the Soviet Union were too intimidated to name their tormentors. . . . Someone has to name these crimes and spot the men responsible even when foolproof evidence is hard to come by.

But old-time habits of censorship were dying hard at Radio Free Europe and Radio Liberty, even under the Reagan administration, and even when it was clear that the only beneficiary of the censor's blue pencil would be the Soviet Union. While I was on an official visit in Washington in November 1985, the *Washington Times* published a ten-point open letter to the president which I had written at the invitation of the editor in the hope that it might assist Reagan in preparing himself for his forthcoming meeting with Mikhail Gorbachev in Geneva ("Mr. President: Some Suggestions," November 13, 1985). The article appeared prominently on the front page of the "Commentary" section, and was (as I subsequently understood) well received in the White House and by the president himself.

Not so in Munich where, on November 14, 1985, in my absence, James Buckley issued instructions to the effect that in any use of my article it should be made clear that the "opinions are the author's and not RFE/RL policy"—a point I had myself made abundantly clear in a note to my by-line. But he went further, directing the two Radios' services to excise six passages because "the article was written with Western audiences in mind. . . . Certain passages might not be well understood by our audiences." I had sent Buckley a courtesy copy of the article before I left for the United States. Had he wished to express his reservations, he could have done so before my departure or got in contact with me in Washington.

Upon my return, a polite but nonetheless bitter row followed. I did not take kindly to being censored; I wrote to members of the board demanding a retraction. On November 22, 1985, Buckley made a verbal apology in front of senior staff but refused to put it in writing. The Radios' "Commonwealth progressives," and ill-wishers in the American East Coast press corps, were delighted.

So great was the gap between Buckley and our troops on the ground that, in the event, our various services refused to broadcast my article in its mutilated condition. George Bailey, speaking for Radio Liberty, registered his protest. "The instructions contained in the note," he wrote to Buckley, "constitute out-and-out censorship . . . they are a classic example of how censorship is managed behind the Iron Curtain" (November 16, 1985). Buckley's attempt to doctor an opinion piece was particularly galling to one who had abolished preemptive political vetting at Radio Free Europe. It contributed to my eventual decision to retire from my post upon the expiration of my contract in the autumn of 1986. By that time, however, Buckley himself had left.

It is still not clear to me what motivated Buckley to make so ill-concealed and self-damaging a move. Lack of self-confidence may have been one of the reasons. He was, as we all knew, unsure of himself, especially in the company of seasoned experts on the Soviet Union and Eastern and Central Europe. With Frank Shakespeare no longer running the board, Buckley may have felt the time had come to show staff and our critics in Congress who exactly was in charge of the two Radios.

But there may also have been a more worrying motivation. Being very much part of the Washington establishment, a former senator and undersecretary of state, Buckley anxiously avoided the pursuit of policies that went beyond the consensual politics of the day in Congress and the State Department. He probably felt it was not for us, and especially not for me, to suggest to the president how to avoid being outwitted by Gorbachev. By November 1985, the American adulation for the general secretary and his wife, Raisa, was in the ascendant. Reagan himself was changing his mind about the "evil empire." My article, with its dire warnings, was out of phase with the prevailing mood in the United States. But that, of course, was the very reason for which I had written it.

One point in my open letter compared the Soviets' expansionism with Hitler's. It was excised by Buckley. "Only last week," Norman Podhoretz commented on the incident, "a reference to Hitler was eliminated by an official of the Reagan administration from a piece scheduled for broadcast to East Europe, lest it be thought that this comparison reflects official policy."[1] Podhoretz was right: communism, in the State Department view, was not to be compared with Nazism. On that point the American bureaucracy shared the Kremlin's platform.

The time was ripe for the abolition or drastic revision of the two Radios' December 1, 1976, Program Policy Guidelines. In Central Europe, the expression of free criticism and conflicting interests began to be heard more and more clearly in both unofficial and official articulations, especially in Poland and Hungary. Absurdly, our Radios were in some ways more inhibited than the unfree media for which we claimed to be acting as substitutes. The previous board's laboriously constructed rules of self-censorship had become farcical. In September 1985 I suggested to the board, via Michael Novak, whom I knew to be sympathetic, a complete change of policy.

> Hungarian information policy . . . is rapidly approaching Western standards. That this has, in large part, happened under RFE's impact is a tribute to our work, but now that the Hungarians have done it, we have an extremely hard time keeping up with Radio Budapest.
>
> Some recent criticisms . . . of Hungarian communist institutions and practices . . . are so open that RFE cannot match them for fear of running into our Guidelines. As a political development, this is much to be welcomed, but it has put us in an absurd situation, Hungarian communist radio and TV being "freer" than the voice of Radio Free Europe.
>
> But the absurdity does not end there. Many of the ideas President Reagan and Secretary Shultz regularly incorporate in their articulations cannot be uttered as our own because they, too, would violate our Guidelines. . . . Reagan and Shultz can be used with "clear attribution" only. Need one say more? (letter to Michael Novak, September 27, 1985)

Almost two years were to elapse—such was Washington's glacial slowness in the last decisive phase of the Cold War—before the guidelines were replaced by a "Professional Code" (1987). But even this slow change ran into bitter opposition. The rumour that new guidelines were being contemplated was enough to cause the local unit of our New York–based Guild of Journalists to attack the very intention— with the support of former vice president Ralph E. Walter, one of the authors of the 1976 guidelines (see Chapter 7). A radical critique of Sovietism, which the board, Bailey, and I represented, seemed to alarm members of our News Division more than the threat of Soviet- ism. Their hopes for the retention of the censorship provisions of the old guidelines were pinned on Gene Pell's impending arrival from his previous post as the director of the Voice of America.[2]

The new rules were certainly an improvement on what had gone before. Our two Radios were no longer required to eschew taking sides in the ideological contest, but their ability to keep up with the growing sense of self-liberation in the target areas was still hampered. Fortu- nately for the outcome of the Cold War, the code was to be honoured more in the breach than in the observance—exactly as the 1976 guide- lines had been. The revolutionary changes in the Soviet Union were a mere two years away.

Enough has been said to show that alternative policy making in the Cold War was a significant adjunct to Western foreign policy and, in many ways, a substitute for it. In both roles its achievements far ex- ceeded expectations. But it would be futile to deny that the very nature of foreign broadcasting also induced some thoroughly foreseen but un- preventable results of a less salutary character. To put it very briefly: we rather oversold the West; but it also has to be said that the East, for its part, was only too keen to be offered an overblown image of what the West was like and could do. In the postcommunist world, disillu- sion inevitably followed.

Under Stalin and Brezhnev, the image of a rich, equitable, and os- tensibly cultured West became a psychological counterweight to re- pression and poverty. "Over there," it was said in the East, stands the Celestial City to which those sentenced to live in socialist squalor can aspire and from which they can draw hope. "Over there" were the lega- tees of their own dormant traditions and the guarantors of their return to a dignified national existence and to Europe.

But this reassuring although decidedly warped vision of the world outside the socialist universe could not be entirely ascribed to a sorely tried population's reaction to communist rule. Before *glasnost* arrived on the scene, most of the reliable information East European and Soviet citizens could glean about the rest of the world (and frequently about their own countries) had reached them in their own language from Western broadcasting stations. These were, for the most part, institutions founded and supervised by men and women of the Western cultural élite and replenished with their peers, of similar learning and sensibility. Many made their names as writers and politicians of distinction and came to occupy leading positions in national governments and international organisations. They were, in other words, rather unrepresentative of the state of American, French, English, or German society as we encounter it in our daily lives, but they were immensely effective—and perhaps for that reason—as international broadcasters. For the appeal of "high culture" in Eastern and Central Europe always reached beyond the intelligentsia and the middle class. In Prague, Budapest, Tallinn, and Warsaw it was always a badge of honour to be, or to be thought to be, well-read and at home in the fields of music and the visual arts. That much of this was a pose did not diminish the serious intent behind it. Even under the dictatorship of the proletariat, the assimilation of the higher values of culture was a mark of bon ton and a prerequisite of acceptance as a serious member of the community. The dated notion of *Proletkult* had no followers.

It was not that members of our Western cultural élites conspired to monopolise the airwaves of their respective countries on behalf of cultural values which they could no longer adequately assert in their own domestic environment. Some did, but they were the exceptions. It was, rather, that international broadcasting was an inherently élitist activity. Foreign broadcasters had to be linguists familiar with the history and thinking of the countries they addressed. That alone would have made them untypical. But they were also heirs to the ethos and scholarship of the founders and high priests of "committed radio." The tastes and values of these men and women stemmed from the seminars and common rooms of Oxford and Cambridge and the Ivy League universities in America. Broadcasting, for them, had little in common with popular journalism, and nothing at all with the entertainment industry.

What emerged at the receiving end was an image of the Western world that was broadly accurate but larger than life. Our communicators did not hide our shortcomings; they painted them in, but only as blots on an otherwise magisterial canvas. The public in the USSR and Eastern Europe, however, did not want to know about our failings. They were hoping, somewhere down the road, to become free, fair, democratic, and compassionate societies imbued with a sense of spiritual culture—"just like the West."[3] It hardly needs saying that such expectations were doomed to be disappointed. One unwelcome result of the disappointment was a petulant withdrawal into nationalism to the cry of "the West can give us little and teach us less." This was, of course, not the whole reaction, but it *was* a significant part of it. It stemmed, as I say, from the juxtaposition, after 1989, of the West's out-size and overdecorated image with the sobering reality, especially in the area of mass culture and hit-parade entertainment. The depreda-tions of Hollywood and of the Western tabloid press came as a shock to most East Europeans. Nothing in Western international broadcast-ing had prepared them for it. Between the summers of 1989 and 1991 they saw the collapse of the Soviet system, but also the evaporation of the dream of a superior and cultured West.

In sum, two mirrors had been held up to Western Europe—one by the East Europeans themselves and another by Western public diplo-macy. Both distorted the real world, and for the best possible reasons. East European morale could not have weathered the long siege of "socialism" without popular belief in an all-providing, unsullied land beyond the hills. Western communicators, on their side, were too over-educated (and a little ashamed) to recognise and describe the full truth about the world *they* were inhabiting. They did speak the truth, but not enough of the whole truth to soften the blow for the East Europeans once the walls came down.

I, too, must have erred into misplaced sophistication. I was led by an ambition to try to make man more perfect—rather than imperfect man more comfortable. I did try to counter the ethos of mass cul-ture by encouraging a mentality of privacy and solitude—thinking and musing rather than acting and sharing. I was looking to the heart more than the belly for improvement. This may have been aiming too high. It may have lured me and my collaborators into too serious and too lofty a conception of what politics was about and what communicators were able to do about the human condition in shortwave broadcasts poorly heard against a background of jamming.

But I have few regrets. In a small village in Slovakia there exists a library stocked entirely with our university broadcasts under com-munism. The volumes on its shelves were the recorded version of our broadcasts, which had been secretly monitored, transcribed, and put between covers. When dialling Western telephone numbers became relatively risk-free, the Slovak "librarians" called to thank us. That is a reward I cherish.

Yet, as the decline of the system was slowly proceeding in Poland and Hungary, another and most interesting phenomenon was claiming our attention in the hard-line states of East Germany and Czechoslo-vakia: Western television, which was now reaching large parts of these two countries, seemed to have become a substitute for freedom rather than a force that would seed demands for political and intellectual liberty, as many expected. Where the regimes stood absolutely firm and dissent was dangerous, the more pliable segments of the population appeared content to satisfy their desire for an alternative way of life vicariously, by watching Western television.

What lessons had to be drawn for surrogate broadcasting? Was the freedom of information an arouser, or a pacifier? We were, of course, making judgements on insufficient evidence and at a time of rapid transition, but I nevertheless ventured an interpretation on the editorial-opinion page of the *New York Times:*[4]

> Unlike radio broadcasts of the kind that Radio Free Europe, the British Broadcasting Corporation and the Voice of America specialize in, television seems to make political oppression easier to tolerate because it carries within it the insidious persuasion that as long as "the box" stands, there are easy escapes from the dominion of Communism. In other words, "the medium is the message"; television *is* freedom; the flickering image blots out the reality of oppression.
>
> Our most persuasive and grotesque evidence of the neutralizing effect of uncensored television comes from the accounts of those East German refugees who, in the licensed exodus of 1984, arrived in especially large numbers from those parts of East Germany that were beyond the reach of West German television. They left, they said, because life under the Communist regime was intolerable without the daily offerings of the West German and American image-makers.
>
> These are astounding facts with important implications for our understanding of Communist societies in a state of imperfect oppression.
>
> I would not like to say without a good deal of further evidence whether "surrogate freedom" explains this curious phenomenon. What is beyond dispute is that our view of how Communist political systems work in Central Europe needs some revision. . . .
>
> Central Europe's perplexing reaction to Western television seems to suggest that certain kinds of unauthorized communication may help to stabilize the existing order rather than upset it.

A few years later, the elemental force of the implosion of the communist system made such fine distinctions seem irrelevant. But in 1985–86, they added to our understanding of the psychology of our audiences' search for freedom behind a porous curtain.

One regret I do have about the outcome of our conflict with communism is the failure of Western governments and private institutions to address domestic opinion with the sort of skill and vigour they employed in talking to the East. We have won a long war against the Soviet system, but I am not sure whether we have won the war against communism and communists. At a philosophical level, all-embracing doctrines of ideology always survive; in a practical sense, however, they can be so discredited that they find it hard to resurface as a live force within an historically meaningful time span.

Despite the unspeakable horrors of the Gulag, despite the administrative slaughters which claimed victims in far larger number than those of Nazism, despite the hegemonic successes of the totalitarian system which nearly engulfed the whole of Europe and much of Asia, despite the poverty, squalor, and humiliation visited upon the individual wherever Leninist communism had established itself—communism as a programme for enforcement in the future has not expired. It continues to lead a parasitical existence on what remains of the European humanistic tradition from which it sprang but which it has so signally betrayed. Sophisticated (or unworldly) academics at Western universities tell us that what went down between 1989 and 1991 was not Marxist communism, but its Russian caricature. Wicked leaders and the legacy of the tsars and the Mongols, we are told, corrupted the blueprint. Yet, it is contended, the ideology of communism has shown its strength by renewing itself from within—Yeltsin, Kravchuk, Kuchma, Iliescu, Shevardnadze, Brazauskas, Gorbunovs, Horn, and other postcommunist leaders have given us communism with a human face. The burial rites, we are warned, have been performed a little too soon. "Socialism has not failed, because it has never been tried."

We have done little to counteract such fantasies. In the East, we seem to have quashed Marxism-Leninism as a source of state power, but we have not neutralised its manifold radiations into Western Europe and America. At our schools and universities, the influence of Marxist and marxisant studies is still powerful. The call of collectivism and the appeal of a vacuous egalitarianism have spread far and wide. Utopia, Soviet style, may have succumbed to its own absurdities, but the Western intelligentsia's thirst for some other seamless solution to all human problems is unslaked and may yet return to punish us in unpredictable forms. For all we know, new-age Trotskyites may be readying their rhetoric for permanent revolution in obscure corners of the world—or at our universities.

Utopia, though shaken, stands undiminished. Ernst Bloch's "principle of hope"[5] renounces the evidence of empirical experience. Our seminar rooms and curricula are not closed to communists of the Leninist persuasion. Their work and ideas are discussable in our drawing rooms in a way that Nazism is not. Lenin, Trotsky, their political children and grandchildren appear to fall within the compass of Western intellectual chic in a way Rosenberg and Farinacci do not. Few people among us would, in the 1990s, boast about their nazi past—yet many are happy to admit that they were, or are, communists. Opprobrium attaches to the first but not the second. One wonders whether we would be judging the two in a more evenhanded manner if Soviet communism, too, had had to be defeated, as Nazism had to, in a long and bloody shooting war. Some of the disorientation among Western intellectuals may be due to the unexpectedly and undeservedly soft landing of the communist system.

The belief doggedly persists that communists are men and women of good intentions who happened to have got things a little confused; idealists who backed the wrong horse; humanists who allowed their enthusiasm for improving the human condition to run away with them. Their identification with the Soviet model, we are told, may have been misguided, but there was no other useable model. There was, however, the menace of Hitler. Hence it would be a mistake to judge communists too harshly. Their way back to the human family should not be barred—the prodigal son is dearer in the sight of God than one who never strayed. Variations on these themes are legion. They coincide in their affirmation of double standards.

I have even heard it suggested that as communists were responsible for bringing ruin upon the countries they once ruled, they now have a special title to return to power, for who could undo the devastation more reliably than the men and women who caused it? In 1993 in Lithuania, Algirdas Brazauskas and his communist team were, in fact, elected to power at least partly on the strength of that perverse argument. So charitable (or bizarre) an attitude was scarcely shown towards the Gauleiters and Storm Troop commanders of the Third Reich. Himmler's men were not put in charge of the rehabilitation of Jews.

The public acceptance of postcommunist attitudes in the East has only served to confirm the notion that communism is somehow different. In the former Soviet empire war crimes and crimes against humanity were committed on a vast scale—but there were no war crimes trials. The communist system collapsed—but there has been no de-Sovietisation. Institutionalised snooping, spying, and denunciations flourished throughout the empire—yet no postcommunist government, with the partial exception of the Czech, has been pressed hard enough by public opinion to cleanse the state completely of that shameful legacy. And even in Germany, where the Gauck Authority performed a notable service in lifting the veil on the Soviet past, the Constitutional Court ruled in May 1995 that spies of the former German Democratic Republic were not liable to prosecution.

At the end of the millennium, it is to questions such as these that Western governments and communicators will have to turn their attention. Turbulence in the Balkans and the Caucasus and disorientation in Russia have confused Western priorities. The predominant inclination is to close the books on the Cold War. The evils of communism are said to have been much exaggerated. But this is a myth that needs debunking. We now know the bulk of the truth about the Soviet system, but that truth cannot always speak for itself. It needs to be formulated—and expressed with conviction.

Our victory over the Soviet Union has not brought us victory over the Soviet mentality or its twin brother, fascism with a Soviet Russian face. Nor has it acted as a corrective to Western credulity and intellectual bias. It would be a pity if we allowed the notion to survive that some other variety of communism, even if not the Soviet Russian model, may yet bring the world more light than darkness.

CHAPTER TWELVE

Dialogues

Disputatious conversations on the airwaves of Radio Free Europe, and the publications resulting from those conversations, were probably my most useful contributions to the Cold War, both before and after my stint as director of the Radio.[1] Like so much else in my life, they happened without forethought or design, and in some ways against my better judgement.

Upon my return from a visiting fellowship in California in 1970, James F. Brown, head of the Research Department of Radio Free Europe, a respected scholar and later my predecessor as director, approached me to see whether I would record a number of spontaneous conversations—"interviews"—with leading Western ecologists and "futurologists." Environmental issues and political crystal gazing were growth industries in those days, and the East Europeans were keen to be informed. *Their* futurology was, of course, writ large in Marxism-Leninism, but wisely, they did not quite trust it. Unbridled industrialisation of the chimney-stack sort was still the dominant creed under communism; the Radio's management wanted to broaden listeners' horizons and warn them of the dangers.

Although I had no firm job at the time (can writing books be considered one?), I was rather lukewarm to Brown's idea. My commitment to myself was to do whatever I could to promote, by the power of words and ideas, the destabilisation of the Soviet system and empire. Time spent on the ecology would divert me from that central concern, even though "green" issues had a profound appeal for me. Unlike some of my friends on the right, I did not consider the protection of the environment as intellectual territory irretrievably relinquished to the radical Left. Also, I abhorred all-purpose punditry and the type of people engaged in it. Could I be a student of communist affairs one day and a credible ecologist the next?

Such was my reluctance to tour the world picking *obiter dicta* off the lips of the great and the wise that while gladly accepting the general idea of collaboration with the Radio, I farmed out the first ten of about two dozen ecological topics to Michael Glenny, a distinguished Oxford scholar of Soviet Russian affairs and a famous translator. He was, at the time, transposing Bulgakov and Solzhenitsyn into English with impressive empathy. Glenny, I knew, could turn his fertile mind to any question and make a success of it, especially when he was running short of funds—an affliction that visited him only too regularly. The ecological fad, I thought, would pass, and I could eventually bend my ad hoc arrangement with the Radio to something more immediately relevant to the undoing of the Soviet system.

Michael Glenny and I had about six months of happy cooperation. Scintillating wit, a panache for the Bohemian life-style, a discerning taste in food and wine, a weakness for women, a thoroughgoing hatred for everything the Soviet Union stood for, as well as a record of courageous work in the service of human rights and dissent on Soviet-controlled territory—these were some of the characteristics of this impish and lovable student of the Russian mind. Glenny died of a heart attack, much before his time, in 1989 in Moscow, perhaps (as I heard it suggested) under the impact of being suddenly given access by the KGB to the very secrets he had spent so much of his life trying to get hold of and decipher. The shock may have been too great. He was in his way one of the first casualties in our ranks of the fall of the Soviet system.

But despite the high quality of Michael Glenny's work, Radio Free Europe wanted to use my name in the billing of the series. Early in 1971 Glenny retired from the project and I began work on the first of those long conversations which eventually superseded (at least within the radius of my microphone) the traditional interview format and were to become my main contribution to the spoken critique of communism (Glenny's pieces are printed together with mine in *Can We Survive Our Future?*). The "interviews" became colloquia, the question-and-answer formula gave way to the spirit of shared enquiry, and length became virtually open-ended. For the purposes of broadcasting, the conversations were divided into ten- or twenty-minute segments and translated by a band of enthusiastic editors[2] into the Radio's various languages. On the printed page, however, they usually appeared as single articles, without further editing.

My resistance to interviewing was short-lived. I carried with me from my Hungarian childhood a love of the peripatetic mode of exchanging ideas. Long and almost weekly walking tours in the Börz-söny, Pilis, and Bükk mountains, "Wandervogel" fashion, were in great vogue in my youth, and the conviction that like-minded men and women could pleasurably identify, and perhaps even resolve, many of the problems of the world in friendly dialogue to the rhythm of their feet, their singing, and the sounds of nature was very much part of my inheritance. For me, the dialogues I was now asked to conduct for radio were not far removed in spirit from those earlier brainstorming sessions in the forests of Hungary.

Eventually, Brown and I decided to go beyond ecological issues and tackle virtually all principal themes in the East-West relationship. We would undertake a scholarly audit of precisely what was understood in the East and in the West by the idea of Stalinism. We asked whether the 1968 Czechoslovak reform movement had a realistic chance of re-newing the appeal of communism, whether the domestication of com-munism in Italy and Spain could serve as models for East and Central Europe, whether—and how—the conflicting interpretations of peace-ful coexistence (détente) could promote peace, whether the alienation of labour in modern societies was common to both capitalism and socialism, and finally, whether the Soviet system was capable of re-forming itself under the treble challenge of industrial backwardness, the dead weight of the Russian tradition, and the intellectual-cultural lead of the West.

Out of these broad themes grew book-length discussions with some of the leading men and women in the thought-generating, policy-making, and policy-interpreting communities. With one exception, these discussions have all appeared between covers.[3] A word might be in order, however, to describe the people involved and how the spoken word came to be deployed on the printed page.

After a slow beginning, I soon found myself in the fortunate position of not having to seek out people for their collaboration because some began to approach me for mine. My first effort, *Can We Survive Our Future?*, did reasonably well; it had gratifying reviews and was put into several languages. So was my joint volume with Arnold Toynbee.[4] Dis-tinguished writers, politicians, and scholars let it be known that they would be happy to be associated with my projects. Their main ambi-tion, however, was not so much to be heard on our airwaves—though many felt that would be a bonus—as to appear on the pages of *En-counter* magazine, at length, and in good company. Some who would perhaps not have made the pages of the journal under their own steam could look forward to having their views promoted in the framework of my projects. For Radio Free Europe, suffering as it unremittingly was from the suspicions and barbs of American progressives, the appearance of so many famous names on its cast list was of immense benefit. The broadcasts, articles, and books resulting from my colloquies with distinguished writers, politicians, and scholars gave the Radio added respectability. No one could claim that Werner Heisenberg, Max Beloff, Golo Mann, Herman Kahn, Maurice Duverger, Dean Rusk, Sir William Hayter, George W. Ball, Johan Jørgen Holst, W. Averell Harriman, George F. Kennan, Lucio Lombardo Radice, Manuel Azcárate, or Milovan Djilas (to name only a few) were making cheap anticommunist propaganda. The Radio's Third Programme, suspended after my resignation in 1965, would now be resumed.

I could, of course, guarantee no one's appearance in the pages of *Encounter*. Melvin J. Lasky, *Encounter*'s famous editor, had a stringent code of practice and suffered fools and even minor lapses in sophistication with singular impatience. I shall have more to say about him in the pages that follow. But the great majority of my conversations for radio did make the journal. They filled, in the eyes of my critics, only too many of its pages, all the way from the early 1970s to its much-lamented closure in 1991. But the editor of *Encounter* was satisfied:

> The sterling merit of "the art of interviewing," as exemplified in the work of George Urban, is almost unprecedented in modern journalism. . . . One can appreciate the iconoclastic interviews of Oriana Fallaci. . . . One can value the recorded conversations of Emil Ludwig with Stalin and Mussolini, and of Edgar Snow with Mao Tse-tung, and still regret their inability to formulate a challenging, not to say a disagreeable, question. Recent American television interviews with the visiting Mikhail Gorbachev were polite to the point of obsequiousness. . . . Unlike most of his fellow-practitioners, Urban is a journalist and historian with wide-ranging scholarly interests; . . . he has been a specialist and a generalist in the fields of social science and literature. He has read the books. . . . Having myself published a number of these texts in *Encounter*, with hectic preludes of corrections on proofs and postponement of schedules, I know how trying for an editor this species of *akribie* [scrupulous exactitude] can be. But that is why, in thinking of the work of George Urban, I have been reminded often of Max Weber's remark that there is a kind of *haut journalisme* which is indeed a form of scholarship and akin to the highest intellectual activities.[5]

Each of my colloquies was preceded by considerable homework. I put forward no problem for discussion to which I had not myself formulated a number of tentative answers. Reading for pleasure is a very different matter from reading with a target in mind. Preparations for my sessions with Arnold Toynbee, for example, took up the best part of a year. Immersing myself in Toynbee's work and sitting down with Toynbee to talk were pleasurable and mind-stretching experiences which I tried to pass on to the listener and reader. Despite the aspersions of Toynbee's numerous critics, even a modest footnote to Toynbee's spectacular life's work would deserve to be remembered— and our "footnote" eventually ran to 113 printed pages. Toynbee was seventy-two, I was fifty; yet a spirit of youthful excitement and joint discovery seemed to pervade our fencing over the meaning of history. Toynbee appeared to thrive in our three mammoth recording sessions. "We both had hard work," he wrote to me on October 7, 1971, "but I found it most enjoyable and valuable." And shortly before the publication of our volume, he added, "From my point of view, our dialogue was very much worth while, but the brunt of the work has been taken by you." This was too generous.

My choice of Arnold Toynbee was not due to his reputation alone. I was genuinely concerned to find out, on behalf of our listeners who had little or no access to Toynbee's work, whether there was a key, a clue, or some other design to history about which the general public and the more run-of-the-mill historians knew nothing. And if a key, or a clue, or a pattern could not be convincingly established, I wanted to know whether a psychological key to Arnold Toynbee himself might explain his search for a key to history. What made history tick and what made Toynbee tick were related questions. They filled me with a keen sense of curiosity. Toynbee proved wide open to questions and comment, and he left me in no doubt that he enjoyed arriving at new concepts on the march and in company. This was a rare phenomenon in the self-conscious and haughty clan of historians.

Similarly, my several (and initially edgy) discussions with Milovan Djilas were preceded by a close reading of his works, his career, and much related literature. I tried to feel my way into his *Geist* as well as his thinking, for I could hardly hope to find a more valid prototype for a revolutionary who had succumbed to the "totalitarian temptation" than he represented—or anyone more sincerely prepared to admit and to overcome it. My meetings with Djilas, both in Belgrade and at my home in Brighton, were confessionals of a kind. "Christ and the Commissar" hints at that nexus.[6]

George Kennan was a man of ennobling presence, a moralist and a gentleman—one with whom I would have been prepared to share a prison cell in the Lubyanka without fear of betrayal. Although I was critical of some of his views, the chance to give a broader audience a glimpse of the sovereignty of Kennan's spirit and of his high-minded *vertu* gave me considerable satisfaction. They were as rare in his native America as they were in Eastern Europe—powerful antidotes to the homogenisation of our culture.

Preparations for my long series on Eurocommunism involved an especially exacting type of research, including familiarisation with the complicated texture of Italian government, life, and letters both under the Christian Democrats and under fascism. Talking to some purpose with such highly sophisticated observers of the Italian scene as the prolific Renzo de Felice (Mussolini's biographer), Rosario Romeo, and Domenico Settembrini was a hazardous undertaking. No matter how familiar one might be with the various reformist heresies in communist history, the devil was, as always, in the details. The ways in which Togliatti and Antonio Gramsci had prepared the ground for Eurocommunism was a vast subject in its own right; so was the ideological link between the early fascist movement and Leninism. Only Italians, with their inimitable love of paradox and self-mockery, could cope with the intricacies of such subjects. My perspective had to be different.

How could one understand the Italian authorship of the soft variety of communism—Eurocommunism—without recalling the Italian origins of the soft variety of right-wing fanaticism? When Mussolini was thundering against the "good-for-nothing . . . mediocre race" of Italians who needed toughening to make them worthy of fascism, he was uttering an early call of the sort Politburo dogmatists would replicate, half a century on, in Moscow, mocking and attacking the Italian Eurocommunists on similar grounds. But to state that parallel alone would have been stating the obvious. The beauty and difficulty lay in pointing to the ramifications of that simple theme and identifying the variations of which it was capable both under fascism and in the context of communism.[7]

The role of the interlocutor could be tricky in the extreme. My task, as I saw it, was to force such nuggets out of the ground as would not normally surface in written communication. The spoken word had its own rules and dynamism. But these inevitably required an occasional show of intellectual innocence, a touch of naivety, or profession of ignorance, either on behalf of the man or woman in the street in search of straightforward information or, more often, in order to induce my interlocutor to make points useful to our confrontation with the Soviet system. At times I had to trap him into doing so. This Socratic irony could be painful, for nothing evokes greater derision or glee among political scientists and historians than a display of naivety by one of their own number. I took that risk quite deliberately in the service of the cause I was espousing.

At times, the heat of the argument propelled me into defending positions I did not believe in. For example, talking to Elie Kedourie about the likelihood of war between states of identical culture and similar social organisation, I found myself contesting Kedourie's view that such similarities do not rule out war.[8] I knew perfectly well that he was right and my advocacy was mistaken. I did myself argue on count-less occasions that almost identical cultures and flourishing economic relations had not prevented war between France, Germany, Britain, and Italy in our own century. Yet, there I was, arguing the opposite with every appearance of conviction, driven by the need to produce a captivating controversy, and mindful of Montaigne's words that "agree-ment is a very tiresome quality in conversation."[9] I was no lawyer, and I hated every minute of behaving like one; but such were the require-ments of my genre.

In a small number of cases, when specifically asked to do so, I had sent written observations ahead of my appearance by way of a navi-gational chart, but it soon transpired that in real life the dykes would not hold and the drift of the argument would take us into unexpected waters. This was just as well, for it was the random element in these conversations that gave them their authenticity and their fascination. Neither of us could foresee the submerged obstacles, nor how some mine left unattended earlier in our engagement might blow up this or that position. As initiator of the game, I had the advantage of vaguely knowing my destination, but this was, luckily, not enough to lessen the hazards of battle.

I am not sure whether it would be fair to my contributors to tell the full story of how a great deal of inconsequential talk and rather loose thinking eventually cohered into dialogues that have been described as challenging. But part of the story can be told.

A few of my interlocutors were print-perfect or nearly so and needed only light editing. But most of them could neither think nor speak fluently "on their feet." I certainly could not. Guided by the spirit of Plato's dialogues, Goethe's *Gespräche* with Eckermann, and Maurice Cranston's *Imaginary Conversations*, I did not hesitate to upgrade what had to be upgraded, my own entries included, although always in scrupulous agreement with my partners in conversation. The message was theirs and theirs alone, but some of the words and arguments were not, or were only partly so.

In almost every case I can remember, I was dissatisfied with either the depth or the intellectual span of the recorded conversation, and frequently both. The stylistic limitations of the unrehearsed spoken word, the absence of cross-references and quotations, the irrelevant interruptions, the sheer chaos of spontaneous exchanges driven by passion and sometimes by personal animus left me with a sense of exasperation. The raw transcripts were mostly shambolic. Arguments and ideas clamoured for inclusion on both sides after the event.

Herman Kahn, for example, after two very substantial meetings in London and Davos, began sending me reams of telex messages from all parts of the world containing rambling afterthoughts on this or that aspect of our topics. Could I somehow shape them into our text? Luigi Barzini, upon receiving for his approval the reformed version of our conversation, wrote to me to say that I had made him sound more learned and philosophical than he was, but he was quite happy to see himself so depicted. This was, of course, modesty going over the top. Barzini's irony, learning, and sophistication were a delight to encounter. He was (as he claimed) watching Italy's sweet ungovernability "without understanding it." Whichever side the Italian communists supported, he presciently told me, would lose the Cold War, or indeed any other.[10]

Many dialogues ended up being recast from scratch, with the sense of what had been said on both sides of course preserved, but with the gaps in reasoning filled in, the argument enriched, the pieces rearranged, and the grammar improved. I could not live with rank imperfection, and most of my partners in dialogue deserved better than to be brought low by the randomness of the spoken word. Arthur Koestler, for example, was rightly celebrated for his lucid thought and fine style in print, but his Hungarian-inflected spoken English, and the difficulty he experienced in formulating ideas under pressure, let him down in his public speaking engagements. I was a friend and an admirer—could I allow him and contributors facing similar limitations to appear less coherent or inspired than they were at their best? I improved the transcripts, within the limits of intellectual integrity. In every case, though, the revamped texts were sent back to my interlocutors for their revision and approval.

Some needed virtually no editorial assistance. Arnold Toynbee—the most gracious of them all—thought and spoke with assurance, charm, clarity, and charity. So deep and multidimensional were the roots of his knowledge that he could afford to make his message simple and compelling. I found no trace in him of that overweening ambition to figure in historiography as a latter-day saint that Lord Dacre (Hugh Trevor-Roper) ascribed to him in a famous and bitter article.[11] Trevor-Roper himself was an inspiring, somewhat dry, but fluent and attractive verbaliser, well able to do without editorial props.[12] He performed magnificently at our Chequers seminar on Germany with Prime Minister Margaret Thatcher on March 24, 1990.[13]

With Sidney Hook I developed a sense of coauthorship by remote control.[14] Over a period of several months after our recording sessions in California in 1987, I sent him a host of supplementary ideas for incorporation; and he retaliated with comments that in turn provoked fresh lines of enquiry. Somewhere our spiralling reconsiderations had to stop. Hook's unfortunate death put an end to them. Large parts of the unedited transcripts have, alas, remained unpublished.

Sidney Hook was an exceptionally unpretentious and courteous interlocutor as well as a warm-hearted host. He had arranged a fellowship for me at the Hoover Institution to make my trip less costly and embarrassed me with public praise. Upon my appointment as director of Radio Free Europe, he had warned me in a letter that people of my sort should stay on the frontline of ideas and not squander their energy running inevitably soulless bureaucratic organisations, even if the cause they were serving was as worthy as the Radio's. He wanted me to join him at the Hoover Institution. I wonder whether I should have been more attentive to his advice.

Of the numerous critics of the Soviet system and the Marxist-Leninist creed, none was more compelling to listen to or more devastating in the overall effect of what he had to say than this intensely motivated, outstanding American. His own roots were in Marxism. He knew what he was talking about. In one of his last notes to me (June 22, 1988) he said, "I am currently writing an open letter to my Soviet friends denouncing the cults of Bukharin, Lenin and Gorbachev and calling for a return to the era following February 1917 with a call for a Constituent Assembly!" Hook died in July 1989, a few months before the "October revolutions" in Eastern Europe. It is heartrending to think that age cheated him of witnessing the collapse of the Soviet system.

I had a decidedly less pleasant experience with Sir Karl Popper, another famous Enlightenment-based critic of communism. Popper needed editing on a grand scale because much of what he had to say was frequently disjointed and rambling. He was intolerant of most things in the realm of ideas except his own "teaching" and unwilling to cooperate in the work of making sense of his spoken statements. Towards the end of his tenure at the London School of Economics he was being jokingly referred to by his students as "the open society and its *enemy*."[15] In our otherwise agreeable conversation, he lived up to his reputation for intolerance. I recast our dialogue as best I could and sent him the cleaned-up version, meanwhile asking whether I had correctly interpreted his intentions, and what I could understand of his words—for Popper's Vienna-flavoured English was not always easy to decipher.

Popper kept me waiting for several months without a reply. My telephone calls were equally unproductive. Finally, about a year on, I decided to remove from my draft everything he had not explicitly uttered (to the extent I was able to make out what it was he *had* uttered) and had a pared-down version broadcast and later published.[16] Still, the tension between us remains clearly detectable in the published text. Popper's age and frailty—he was over ninety when I saw him in his home near London—may explain a lot. He was hospitable and, outwardly at least, pleasant enough; but he probably expected to find in me a reverential disciple, not a hardened critic with views in many respects different from his own. So ended my short association with a man whose early books I admired, but whose charm I found to be in inverse proportion to his fame and achievements.

The terror of seeing their spoken and often ill-considered words in cold print did grip one or two of my contributors. In noncontroversial cases I accepted second thoughts without demur, but whenever they struck at substance, I insisted on sticking to the original statement or on indicating that a change of mind had taken place. The best example was an observation made by Lucio Lombardo Radice, then a member of the Central Committee of the Italian Communist Party, in the course of our two long meetings in Rome in 1977.

One of the great questions preoccupying the Western world in those days was the future loyalty of the reforming West European Communist Parties. Would they, if they formed a government or became partners in a coalition government, stay loyal to the Atlantic Alliance in an East-West confrontation? Progressives on our side were claiming that the Italian Communist Party had undergone fundamental change and would honour Italy's international commitments, including the mili-

tary ones. I wanted to test that hypothesis. Radice was a Eurocommunist of sorts and a respected member of the communist hierarchy. I
asked him: "Suppose there is, in 1978, or 1984, or whenever, a grave
international crisis between the Soviet Union and the West. Suppose,
further, that the Communist Parties of Italy and France have by then
come to power, or to share power, and would therefore have to make
a quick decision whether to stay loyal to the Western Alliance, or not
to stay loyal to it. What would you do?"

Radice, in the original recording, gave the following answer: "We
would choose the Soviet side, of course, and we would do so on
grounds of principle."

But when he saw the transcript, Radice—understandably—got cold
feet. He had said something highly damaging to the acceptability of
Eurocommunism and was eager to undo it. He asked me to delete
his original words and substitute, in the version I was preparing for
radio, a much milder statement: "Generally speaking—and I am going
to qualify this—we would be on the Soviet side of the fence. If there
is an imperialist aggression with the avowed objective of rolling back
socialism, we would feel entirely absolved of any obligation of 'loyalty' to the 'defensive' character of NATO and take the side of the Soviet
Union. But we would, in such an extreme emergency, also do our ut-
most to restore peace."

When it came to publication in *Encounter* magazine, Radice got
even more apprehensive, requesting a further dilution of his statement:
"It depends. If there is an imperialist aggression with the avowed objective of rolling back socialism . . . we would take the side of the
Soviet Union."

I accepted Radice's second thoughts for the text that was to be
broadcast, because he was the first leading Eurocommunist I had invited to talk with me for the Radio and I did not want to frighten away
other Eurocommunists by a public wrangle. In *Encounter* magazine,
however (and that was the version that mattered), Lasky and I decided
to use Radice's watered-down formulation in the main text, but also
to append a footnote quoting the give-away words he had originally
spoken:

"We would choose the Soviet side, of course."

That footnote made a bit of contemporary history. Reprinted and
discussed worldwide, it did nothing to promote the credibility of Eurocommunism.[17]

In one memorable case I had to write the entire conversation myself. Being close to completing my series on Eurocommunism in 1977,
I sought to obtain a concluding conversational statement from the
Church through Father Bartolomeo Sorge, S.J., then editor of the influential Vatican journal *Civiltà Cattolica* and a close adviser of Pope
Paul VI. Sorge was closeted with the Pope on the morning of our appointment, and by the time he emerged to see me, his busy schedule
ruled out a proper colloquy. We talked for a while in general terms.
He knew that I had read his recent studies and articles and asked with
apologies whether, *faute de mieux,* I would be prepared to "ghost" the
dialogue as there was no time to do the real thing.

The Sorge colloquy was a difficult one. I wanted to shed some light
on the Church's growing détente with (or, many feared, appeasement
of) the communist regimes in Eastern Europe under Pope Paul VI and
represent the feelings of those millions of Christians who could not
understand why the physical self-preservation of the Church seemed
more important to the Vatican than ministering to the spiritual, including the political, needs of the faithful under oppression. Poland,
of course, was the significant exception. The Holy See itself was split
about the rights and wrongs of the concessions made or about to be
made, and it was even more at sixes and sevens over the sensitive
question of whether, and if so on what doctrinal or practical grounds,
Christians and communists could live in political symbiosis in Eastern and, indeed, in Western Europe; for the suggested creation of "an
opening to the left" was a controversial Italian problem, too, and very
much at the forefront of attention at the Vatican.

Closely related to this group of questions was a fear which was
occupying the minds of many Christians in the East. The Church
and the communist regimes, they charged, were sharing an unspoken
agenda: both were committed to an authoritarian and conservative
moral and social order. Both, it was claimed, saw liberalism as their
real antagonist—liberalism especially in its Western, permissive, and
allegedly corrupting forms. What did Rome have to say about this supposedly joint platform?

There was room here for fierce debate. I was in the fortunate position of having a good deal of sympathy with both sides. I shared the
view widely held among serious Christians that faith thrives under
oppression. At the same time, I could see that the Church's moral
teaching—especially where aggression, torture, brainwashing, hostage

taking, and genocide were concerned—could not be upheld if there was no organised Church to uphold it.

My own heart was in noncooperation with the communist regimes. I did not really believe that they and the Church were anywhere near sharing a conservative moral platform. But I did make a case for both sides with the dedication the seriousness of the topic clearly demanded. *I* certainly learnt a great deal from this conversation with myself.

Surprisingly, the text I eventually sent Father Sorge for his comments came back with his approval and without a single revision. That is how "Will Eurocommunists and Eurocatholics Converge?" was born.[18] That benign violation of what is intellectually right is, *mutatis mutandis,* also the key to my introductory motto to *Stalinism* and indeed to much of my nine-volume dialogue work.

> CALLICLES: Couldn't you finish the argument alone, either in a continuous speech or answering your questions yourself?
> SOCRATES: "One man doing the work of two," to quote Epicharmus? It looks as if it will have to be like that.[19]

CHAPTER THIRTEEN

Companions

MELVIN J. LASKY

C an words describe a volcano in near-permanent eruption? Such was Melvin J. Lasky, senior editor of *Encounter* magazine, in thought and character. Because Lasky's monthly journal was a powerful inducement for some of the most intriguing minds of our time to join the network of our Radio University broadcasts, I will attempt to say something about this central figure of the Western world's contest of ideas with the Soviet system.

Despite our different backgrounds and temperaments, Lasky and I became close friends. We shared the expectation that Sovietism had to be dispatched and could be dispatched in our lifetime without war. Starting in about 1965, we cooperated on a variety of projects—conferences, symposia, and publications—and with the assistance of the Congress for Cultural Freedom, promoted Britain's entry into the European Economic Community. It was through him that I met Ignazio Silone, John Strachey, Michael Josselson, Denis de Rougemont, Sidney Hook, Jeane Kirkpatrick, Max Kampelman, Luigi Barzini, and other like-minded men and women of eminence, influence, and a stomach for battle.

Lasky was larger than life—not everyone's choice for intellectual partnership or a quiet existence. Compared with Leopold Labedz, with whom Lasky maintained a stormy love-hate relationship (all the "love" came from Lasky's side), he was a model of composure; but then, the brilliant Labedz, with his intolerance and penchant for the overkill, belonged to a class entirely his own. Lasky stormed but seldom sulked or fretted, but even he had a didactic streak which made him few friends. Lecturing people in high office or at the peak of their fame is a risky undertaking. In his younger years, Lasky tended to pay scant attention to this sensitive aspect of human relations. Overwhelmed by the conviction that nothing should stand in the way of the truth as he saw it (and in almost every case I can remember, he saw it "right"), he tended to play his notes fortissimo when quieter sounds might have achieved as much or more.

Happily for his Anglo-American magazine and the world of letters, Lasky never quite fitted into the unenterprising and underpowered culture of middle-class Britain. In British eyes, his respect for ideas and for naked intellectual attainment was outlandish and somewhat suspect. His mind worked too fast and his information base was too rich and too international for off-shore consumption, but he suited me down to the ground in most things. He was a combat historian; so was I. His great strength was his feel for ideas in the making. A crusader of both the will and the intellect, he was not a crusader, much less a hater, by temperament. He lacked Schadenfreude and any sense of mockery or self-righteousness. "Kill your enemy if you must, but don't insult him." The tone he struck was a "serious call" which frivolous minds scorned and rejected but few managed to ignore.

Leninism, Stalinism, and the false consciousness they generated in Western thinking in one guise or another drew Lasky's sharpest fire. He believed them to be not only hostile to human emancipation and dignity but responsible for cheating the world of the prospect of liberty *in the name and in the language of liberty*. It was this global confidence trick that engaged all Lasky's energies. From it followed his long preoccupation with utopia[1] and his wrestling with the vocabulary of the "sweet dream" and the sweet but menacing dreamers. And it is precisely because Lasky's own life was a *carrefour* for the competing calls of passion and reason that his final espousal of moderation, balance, and prudence carries so much conviction. In the final days of *Encounter* magazine this man who had chosen the abolition of slavery as the topic for his master's dissertation at the University of Michigan observed with satisfaction that Soviet totalitarianism had gone down not because it had been defeated by some counterutopia but because the system had failed to answer the call of such unspectacular but essential public virtues as tolerance, pluralism, and individual freedom.

Lasky's moral courage was matched by his ability to identify with ideas that included those he criticised and ultimately rejected. Many contributors to his magazine had the perplexing pleasure of having their own thoughts explained to them by the magazine's editor in un-

expected ways and often in a more fruitful manner than they would
have thought possible. Like some seventeenth-century master of the
fugue, Lasky could take a melody and surround it with voices both contrasting and imitative until, at the end of spectacular variations, the
original theme would return to rest in the original key—enriched and
purified. He did so to amuse himself—*varietas delectat*—but he would,
once he had accepted a manuscript, never interfere with its wording.
In this, he was wholly un-American.

Part of Lasky's penchant for the polyphonic presentation of ideas
was mere playfulness—the mark of a restless intelligence that finds
it more congenial to internalise and develop received themes than to
put forward entirely new ones. This imaginary conversation with me
about the art of the interview is one memorable example. But part
of it—most of it—seemed to flow from an instinctive comprehension
that ideas must be grappled with and grasped from within before they
can be properly understood and that understanding requires exposing
them, now from this, now from that angle, to the searchlights of feeling and intellect. Lasky never allowed this many-sided apprehension
to jeopardise his single-minded moral commitment, but he was aware
that in the practical affairs of men, moral purpose is ineffectual without the ability to fashion what is right into what is incisive and memorable. His contempt for one-dimensional State Department prose was
second only to his scorn for the sound bites and thought bites of television pundits and politicians.

But of all the uncommon virtues which lift a blue-pencil man to
the status of a creative editor, the ability to connect is the rarest. Lasky
possessed the uncanny gift of sensing what belonged together or would
eventually do so, before lesser minds could see a pattern. He was a
seismogram before the earthquake—a lie detector preempting the liar.
Even his exasperating habit of not answering contributors' letters but
then rushing their words into print at the relevant moment was an
idiosyncratic way of responding to bleeps on his private radar screen.
Essays, reports, and interviews from diverse parts of the intellectual
world cohered under Lasky's baton into meaningful scores. I often
wondered whether the passionate intellectual behind *Encounter*'s editorial desk had a hot line to history, or whether it was history that, for
cunning reasons of its own, did Lasky's bidding. That I had reason so
to wonder is surely the highest tribute I can pay Lasky as a maker of
the political mood of our time.

"The mind takes its bias from the place of its birth," Virginia Woolf

observes in an essay on the Russian classics. Lasky's weaknesses (if
that is what they were) were weaknesses of omission rather than commission. They stemmed from the secular liberalism of an erstwhile
social democrat and from the New York urban milieu in which he had
grown up. These explain some of the ground *Encounter* left uncovered
or thinly covered over the years. Two of them strike me as important because *Encounter's* silence about them has not been justified by
the real world. The first was the magazine's neglect both of the role
of Christianity and the personality of Pope John Paul II, as elements
of resistance to the philosophical claims of communism, and of the
hopes attached to Christian forms of democracy in both communist
and postcommunist Central Europe and Russia. The second was the
environmental skein of problems. *Encounter* was slow to respond to
the world's ecological concerns because these were thought to be items
on the hidden agenda of the "lunatic Left," and anachronistic to boot.

Such omissions, however, do not take away from Lasky's editorial achievement, and to complain about them is to misunderstand
his position. The intellectuals behind *Encounter*—and for a turbulent
decade before that (1948 to 1958), his journal *Monat* in Berlin—and
the Congress for Cultural Freedom, which was associated with both,
did not set out to look at our civilisation with the eyes of disinterested observers. Their purpose was to reclaim the political heritage
of the Enlightenment from the disaster which had befallen it in 1917,
and specifically, to challenge Leninism-Stalinism on its own ground.
In this they succeeded beyond the most sanguine expectations. There
is no finer testimony to *Encounter's* "rightness" over the decades than
the revelations reaching us daily from the lips and pens of Central and
East European writers and politicians.

As the motivating force behind *Encounter* and its extraordinary network, Lasky had to swallow more than an editor's fair share of intrigue
and misrepresentation. Some of his detractors inveighed against him
because he was an American heading Britain's foremost political and
intellectual journal; others, in America, thought he was too European
to qualify for long-term U.S. support; yet others resented it that his
early, "premature," exposure of the lies and crimes of the Soviet system
turned out to be well founded. Turncoats and time servers detested his
consistency; appeasers loathed him for his courage. Lasky committed
the unpardonable offence of being right before his time.

After the closure of *Encounter* magazine in 1990, Lasky and his
German-born wife, the novelist Helga Hegewisch, moved to Berlin,

where in the aftermath of the war Lasky had earned the respect and friendship of leading German politicians and intellectuals with his fighting resistance to the spread of Soviet influence. It was a move made not a day too soon. In Britain, Lasky's role in the Cold War went largely unrecognised, whereas in Germany he was as much in the public eye at the end of the Cold War as he had been at its beginning. A psychological factor also militated for domicile on the Continent. Lasky identified himself fully with the culture of Europe and especially with German thought and letters. In Berlin, he was spared daily encounters with the increasingly hysterical reactions of some of the English political class to the European Union and all things German—fruits of Margaret Thatcher's planting that reached their poisonous maturity with the xenophobia surrounding the beef crisis and the European football championships under John Major's administration in 1996.

I witnessed time and again how little Lasky allowed his humanity to be compromised by the animus of his critics—or his friends. He remained dignified in the face of ugly personal attacks and impervious to the barbs of those who misrepresented or maligned the ideas and institutions he stood for. He was, it is true, intolerant of the mediocre message, but never of the imperfect messenger. I often puzzle over this largesse of spirit in a man who was anything but naive or unworldly. Clearly, he could "do no other." An innate generosity helped him to ignore past wrongs and present hardships and to harness diverse people and ideas to the never-ending struggle against mendacity and violence. Therein lies his greatest achievement. When the story of the collapse of modern utopias comes to be written, his impact will be seen as central, seminal, and decisive.

MILOVAN DJILAS

I first met Milovan Djilas in 1977, in his modest apartment on the second floor of No. 8 Palmoticeva Street in Belgrade. The Soviet Union under Brezhnev was on the march at the time, and Western leaders felt they could at best slow down but not reverse the relentless spread of Soviet hegemony. In the Western chancelleries, the spirit of détente was in the ascendant, and only hopeless cold warriors would try to pick holes in a system with which, we were told, we had to live in amicable symbiosis. With Tito still firmly in charge of Yugoslavia, Djilas was under virtual house arrest. Our correspondence, our telephone conversations, and our personal movements were all monitored.

I last saw Djilas in 1991, again in Belgrade, after the first free Serbian elections, which fatefully confirmed the communist ultranationalist Slobodan Milošević in power. The Soviet system and empire had fallen apart. The Yugoslav army's onslaught on Slovenia and Croatia was yet to come, but Serb factional violence had already claimed its first victims in Croatian Krajina. Yugoslavia was on the verge of civil war. An historic epoch, which Djilas had helped to create and then to destroy, was coming to an end.

That first Belgrade encounter was enough to make me feel that despite our political differences and very different cultures, Djilas and I simply liked each other. I first recoiled from the hands and eyes that had created or overseen so much vicious propaganda and bloodshed, but Djilas's melancholy contrition in his books and in private conversation grew on me as I got to know him better. He on his part seemed to sense both the judgmental element in my attitude to him and my eventual understanding. After our first and most difficult conversation, I greatly enjoyed wrestling with this famous protoheretic of the faith. Fortunately, Djilas was not easily offended—on the contrary, he seemed to thrive on my often blunt questioning. "You have, during our many conversations over the years, witnessed my 'fall' and given it a dimension I found new and challenging," he wrote to me in 1987. A generous supply of steaming coffee and Central European cakes, which Djilas's wife, Stefania, continued to put on our table while we were digging for the roots of communist heresy, helped to make things very civilised between us.

This fortunate chemistry was especially helpful when, after our first joint publication in *Encounter* magazine in December 1979, I began receiving anonymous threats to the life of Djilas's son Aleksa, and indirectly to my own life. The letters appeared to be coming from American survivors of Tito's great massacres of Yugoslav refugees in Slovenia in 1945, forcibly returned to Slovenia from Carinthia by British troops in 1945. Djilas and I discussed these killings on the pages of *Encounter*. He agreed that many thousands had been put to death but denied any personal responsibility. The survivors, however, now wanted to pin responsibility on him, and for a much larger number—hundreds, rather than tens, of thousands—than were generally believed to have been shot by the Partisans. Alexander Solzhenitsyn, Nikolai Tolstoy, and Nicholas Bethell devoted much thought and research to this terrible aftermath of World War II.[2] The letter writers' demand was that I should "make" Djilas admit his crimes in a subsequent dialogue, or else Aleksa would pay with his life and I might fare no better.

In reality, as Djilas's wife soon discovered from former Partisan colleagues in the Belgrade police, the threatening letters were the work
not of aggrieved émigrés in the United States but of the Yugoslav secret
police, which was trying to intimidate Aleksa for his anti-Titoist activities abroad. But the threats were enough to usher in two years
of anxiety for the Djilas family and my own. To forestall surprises,
Scotland Yard installed a shortwave radio transmitter in my study in
Brighton, and put Aleksa Djilas, then living in London, under police
protection. But Aleksa, a chip off the old block, was too proud to accept protection. His campaign against Tito's regime was in full flood,
and he would not be deflected from it. An element of overconfidence
in his character added to the security problem.

I remember doing my best one hot weekend to dissuade Aleksa
from addressing a London conference of émigré liberals. The would-
be assassins had just warned Milovan Djilas in Belgrade by telephone
that that night they would strike and kill his son. Djilas got in touch
with me, and I with the police. But Aleksa would heed advice neither
from Scotland Yard nor from me. He proceeded to speak at the émigré meeting, with Scotland Yard discreetly present to shield him. But
our alarm ended in an anticlimax—nothing at all happened, then or
later. Aleksa's foes in Belgrade were content with a warning. In 1980
Tito died. My personal affection for Milovan Djilas and his wife stems
from the shared anxiety of those strenuous months.

Some vignettes of my nexus with Djilas stand out in my memory.
He was as ready to admit his Stalinist past and the wrongs committed
under Stalinism in conversation as he was in his books. No sooner did
I take him back to statements he had made as a fervent communist
than Djilas would score one better: "Ah, but you've heard nothing yet,"
and he would then throw at me even more damaging evidence against
himself than I had mustered.

Hadn't he been an especially articulate voice in the chorus adulating
Stalin and maligning the West—a chief propagandist? "Oh yes, I *loved*
Stalin, I sincerely loved the Soviet Union without reservations. Nothing the Russians did was too absurd for us to rationalise and defend."
Did the Soviet annexation of the Baltic states and parts of Finland give
him pause? "Not at all. Personally, I managed to convince myself that
the Finnish people were being liberated by the Red Army . . . that Finland was part of a capitalist plot against the 'fortress of socialism' and
that the Finnish peace treaty with the USSR detached only those bits

of Finnish territory which were essential for the security of Leningrad and Murmansk. I managed to suppress any embryonic doubt I might have had about the overall justice of Soviet policy."

How did he feel about the incorporation of the Baltic republics? "We thought of these countries as territories wrongly torn out of the flesh of Russia at the end of a lost war, and now justly reintegrated to the benefit of world socialism. . . . The partition of Poland seemed to me especially worthy of support."[3] And didn't he write in *Borba* in November 1942: "Can there be any greater honour and happiness than to feel that one's closest and most beloved friend is Stalin? . . . Stalin is the bitterest enemy of all that is inhuman, he is deeply concerned, he is the wisest person, he nurtures human kindness. . . . The Soviet Union is the only country without hidden motives. . . . Stalin is the only statesman with a pure conscience and an unselfish heart"?

And didn't he then say, twenty years on, that Stalin was the greatest criminal of all time?

Oh yes, he did, Djilas would say; he had been a Stalinist, as all communists had at the time. "My Stalinism is on the record. We *were* fanatics—and had to be."[4] I found Djilas's admissions and repentance sincere and enormously impressive.

Another mental image vivid in my mind is of Djilas's inner struggle for higher justification. He had embraced communism for entirely moral reasons and then changed fronts to oppose communism for moral reasons. But his choices in both cases were surrounded by scruples of a very similar nature which he tried hard to suppress. Future historians will do well to think of Djilas not only as the most influential postwar heretic of communism and author of *The New Class* but also as an archetypal rebel and counterrebel. Driven by an unswerving idealism, he found satisfaction in being neither.

We can trace early signs of his heresy in many of his outwardly faultless orthodox communist writings. Even late in life he often qualified his *mea culpa* with impassioned recitals of the historical and psychological reasons that had made him join the movement in the first place. There was, in his terms, no break in the spirit of his commitment—only in his career. In his final years he accepted the futility of utopian pursuits and would have no truck with any notion of expediency in the service of "higher" ends. But the glow of single-minded dedication and the romanticism of "the struggle" retained their magic for him. In 1991 he said he had no message for the younger generation, much less for mankind; but if he were pressed for a lapidary statement, he would say: "Fight and be fully stretched in the service of some great idea, but be aware that you can never attain it."

Djilas's burning fanaticism in his first incarnation was a Jacobin affair. When I put it to him in 1979 that temperamentally he was a rebel first and a communist only second, he did not demur: "Revolutionaries are *born*. They don't need books to teach them revolution. Tito is another example. He too was a rebel by nature. If communism . . . had not existed, he would have found an outlet in some other idealistic struggle. . . . In different historical situations we would have supported totally different revolutionary or even nationalistic movements. I could . . . easily see myself as a Serb nationalist in 1914 fighting Austria-Hungary in the name of our national revolution."

Would Djilas have reached for his gun to bring about a greater Serbia had he been eighteen when Yugoslavia began to disintegrate and had the Montenegrin fire been stirring in his blood? I very much doubt it. Towards the end of his life Djilas totally condemned Slobodan Milošević's fascist posturing and the genocidal work of his commandos. His indictment of the Bosnian Serbs in Pale was no less severe.

When I suggested to him that he was not only a born rebel but a Montenegrin rebel, at that, who happened to have found a handy package of rationalisations in Leninism, Djilas again outbid me: "Yes, most Montenegrin revolutionaries joined the communist movement for exactly the same reasons I did. As a young communist I rejected the old regime with the same uncompromising resolve as I now reject communism. I was, and I am, a Montenegrin!"

Djilas's struggle for moral, and I'm almost inclined to say divine, sanction comes out most clearly in his account of the turbulence that enveloped him in the spring of 1943, after he had slit the throat of an unarmed German prisoner, clubbed him to death with a rifle butt, and then handed his knife to a comrade to stab another.

The night after the killing, Djilas had a vision of Christ—"the one from the frescoes and icons, with a silky beard and a look of pity." He saw himself addressing Christ, seeking His reassurance that the cause he was fighting for was noble and just. Djilas does not tell us whether he received that reassurance, but he found himself enveloped "in some safe and glowing warmth" which inspired a feeling of "calm and courage."

I put it to Djilas that he must have been suffering from a deep sense of unease, even guilt. Was he seeking forgiveness?

"The day's events were gruelling," he said. "Many of my comrades around me lost their lives. The horror of all this must have released a hidden strain of religious feeling in me."

Was he troubled by any sense of remorse about the killings?

"No remorse, none at all. But after the day's fighting, I began, slowly but perceptibly, to take a larger, more humane, and more forgiving view. . . . The analytical rigour of the communist leader and the passionate resolve of the typical Montenegrin were still alive in my mind; but they began to be tempered by a gentler consciousness."

Wasn't his vision of a gentle Christ a religious experience?

"Oh, absolutely; for a long time, I could not come to terms with it. Had I ceased to be a communist? . . . Was I suffering from hallucinations? I was deeply ashamed of the apparition of Christ and tried to ignore it—until I wrote *Wartime*. . . . Let future historians make of it what they will."[5]

In his final years, Djilas, as I say, appeared to be reconciled to limited horizons and a cautious vocabulary. When I asked him in 1991 whether he would accept Kant's warning that "out of the crooked timber of humanity no straight thing can ever be made," Djilas said: "Yes, communism tried to do just that—to straighten out the crooked timber—but it has dismally failed."

Was it at all right to try? Is it ever right to try? I wondered. "I'm not even sure whether it would be a good thing if the crooked timber . . . *could* be straightened out completely," he said. "Would you or I like to live in a society of unadulterated goodwill? . . . I think we need a certain amount of wickedness in the world to sharpen our minds and test our swords against." Whether this was an unconscious recognition of felix culpa or a new formulation of the dialectic, who can say. Although an atheist, Djilas was no stranger to the notion of atonement.

At an advanced age, he paid a visit at a monastery to a childhood friend turned monk. Djilas was struck by the beauty and tranquillity of the religious environment. Would he like to come and live there? the monk asked. "I've committed far too many sins for that," Djilas replied; but his friend insisted: "The Church forgives your sins provided you sin no more." "If that is the price of admission, I think I might qualify because one of the great weaknesses of my life has been precisely that I once sinned profusely—but then stopped sinning."

That Djilas should have associated his career as a communist with the notion of sin strikes me as pregnant with meaning. It opens a wide field—a minefield—to future research.

Djilas's words did not take *me* by surprise. They had been prefigured by his remorseful meditations in *Wartime* about the cruelty of war and the very ordinary, nonideological roots of collective fanaticism. Such thoughts, he tells us, "cropped up whenever any violence threatened me, and became a reality of my suppressed and hidden spiritual self."

Soon after the publication of *Rise and Fall*, Djilas wrote a dedication into my copy: "As further evidence that my 'fall' was more glorious than my 'rise.'" Was this meant to be read as a summing up of the story of his life? I wondered. "Those who are seen by the world and the church to which they once belonged as heretics," he reflected, "usually get better billing in history than those who are not. In that sense, my 'fall' was more glorious than my 'rise.'"

This was true, but it was saying too little. Djilas has received outstanding billing in history because he was the first in the postwar world to show up from within the crimes and depredations of the Soviet system. He was more than a heretic. Like many a schismatic before him, he was also a counterprophet and global public prosecutor. His "fall" was his elevation because it served to point the way for those in the world's communist parties who, without him, would have lacked the strength to fashion doubt into negation and then into resistance. Yet, my personal image of Djilas remains that of a lonely soul wrestling with his anticommunism almost as much as with his erstwhile communism.

He embraced and then repudiated the great totalitarian delusion of our time, but I suspect that at heart his quarrel was always with human nature itself—with the inherited facts of history, race, birth, and culture; with our inability to learn from our errors; with collective memories that are either too long or too short; with the fragility of human resolve; and with the long arm of guilt by association. He was a man of religion without a religion but wide open to the call of religiosity.

The key to our friendship (if I may call it that) was not so much Djilas's outward story—though that was instructive enough—as our shared interest in the psychological way stations along a tormented believer's path from rebellion to rebellion.

ALEXANDER ZINOVIEV

Zinoviev intrigued me from the day of his arrival in Western Europe, because he claimed to be the proud owner of an incontrovertible theory of how the Soviet system worked. Our fierce arguments on the air (later printed in *Encounter* and in book form[6]) centred on this point. Despite his splendid satires of the hubris of the Soviet bureaucracy, of Soviet corruption and backwardness, Zinoviev believed that the system was cast in concrete and would last "a thousand years." "We can assume for all practical purposes," he observed, "that the Soviet system is here for the rest of human history."[7] I could never quite make up my mind whether Zinoviev really felt this to be the truth, on the basis of sociological models and calculations he alone seemed able to understand, or whether he was merely trying to shock the Western bourgeoisie. He came late as an émigré; his dissent in the Soviet Union was virtually unknown outside Moscow. The normal thing for exiled or self-exiled people of his background to do was to rush into print upon arrival and mobilise Western opinion by revealing yet another repulsive aspect of the Soviet organisation of society. Not so for Zinoviev.

He, too, left or had to leave the USSR because he did not feel free enough in the Soviet system, but once here, he surprised us all by advocating, in the guise of "scientific" analyses, the great human advantages, even the peculiar "freedoms," of communism as practised in the USSR. If this tactic was designed to make him stand out from the "normal" Soviet émigré intellectual and attract attention, it certainly succeeded. What could be more astonishing than a dissident who positively liked the system from which he had dissented and who procured a living as well as considerable fun by mocking it?

Whatever the reason (and one could adduce many others), Zinoviev revelled in being caught between hating and loving communist society and in having to explain his self-created dilemma to the world and to himself. His contempt for any Western explanation of Sovietism helped him over many hurdles, for what could be simpler and more pleasing than to assert that the Soviet Russian mind was sui generis and thus excluded from Western comprehension? And this he did with relish. If Westerners were generically incapable of meaningful study, then there was no need to argue with them, and Zinoviev's theory stood uncontested and incontestable.

Under the Soviet system, Zinoviev tells us, no one gets bogged down in the swamps of Western taxation because there are no tax returns and there is no income tax. This situation is immeasurably better than that of Western societies which are governed by the rule of law. Concentration camps and labour camps are not typical of Soviet rule, he claims; rather, "the concentration camp is a useful arena for observing the manifestations of the laws of communality." Compulsory attachment to a work commune "is not perceived as a lack of freedom."

Collective life in the commune is "intimate" and enjoyable. Manifold activities bind the commune into "the superpersonality of communist society; into the kind of 'we' that has the right to regard itself as an 'I.'" Under communist rule, Zinoviev states, "large sections of the population feel that the communist situation is advantageous for them; and having tasted it in practice, they can no longer give it up."[8] Soviet earning power, too, attracted Zinoviev's admiration, even though he was speaking from prosperous West Germany.

"The degree of remuneration of the most active and productive segment of the population in communist society has a tendency to grow, while the degree of its exploitation diminishes. Moreover, the degree of remuneration is here higher than for corresponding people in Western countries, and the degree of exploitation is lower. This is the basic advantage that Communism has over Western society and the reason for its attraction for millions of people on this planet." Even the absence of crucial individual freedoms (the rights to organise, publish, and protest) did not induce Zinoviev to criticise Soviet society. "It isn't at all as if some evil rulers were deliberately depriving people of certain natural and generally recognised freedoms. No, the real fact is that Soviet society at its very foundations doesn't need freedoms of this kind and is even hostile towards them. To Soviet people these are alien phenomena."[9]

Not to put too fine a point on it, Alexander Zinoviev is a highly idiosyncratic thinker. The complexities of his thought and character often get the better of him. At home he was yearning for the West and probably saw himself as a Westerniser. In the West he soon discovered (what some of us had known all along) that he was a Soviet Man through and through. The soulless pragmatism of the Occident made him, as he often told me, yearn for the cosy familiarity of his Moscow commune. He loved Stalin, yet he fought him and went to prison for opposing him. The slaughter of millions under the dictator struck him not so much as criminal as merely "tragic." "Some people perished," he observed to me, "others made good. . . . Morality does not enter the picture. History happened as it happened."[10]

These oscillations and inconsistencies in Zinoviev's writings and table talk amused but also enraged me. He was a rough diamond if ever there has been one—a muzhik at heart with enormous pretensions to learning and wisdom. I first met him in Tongue, at the northwestern tip of Scotland, in the country home of Charles Janson and his wife, Elizabeth, Countess of Sutherland. My wife, Patricia, and I repaired there, together with Iain and Elizabeth Elliot, for a long Soviet–East European weekend in the summer of 1982.[11] High talk in magnificent surroundings and a meeting with the Zinovievs (Alexander, his wife, Olga, and their daughter Paulina) were the purpose of our gathering. Charles Janson was, by then, fully persuaded that Western Sovietology could not explain Sovietism. Could Zinoviev provide the authentic key to it?

Unlike Amalrik and Solzhenitsyn, Zinoviev had been tepidly received in the West. That may have been one of Charles Janson's reasons for embracing him. He may also have detected in Zinoviev something of the proverbial Russian "holy fool," but because the signs were reversed, an especially intriguing one. A tame homo sovieticus in Caledonia appealed to my imagination, too.

Janson was (and is) one of the most sophisticated, multilingual students of Soviet affairs I have known, as well as a connoisseur of classical music (always a huge plus in my estimation) and a man of great learning. He knew his Russia, including its language, better than most. He was at the time the chief sponsor of *Soviet Analyst,* of which Elliot was the editor. If Janson and Elliot took so intense an interest in Zinoviev, I felt we all should.

Whatever Janson's precise reasons, Zinoviev undoubtedly appealed to him as *the* man with a plausible theory to account for the otherwise inexplicable durability of the Soviet system. Once we knew the real nature of the beast, it might be easier to deal with it. Zinoviev's pronouncements, moreover, came straight from the horse's mouth; he was articulating things about Soviet society that confirmed Janson's feeling that Russian culture and Soviet culture were in rare harmony and richly deserving of each other. Charles was profoundly convinced of the barbaric antecedents of Sovietism in Russian history, and although he looked upon Zinoviev as a weird genius of sorts, he was happy to see the overall image of a society permanently in the gutter, as he often put it, so authentically confirmed by his protégé.

For Zinoviev did, after a time, become Janson's protégé. His books, with the exception of *Yawning Heights* (1976), did not sell in the United States and Britain, although they did well in France, Italy, and the German-speaking countries. Zinoviev was too ideological for the pragmatic reader, and it was unkindly said about him that once you had read one of his satires, you had read them all.

Charles Janson often came to Zinoviev's rescue. He also translated, with enormous skill and dedication, *The Reality of Communism,* but my hope that this book would finally give us the precise model of communist society Zinoviev had so often spoken about was to be disappointed. All the book offers is a series of interesting but by no means strikingly new sketches of how communist society works and how we should understand it. It claims to be scientific and value-free but, as I have tried to show, it is not. Zinoviev's main handicap here is one that has frustrated the ambitions of other Soviet émigrés too: his poor knowledge of Western Sovietological scholarship. He had not read the bulk of American and West European scholarly literature and was constantly reinventing the wheel. This came out in my own long conversations with him; and what he had read he despised. Western scholars, he argued, should adopt his methodology. "The methods they now use, if indeed they use any, are deplorable. Their judgements are chaotic."[12] *The Reality of Communism* is therefore more a recognition than a shock, and since the collapse of the Soviet system, its prognostications are embarrassingly irrelevant. What was new in the book was Zinoviev's veiled but clearly discernible approval of some of the (for us) most repulsive features of the totalitarian state.

Time and again he claimed that he was no apologist of the Soviet system; he was merely offering analyses, not passing judgement. Yet my own talks with him proved the opposite to be the case. Under the pressure of my questioning he probably let slip more than he had intended. When shown my edited transcript, he was unhappy and tried to induce me to have a revised version printed. But, while accepting minor revisions, I refused changes in substance. When the transcript came to publication in book form, Zinoviev asked for an explanatory epilogue to be appended to "put the record straight." I readily agreed. "Too many readers," he wrote, "interpreted my statements tendentiously and saw in them what was not in fact there. One of the reasons for this lies in readers' confusing my personal attitude towards various aspects of life with my comments as a detached observer of the same. This confusion is particularly apparent in Vladimir Bukovsky's response to my comment that, given a free choice, the vast majority of the Soviet population would prefer Brezhnev to Solzhenitsyn. He took this to mean that I prefer Brezhnev to Solzhenitsyn."[13]

I rest my case.[14]

Zinoviev puzzled me as an individual. Stocky and short-necked, he was the very epitome of the run-of-the-mill Russian. A long life spent thinking and writing about difficult things had left few marks on his face, but his sad eyes betrayed suffering. He commanded at the time no foreign language except a fractured English. Flashes of brilliant insight were oddly sorted in his conversation with morose introspection and long silences. In the heat of argument his lips and eyes were ill-coordinated—the first uttering polite words, the second displaying signs of an all-consuming anger. His extraordinary paintings—of rats and other predators doing exceptionally unpleasant things to one another—do not, in my view, confirm the opinion, widely held among his former students and some readers, that Zinoviev was somehow "mad."[15] But despite his cool exterior, I do think he was, as geniuses have every right to be, high-strung and deeply worried. Time and again I found him tiptoeing around booby traps of his own laying.

He repelled and charmed me at different times. A lecture for broadcasting staff which I chaired for him at Radio Free Europe in 1984 left his audience in confusion. In our personal dealings he was always pleasant, not least because the uneven surfaces in his character were being smoothed out by his highly intelligent wife. He was turbulent as only Russians can be. His attempt to explain the Soviet system according to methods and models of his own devising showed the brilliance as well as the weaknesses of a man risen from the peasantry to the pinnacles of the world of learning in less than three decades. Despite his unusual gifts, he was boxing above his weight.

IGNAZIO SILONE

Of all ex-communist men of letters, Ignazio Silone was the one I respected most. *Fontamara* and *Bread and Wine* were masterpieces. A tormented believer with his soul and imagination rooted in the Middle Ages, Silone's inner debate over communism was another side of his quest for faith as a Catholic. I was drawn to him by his indefatigable search for right and wrong in public affairs. What could be more absurd and therefore more attractive in our amoral and de-Christianising century? His spiritual journey was a symbol of what was happening to numerous Christians in Central and Eastern Europe and was thus profoundly linked to our broadcasting. It is to him that we owe the words: "The final struggle will be between the communists and the ex-communists"—a forecast for which his own life became a significant metaphor.

In the autumn of 1963, on a visit to the Italian capital, I invited Silone to write a series of talks for the Radio and spend a few days with our staff in Munich. I felt his presence would enlarge the horizons and boost the morale of our commentators. There was too much incestuous sociology in the editorial councils of Radio Free Europe. The intellectual isolation of our staff worried me. We needed to open the windows so that independent thinking could waft in. Who was more qualified to do it than this celebrated Italian of vast learning and penetrating wit? Silone wore his learning lightly; he was a chosen soul, a latter-day hermit from the Abruzzi—introspective, loyal, self-denying, rough, generous, and of small speech, not unlike the saintly Pope Celestine V he later exalted in *The Story of a Humble Christian*. He was one of those men who hunger and thirst after righteousness, but have gone out of the temple to find it. What a fine force to balance the superficiality and cynicism of journalists.

Silone needed little persuading. He shared the broad ideological objectives of the Radio. We were, for him, one of the few remaining refuges of the spirit, whether in Eastern or in Western Europe. We promised to provide a vibrant and receptive audience, which he needed as much as we needed him as an inspiration. Silone was preoccupied at the time with the shortcomings of the Western welfare state and was "rethinking Progress." We spent a long afternoon circling round impressions and ideas that might go into his broadcasts.

Socialism conjured up two contrasting images in his mind—the Stalinist system, which was clearly repugnant, and the cradle-to-grave kind of Western welfare state. He was not against the latter, but what could welfarism offer beyond creature needs and comforts? The poor, of course, had to be looked after—no righteousness sprang from poverty. Yet, like John Maynard Keynes before him, he dreaded the enervating effects of universal leisure and prosperity. When all our material needs are satisfied, what then? Satiety and the freedom to do nothing would confront us, and especially the Marxist conception of man, with all the tragedy of human limitations. Only fools would expect the affluent and the idle to devote their time to harmless pursuits or the cultivation of their minds. The prophets of social emancipation were reckoning without the old Adam. There were no magic buttons that economists and sociologists could push to usher in a state of human felicity. Nor could one legislate for it.

The fashionable conception of man which reduced him to his digestive and sexual functions repelled Silone. Human beings, he said, were just as capable of rebellion under conditions of sybaritic wealth as under those of want and oppression. "When we are no longer persecuted, shall we persecute others, in turn?" he quoted from one of his characters in *Bread and Wine;* "And if ever a time should come when we're able to eat our fill, day after day, will we have nothing else to do but concentrate on our digestions?" He was expressing a view that was to be widely held in 1968 and after by a whole generation of student-rebels at Western universities. The tone and shallowness of intellectual discussion distressed him no less. Had he foreseen what was to follow in the tabloid press, in the video industry and on satellite television in the 1980s and 1990s, he would have counted his blessings.

To questions such as these Silone's five Radio Free Europe keynote lectures for 1964 were eventually devoted. We broadcast them under the title of "Bread Alone?" The exercise was well timed, for Nikita Khrushchev had announced the impending arrival of universal prosperity in the Soviet Union (the USSR, he predicted, would overtake America), and it was a nice question whether a prosperous Soviet proletariat, with leisure on its hands, mightn't find itself engulfed by the same boredom, frustration, and vacuity that appeared to be threatening Scandinavia and the United States. Things did not quite work out that way.

In June 1964, Silone and his high-powered wife, Darina Laracy (an Anglo-Irish writer and Silone's translator), spent a few days at the Radio in Munich apropos of Silone's lectures. The day after the launch of the Radio's series, my wife and I had the Silones to ourselves. I cannot say we had an easy time of it. Silone was stiff and distant. Small talk and courtesies were not in his social repertoire. In theory, I rather liked his earthy severity; I, too, tended to be taciturn—but two big silences did not make for a happy visit. We were also hampered by Silone's poor spoken English and my poor Italian. But what hampered and irritated him most, I thought, was his enforced reliance on his wife as his translator and chaperone. In Munich, at least, he seemed helpless without her.

My wife and I spent the day driving the Silones around in Bavaria and the Tirol. Darina was sitting next to me in our small V.W. Beetle, with Silone and Patricia in the back. Given the size of the vehicle, we were virtually sitting in one another's laps. Darina, trusting that Silone in the back would either not hear or not understand, embarrassed me with indiscreet observations in English about her husband. Time and again, I tried to divert her attention to the landscape and the outstanding work she had done translating Silone's lectures into English—but to no avail. I held Silone in the highest esteem for his literary and spiritual qualities; I did not want to hear about his private shortcomings. Our pleasure drive turned into a minor nightmare.

Attending a conference in Rome in January 1966, I saw the Silones again. The favourable reception of Silone's lectures visibly pleased him, yet his strange relationship with Darina cast a pall over our reunion. He gave me lunch at a fashionable seafood restaurant where he was a much respected patron, but for the best part of an hour and a half Silone was sunk in silence. Every time I attempted to broach some topic with him in German or English, Darina would butt in to translate. That was enough to foreclose any conversation, for Silone would not respond to anything coming from the lips of his wife. Whether this refusal was the result of a recent quarrel or a sign of normal jealousy between spouses of the same profession I could not tell. Silone was now barricaded in his private universe and seemed at times bored, at times irritated, but I gathered from the look in his eyes, his handshake, and the dedications he wrote into the books he gave me after lunch that it was not me he resented—it was his wife. Darina's interruptions, however, were not the sole cause of our discomfort: at sixty-six, Silone was taking driving lessons, I suppose to make himself independent from his wife. That, too, proved to be a lively bone of contention between them; I had no choice but to play the pained impartial observer.

I was to leave Rome by train the following day. Darina insisted on driving me to the Termini station. She said she wanted to talk to me privately. I had rather feared that she might. We sat in the station buffet for an interminable half hour.

"Don't be deceived by Silone"—she never referred to her husband by his Christian name—"there is no real genius there. Not now, anyway. He has written himself out. Were it not for his volte face on communism, Silone's name would hardly be known. Do you know what drives him to go on? Frustration, pure impotence, pus, pus! Outsiders can't see that, but I can. That's also the reason he wants to drive a car now—to get rid of his anger with himself. The genius is gone. All that's left is implosion, sickness, and pus. Please remember that." And she continued enlarging on her theme, to my immense dismay and embarrassment. Why she favoured me with these disclosures is still a mystery to me.

Having unloaded a burden that must have been distressing her, Darina handed me a copy of *Uscita di Sicurezza* which incorporated Silone's Radio Free Europe lectures, pointing on one page to the fading remains of a drop of blood: "You see, I was sweating blood to get this into English for you." A joke? A reproach? A token of affection? I wasn't sure.

Some weeks after Silone's death in August 1978, Darina appeared in England looking for someone to sort and edit Silone's papers. She got in touch with me—could I recommend a suitable person? We met in London at the Café de Paris. She was dressed in widow's weeds and looked distressed. She reminisced for a while about her recent visit to India where she had been the guest of Indira Gandhi—a close personal friend. The final days of Silone? Well, he wouldn't trust Italian medicine, she said, and insisted on being treated in Switzerland. And that's where he died. Otherwise—oh yes, a genius in his way, and a great fighter. But I could detect little genuine grief in her voice.

I respected and in some ways loved Silone because he was a Franciscan at heart and the antithesis of an easy optimist. He embraced suffering with the willingness of the early martyrs and took Original Sin and the temptation of power as daily realities in our lives. He was an advocate of things that sit uncomfortably with the consciences of our time: that the Church, before it can rise again, may have to "rot away completely"; that to resist injustice is a sacrosanct Christian duty; that good ends cannot justify tainted means; that a Christian should never bless the standards or weapons destined for war; that the root of all evil lies in the lure of power; that human souls alone are immortal— not kingdoms, not sovereignties, not nations.

In the Bosnian Serb massacres of the mid-1990s Silone would have recognised the timeless relevance of his creed. He would have repeated, I rather think, what he wrote from exile in 1944: "In the sacred history of man on earth, it is still, alas, Good Friday. The spirit of man is still forced to save itself in hiding."

ARTHUR KOESTLER

Like so many others of my generation, I was awed by the unforgiving logic of Investigating Magistrate Gletkin's argument in *Darkness at Noon*. Its author, Arthur Koestler, made a far more convincing case for communism Soviet style than any communist party or any communist dead or alive. There were lessons to be learnt. "I knew one man of first-rate powers, but without previous acquaintance with communist doctrine, who as late as the nineteen-forties was definitely influenced in a *procommunist* direction by reading *Darkness at Noon*. 'But what *is* the answer to Gletkin?' he used to say."[16]

Koestler's book, intelligently and imaginatively read, was the answer, and that is how it left its imprint on the Western imagination. As the Red Army was advancing into Central Europe in 1945 and communism was in the ascendant in Western Europe, it was precisely the seamless consistency of Gletkin's reasoning that swayed Western Europe against succumbing to the totalitarian temptation. The spectacle of doing the party a final service through a macabre confession to crimes never committed sent up a warning which even Solzhenitsyn's books would not quite equal three decades on. When *Darkness at Noon* appeared in French, there were riots in the streets of Paris and the danger of a French communist takeover receded. Seldom has a small volume had more far-reaching repercussions.

Koestler and John Strachey were my choices as curtain-raising contributors to Radio Free Europe's freshly created Third Programme broadcasts, of which I became the first director in 1962. I was intrigued by Koestler's mind, his life story as a communist and an anticommunist, and his attitude towards his native Hungary. I never became a close friend—rather a student of Koestlerism and an admirer of that extraordinary intellectual transformer station of which Koestler was the enviable owner.

Koestler's power as a fighter and thinker struck me as the obverse of his personal shyness. He was small, hesitant, visibly tormented, and nervous when unaided by alcohol. In his autobiography he recalls, "A shrewd Comintern agent said to me: 'We all have inferiority complexes of various sizes, but yours isn't a complex—it's a cathedral.'"[17] In the summer of 1962 I found him ensconced in his chalet (Schreiberhäusl) in the Tirolean village of Alpbach in Austria, on familiar *du* terms with the local peasants and religiously in attendance at every village wedding and funeral.

He had by then emptied his pockets as a critic of communism and was anxious to do justice to nonrational ways of perceiving reality such as the painter's and the monk's experience. Reason alone was now a defective compass for him. He had written *The Trail of the Dinosaur, The Sleepwalker,* and *The Act of Creation.* He was after some "oceanic" feeling, "the sense of participation in the mystery of the infinite."[18] Embracing Alpbach and the surrounding mountains was one practical way of attaining that mystery. Koestler was going native. He kept an exasperated George Mikes waiting in the village for two whole days because he had to attend a local christening with its snowballing revelries. This was a deliberate snub to the city ways and narrow, jocular pragmatism Mikes represented. Poor George Mikes, believing himself to be a close friend, did not realise that he was at the receiving end of an ideological statement. I sympathised with this side of Koestler's changing persona more than with any other.

After a great deal of procrastination, Koestler and I set out to discuss *Darkness at Noon* but covered much wider ground. Cynthia, Koestler's young secretary (as she then was), was on hand to help the proceedings and entertain my wife. Koestler and I spent the day locked in his study with the Alpbach valley stretching out before us on one side of his house, and a mountain slope covered in a tapestry of wildflowers on the other. All was calm and silent—only Koestler was agitated. He offered me some Librium™, as though swallowing tranquillisers were the natural prelude to conversation, and took some himself. Like most good actors, he was struggling with stage fright.

I will not go over the results of our colloquy again, for they appeared in "A Conversation," in *Talking to Eastern Europe*. But bits of our incidental conversations then and in later years may offer the student of Arthur Koestler's work clues to his thinking.

I was surprised by Koestler's emotional identification with Hungary. Only his very early roots had been there. He had spent most of his life in Austria, Germany, France, and England—a cosmopolitan to the tips of his fingers. He spoke Hungarian imperfectly and with a foreign accent, but he was eager to speak it when given half an opportunity. He tried it on me too. He was devoted as a youth to Endre Ady—a difficult turn-of-the-century poet—and later to Attila József, some of whose poems he had translated into English.[19] His deracination worried him. "Though I had the good fortune to be brought up bilingually and to leave Hungary as a child, I have paid the penalty which the loss of one's cultural roots entails," he wrote in *The Invisible Writing*.[20] I heard from Cynthia that on one occasion, under Rákosi, when Hungary was still sealed off by the Iron Curtain, Koestler drove her to the Austro-Hungarian border near the Neusiedler See and took rooms in a Hungarian-style inn virtually on the frontier. "Over there," he said to her, "is my native land," and tears welled up in his eyes.

Koestler's sentimental attachment seemed curious. His family had left Hungary when he was eleven or twelve (returning, though, from time to time for long periods up to 1919), and we learn from Mamaine, his second wife, that Koestler's Austrian mother would not allow him to mix with Hungarian playmates because they were not "well brought up enough."[21] Koestler himself tells us that she "never ceased to regard the Magyars as a nation of barbarians" and never took the trouble to learn their language properly. "I was an only child and a lonely child."[22] Koestler deeply resented his mother, and probably for that reason.[23]

In 1956, too, at the time of the suppression of the Hungarian Revolution, Koestler's emotions got the better of him. At a protest meeting I attended in Red Lion Square in London, Koestler was on the podium as one of a mixed panel of English and Hungarian speakers. But when his turn came, I saw him swallowing heavily, suppressing his tears, seemingly incapable of uttering a word. "Koestler, Koestler," many in the audience chanted in rhythm, but Koestler remained silent. On the night of October 23, 1956, he is said to have thrown bricks through the windows of the Hungarian Embassy.[24]

I could never quite suppress my suspicion that—despite his early Zionism and support of the Jewish state—Koestler was looking, for unspoken reasons of his own, for some ancient link connecting Jews and Hungarians. Later on, when his book *The Thirteenth Tribe: The Khazar Empire and Its Heritage*, appeared, I saw my suspicion confirmed. But already in the 1960s I could detect in his table talk a tacit belief that the intellectual brilliance and international influence of Hungarians and Jews, and especially of Hungarian Jews or Jewish Hungarians, was due to some unexplained but clearly ancient affinity between the two peoples. The theory propounded in his book—that the Judaising Khazars and the Hungarian tribes of the ninth century underwent a merger—corroborated my feeling. "It looks as if the Magyars had received—metaphorically and perhaps literally—a blood transfusion from the Khazars," he wrote. "There may have been one or more tribal chieftains among [the Magyars] who practised a Judaism of sorts—we remember the Byzantine chronicler, John Cinnamus, mentioning Jewish troops fighting in the Hungarian army."[25]

Koestler went to great lengths to prove the connection, but if my reading is correct, the psychological drive to do so was simple: he admired the inspiration he thought he had received from the Hungarian environment into which he had been born yet could not quite disavow his Jewish descent, try though he did. Instead, he tried to put flesh on the bones of an earlier (and apparently unproven) hypothesis that the bulk of European Jewry was not of Semitic but of Hunnish and Turanian origins and that today's Hungarians in particular were of a mixed Khazar-Magyar race. I never put it to Koestler in so many words, but his frequently mocking reference to the "chosen race"—which according to his mood meant either the Magyars or the Jews—betrayed his desire to see the two as a single phenomenon of which he, Koestler, was by implication a late offspring. His book struck me as an attempt to detach himself from the Semitic association.[26]

When John Strachey and his wife, Celia, visited us in Munich in March 1963 to launch his series *The Challenge of Democracy* in our Third Programme Radio University broadcasts,[27] Koestler's name was never far from our lips. I told Strachey about my talks with Koestler, but Strachey's own had been much more intense and telling. He had been Koestler's commanding officer during World War II at an RAF fighter station and remained a close friend up to Strachey's untimely death in July 1963. "One day a pilot opened the door of the Mess and said, with disinterest, 'Someone to see the Adjutant.' There entered the rumpled, battle-dressed figure of Private Koestler of the Pioneer Corps, surely one of the oddest men ever to dig a British latrine."[28]

My wife and I gave the Stracheys a tour of Bavaria. On a late winter's day, in glorious sunshine, we lunched in the hills overlooking the Tegernsee. Strachey was greatly impressed by the wealth and orderliness of Germany. For me it was gratifying to have a man of Strachey's stature and background at the birth of my Radio University enterprise. Strachey had held down three ministerial appointments in postwar Labour governments and was being groomed for high office in the next. Even his scepticism about European unification was forgiveable.[29] The precision and lucidity of Strachey's thought were as striking as his readiness to re-examine and reject his left socialist past. I could have found no one more qualified to talk to members of the apparat in Eastern and Central Europe. Now that we had a common friend in Koestler and that Strachey was aware of my own Hungarian background, he enlarged on a theme that was clearly close to his heart: the central importance of Hungarians to the world of the intellect.

"Koestler was a member of that unpardonably brilliant Hungarian emigration which has peopled the universities, the publishing houses, the laboratories, and the authors' societies of the West. Why this particular little country should have become, as it were, radioactive and have thrown off these stimulating, if irritant, human particles is unknown. But it did so. For what Europe as a whole is to the world, namely something small, intelligent, aggravating, and indispensable, Central Europe is to Europe. In turn, what Central Europe is to Europe, Hungary is to Central Europe: and finally, perhaps, what Hungary is to Central Europe, Arthur Koestler is to Hungary."[30]

These fine words were, of course, not meant to be taken seriously, but even as a well-meaning hyperbole they were wide of the mark. In

the 1940s, the 1950s, and the early 1960s, Koestler certainly had intellectual chic among wavering socialists and liberals in the West, but in
Hungary he was almost unknown, and when details of his books began
to pierce the Curtain via radio, the public response was small. The
whole notion of idealistic communism struck no chord among Hungarians because they had virtually no experience of idealistic communists. They accepted, if they had to, the practical necessity of serving
a régime imposed on them by the power of the Red Army, and under
János Kádár they even found reasons for believing that their compliance did not imply the betrayal of their nation. But very few identified with the kind of restless intellectual idealism that had made
Koestler into a communist, and hence very few were interested in finding out how this idealistic guardian of the faith had fallen into apostasy.
Koestler's problems were not those of the Hungarian intelligentsia,
not even the communist intelligentsia. What did matter, and mattered
greatly throughout the East, was the spectacle of important communists and left socialists such as Koestler, Silone, and Strachey breaking
ranks and lifting the veil off the mendacity, failures, and malpractices
of communist regimes. Only a few were seized by the desire to tangle
with theological polemics. Those few, however, were important to the
extent that they occupied key positions in the state and party hierarchies.

It so happened that the transcripts of my discussion with Koestler
were garbled; I drove to Alpbach again to clear up some points and
add others. I took my son Andrew with me to let him catch a glimpse
of the great man. We met for lunch at the Hotel Post. I found Arthur
in his cups.

"Why," he was waving a cable in my face, "look at this, George, my
life's ambition is being fulfilled—an invitation to take up a professor-
ship of neuropsychology at Stanford in California! We are celebrating." And Koestler went on to explain that he regarded his long feud
with communism as no more than a diversion from his real purpose
in life—to try to delve under the surface of human behaviour and see
how man's flawed moral sense could be made to match his technological and scientific achievements. I tried to argue, without the slightest
hope of success, that his name would be always associated with his
great books about communism, whatever the brilliance of his other
works might be. But Koestler would not have that. The wrangle with
communism—well, that was old hat. He had other and more important things to do. Holding down a chair at a famous university in

his original profession, psychology—now *that*, he said, was achieving something—*that* was getting at the basic *Problematik* of man.

"Incidentally," I said to him, "if psychology is your forte, why is it that well-known people trying to make an appointment with you have such difficulty seeing you, while unknown writers, even students, find you quite accessible?"

"Very simple," he said, "an established man will not go away feeling that he is inadequate because I refused to see him, but a young man might. My refusal might prejudice his self-confidence, his self-respect, and his future. I would not want to have that on my conscience. I have open doors for the young and anyone still struggling."

This, too, was Arthur Koestler, a man more often seen in the company of friends such as Camus, Crossman, Sartre, the Rothschilds, and von Neumann than with the poor and humble.

One of the perplexing features of my acquaintance with Koestler was the impersonal and almost deliberately detached respect in which I saw Cynthia holding him, outwardly at least. She was his secretary, companion, and finally wife, and there was no doubt that a deep bond of love existed between them, but in whichever set of roles I happened to see them, the courteous formality predominated. Of course, their togetherness was a state to which Cynthia had long aspired, and there was a large age difference. Nevertheless, even to me she would say over the telephone: "'Mr. Koestler' will be with you in a minute," and she only very occasionally called him Arthur in my presence. Perhaps this was her way of indicating to the world that work and personal life could be kept apart; perhaps it was just another way of demonstrating her devotion.

We do not know what passed between Arthur and Cynthia Koestler on the night of their suicide (March 2–3, 1983). It is clear from the note Koestler left behind that he expected Cynthia to survive him;[31] yet she took her own young life when he took his, using the means he did. Koestler's universe must have struck her as the only one worth inhabiting, and it *was* a universe worth inhabiting. But was it worth dying for?

The words that must have been spoken between the author of Gletkin's remorseless reasoning and Cynthia, his wife and disciple, have been exercising my imagination since the day of their suicide. Was Koestler's a calm departure befitting a philosopher who has been preparing himself for death all his life, such as Plato describes in *Phaedo*? Was Cynthia's? Did the irreversibility of it all cause him, or her, to hesitate in the final hours? Did Koestler know that his wife was going to join him? Did an oceanic feeling of submission to a higher reality irrupt before consciousness was lost, as Koestler so fervently desired? We do not know. Here lie elements for an existentialist postscript to one of the strangest and most fruitful lives in intellectual history.

MARGARET THATCHER

My relationship with Margaret Thatcher was of a very different kind; in *Diplomacy and Disillusion* I describe it at length. But Margaret Thatcher as a comrade in arms in the Cold War merits a vignette in her own right. She gave my attitude towards the Soviet system an exhilaratingly fresh focus, and in a small way I may have added something to hers.

Margaret Thatcher's education in foreign affairs had been modest. Her degrees in chemistry and law and her long preoccupation with domestic politics had not prepared her for dealing with foreigners or understanding foreign cultures. Least of all had she been educated to think of ideology as a motivating force for foreign policy. As a patriot and an avowed nationalist, she had an instinctive feel for what might hurt British power, prestige, and economic influence, and within those limits she did have a visceral appreciation of why a Soviet superpower with nuclear arms was a threat to Britain and the Atlantic alliance. But unlike Ronald Reagan, who wanted to know little more, she was keen to become a hands-on manager in foreign affairs, too, and to understand what precisely constituted the broad intellectual challenge to liberal democracy. For that, she needed assistance. Whether in government or out of office, she was never too proud to ask for it.

Early in her first term, I was one of those East European–Soviet "experts" she consulted; and later on, over a period of thirteen years, she sent for me from time to time for advice and speech-writing assistance. Her distrust of the British Foreign Office was profound. She hated the jargon and circumlocutions of British diplomats. Of the numerous invertebrates in British public service, these she rated lowest—and this although she was loyally served by two able Foreign Office assistants, (Sir) John Coles and later (Sir) Charles Powell—the latter of more lasting fame as her (in my view) misguided backseat driver on German policy in the late 1980s.

Margaret Thatcher thoroughly enjoyed arguing, even crossing swords, with her private advisers. In our company she could test her ideas without fear of losing face and indulge her taste for informality and a good fight. Unlike members of the government or mandarins of the civil service, we were wholly independent, receiving no pay, owing her nothing, and expecting nothing from her. There were, of course, compensations; for me, being regularly in touch with so resolute and intellectually demanding a person in high office was reward enough. I cherished the freedom to put my views to her in support of causes I deeply believed in, and in a way that turned out to have some practical effect. Working with and for the lady was a labour of love, but that was good enough for me.

I was, to be sure, no card-carrying Thatcherite, nor even a member of the Conservative Party—or any other. My dedication to Margaret Thatcher (for that is what it began with) had two pragmatic sources: first, my fear that without more informed policies and greater resolve, we might gradually succumb, as we had begun to under détente in the 1970s, to an aggressive Soviet imperialism; and second, my recognition of the need to instil ambition, discipline, and grit into underperforming and backward-looking Britain, gripped as it was by an enervating complacency. How the British malaise might be cured, however, gave me few sleepless nights. I had a suspicion that in the short or medium term, it just could not; but I also believed that if anyone could administer the bitter medicine, it was Margaret Thatcher.

Although in addition to being an occasional adviser on foreign policy I was also a longtime member of the board of directors of Margaret Thatcher's own domestically oriented think tank, the Centre for Policy Studies, I seldom meddled in the domestic debate. I was, of course, strongly supportive of Margaret Thatcher's two great achievements: the demolition of the power of the unions and the privatisation of certain (though not all) publicly owned, loss-making industries, provided privatisation were carried out in a competitive environment. At the same time, however, I was critical of her failure, despite valiant efforts, to reform the inequitable English legal system, which denied large swathes of the population proper access to justice, and her failure to rescue the young from the curse of a peculiarly English, self-perpetuating kind of ignorance and undereducation. But that was as far as my concern with Thatcherism on the home front went.

About defeating the Soviet system, however, I felt passionately. So did the prime minister; and it was almost exclusively in the context of how best to fight the Cold War that she enlisted my ideas and I was able to assist her. It was an intermittent but incandescent and stimulating cooperation. Her impatience and single-mindedness thoroughly agreed with my own temperament. She was a perfectionist; so, to the discomfort of those within my personal environment, was I.

We shared the view that our great contest with the Soviet Union was not just about power and security but about conflicting conceptions of the state and the individual in human affairs. For all their egregious shortcomings, the Western democracies were sustaining freedom of choice, the worth of the individual, the dignity of labour, the openness of history, and other philosophical values of a humanistic or Christian inspiration at the centre of their activities. These aims could not always be easily fitted into the agenda of pragmatic political parties or made accessible to the minds of myopic electorates, and in Western Europe at least it was also unfashionable to attempt to do so. They were nevertheless the true marks of open, as distinct from closed, societies, and we had to say so again and again. No "moral equivalence" existed between the killing fields of communist tyrants and the prejudicial treatment of North African Muslims in France, as the Marxists were implying. With all our vast imperfections, the choice was clearcut and had to be shown to be clear-cut in the frosty debates of the Cold War. Such were, in brief, some of the ideas that informed my co-operation with the British prime minister.

The Soviet definitions of *détente* and *peaceful coexistence* were special grist to our mill—they had been grist to mine for a long time. Margaret Thatcher agreed with the Soviet leaders that a shooting war had to be ruled out, but she also agreed, with enthusiasm, that in the field of verbal warfare, in the international contest of ideas, no holds were barred. We had truth on our side, the better case, the better arguments—why did we not take the offensive? And she did take the offensive, though not without reaping criticism and abuse at home, and at times even within her own party. I did my bit to endorse and embroider on her pleasing belligerence. Margaret Thatcher's Winston Churchill Award speech in Washington in September 1983, for example, bore Hugh Thomas's[32] and my own fingerprints. By the still prevailing standards of détente, it was a tough statement.

At home, the speech was greeted by a chorus of approval—and howls of indignation. Was Margaret Thatcher trying to provoke our powerful neighbour, with whom we had to live in peace or face nuclear extinction? Michael Foot accused her of "throwing faggots onto the flames";[33] and a *Guardian* editorial observed: "It is not simply that the Iron Lady is unflinching in the fray: she seems almost to glory in its challenges. There is not just Churchill in her rhetoric: there is Harry before Agincourt, even Richard the Lionheart. . . . But . . . once you begin to talk about your antagonist in the language of the third crusade, it becomes difficult ever to escape from it."[34] Even Enoch Powell of the far Right weighed in, interestingly enough, in the pages of the *Guardian*, with the argument that the American view of a hostile and expansionist USSR was "self-serving and all wrong." That the prime minister should have gone along with it "challenges, if it does not defeat, comprehension."[35] Such was the mood in Britain among Margaret Thatcher's most influential friends and critics alike. But in public opinion she was riding high and seemed indestructible.

Towards the end of the Cold War, however, Margaret Thatcher began to lose her bearings in foreign affairs and was doing no better at home. She had developed a proprietary interest in the political survival of Mikhail Gorbachev and was attempting, without success, to slow down the disintegration of the Soviet Union. Gorbachev, she claimed with a touch of arrogance, had been her discovery. She had "spotted" him among the leadership aspirants in Moscow. It was she who had coined the phrase "We can do business with him." As long as he was at the helm, we could, she thought, be assured of orderly reform. And that was all she really wanted. She had no sympathy for Ukrainian independence or the rapid restoration of the sovereignty of the Baltic nations, even though Britain had never recognised their incorporation into the USSR. Should Texas be independent? Why, then, Armenia? When in 1990 I described to her in hopeful terms the growing insubordination of certain military commands in Ukraine and Moldova, she was appalled. No, no—she said—the collapse of the Soviet state would destroy the balance between NATO and the Warsaw Pact and usher in chaos. Worse, it might bring about the reunification of Germany. At once, the old enemy-image began to surface in her thinking as though time had stood still since 1945.

Margaret Thatcher's Euro-complex and Germanophobia distressed me. Her fear of Germany and her distrust of the German people were but the latter-day signs of a long-running Anglo-German psychodrama, which people outside the British Isles have always found hard to understand. Ogre images of Germany—and of much of Europe for that matter—proliferated in the prime minister's mind. She distrusted Chancellor Helmut Kohl because he was a "plodding" Teuton, and rich to boot; Jacques Delors because he was a French socialist centraliser, "throwing his weight around" from Brussels; Presidents Valéry Giscard d'Estaing and François Mitterrand because they were failing to "stand up" to the Germans. Smaller fry on the Continent fared no better.

Her experiences during the war, when she was a teenager living near an airbase of the RAF bomber command, with its nightly casualties, were carefully nursed in her memory. The Germans were people who killed British airmen; the Germans were the people who had bombed Grantham—such, under the diplomatic surface, were the psychological springs of Margaret Thatcher's European policy in the 1980s. That the British people, unlike the French or the Dutch, had no personal "German experience" at the day-to-day level because they had escaped occupation added a dimension of fantasy to their, and especially to some of their leaders', judgement of what Germany and the Germans were about as a civil society at the end of our century. I found this sad beyond words and frightening for the future of Europe.

Of the German Federal Republic's forty-five-year-old educational and cultural record, of German life, letters, music, painting, jurisdiction, and social policy, Margaret Thatcher knew little. Those scraps of selected knowledge that pass for information in the minds of older members of the British middle class (those under fifty know better), and from which their stereotypes of foreign nations are drawn, luxuriated in her imagination. In a private citizen, such prejudices would have been amusing. In a prime minister, they were a menace to the national interest. In the summer of 1990, under great pressure, she dismissed Nicholas Ridley, a close friend and a minister in her government, for publicly holding them, but her own prejudices remained unchanged. Within a few months, they caused her fall.

By the time Margaret Thatcher called her March 1990 Chequers seminar on Germany, her aversion to German unification had become a policy—and her general suspicion of how Germany might behave if Soviet power collapsed, very outspoken. Our seminar group did its best, during a long day's discussions, to correct Margaret Thatcher's misperceptions, but I cannot say we succeeded. A few days after our meeting, Lord Dacre wrote to me: "As for Mrs. T. . . . , I think that, having heard us all, she will be of the same opinion still."

Meanwhile, the prime minister was trying to stop, and then to slow down, the momentum of reunification, appealing for support to both Gorbachev and Mitterrand. After some hesitation, however, neither was prepared to return to the kind of balance-of-power politics that had cost the world so dear but that Margaret Thatcher still favoured.

Suddenly, she found herself out of phase not only with the Russians but also and most emphatically with the U.S. administration. To her dismay, in October 1990, Germany was reunified on Western terms, but with Britain watching from the sidelines. "If there is one instance on which a foreign policy I pursued met with unambiguous failure, it was my policy on German reunification," she ruefully admits in her memoirs.[36]

Looking at the Thatcher phenomenon from a larger perspective, we are struck by a disjunction between Margaret Thatcher's own character and the British "national character" as usually identified by the world in the late twentieth century. Margaret Thatcher was in the tradition of those eighteenth- and nineteenth-century British pioneers who invented engines, built bridges, and expanded the empire. Yet, in 1979 she was elected (on a minority vote, to be sure) by a nation of underachievers—a population uncomfortable with the notion of competition, hard work, discipline, punctiliousness, and independence from an all-providing welfare state. In almost any other country—certainly in Japan, the new Far Eastern states, Germany, even the United States—she would have released more robust responses in the population than she did in her own. When the novelty of Thatcherism wore off and the costs had to be counted, her ambition to propel Britain into a state of modernity and self-reliance began to founder on the same obstacles of short-termism, national complacency, undereducation, and plain indolence that had undermined Britain's status in the world throughout the twentieth century.

Margaret Thatcher's good fortune was her gender. It enabled her to last better and gave her message greater splendour than any male counterpart in No. 10 Downing Street could have hoped to achieve. Her tragedy was that the country which history dealt her to lead had grown very different from the one that so powerfully retained its hold on her imagination. A disciplinarian and Prussian at heart, she became a misfit in her own land.

But greater than her own was the tragedy of Britain as a medium-size power under her leadership. Dean Acheson's famous warning at West Point Military Academy on December 5, 1962—"Great Britain has lost an empire and has not yet found a role—that is, a role apart from Europe, a role based on a 'special relationship' with the United States, a role based on being the head of a 'commonwealth' which has no political structure, or unity, or strength and enjoys a fragile and precarious economic relationship by means of the sterling area and preferences in the British market—this role is about played out"—lost none of its relevance in 1979, when Margaret Thatcher was elected to power, or 1990, when she was ejected from it. In the intervening eleven years she did nothing to strengthen Britain's standing in the European Community as a constructive and bona fide member—indeed she did everything to weaken it, to alienate her partners, and to implant the idea in the minds of the British people that European unification was solely about an enlarged market and increasing prosperity. Beyond the market she could not see and did not want her countrymen and countrywomen to see, even though the "special relationship" with America was defunct, the commonwealth all but meaningless, and the sterling area dead. Britain as a storehouse of fresh ideas in world affairs remained as empty under her rule as it had been since the demise of the empire.

Building a powerful European Union with a distinct voice would have been a task commensurate with Margaret Thatcher's resolve and her high opinion of herself. She commanded enough respect at home and abroad during much of her time in office to make British membership a success, and to secure for herself a place in the British and perhaps the European pantheon. Some of her advisers attempted repeatedly to bring this home to her; but the tyranny of the past proved too strong. She was a prisoner of history. "Don't forget: Britain *won* the war," she would exclaim; "de Gaulle was right in 1963 to judge us to be wholly unlike the Continental nations." British mythology was by now playing havoc with Margaret Thatcher's judgement and was to have a similarly dire influence on her political children—the Europhobic, anti-German Conservative far Right of the 1990s.

In her third term, and in her afterlife as a media star, Margaret Thatcher revealed herself as a balance-of-power politician of the old school—narrow-gauged, petulant, xenophobic, and with the exception of her stand on Bosnia, lacking in any larger vision beyond the promotion abroad of Thatcherism. At the end of the millennium, after eighteen years of Conservative rule of which hers embraced eleven, Britain's "role" in the world is no more clearly conceived than it was in 1962, when Dean Acheson uttered his ungraciously received warning.

CHAPTER FOURTEEN

1956 Reconsidered

Having looked at the strengths and achievements of surrogate broadcasting, I will proceed to put a specimen of its weaknesses under the microscope—the record of Radio Free Europe broadcasting during the period of the Hungarian uprising of October–November 1956.

My own participation in the Western broadcasting effort in 1956 was modest. It took the form (as the reader will be aware) of holding down a junior post in the European Service of the BBC at Bush House, in London, but I was also closely observing the work of Radio Free Europe. I had paid a couple of visits to the station, and soon after the Radio's inauguration in 1951, I had been asked to share with the Radio's management my impressions of the political acumen and intellectual quality of the transmissions. My occasional stints as a private monitor, as well as my personal interest in what line the new station was taking, turned me into a regular listener. Running comparisons with our broadcasts from the BBC were of considerable assistance in my own work.

My monitoring credentials included time spent on the BBC's behalf at an American-protected refugee camp in Wels, Austria, with the express purpose of testing on the spot how freshly arrived defectors reacted to transmissions in their native languages from the BBC. The Soviet bloc was sealed off, and it was impossible to conduct audience research inside our target countries. My limited effort was a partial substitute. Upon my return to London I passed on my impressions at a BBC staff conference. One of my conclusions was that only highly educated members of our audience could tell one Western radio station from another. In the minds of average listeners, all Western broadcasting existed as one big blur, usually referred to as "the radios," the

"Western stations," or the "voices." For the BBC, this was unwelcome news, but it was accepted with good grace on the unspoken premise that the BBC had never seen it as its task to influence the lower reaches of humanity. Those were élitist times, and the BBC was an élitist institution.

The best-known and most frequently criticised item in the record of surrogate public diplomacy is Radio Free Europe's alleged failure to deal responsibly with the 1956 Hungarian Revolution. Radio Free Europe, it has been said, incited the Hungarian people to rise and then encouraged them to resist the Soviet attempt to put the uprising down. Worse, the Radio did so while holding out promises of Western armed assistance.

As a BBC man, I wrote about these accusations in *The Nineteen Days* in 1957, in the immediate aftermath of the revolution.[1] Most of the judgements I made in that investigation have, I believe, stood the test of time, but certain aspects of the story now need retelling in the light of evidence that has become available since the fall of the Soviet system.

Let me say by way of a prefatory summary: between October 24 and November 4, 1956, the Radio did indeed broadcast materials with the clear purpose of endorsing the Hungarian insurgents' political will to free themselves from the communist system and Soviet tutelage. In retrospect, these broadcasts were clear acts of incitement, by the peaceable standards of Western liberal democracy. But there is no evidence to support the accusation that Radio Free Europe had anything to do with *causing* the revolution to break out on October 23, 1956. Indeed, immediately after the violent upheavals in Poznan, the Radio warned Hungarians (June 28–29) to keep "calm" and remain "disciplined." Nor are there grounds supporting the charge that after the second Soviet military intervention, on November 4, 1956, Radio Free Europe pledged Western military assistance.[2] No such pledge was given.

Yet the nonspecific impression has gained ground both in the West and in Hungary itself that throughout the period of the revolution and its suppression, Radio Free Europe was stoking the fires of national disaffection and must, therefore, be held responsible for the length and intensity of the fighting and the resulting casualties. What are we to make of this generalised charge?

Re-examination of the evidence shows that between October 24 and November 4, 1956, the Radio broadcast a large number of editorial comments, personal exhortations, military analyses, and excerpts taken from articles in the Western media, all of which expressed admiration for the insurgents and moral support for the uprising. After November 4, 1956, the Radio also rebroadcast the resolutions and appeals for help of the various insurgent radio stations and revolutionary councils from all parts of the country.[3] Poorly heard against the jamming, these rebroadcasts, taken together with the Radio's own comments, left the revolutionaries with the impression that the Radio identified itself unreservedly with their objectives.

But in the heat of battle, the insurgents, sensing victory, then went a step further, and assumed that behind this American-sponsored Radio's militant sympathies must lie a corresponding American resolve to translate words into action. That the Radio was a "private" organisation, deniable vis-à-vis Congress and world public opinion if the U.S. interest so required, did not cross the minds of most revolutionaries. The same idealism that had moved them to rise against overwhelming odds also made them incapable of comprehending the cool detachment of the U.S. government. They were, as they had to be, optimists to the last. Some of the Munich broadcasters themselves found it hard to grasp the brutal truth.

One of the first American staff members of Radio Free Europe (he had joined in 1951) noted in his reminiscences: "Most of us at the Radio could not believe that such statements [as the American calls for roll-back and liberation] could be made by the highest U.S. Government officials without there being a sincere policy of bringing every conceivable pressure short of outright warfare to push the Soviets out of Eastern Europe. But U.S. behaviour during the 1956 Revolution proved the cynics right."[4]

Because my partial endorsement of the claim that irresponsibility and lack of control were rife in 1956 in the Radio's political management is a serious one, I owe it to the reader to provide the evidence. That, in turn, demands a note about my sources.

For the best part of four decades, historians as well as Radio Free Europe's own staff had been looking for the oral and written record of the Radio's 1956 Hungarian-language broadcasts—but nothing could be found. Both the original typescripts and the tape-recorded sound-evidence were said to have been destroyed, and it was widely assumed that the destruction had been ordered by the American security authorities, to forestall embarrassment.

Approaches made by historians to the German Bundesarchiv (federal archive) in Koblenz were fruitless. In 1956–57 the Adenauer government ordered an enquiry to establish whether the Radio had, as was widely believed, incited the Hungarians to rise against their rulers —but on January 25, 1957, Chancellor Konrad Adenauer himself returned a "not guilty" verdict. I assumed that eventually the materials on which the German investigation had been based must have been passed on to the Bundesarchiv for safe keeping; but repeatedly, representatives of the Bundesarchiv denied any knowledge of them. Requests addressed to American sources proved equally futile.

After the collapse of the Soviet system I decided to rake through the field once again. On August 27, 1993, William Raedemakers, the Radio Free Europe policy adviser's assistant for Hungarian affairs (as well as a broadcaster in his own right) told me that by the end of November 1956 he himself had been unable to retrieve the tapes of his own comments, because all recorded evidence of what had been transmitted during the critical weeks had been destroyed. Raedemakers, with his background in American security, was the most authentic witness I had yet encountered. The Radio's archivist, who had apparently seen (or overseen) the destruction, was a friend of his, whose testimony he trusted. I had no reason to doubt Raedemakers's account.

Yet in Budapest, after a long trawl, I managed in October 1993, with the cooperation of Géza Jeszenszky, then Hungarian foreign minister, and Magdaléna Cséve, head of the Hungarian (Budapest) Radio's sound archives, to retrieve several hours of Radio Free Europe's Hungarian-language broadcasts. These were materials which had been monitored by the communist authorities in 1956 for their senior officials in Budapest, Prague, and Bucharest and then deposited in the archives of Radio Budapest. I chose the Budapest venue on the assumption that even if no record had survived in Western Europe or the United States, there was a reasonable chance that the Radio Free Europe transmissions monitored by the communist authorities for their own information would turn up in postcommunist Hungary. And so they did.

With this small treasure in hand I then proceeded to go through Radio Free Europe's own files in Munich. Here, too, I had been assured by all and sundry (including the Radio's senior officers) that thoroughgoing searches had failed to unearth either typescripts or tapes from the 1956 period. All the greater, then, was my astonishment when on the very first day of my work in Munich I came upon a fine hoard of typescripts in the Radio's archives, neatly stored in file boxes, clearly labelled, and possibly unread. How they had escaped destruction and then the eyes of earlier researchers puzzled me. I came away with photocopies of the entire—though I believe still incomplete—collection.

But an even greater surprise was in store for me. In the summer of 1995, György Vámos, the new head of the recorded sound archives of Hungarian Radio, stumbled (as he claims) upon the entire sound record of Radio Free Europe's 1956 Hungarian-language broadcasts, in one of the apparently unvisited backrooms of the German Bundesarchiv.[5] He secured release of the holdings, and Hungarian Radio began to grant historians, journalists, and, ironically, Radio Free Europe itself limited access to it. I was one of the early beneficiaries. Had I anticipated this fortunate outcome, I could have saved myself a great deal of work and expense.

Why Bundesarchiv officials agreed to release these tape recordings to Hungarian Radio, after having denied access for more than four decades to bona fide historians and Radio Free Europe itself, must remain a matter of conjecture. That officials of the archive had no knowledge of their holdings seems improbable. They may have decided against releasing the tapes to Radio Free Europe alone on the reasoning that given the damaging character of some of the recordings, Radio Free Europe might withhold them from the general public for a second time, even though the Cold War was over. Hungarian (Budapest) Radio was much less likely to be economical with exposure. And indeed, beginning in the fall of 1995 under the socialist-led coalition government of Gyula Horn, long extracts from these 1956 transmissions were rebroadcast to the Hungarian public to mark the anniversary of various phases of the revolution—without any "we told you so" emphasis. But in the volatile climate of Central European politics it would be a bold man indeed who predicted that these broadcasts would not one day become a political football in as yet unforeseeable circumstances.

What exactly did Radio Free Europe tell its Hungarian audiences in those critical days?

Appeals on October 24, 1956

Soldiers, policemen! Don't fire on the people who are fighting for their freedom! He who raises his weapon against the demonstrators is a murderer! Think how you'll have to answer for your actions!—
UNIDENTIFIED FEMALE VOICE

Members of the armed forces and party functionaries! Your place is on the side of the people! He who turns against his people in this struggle between the people and the regime, is a traitor of his nation! [*hazaáruló*]—UNIDENTIFIED FEMALE VOICE

The fight for freedom is being waged by the whole people! Anyone siding with the oppressors in this battle turns himself against the people!—UNIDENTIFIED FEMALE VOICE

The East Berlin German police and the Polish police in Poznan did not fire on the people! He who turns his weapon on Hungarians will be brought to punishment! [*megbűnhődik*]—UNIDENTIFIED FEMALE VOICE

Gerő is again First Secretary of the Party! It was Gerő who ordered [the police] to fire on the people! Gerő must perish! [*pusztulnia kell*]— UNIDENTIFIED MALE VOICE

Members of the courts-martial! Imposing sentences of death is unwarranted and unlawful! You will have to answer for them! The final verdict will be spoken by the people!—VOICE OF IMRE MIKES

It was Ernő Gerő who ordered the armed forces onto the streets! Ernő Gerő has fled to the protection of Soviet tanks! Ernő Gerő is the enemy of the people! [*a nép ellensége*]—VOICE OF IMRE MIKES

The party leadership has turned to the workers, urging them to help in the suppression of the fight for freedom. Workers! Your responsibility is enormous! The freedom fighters are battling for your freedom too! The interests, the past, and the future of the working class demand your solidarity!—UNIDENTIFIED MALE VOICE

(These appeals were broadcast fifty-seven times during the day.)
From the Radio's comments:

There will be no peace, no calm, and no public order until the Stalinist criminals are duly punished. The Hungarian people will not give up until the Stalinists have been brought to account. The youth of Hungary, the Hungarian workers, the peasants, and the intelligentsia demand the immediate indictment and removal of all Stalinists.— "JANUS" (IMRE VÁMOS), OCTOBER 25, 1956

The Hungarian people have given evidence on the barricades on this blood-soaked Wednesday and blood-soaked Thursday that for them nothing is impossible. Let the Haynaus of Pest and their blood-judges and hangmen realise that not a single life will remain unavenged and that the sovereign nation will not hesitate to do the impossible should the punishment [of these men] so require.—"GALLICUS" (IMRE MIKES), OCTOBER 25, 1956

There is to be no cooperation with communists. From today on, there are to be no communists in Hungary, only murderers. There are only Muscovite leaders who have to be avoided with horror or brought to account in the name of morality and the law they have violated.— "BALÁZS BALOGH" (LÁSZLÓ BÉRY), OCTOBER 27, 1956

In the depots of the People's Army there are probably enough ammunition and fuel; there are enough spare arms and other *matériel* to enable the People's Army to fight for two or three weeks. It is fortunate that the bulk of these materials are kept in decentralised storage places in different parts of the country. The nationally inspired local organs have, therefore, two tasks facing them. First, they must do everything in their power to ensure that the Soviet and Soviet-supported communist forces do not get hold of these stores. Second, they must see to it that the troops of the nation can resupply themselves from these stores. . . . All railway lines and other means of communication that support the Soviet troop movements must be destroyed; their telecommunications must be disrupted. It was precisely the Russians who, fourteen years ago, provided us with a model for how a nationally inspired hinterland can paralyse a vast military power's ability to fight—if, that is, all the tasks I've just listed are carried out with skill and courage.—"COLONEL BELL" (JULIÁN BORSÁNYI), OCTOBER 27, 1956

He who holds the weapons holds power. We repeat, therefore, for the hundredth time and will go on repeating it a hundred times again: the victorious people should hold on to their weapons because this alone can guarantee their power.[6]—"GALLICUS" (IMRE MIKES), OCTOBER 28, 1956

Imre Nagy was bluffing when he made his pledge, and the pledge was shot to pieces by the Soviet Union within hours. . . . What sort of a man is it that can lie with so much determination and so irresponsibly in these blood-soaked, difficult times?—"BALÁZS BALOGH" (LÁSZLÓ BÉRY), OCTOBER 29, 1956

If our victorious revolution surrenders its weapons before it has attained its goal, before the nation has become master in its own house; if it abandons its blood-soaked, sacred ramparts before it has turned the sacrifices of its martyrs into the golden currency of freedom, then tyranny may have lost the war but won the peace. It will have won the slavery of the nation. . . . Hungary's fate depends on this: after your triumph, you must not throw away your victory.—"GALLICUS" (IMRE MIKES), OCTOBER 29, 1956

Hungarians! You may have been victorious, and you are now subjected to a barrage of wonderful words, promises, and assurances; but you have as yet attained little that is tangible. . . . Hang on, then, to your weapons . . . preserve the spirit of permanent revolution. We don't want you to use your weapons; we want only to make sure that your use of them [in recent days] will not prove to have been in vain; that your children's death on the barricades will not prove to have been for nothing.—"GALLICUS" (IMRE MIKES), OCTOBER 30, 1956

The revolution is in danger. . . . [The new] police forces should be controlled—neither by the "peace government" [under the rule] of the Soviet legions nor by the courts-martial but by yourselves. They should be under the control of the most reliable and toughest fighters for Hungarian freedom. See to it that this becomes a fait accompli on the whole territory of the nation with the agreement of all. It is on this that your future depends. It is up to you whether Hungarian liberty bleeds to death in their [the Soviets'] torture chambers or whether the force of the victorious people liquidates the alien despotism.—"GALLICUS" (IMRE MIKES), OCTOBER 30, 1956

The Soviet forces deployed against Hungary are not invincible. The troops available [to the Soviets] have been used up. . . . Therefore, you don't have to reckon with the whole power of the Soviet armed forces but only with those [forces] which . . . have been detailed to restore order. The Hungarian forces are superior to these. According to any cool and rational calculation, the Hungarian army can stand up to the Soviet forces and achieve victory. . . . Every weapon that is not being used now will turn against its holder. Every weapon that procrastinates will fall victim to the [Nagy] government's deceptive tactics. Procrastination means inactivity in the face of the murder of our brothers, sisters, parents, and children by Soviet soldiers and units of the AVH.— "BALÁZS BALOGH" (LÁSZLÓ BÉRY), OCTOBER 30, 1956

We cannot tell at the moment how János Kádár got himself into the company of traitors. But if he volunteered to join them, then he too deserves no mercy. All the tortures and sufferings he underwent for eight years in Rákosi's prison cannot make up for his treason.—JÓZSEF MOLNÁR, NOVEMBER 4, 1956

At least two further military commentaries, broadcast on October 28 and 30, 1956, under the pseudonym of "Colonel Bell"—pen name of the former Hungarian lieutenant colonel Julián Borsányi of the precommunist Hungarian General Staff—provided information on methods of guerrilla warfare. The wartime techniques of the Yugoslav partisans were recommended. In his correspondence with the Radio's management, Borsányi relates that the order for such comments was handed him by the director of the Radio's Hungarian Service and indirectly, as he thought, by William E. Griffith, the American policy adviser. Borsányi claims to have refused, but the commentaries, written by a more cooperative journalist using Borsányi's pen name, were put on air regardless. In Hungary, "Colonel Bell's" views were widely believed to represent American thinking; hence his advice had far-reaching consequences. I had heard one of these broadcasts myself and discussed it in *The Nineteen Days* (pp. 270–271). Borsányi recalls:

> On 28 October 1956, I received instructions from Andor Gellért, Head of the Hungarian Broadcasting Department, to write, in the framework of my military programmes and in the form of a series, guidelines for the population, and especially for the young, telling them how to fight a partisan war, how to build barricades, how to overcome armoured vehicles, etc. The activities of the Yugoslav partisans in the Second World War were to serve as my models. The suggestion for the series was said to have come from Mr Griffith, the so-called "political advisor." I turned the order down. . . . It was passed on to a colleague, and the broadcasts were then mounted under my pen-name, as programmes by "Colonel Bell," using the same announcer as was normally used to voice my programmes exclusively.[7]

Such advice and encouragement were heavily reinforced by wishful thinking on the part of the hard-pressed young fighters. They wanted to—they had to—believe that they were not alone. "The fact must be faced," I wrote in 1957, "that the most scrupulous avoidance of incitement was locally offset by a tacit assumption that as soon as Western opinion was offered on air, the West took on moral responsibility for helping or failing to help in the overthrow of a system which it was so persistent in condemning. This may be faulty logic, or it may be wishful thinking, but there can be no escaping the truth that in the psychological climate of what must be considered wartime conditions everything the free world said in its broadcasts was liable to incite or, at least, raise false hopes on a very large scale. One cannot condemn a murderer for ten years without, sooner or later, being asked to help in his arrest."[8]

But there was, as we have seen, no "scrupulous avoidance of incitement." Supposing, however, that Radio Free Europe *had* confined itself to bland observations throughout the period—the perceptions in the minds of listeners would still not have been very different. Given Radio Free Europe's mandate—and a similar mentality which informed the broadcasts of the Central European Service of the BBC—a "positional" kind of incitement was inevitable. Surrogate broadcasting from Munich and BBC broadcasting in the languages of Central and Eastern Europe from London were a form of encouragement simply because they, and the sentiments they reflected, existed. Incredibly, the risk of being misinterpreted in a revolutionary environment had not been foreseen. Sándor Márai, one of Hungary's most distinguished writers, noted in his diary immediately after the revolution: "It is not true that the radios incited to rebellion. This is a stupid and evil thing to say and is spread by the Russians. . . . But it *is* true that for many years every Western radio, every newspaper, and every statesman—everyone—has been telling us that there is [such a thing as] Western solidarity."[9]

An even more sobering testimony, by a twenty-six-year-old Hungarian, appears in James A. Michener's book *The Bridge at Andau:*

"Then you set up Radio Free Europe in 1950 and you got right down to the business of freedom. You had eleven separate stations which broadcast one thousand hours of encouragement a week from Frankfurt, Munich and Lisbon. RFE told us many times, 'Our purpose is to keep opposition to communism alive among the people of the slave states behind the iron curtain. We want to help such people gradually to make themselves strong enough to throw off the Soviet yoke.' . . .

"Next, to make your message even more clear, you began to launch balloons to fly over our country bearing leaflets and aluminum medals. I got one with a Liberty Bell on it and the legend 'Hungarians for Freedom—All the Free World for the Hungarians.'

"These balloons were very important to our psychological reactions. I remember thinking at the time, 'At last something tangible. Something more than words. If America could reach us with these aluminum medals, why couldn't they reach us with parachute supplies if a revolution started. Obviously, America intends to help us.'

"In 1952 all of your radio stations broadcast over and over the promises made in your election campaign. We were told that America was to roll back the iron curtain. You would stimulate a desire for freedom among the eight hundred million under communist domination. We were assured many times that your President would find ways to make the Russians want peace. The speeches of your leaders were quoted to us day after day . . .

"Words like 'freedom,' 'struggle for national honor,' 'roll-back,' and 'liberation' have meanings. They stand for something. Believe me when I say that you cannot tell Hungarians or Bulgarians and Poles every day for six years to love liberty and then sit back philosophically and say, 'But the Hungarians and Bulgarians and Poles mustn't do anything about liberty. They must remember that we're only using words.' Such words, to a man in chains, are not merely words. They are the weapons whereby he can break chains . . .

"If America wants to flood Eastern and Central Europe with these words, it must acknowledge ultimate responsibility for them. Otherwise you are inciting nations to commit suicide."[10]

Where Radio Free Europe's American and Hungarian editorial staffs went especially wrong was in their evaluation of the forces at work in Hungary after October 23, 1956. They misheard the voices of a country just emerging from Stalinism and misjudged the appeal of Imre Nagy and his associates. Some of the Radio's commentators, in line with the spirit of the Radio's policy handbook and of guidances received both from the New York headquarters and from William E. Griffith, the Munich policy adviser,[11] continued to attack Nagy, mostly in vitriolic language, almost up to the eve of the second Soviet intervention on November 4, 1956, by which time Nagy had renounced the Warsaw Pact, declared Hungary's neutrality, restored the multiparty system, included leading anticommunists in his government, and become a national hero:

So this was Imre Nagy's first action: bullets, the hangman's rope, persecution, Soviet troops and terror! . . . With his first act, Imre Nagy has tied himself to the political corpse of Rákosi. . . . With the courts-martial he has signed his own . . . certificate of political immorality.— EMIL CSONKA, OCTOBER 24, 1956

Imre Nagy has contributed to the deployment of Soviet troops. . . . This step can already be listed as one of the great betrayals of Hungarian history, a betrayal that will probably be notoriously remembered for centuries!—ANDOR GELLÉRT, OCTOBER 25, 1956

Soviet tanks are arriving at the behest of Imre Nagy, whose hands are steeped in Hungarian blood. You, Imre Nagy, must halt and go down on your knees as a penitent sinner before the nation. . . . If you still want to give some meaning to your misguided life, then there is only one duty left for you to perform: you must shout "Stop" to the Soviet mercenaries whom you have vilely let loose on the nation. And then: put up your hands and surrender to the overwhelming will of the nation.— MIKLÓS AYTAY, OCTOBER 26, 1956

Either Imre Nagy lives or the nation dies! [sic] Tertium non datur! There is no other alternative.—IMRE MIKES, OCTOBER 26, 1956

Can a leader command any credibility or authority who makes common cause with yesterday's gaolers against the nation in order to preserve the spoils of power? That is what Imre Nagy has done. In the midst of a decisive crisis, suddenly the old Muscovite reappeared in him. Obeying the orders of the lords of the Kremlin, he joined the side of the Stalinist Gerő so that he could help in saving the despotic rule of the Hungarian proconsuls of Soviet imperialism.

János Kádár and Imre Nagy are Moscow's agents every bit as much as were their predecessors. They, too, have been appointed as puppets by Mikoyan and Suslov.—SÁNDOR KŐRÖSI-KRIZSÁN, OCTOBER 26, 1956

Who is the illegal aggressor in Hungary? Imre Nagy, the traitor and nation-killer and his guilty government. Who is the murderer? Imre Nagy and his traitor government.—FATHER KÁROLY FÁBIÁN, OCTOBER 27, 1956

Imre Nagy has shown himself to be a foul Muscovite. He has organised a bloodbath in the country. Hands on which the blood of thousands is now drying, blood which history will never wash away—such hands cannot [be fit to] govern.—ZOLTÁN NÉMETH, OCTOBER 27, 1956

The freedom fighters . . . realise that if they take a single step backward, they will be inviting, through Imre Nagy's system, the return of the past of accursed memory.—ZOLTÁN KOVÁCS, OCTOBER 29, 1956

The people-killer Imre Nagy and the bloody-handed party leadership have not mustered the humanity and Hungarian decency to resign! . . . The blood-stained Budapest government's promise of a cease-fire was foul treason. The strike of our brother-workers is the strongest weapon against the nation-exterminating [Nagy] government.— ZOLTÁN NÉMETH, OCTOBER 30, 1956

"The Primate is free!"
     . . . but the question arises: Has this people, whose sons and daughters have attained the glory of heroes, a leader? Everything suggested some invisible, wise, and ingenious leadership, yet no one knew where it was coming from. Now here is the answer to that question: József Mindszenty! . . . Our youth . . . our people . . . were the people of Mindszenty. . . . A reborn Hungary, and the appointed leader sent by God, have met each other in these hours.—"BALÁZS BALOGH" (LÁSZLÓ BÉRY), OCTOBER 31, 1956

The Hungarian peasantry does not want Imre Nagy's system. If Imre Nagy survives the present situation, what guarantee is there that the ordeals of the past years will not revisit us?—FARMERS' PROGRAMME, NOVEMBER 1, 1956

For a publicly funded "alternative home service" to broadcast views such as these in language so provocative was a mistake, the more remarkable because the Radio's Polish Service avoided making a like misjudgement about Wladyslaw Gomulka. True, the Radio's Poles under Jan Novak (a hero of the wartime Polish Home Army) had the fate of the abortive 1944 Warsaw Uprising in mind as a tragic disincentive. They were, further, induced to support Gomulka because, through the defection of two leading communist security officials— Jozef Swiatlo and Seweryn Bialer—they were well aware of the struggle for fresh policies within the Polish Communist Party of which Gomulka was the leader. No such legacy and no such inside knowledge informed the transmissions of the Radio's Hungarian Service.

Nonetheless, the Radio's mandate was to detect and then to identify itself with the will of the nation. No matter how unsavoury and uncertain the Hungarian nation's identification with Imre Nagy might have seemed to the Radio's controllers, he was, in the circumstances, undoubtedly the symbol of reform and of an improved future, not unlike Gomulka in his confrontation with Khrushchev, Molotov, Kaganovich, and Mikoyan in Warsaw. Because the Radio's American and Hungarian policy makers failed to understand this in time, some of them picked Cardinal Mindszenty as the repository of Hungarian nationhood and the country's potential leader. But Mindszenty, barely out of detention, had no broad appeal or effective following, despite Pope Pius XII's immediate endorsement of him in an encyclical of November 1, 1956.[12] Imre Nagy continued to be berated by the Radio as a lifelong Muscovite with a shady past (true) who had changed sides only to disarm the insurgents and betray the revolution (untrue). As evidence accumulated to the contrary, and János Kádár's Soviet-sponsored countergovernment appeared on the scene on November 4, Radio Free Europe began to change course, but by then the damage had been done. An especially colourful Radio Free Europe broadcast ran:

> The happy people of the world's largest city, enjoying as they do the blessings of freedom, are paying tribute [here in New York] to Hungarian heroism and Hungary's now reconfirmed legendary love of liberty. . . . The placards I can see carry these words in English and Hungarian: "Patriots are being murdered by Russian tanks in the streets of Budapest on the orders of traitors. The Muscovites will not evade the judgement and wrath of history." Another slogan reads: "The last gasps of the Hungarian martyrs reverberate throughout the world. Their last breath is like thunder; it says: Russians go home! And perish the Muscovite leaders!" It was with these words on their lips that hundreds of our martyrs died, and I can now hear the voices of American Hungarians chanting: "Murderers, murderers, murderers!"
>
> American university students [are also present]. Governed by their trust in justice and historical responsibility, they condemn with the greatest resolve the betrayal of the [Hungarian] nation by the Budapest communist government and the irrefutable fact that Imre Nagy and his associates appealed for the help of the Red Army in order to protect their own lives, put fear into the public, and drown the national uprising in blood.

In Poland there has been no Polish Muscovite leader! In Budapest the blood of the martyrs will return to haunt Imre Nagy, Kádár, and their associates. In the American view, Imre Nagy's self-debasement [elaljasodása] and his betrayal of his Hungarian identity [magyarság-tól elfajzása] reached their climax when, in the midst of the killings by the Red Army which he had unleashed, he had the nerve to cause the [Budapest] Radio to tell the world that the Hungarian people considered the Soviet Russian murderers to be their friends and the slaughter of Hungarians an act of friendship.[13]

The suppression of Hungary was followed by a purge of the Radio's senior officials. Under one head or another, they were released, retired, or encouraged to retire from service, among them Richard Condon, the European director of Radio Free Europe; William E. Griffith, policy adviser; Andor Gellért, head of the Hungarian Service; and thirteen Hungarian members of staff. Of the latter, however, some of those most compromised (Béry, Mikes, Csonka, Borsányi, Németh, János Ölvedi) were not removed and were still active as full-time commentators ("editors") during my first stint in Munich in 1960–65.

Could their misjudgements have been avoided under the prevailing conditions? I concur with the view widely held by observers: that for the first two or three days of the revolution it was indeed extremely difficult to tell whether Imre Nagy would turn out to be a bona fide national leader or an unswerving Muscovite who might, at the appropriate moment, deliver the revolutionaries into the hands of the Soviet or Soviet-controlled Hungarian authorities. Nagy himself was hesitant and confused. On October 24, 1956, summary jurisdiction was declared over Radio Budapest in the name of Nagy as the new prime minister. The next day, October 25, he described the insurgents as provocateurs, looters, rumour-mongers, inciters, and counterrevolutionaries and insisted that it was to secure the vital interests of Hungary's "socialist order" that Soviet troops had been called to Budapest. Late that night Anastas I. Mikoyan and Mikhail A. Suslov reported to the CPSU Central Committee: "Imre Nagy urged us [earlier in the day] to increase the strength of our troops in Budapest, especially the infantry." Yet to their consternation, later in the day Nagy declared "the very opposite" in a radio broadcast, announcing his government's decision to initiate talks with the Soviet Union "with a view to the withdrawal of Soviet forces" from Hungary.[14] Eyewitness accounts report the same indecision. András Hegedüs tells us that although on the night of October 23–24 Imre Nagy had verbally agreed with other government and party leaders that Soviet troops should be called in to restore order in Budapest, he subsequently refused, as prime minister, to sign a written invitation. "The appearance of Soviet tanks promised to be a solution. We unanimously agreed. . . . Imre Nagy agreed too. . . . There he sat in an armchair, exhausted. The situation was desperate; he was not responding. He didn't say 'no.' None of us did. . . . But Imre Nagy didn't sign. He was marking time. He did not say he would not sign, but neither did he say that he would."

Eventually Hegedüs signed the predated document, "probably," as he recalls, on October 26, even though he was no longer prime minister.[15]

The speed of events, sheer confusion, the rumour mills, and cluelessness inside what was left of the Communist Party were additional invitations to anyone in the West who cared to do so to enact his pet political scenario and muster evidence to prove that Nagy was at heart more of a patriot than a communist—or the opposite. The Soviet leaders were not much wiser. On October 27, Anastas I. Mikoyan and Mikhail A. Suslov, reporting from Budapest, expressed their confidence that the new multiparty government, headed by Nagy, was "reliable and in the social sense more authoritative."[16]

But this was not how an important segment of the Soviet leadership saw Nagy and his supporters. On October 28 and again on October 30, October 31, and November 1, the Mikoyan-Suslov line, suggesting, initially, an amicable settlement and pleading for patience before a second Soviet military intervention would be considered, was strongly opposed by the old guard (Kliment E. Voroshilov, Vyacheslav M. Molotov, Lazar M. Kaganovich, Nikolai A. Bulganin, Georgy K. Zhukov, Yekaterina A. Furtseva): "The international situation has changed. If we don't take certain measures, we shall lose Hungary" (Bulganin). "I don't agree with Comrade Mikoyan's suggestion that we should support the present government. We need resolute action. Catch all the scoundrels. Disarm the counterrevolution" (Zhukov). "If we don't take determined action, things will fall apart in Czechoslovakia, too. Use military force to restore order" (Dmitry T. Shepilov). "We should call Mikoyan to the telephone and tell him: 'The Politburo of the Central Committee of the Hungarian Workers' Party should act resolutely, or else we are going to act for it. It may well be that we ourselves will appoint a government'" (Bulganin).

Khrushchev himself, appalled by the spectre of disunity in the Presidium and impressed by the noninterventionist attitude of the Chinese, limited himself to putting forward a choice of scenarios for Soviet action, coming down, however, at least on October 28, on the side of endorsing Imre Nagy and his then government. "We have much to answer for," he ruefully observed.[17] Radio Free Europe's controllers were not alone in wondering where exactly Imre Nagy stood during the first phase of the uprising, and where the Soviet leadership thought he stood.

The political atmosphere in which Radio Free Europe had been born and reared certainly militated against extending the benefit of the doubt to Muscovite communists of whatever description. Imre Nagy was widely rumoured to have been an OGPU and then an NKVD agent in the 1930s and 1940s, responsible for the liquidation of several of his close comrades—and so he had been, under the code name of Volodya.[18] It must have seemed preposterous to the Radio's management that after what at first appeared to be the victorious conclusion of the Hungarian Revolution, and after the Soviet government's declaration that it would withdraw from Budapest and possibly all of Hungary if requested to do so (October 30, 1956), power might be retained by old Leninists or passed back into their hands. The Hungarians had achieved something that had previously appeared impossible—the surrender of communist power, the neutralisation of the Red Army, and the defection of a (small) number of Soviet troops.[19] Blood had been shed—there had to be wholesale change.

This, too, was the mood of the Western public. Liberation and rollback were in the air. Eisenhower and Dulles had called for no less during the 1952 election campaign, and they maintained their rhetoric over the ensuing four years. The Western press, radio, and television were in a state of euphoria, heaping praise on the boy-revolutionaries of Budapest, applauding their triumph over Soviet tanks in the first phase of the uprising, and then eulogising their heroism when tragedy began to engulf Budapest in the second. These public reactions were hourly reported back to the Hungarians by the whole machinery of Western radio and television—not least, of course, by Radio Free Europe and the BBC. No East European event had so mobilised Western opinion since the Bolshevik coup, and few events have done so since. It would have been contrary to the whole thrust of Western public thinking to expect Radio Free Europe not to demand the end of the communist dictatorship.

No less important, the world communist movement was coming under serious pressure. The nightly spectacle on Western television screens of Hungarian workers marching against the "workers' state" and being mown down for their pains by "workers' tanks" from the Soviet Union damaged the cohesion of the Western communist parties, in many cases beyond repair. In France, Italy, Britain, Belgium, Holland, and Spain, old communists were leaving the party in protest. In this climate of Western opinion, could the Radio back the Muscovite Imre Nagy, a longtime member of Rákosi's Politburo and an accomplice in Hungary's fraudulent communist takeover in 1947–49? All broadcast reviews of the world press—from the two communist *Daily Worker*'s (in London and New York) to the Vatican's *Osservatore Romano*—sounded like ringing endorsements of the Hungarian uprising and proclaimed the apotheosis of its young fighters; there was no need for encouragement by the Central Intelligence Agency.

This mood of no compromise was compounded by the broadcasters' individual feelings of solidarity with their kith and kin in Hungary (the BBC's staff were of a very similar disposition). Distance and the inability to participate gave their enthusiasm a nineteenth-century "spring of nations" flavour. Their commentaries, extravagant and florid to Western ears, were inspired by understandable paroxysms of sentiment—fear that the small Hungarian nation would be swamped by the Soviet superstate and pride that the small nation had courage enough to take on Goliath and get the better of him after only a couple of days' fighting. Few in the Radio's American management had the heart or the willpower to quarrel with such sentiments, much less to muffle either the broadcasters' or the Hungarian nation's strangled cry after the second Soviet invasion. The Radio's mandate required that its broadcasters should think and feel with their audiences as though they were operating from "home." This was, arguably, exactly what they were doing, cautionary guidances from New York notwithstanding.

Political unpreparedness and confusion in the chain of command added to the Radio's difficulties. Its principal analysts and commentators were taken by surprise, as were all Western governments, and were as little able to form adequate judgements about—or, for some time, even to ascertain—what was happening in Hungary. Editorial control was in the hands of the almost autonomous Hungarian service, though guidances from New York and the Munich policy adviser were in circulation. American management exercised only loose and mainly retrospective control. Editorial comments were uncoordinated and often specific to the worldview of individual writers. William E. Griffith, the policy adviser, though the key figure in the Radio's formulation of policy and one privy, in my judgement, to the views of CIA and State Department officials, had no formal powers to hire and fire. William Raedemakers, his assistant for Hungarian affairs, absented himself from his desk at the height of the revolution to send despatches from Hungary to an American newspaper, with the Radio's eventual cooperation.

The Radio was young and inexperienced. After barely five years of broadcasting, its management was still testing the instruments and boundary lines of the Cold War and was simply not up to the task of responding with clarity or finesse to its first great challenge. Hungary, its baptism by fire, cost it dear.

But the Hungarian Service of Radio Free Europe could have played things differently, as its Polish Service had done a few days earlier. Had the political legacy and maudlin yet pugnacious vocabulary of Hungarian society under Miklós Horthy not formed the dominant "culture" of Radio Free Europe's Hungarian service, its commentators might have embraced more enthusiastically than they did the vast significance of the Twentieth Party Congress of the Soviet Communist Party in February 1956, and especially Khrushchev's revelations about the crimes of Stalin, news of which was circulating freely. That was the banner under which the Hungarian university students had launched their first demands for radical reforms, and which the Radio, too, could have fully adopted.

It cannot be said that the Radio paid insufficient attention, as far as general policy guidance was concerned, to this self-inflicted breach in the Soviet defences. A special guidance of March 27, 1956 ("Twentieth Congress CPSU"), made a well thought out and eloquent case for applying the idea of de-Stalinisation blocwide: "In each country, our peoples have the right to look at what is most abusive and ask, 'Is this not Stalinism? If yes, when is it to be abolished? When are we to have opposition parties? A free press? Free elections? Dissolution of collective farms? Free trade unions? More and better consumer goods? Free travel?'"[20]

But there was a reluctance among the Radio's more right-wing Hungarian commentators to make full and speedy use of the weapons thus handed them by Moscow. Some found it distasteful to employ arguments of a deeply ideological, communist provenance for the liberation of the Hungarian nation; others suspected an ambush of the kind that was to materialise in China not many months later under the rubric of "Let a hundred flowers bloom and a hundred schools of thought contend," with dire consequences for those who took the party's encouragement of intellectual freedom at face value. But, whether for reasons well founded or ill judged, the message of the Twentieth Party Congress was not exploited to the hilt in the spirit of the Radio's own guidance or indeed in the spirit of the time.

Radio management would have done well to recognise without delay the implications of Gomulka's rehabilitation and popular acceptance in Poland, and the enthusiasm with which Hungary's mushrooming student circles, schoolchildren's parliaments, dissident intellectual associations, and other "assemblies" were adopting and then beginning to apply the Polish example to Hungarian conditions, the culmination of the trend being the demand for Imre Nagy's return to power.

On the morning of October 23, only hours before the students' mass protest began in Budapest in front of the statue of the Polish general Bem, a commander in the 1848 Hungarian Revolution, the Hungarian press, including the Communist Party's official daily *Szabad Nép,* had reproduced verbatim Wladyslaw Gomulka's radical demands for de-Stalinisation and national independence.[21] The message was clear: for Warsaw, read Budapest; for Gomulka, read Nagy. The inevitably semi-communist vocabulary in which that message was cast should not have blinded the Radio's editors to its real meaning. The early humanists of the fifteenth century still couched their "dissent" in the language of the Middle Ages, for there was no other.

Earlier in October, the Radio should have made better use than it did of the loud public approval of the rehabilitation and spectacular reburial of László Rajk and his associates. Some two hundred thousand Hungarians marched past Rajk's coffin, and Imre Nagy demonstratively kissed Rajk's widow in a supreme gesture of solidarity with the executed "national" communist. The fallibility of the Leninist system was now on public display. Could its "legitimacy" survive so severe a humiliation?

Ernő Gerő, first secretary, in October 1956, of the Hungarian Workers' Party, had (as we now know from postcommunist revelations) a more precise understanding of what was in store for Hungarian Communism than either Radio Free Europe or most informed Western observers had. In a long and almost confessional conversation with Soviet Ambassador Yuri V. Andropov (October 12, 1956), Gerő repeatedly pointed to the repercussions arising from Rajk's reburial and predicted the disaster that would, in fact, engulf the Communist system only nine days later. In Andropov's words:

> Since the reinterment of the remains of Rajk [Gerő related], the oppositionists are behaving with particular insolence. They are openly demanding the return of Nagy to the Politburo and the trial of Rákosi and Farkas. . . . Comrade Gerő believes that the reburial of Rajk has gravely damaged the party leadership, whose authority was, in any case, not very high. A situation has arisen in which the Politburo is unable to have any impact on the solution of a whole series of questions. . . .
>
> At the end of our conversation, Comrade Gerő returned to the domestic political scene. It was obvious that this was both worrying and depressing him. He said he would not want to be accused of panic mongering but he must ask us, once again, to understand that the situation in the country was "very serious and getting worse." . . .
>
> I formed the impression from his words that Comrade Gerő was considerably nervous and uncertain. When asked how he and other members of the Politburo were proposing to overcome the difficulties he had outlined, Comrade Gerő said that for the time being neither he nor any of the other comrades could see a way out.[22]

Naturally, the policy makers of Radio Free Europe were not privy to these views of the country's supreme power holder. But the signs were everywhere around them. On October 13, 1956, Nagy was reinstated as a party member, and by October 23 demands for his leadership were on the programme of a large variety of dissident "socialist" assemblies, few—perhaps none—of which could be mistaken for old-fashioned communist "front" organisations. To dismiss them as, at best, the expression of arcane quarrels among communists, was to ignore their potential for undermining the system from within. Behind the esoteric arguments, voices demanding the demolition of the entire communist system and Hungary's disentanglement from the Warsaw Pact could hardly be missed.

The BBC avoided making that particular error—but it had, of course, the much easier task of having to cover Hungarian events only in fifteen- or thirty-minute bulletins. Nor was the Hungarian Department in Bush House perceived to be a surrogate Hungarian radio—even though in many ways it was. Radio Free Europe, by contrast, was on air almost around the clock. The BBC began supporting Imre Nagy on October 23, 1956, as "a natural and popular choice in Hungary for the role that Gomulka has assumed in Poland," and backed him without hesitation throughout the revolution.

London, as represented by the Central European Service of the BBC, undoubtedly acquitted itself better than the Americans and Hungarians working together at Radio Free Europe. But the success of the BBC's editorial policy was as little due to or typical of the wisdom of the British political class as the failure of Radio Free Europe was due to the unwisdom of the American. Both were predominantly the work of unofficial policy élites which proceeded with circumspection in one case, but with insufficient insight and maturity in the other.

Forty years on, in Budapest, William E. Griffith admitted as much, without clearly allowing, however, that the Radio's deficiencies were preventable, and that the responsibility for not having forestalled them was in great part his own. As linchpin of the entire organisation in Munich in the 1950s, he was in a position to forewarn, guide, dissuade, and veto, even though formally, as I say, he did not possess the powers to do so. Griffith's intellectual brilliance, of which I was an unstinting admirer from the moment he took up his position in Munich—he was an intellectual's intellectual if there has ever been one—was lacking an element of historical seriousness. His well-furnished mind, his delight in mental fireworks, and his superb recall were so much in the service of the kind of intellectual display that impresses a postgraduate seminar that he seemed to be unprepared for the grave responsibility that suddenly came to rest on his shoulders in October 1956. Only thus can we explain that even with the hindsight of four decades, Griffith maintains a scholarly detachment from the Radio's record in 1956, as though the events he describes in 1996 had been the work, not of himself, but of people and forces under no one's control.

"The Desk [Radio Free Europe's Hungarian station] was politically too right wing," Griffith stated. "Its tone before and during the revolution was . . . too emotional and too didactic. . . . [Members of the Hungarian desk] transgressed against the overriding importance of objectivity and therefore of credibility. . . . During the revolution, my post-revolution analysis revealed, there were roughly an equal number of scripts which implemented policy well and those which did not. There were a few scripts which . . . clearly implied that foreign aid, perhaps military, would be forthcoming. . . . RFE's coverage of Imre Nagy and its polemics against him were probably its major policy error during the revolution, although they were in accordance with guidance from RFE New York and Munich. . . . RFE had been set up on the basis not of pre- but of postreview of broadcasts by the American staff. In retrospect, Hungarian programs during the revolution should have had American review before broadcast, especially because the English summaries of programs discussed at morning policy meetings before broadcast often did not reflect their actual content."[23]

Such public self-criticisms deserve respect, but they would have been more impressive had they been couched in the first person singular and made in good time, during the revolution, rather than only after evidence of the Radio's 1956 Hungarian broadcasts had unexpectedly come to light.

The irony is that on December 5, 1956, Griffith did write a thoroughgoing review of what had gone wrong in the Hungarian Service under his stewardship (see Appendix C). Addressed to the director and written for internal use only, this remarkably frank, indeed self-incriminating, twenty-four-page document was not allowed to reach the public until the end of 1996 and may have been withheld from the 1956–57 American and German government investigations too.

In it, Griffith lists violation after violation of the Radio's guidelines, as well as of his own guidances and verbal advice, by individual members of the Hungarian Service, not least, as he claims, because of the poor leadership and eventual illness of Andor Gellért, head of the Hungarian Service. He produces evidence that in the period between October 23 and November 4 (less so later), Radio Free Europe's Hungarian broadcasters were apparently under no one's effective supervision and were inciting the population either to fight or not to give up fighting the communist system. Some, he tells us, gave precise instructions for how military resistance might best be organised; others held out promises of foreign aid and even Western military intervention. Throughout his memorandum, Griffith stresses the irresponsibility and unprofessionalism of the providers of such advice and expresses surprise that after five years with the Radio, its Hungarian editors should have learnt so little about "radio broadcasting and political warfare techniques."

He insists that he and his associates were given misleading assurances about the implementation of their guidances, and were generally kept in the dark about what precisely was being put on air in Hungarian. He speaks in the tones of an outside observer. Up to a late date in the uprising, he tells us, there were no prebroadcast script controls, and the digests provided before or after the transmissions were misleading or downright false. An acute shortage of translators, he claims, aggravated the crisis. Even the Radio's much misunderstood quotation from the November 4 issue of the London *Observer*, and the comments based on it, are put down to the irresponsibility of a single Hungarian broadcaster, Zoltán Thury. Griffith and his office allegedly learnt about them only after they had been transmitted (the text of this broadcast is given later in the chapter).

How did it come about that once a revolutionary crisis had begun to engulf Hungary, the Radio's policy managers did not ensure that they had precise, hour-by-hour control over what was being transmitted? It is hard to imagine a military campaign in which the commanding officer has no knowledge of what is being ordered in his name at divisional levels. Political warfare is no different even if allowance is made for the kind of special flexibility "surrogate" radio demands from its practitioners. But even if we were to accept Griffith's plea that the Radio's original structure (autonomy of the national "desks") made it difficult for the policy adviser to gain precise knowledge of what was being said in the Radio's various languages, his responsibility for the breakdown of control is nonetheless clear. It happened on his watch.

Radio Free Europe was heard worldwide. It had language correspondents and numerous stringers in all major capitals. Their feedback was available to anyone who cared to ask for it. I was myself an earwitness in London to some highly irresponsible RFE broadcasting. In *The Nineteen Days* I recorded: "The military correspondent of Radio Free Europe, for instance, volunteered information on methods of guerrilla warfare. The effect created by Radio Free Europe's short, dramatic slogans, preceded and followed by music, and often formulated in the first person plural, was liable to mislead listeners" (pp. 270–271). Throughout Germany, too, expatriate Hungarians were avidly following the Radio's broadcasts. A small ad hoc group of extramural Munich Hungarians would have provided the policy adviser with instant monitoring information had he acted on the suspicion that members of the Hungarian Service might be misinforming him. Staff at the U.S. embassy in Budapest were listening. There was, and could be, no excuse for failing to obtain full and timely knowledge of what was being said by the Radio's Hungarian commentators a few doors down the corridor. If only the will to know and the will to control had existed.

William E. Griffith was perhaps the most sophisticated policy maker in international broadcasting at the time. His associates were of comparable calibre. Several went on to occupy distinguished posts

in the U.S. government, at the universities, or in the media: Paul
Henze, Herbert Ritvo, William Raedemakers, Ralph E. Walter, Ernest
Schneider, and others. It cannot be supposed that the content, language, and tone of the Hungarian Service's broadcasts during the critical period remained unknown or only partly known to such shrewd
men until after Griffith's postrevolutionary audit on December 5, 1956.
Griffith's apologia in September 1996 is, then, entirely consistent with
the case he made in December 1956, and just as unconvincing.

It is just possible to argue that in Hungary, too, a compromise solution might have emerged in the spirit of Gomulka's Poland and the
Soviet government's declaration of October 30, had the Anglo-French
invasion of Suez on October 30 not muddied the international waters
and bestowed on the Kremlin an unexpected psychological advantage
for its attack on Hungary on November 4. But the case is a weak one.

Certainly the Anglo-French attack distracted attention from Hungary. "In Moscow the French and British are practically isolated among
the Western diplomats, the majority of whom condemn the attack on
Egypt," Veljko Mićunović reports in *Moscow Diary*. "It is not that they
have any understanding for Egypt or Nasser but that this 'stupid war'
makes it impossible for the West to make better use of events in Hungary against the Soviet Union." And it did make it easier for the Soviet
leaders to suppress the Hungarian uprising: "Khrushchev said that
British and French aggressive pressure on Egypt provided a favorable
moment for a further intervention by Soviet troops. It would help the
Russians. There would be confusion and uproar in the West and the
United Nations, but it would be less at a time when Britain, France,
and Israel were waging a war against Egypt."[24]

The Hungarians themselves, uncertain whether the arrival of fresh
Soviet forces between November 1 and 4 was a prelude to a second
Soviet attack or a move to cover the evacuation of the original Soviet
garrisons, would have agreed with Khrushchev. Hoping that it was the
second, they nevertheless expected the first. In one of the most penetrating despatches of the period, Victor Zorza wrote from Budapest
two days before the second Soviet attack:

> Against the mailed fist of Soviet military might the Hungarians can
> now put up only their indomitable spirit. The anguish in their minds
> takes them into tortuous byways of speculation which may cause pain
> to those in England who have applauded and admired from afar this

nation's courage and, as some might have said, recklessness. For many here believe, wrong as they might be, that in their hour of need England has betrayed not only her own traditions but also the conscience of mankind by choosing this moment to fish in the troubled waters of Israeli-Egyptian enmity. . . . They go farther, and speculate about the possibility of some unspoken and only dimly apprehended arrangement whereby the Russians will be left to do as they like to the Hungarians, so long as Britain is left to do as it likes in Egypt.[25]

There appears to have been no such Anglo-Soviet collusion, but the suspicion of Western betrayal was enough to make the Hungarian people accept János Kádár and his quisling group faster and with fewer reservations than might otherwise have been the case.[26]

After much hesitation and consultation with the Chinese leaders at Lipky near Moscow (October 30, 1956), Khrushchev and his team decided to crush the Hungarians through a second military intervention, regardless of Suez. Khrushchev reports:

We sat up the whole night, weighing the pros and cons of whether or not we should apply armed force to Hungary. First Liu Shao-chi said it wasn't necessary; we should get out of Hungary, he said, and let the working class build itself up and deal with the counterrevolutionaries on its own. We agreed.

But then, after reaching this agreement, we started discussing the situation again, and someone warned of the danger that the working class might take a fancy to counterrevolution. The youth in Hungary was especially susceptible.

I don't know how many times we changed our minds back and forth. . . . When I climbed into bed that morning, I found I was still too preoccupied with the whole problem to rest. It was like a nail in my head and it kept me from being able to sleep.

Later in the morning . . . I then told the Presidium what the consequences might be if we didn't lend a helping hand to the Hungarian working class before the counterrevolutionary elements closed ranks. After long deliberation, the Presidium decided that it would be unforgivable, simply unforgivable, if we stood by and refused to assist the Hungarian comrades.[27]

Khrushchev and his colleagues felt, not unreasonably from their point of view, that if Hungary were allowed to secede from the empire, wholesale disintegration might follow. They thought they could afford to tolerate neither the retreat of communism as an ideology nor the loss of any part of Soviet-controlled territory. At the Soviet leadership's hastily called meeting with Tito at Brioni on November 2–3, 1956, Khrushchev

mentioned Imre Nagy's appeal to the United Nations and the four powers and the withdrawal from the Warsaw Pact. It was a question of whether capitalism would be restored in Hungary. . . . "What is there left for us to do?," Khrushchev asked, meaning the Soviet Union. "If we let things take their course, the West would say we are either stupid or weak, and that's one and the same thing. We cannot possibly permit it, either as communists and internationalists or as the Soviet state. We would have capitalists on the frontier of the Soviet Union." He said they had assembled sufficient troops and that they had decided to put a stop to what was going on in Hungary. They still needed a couple of days.[28]

In the early hours of Sunday, November 4, 1956, Soviet forces attacked Budapest. At 0420 Imre Nagy, the prime minister, announced the invasion over Budapest Radio and appealed to the United Nations. At 0656 the Hungarian Writers' Union sent an SOS signal to the world for immediate help. At 0724 Budapest Radio went off the air.

In the late afternoon (at 1804), the Hungarian Service of Radio Free Europe broadcast, as part of a press review built into a news bulletin, the following (front-page) report from the November 4, 1956, issue of the London liberal *Observer* (given here in full):

Hungary: Grave Fears in Washington
US May Be Forced to Intervene
By Our Diplomatic Correspondent
Washington, November 1

Although the latest reports from Hungary indicate a possible Russian readiness to withdraw, Washington is still inclined to take a gloomy view.

"The Russians may have moved all these troops in to have a stronger negotiating hand or to protect their lines of communication while they withdraw," a high American government official said today, "but we still have reasons to fear the Russians have decided to drown the Hungarian revolution in blood.

"If our fears materialise and the Hungarians manage to hold out for three or four days, the pressure on America to help militarily might become irresistible.

"There are people inside the National Security Council who have already urged that we use tactical atomic weapons on Russian lines of communication to help Hungary.

"The President, being constitutionally minded, will do no such thing without Congressional approval, and Congressmen will not vote for war, not at least until after the election on Tuesday. If the Hungarians are still fighting on Wednesday, we will be closer to a world war than we have been since August, 1939."

But not the whole of the *Observer*'s despatch was put on air, nor was the piece fairly summarised. The *Observer*'s reference to tactical atomic weapons was omitted, but the prospect of armed intervention was implicitly sharpened. The listener heard the following version of the report [given here in verbatim, un-Englished translation].

The English *Observer* publishes this morning a situation analysis by its Washington correspondent. The report was written before this morning's Soviet attack. The *Observer*'s correspondent nevertheless notes that the Russians will probably decide to drown the Hungarian revolution in blood. The article then continues: "Should the Soviet army really attack Hungary—should this fear of ours become a reality, with the Hungarians holding out for three to four days—then an irresistible pressure will build up in the United States on the government to move Washington to provide military assistance for the freedom fighters."

This is what the *Observer* reports in today's issue. The paper notes that the American Congress cannot vote for war until after the presidential election. It then continues: "Should the Hungarians still be fighting on Wednesday, we shall be closer to a world war than we have been at any time since 1939."

Reports from London, Paris, Washington, and other Western sources show that the responses of Western public opinion to the Hungarian events surpass anything imaginable. It is expected in the Western capitals that Western sympathy and solidarity will be given practical expression within hours.

The *Observer*'s despatch and the decision to broadcast it in doctored form will continue to cause controversy. No rational student of history would judge that a single, badly heard broadcast (even once repeated) could have fashioned wishful thinking into prolonged armed resistance. The Soviet leaders themselves, in their inner councils, as distinct from their propaganda, never claimed (as far as we know) that Radio Free Europe's broadcasts were specifically responsible for the Hungarian Revolution or the Hungarian nation's resistance to Soviet intervention either on October 23–24 or on and after November 4, 1956. Yet the question remains: Should such sibylline language have been entrusted to the imperfect medium of short-wave radio? Could a population fighting for its life be expected to tell a press review from the Radio's own commentary—the anonymous opinions of a journalist from official American policy? Was America going to war over Hungary? Were the Hungarians *expected* to go on fighting?

The *Observer*'s report could be heard only intermittently through the Soviet interference; Soviet tanks were pushing their way into Budapest; all airfields and provincial centres of communication were under Soviet guard; Soviet paratroops were landing; the Hungarians were fighting back. In the ensuing confusion, the *Observer*'s words, repeated through the grapevine, were pared down to convey a simple message: "Hold out until Eisenhower is re-elected." That was, in part at least, what moved several of the improvised, underground radio transmitters (Radio Róka, Radio Csokonay, Radio Rajk, Radio Rákóczi, Radio Vác, Radio Dunapentele, and others) to make desperate appeals to the Western leaders through Radio Free Europe, but also directly *to* Radio Free Europe, for military intervention.

"The quality of the reception was extremely poor," an earwitness reports, "and the jamming made things worse. Dribs and drabs of condemnation [of the Soviet invasion] reached us through the ether from several countries—commentaries, press reviews, words, and again just words. Empty protestations followed about oppression, slogans about freedom and the terror. The jamming became so bad that for about a quarter of an hour only single Hungarian words got through; then, a little more clearly, these fragments: 'If the Hungarians are able to hold out . . . to provide military assistance,' followed by another voice apparently summarising and commenting on what had gone before: 'If the Hungarians can hold out until the Presidential election, a soldier-president will again head the United States, and military help can be expected.' These were roughly the words from which listeners inferred that America was, through Radio Free Europe, encouraging the Hungarians to hold out."[29]

What followed was heartrending and is well documented. The insurgents were now clutching at straws, still believing that the "cultured West" would keep faith with them, and imagining that Radio Free Europe had the power to help them militarily as well as morally.

> Radio Free Europe! Urgent, urgent! . . . Acknowledging your broadcast! Received! Thanks! This is the Hungarian army radio called Rákóczi. If you are receiving our broadcasts, acknowledge to Radio Rákóczi. We are breaking off, for we are in immediate danger! We ask urgently for immediate help! Free Europe! Free Europe!—NOVEMBER 4, RADIO RÁKÓCZI, 1435, LOCATION UNKNOWN

Special appeal to Radio Free Europe: Early this morning Soviet troops launched a general attack on Hungary. We are requesting you to send immediate military aid in the form of parachute troops over the trans-Danubian provinces. SOS! Save Our Souls!—NOVEMBER 4, 1234, UNIDENTIFIED FREE RADIO, IN MORSE CODE

Attention, Radio Free Europe, hello, attention! This is Róka speaking . . . Continuous bombing . . . Help, help, help! Radio Rákóczi, Hungary, repeat . . . Please forward our request to the Geneva Red Cross. Tell them to intervene immediately. Several hospitals are in flames . . . Radio Budapest is in the hands of traitors . . . Radio Free Europe, forward it, please forward it! Forward our request. Forward our news. Help! Help!—NOVEMBER 4, RADIO RÁKÓCZI, 1348

Radio Free Europe, call on the Hungarian people! . . . Tell them that they should demonstrate and demand free elections and the resignation of the Kádár puppet government.—NOVEMBER 5, RADIO CSOKONAY, 2015

Urgent flash! Attention, attention! We desperately need guns, ammunition, and food parachuted in around Dunapentele. Attention! Attention! Munich! Munich! Take immediate action! Attention! Attention! Take immediate action! The Soviet troops called on us to lay down our arms. We will not comply with that call. If necessary, we will keep on fighting for the freedom of Hungary against the foreign occupiers to the last drop of our blood. Attention! Attention! Take urgent action!— NOVEMBER 6, RADIO RÁKÓCZI, 1505

Radio Free Europe! Attention! Attention! . . . An appeal to the United Nations . . . Free Europe, Munich . . . Attention! We ask you to repeat in Russian the following appeal to Soviet soldiers in Hungary . . . Radio Free Europe, attention, attention! . . . Radio Rákóczi calling Munich, Munich! Please tell us on . . . which wavelengths Hungarian radio stations are broadcasting. We are isolated, we want to contact them . . . Attention, attention, Munich!—NOVEMBER 7, RADIO RÁKÓCZI, 1015 AND 1115

This, I believe, is the historical context in which Radio Free Europe's responsibility for what happened in Hungary and in the minds of Hungarians on and after November 4, 1956, has to be understood. In the feverish atmosphere prevailing throughout the country, the promise of intervention was what the majority of Hungarians wanted to hear from Radio Free Europe. And many thought they did. The *Observer*'s partially inaudible and inaccurately summarised report elevated American speculation to the status of an international commitment in the minds of desperate listeners. But that, though important, is hardly the main point. The insurgents addressed their cry for help to the Radio not only, and perhaps not even principally, because they had drawn wishful conclusions from a single (though repeated) broadcast, but because they took Radio Free Europe to be something it was not. And that was an American public responsibility—a case of confusion in the mission and management of the Radio as it then existed.

By the crucial early hours of November 4, whatever the Radio was saying was liable to cause tragic but unavoidable misinterpretations. And the misinterpretations were profound, with far-reaching consequences. When asked "whether American broadcasts had given the impression that the United States was willing to fight to save Hungary, fully half of the [Hungarian refugee] respondents gave affirmative answers and only a little more than one third denied it."[30]

But how was a free Western radio station to conduct itself? Foreign broadcasting from the "free world" had to be free. It would have been wrong and unimaginable to omit the influential *Observer*'s despatch from the Radio's press review, or to exclude similar articulations of world opinion from the Radio's various bulletins and discussion programmes on the grounds that they might give rise to misunderstanding.

Among those who badly misinterpreted the Radio's mandate and broadcasts was Major General Béla Király, commander of the National Guard and the leading figure of the military resistance. He claims to have heard a message personally addressed to him by Radio Free Europe, calling on him and the troops under his command "to fight the Russians to the last as my patriotic duty." Radio Free Europe's announcer, he said in a television interview, "made no definite promise that the American Marines would be arriving, or anything of the kind, but the message was so powerful that I was extremely confused, because we believed that Radio Free Europe was a voice of the American government; consequently, if that voice encourages me to resist, there must be a government decision or plan behind it."[31]

The accuracy of General Király's recall is open to doubt. In his autobiographical book *Honvédségből Néphadsereg* (From the Honvéd Army to the People's Army), he makes no mention of such a Radio Free Europe broadcast or any other Western message addressed to him personally. Indeed, describing the prospects of military resistance in Budapest on November 4, 1956, he writes: "We Hungarians had no resources to mount a counterattack, and we did not seek and could not expect any help from abroad." And later: "Our hope was that if before the conclusion of the American [presidential] election the Soviets did not manage to suppress our country completely, the re-elected president might, basing himself on America's political, material and moral power, take up a forceful position in the U.N. Perhaps he might put an end to the war in Suez, using political and economic—not military—means, and might, using the same means, induce the Soviet Union, too, to end its aggression against us."[32]

In the sound-documentation I examined, I found one personal reference to Király's role in the fighting. It occurs in a comment by "Colonel Bell," the Radio's Hungarian military correspondent (November 4–5), in which Bell complained that the revolutionaries' fighting units lacked a central command structure. The defence of Hungary's border with Austria (Colonel Bell noted) had been left in the hands of the old Communist Party generals. This was making it possible for relatively small Soviet forces to block the border and catch the freedom fighters "in a mousetrap." "Major General Béla Király, that superbly trained and deeply Hungarian-spirited soldier (*lángoló, magyar érzésű*) could do a lot to put this right." These words, though suggestive, could hardly be interpreted as a message instructing Király to "fight the Russians to the last as my patriotic duty."

Radio Free Europe's controllers were quick to learn from the Hungarian fiasco. A frontal challenge to the Soviet or Soviet-controlled system had to be ruled out as irresponsible and unprofitable. Hence, in 1968, the Radio recognised and then clearly supported the Czechoslovak reform movement led by Alexander Dubček. Earlier in the 1960s, it had given prominence to the ideological significance of Chinese revisionism and added to its centrifugal power. It recognised and amplified the impact of the Italian communist leader Palmiro Togliatti and communist polycentrism and flirted for a while with Eurocommunism as a potential force for liberalisation. It even provided cautious support for Nicolai Ceauşescu in the first years of his presidency because he appeared to be a reformer of sorts who enjoyed a measure of public approval. Gradually, the Radio also accepted, without ceasing to criticise him, János Kádár, despite his treacherous role in 1956 and his responsibility for the mass executions that followed his installation as Moscow's proconsul. The Radio did so because, beginning with the early 1960s, many Hungarians appeared to see Kádár as the least of several evils and because the Western world was making its peace with him. Most important, in 1985, the Radio recognised, after much initial scepticism (which I myself at first encouraged), the enormous importance of Mikhail Gorbachev.

But the Radio did all these things guided by the unofficial prin-

ciple that whatever served to undermine the monolithic control of the
party and the communist state would weaken and eventually destroy
the entire system. It was a tactic that paid dividends. I stress the word
"unofficial" again, because a narrow interpretation of the Radio's 1976
guidelines would have debarred it altogether from working for the
elimination of the Soviet system and empire.

The Hungarians dented the Soviet monolith before their time. In
the short term, they lost out and paid a heavy price for their daring, but
they were storing up precious reserves of morale for the future. Such
reserves, we are told by one of their famous late nineteenth-century
writers, are "the moral capital of nations—not the size they really are
but the size they are believed to be."[33] In 1989–90, when self-liberation
was achieved, the Hungarians, the Poles, and to some extent the Czechs
were in a position to begin their long climb to stable democratic conditions from a ledge which the nonrebellious Russians, Romanians, and
Bulgarians had not reached or even attempted.[34]

In sum, despite the 1956 Hungarian debacle, surrogate broadcasting pioneered by Radio Free Europe has amply proved its worth; and
with the 1975 Helsinki Final Act its legitimacy has been implicitly
recognised by the international community. Before Helsinki, it could
legitimately be argued that surrogate radio constituted unlawful interference in a sovereign country's internal affairs. But the Helsinki Final
Act and the follow-up agreements signed in Belgrade, Madrid, and
Paris made it clear that the demarcation line traditionally drawn between domestic and international concerns no longer existed. Self-
determination and the human rights and fundamental freedoms both
of the individual and of national and religious minorities were solemnly affirmed and recourse to effective remedies pledged should
those rights be violated. This was an epoch-making achievement, even
though it did not carry the force of international law. Any Western surrogate diplomacy vis-à-vis closed societies now or in the future will
no longer have to operate by stealth or on sufferance but will be entitled to declare its hand openly as the human rights component of
solemn international agreements. That these splendid commitments
were ignored with impunity in the 1991–95 Balkan wars stands as an
indictment of Western political will but does not invalidate the principles which the commitments express.

Nothing surprised the Western public more about the Hungarians'
great fight for liberty than their dedication and apparent naivety in the

face of hopeless odds. There has always been an inclination in Hungarian life and letters to believe with the ancient Greeks that the mere knowledge of the right course of action leads ineluctably to choice of the right course of action. In 1956, some of that thinking was projected onto the "cultured" West. It was a hazardous projection.

Two conflicting frames of mind were at work—balance-of-power politics and hard realism on the one side and libertarian idealism with its roots in the nineteenth century on the other. In Poland and Hungary there re-emerged, after the Twentieth Party Congress of the CPSU, a strong feeling of "national honour"—two unfashionable words I employ with caution for they are easily misunderstood. The Poles and Hungarians had lost the war and lost the peace, and they had very little left to lose. Rebellion for them was a deeply felt need as well as a policy. When the Muscovite edifice began to tremble, the Hungarians believed their time had come. Without a firm plan—without, indeed, any plan at all—they rose against an oppressive and imported ideology, drawing inspiration from 1848 and earlier models of Hungarian resistance to imposed rule.

What were their assumptions? They believed that the wrong of despotism was too great a wrong to come to terms with—that free men and women worldwide had a responsibility to help them to defeat it. With an almost childlike confidence in the manifest good of their cause, they expected active solidarity from what they imagined were like-minded people and governments in Western Europe and America. They trusted the commitments made in American electoral campaigns, believing that so much tough talk did not make sense unless, when the time for action came, the United States would honour its rhetoric. Not realising, moreover, that French and British imperial ambitions—and duplicity—were still robust enough in the Middle East to obscure in the eyes of the world the Hungarians' clear-cut challenge to the Kremlin, they believed that the West would be eager to exploit the hole they were opening in the side of the Soviet colossus.

These conceptions were at odds with reality as the West understood it, and were fraught with grave consequences for the "peace-breakers." But the defiance and hope that drove the youth of Hungary had a flavour of heroism about them which still inspires.

Incomprehension, however, went still further. Neither the Hungarians nor the other East and Central Europeans under communist rule understood the extent to which some of the Western intelligentsia had come under the influence of progressivist ideology. A revolution against "socialist" rule struck Western progressives as hard to comprehend; national flag-waving was suspect. Nor did the East and Central Europeans quite share the Western fear of nuclear war or understand Western society's unconcern for the victims of Yalta, despite the rhetoric; the fickleness and minimal attention span in Western public opinion; the commercialisation of Western opinion formation; the myopia induced by the four- to five-year electoral cycle; or the spinelessness, not to say occupational mendacity, of Western politicians. Least of all did East and Central Europeans realise that after a spectacular start, the American people's identification with the hungry and oppressed had a way of running out of steam. "Short-distance crusading" was the phrase mockingly coined by Sovietologists to express their scorn.

Looking back over the last four decades, it is hard to avoid the conclusion that very little has changed. The sorry spectacle of the fumbling Dwight D. Eisenhower and ham-fisted Anthony Eden—which filled Western television screens in those not very distant days—offered a preview of what was to follow in the Balkans thirty-five years on, with George Bush, James Baker, John Major, Douglas Hurd, Cyrus Vance, Malcolm Rifkind, Douglas Hogg, (Lord) David Owen, and Boutros Boutros-Ghali leading Western policy in Bosnia into first human disaster and then lasting ignominy. The puzzlement of the East and Central Europeans is as justified in the light of the Balkan disaster as it was in 1956 in the light of the suppression of Hungary, for Western attitudes have indeed been rich in paradox. When the Soviet Union was strong, its restive satellites were denied effective Western political support because no one wanted to provoke their powerful masters in Moscow. When the Soviet Union ceased to exist, the East and Central European nations were denied effective aid or intervention because the new Russia was weak, touchy, and unsettled and had to be humoured. Heads or tails, they were destined to be the losers. The times were great— the arbiters running the affairs of the Western nations were small. Whether the expansion of NATO and of the European Union will make up for so many missed opportunities remains to be seen.

In 1956—as later in the Balkans—the West was unready for action but expert at obfuscation. Caught by surprise by every change in the fortunes of communism, it remained a spectator. It was caught unawares by Yugoslavia's expulsion from the Cominform, by the 1953 Berlin uprising, by the 1956 Polish upheavals, by the Hungarian Revolution, by the construction of the Berlin Wall, by the 1968 occupation of Czechoslovakia, by the rise and suppression of Solidarity, by the invasion of Afghanistan, by the demolition of the Berlin Wall, by the collapse of East Germany, and finally by the fall of the Soviet empire itself.

Eyeless and puzzled, Western governments moved nervously from one soothing formula to another, mouthing incantations about détente, recognising East Germany as a "sovereign nation," offering aid and trade to Stalinist governments, declaring, after Afghanistan, that détente could be compartmentalised ("your aggression will not weaken our cooperation"), pooh-poohing any idea that international terrorism had its bases and protectors in the communist East, and generally speaking, following the dictionary definitions of complacency and appeasement to the letter. And when the thoroughly—though not precisely—predicted self-liquidation of the Soviet system brought Western leaders face to face with the need for peacemaking, whether among the ruins of Yugoslavia or of the Soviet Union, they were, once again, taken aback and unprepared.

I have no doubt that Moscow's nuclear arsenal notwithstanding, the peaceful disintegration of the Soviet system could have been advanced by decades if the Western leaders had shown a modicum of imagination in their dealings with the Soviet phenomenon and had educated our public opinion accordingly.

The profound damage done, in 1993–95, to Radio Free Europe as an intellectually independent, multinational radio station on West European soil, and the conditional survival of Radio Liberty at their reduced joint headquarters in Prague, were two of many American signals to the world that the sole remaining superpower was unprepared to shoulder the more subtle of its global responsibilities and was confused, to boot, about its national interests. That the United States seemed prepared to relinquish two powerful tools of influence in a volatile international environment, for reasons posterity will surely judge to have been frivolous and trivial, was astonishing.

To European eyes it was even more astonishing that American Republicans and Democrats apparently cooperated, although for different and even conflicting reasons, in preparing the ground for the two Radios' liquidation as independent institutions: the Republicans wanted to cut public spending, reduce the power and prestige of the federal bureaucracies, and put the Europeans in their place; many Clinton Democrats were determined to bring the American intelligentsia's long campaign against a hated "instrument of the Cold War" to a victorious conclusion.

The severe reduction of Radio Free Europe and Radio Liberty and their prospective closure in 1999 was the joint work of the United States Advisory Commission on Public Diplomacy and Senator Russell D. Feingold (Democrat, Wisconsin), acting, as far as I am aware, independently of each other. In 1990 the commission recommended the "consolidation and the phaseout of some surrogate broadcasting services." In 1993 it urged that "plans to phase out Radio Free Europe/Radio Liberty should be implemented."

On January 25, 1994, in "a deficit reduction victory," Senator Feingold took the commission's recommendations a step further. His amendment on overseas broadcasting won Senate approval, and the two Radios' operating funds were cut by 64 percent, from $210 million to a maximum of $75 million per annum. The legislation stipulated the termination of all federal funding of the two Radios by 1999—a provision Feingold described as "critical." For the Radios, the 1994 cuts were ruinous; yet the annual savings for the U.S. taxpayer barely equalled the cost of two fighter aircraft.

Feingold's original bill was his maiden Senate initiative. He introduced it on January 21, 1993, the first day of his career as a young senator. "With the end of the Cold War, and with our federal deficit," he said on the day of his Senate "victory," "we have to cut back, prioritize our spending, and eliminate waste and abuse. We simply can't afford to continue paying for so much surrogate broadcasting into countries which have access to other sources of credible information, like CNN."[35]

This hasty retrenchment may have been in harmony with the United States' reviving sense of isolationism, but it was gravely out of joint with the demands of the real world. Republicans and Democrats shared the belief that by 1993–94 democracy and liberty in Central Europe and Russia had made sufficient advances to render broadcasting of the kind and size the Radios were providing no longer justified. Protestations to the contrary by the presidents and prime ministers of almost every ex-communist country were ignored—a surprising state of affairs in a land whose powerful business community relies so heavily on opinion polls and market research. This time the "buyer's" voice was not allowed to be heard. As often before in American history, the legislators' knowledge of European affairs was slight and their judgements were formed almost exclusively in response to domestic concerns. The larger picture escaped them.

With the collapse of communism, Soviet rule had indeed come to an end—but not the "culture" of Sovietism. The shop signs were being changed, but not the spirit behind them. Where so many had to be or chose to be collaborators or accomplices, the road to recovery could only be long and tortuous. So much remained unmentionable about the twilight world of totalitarianism that the growth of liberty was impeded by innumerable inhibitions. The two Radios could have continued to play a vital role in helping democratic ways of being and thinking, and a decent sense of the common good, to establish or re-establish themselves. Funding to empower the Radios to do so, *with their independent status intact,* would have been money well spent. There would have been no better way of investing any American "peace dividend." But impatience and the mentality of American exceptionalism dictated otherwise.

Under the 1994 International Broadcasting Act, the principle of nongovernmental surrogate broadcasting, which had been at the very heart of the two Radios' remarkable record, was abandoned. What remained of the two stations was put under the policy control and supervision of a new board, responsible through the United States Information Agency to the American government. Radio Free Europe and Radio Liberty, now on a par with the Voice of America and Worldnet Television, were listed as two "international broadcasting services of the United States Government." With a single stroke of the legislators' pen the sophisticated formula of unofficial "home service" radio across international boundaries was killed.

Appendix A
STASI and the Carlos Group

The following documentation, retrieved from the STASI files of the former German Democratic Republic, sheds revealing light on the East and Central European, Soviet, and Cuban involvement in international terrorism in the 1970s and 1980s, including the attempt to blow up Radio Free Europe. Separat is the code name for the "Carlos" group.

Deputy Minister   Berlin, 29.4 1981
Agreed, Mielke [overwritten by hand][1]   VNE 3120/81
                                                   Top Secret

Personal
To the Comrade Minister

Enclosed I present to you the report of Division 22 on the consultation held in Berlin on 24–25 April 1981 with Comrade Lieut.-Col. VARGA, head of the 8th Division of the Main Administration No. 2 in the fraternal organ[2] of the Hungarian People's Republic, concerning operation "Separat." Comrade VARGA handed over a "documentation about the preparation of an attack by 'Separat' on Radio 'Free Europe' in Munich," the contents of which had been clandestinely obtained by the Hungarian comrades. This confirms the Hungarian comrades' indication, passed on to you by myself on 30 March 1981, of "Separat" 's involvement.

I request you to take note of this report. The documentation will be evaluated and filed with operation "Separat" materials.

The basic line represented at the consultation by the head of Division 22, Comrade Colonel DAHL, and agreed in advance, continues to have my support. I suggest that it should be maintained and work on its execution continued.

The Hungarian comrades consider multilateral consultation on the problem of "Separat" no longer necessary at the present time. My view is that the MfS [Ministry for State Security] can go along with this opinion.

Stellvertreter des Ministers *[handwritten signature]*

Berlin, 29. 4. 1981
VNE 3120/81

Streng geheim!

Persönlich

Genossen Minister

Beiliegend überreiche ich Ihnen den Bericht der Abteilung XXII über die in Berlin am 24./25. 4. 1981 erfolgte
Konsultation mit dem Genossen OSL VARGA, Leiter der
8. Abteilung in der 2. Hauptverwaltung im Bruderorgan
der Ungarischen Volksrepublik zum Vorgang "Separat".
Genosse VARGA übergab eine "Dokumentation über die Vor-
bereitung eines Anschlages auf den Sender 'Freies Europa'
in München durch 'Separat'", deren Inhalt die ungarischen
Genossen konspirativ beschafft haben. Damit bestätigt sich
der Ihnen bereits am 30. 3. 1981 von mir übergebene Hin-
weis der ungarischen Genossen auf die Tatbeteiligung von
"Separat".

Ich bitte Sie, den Bericht zur Kenntnis zu nehmen. Die
Dokumentation wird ausgewertet und dem Vorgang "Separat"
zugeordnet.

Die vom Leiter der Abteilung XXII, Genossen Oberst DAHL,
in der Konsultation vertretene, vorher abgestimmte Grund-
linie findet weiter meine Zustimmung. Ich schlage vor, sie
beizubehalten und weiter an ihrer Durchsetzung zu arbeiten.

Die ungarischen Genossen halten eine multilaterale Beratung
zur Problematik "Separat" zum gegenwärtigen Zeitpunkt nicht
mehr für erforderlich. Dieser Meinung kann sich meines Er-
achtens auch das MfS anschließen. Von unserer Seite werden zum
weiteren Vorgehen noch Konsultationen mit den kubanischen Genossen und mit dem KfS der UdSSR geführt. Mit den kubanischen
Genossen ist beabsichtigt zu prüfen, ob den Mitgliedern von
"Separat" in Lateinamerika eine für sie akzeptable Perspek-
tive geboten werden kann.

Anlage

6 Blatt

[handwritten signature]
Neiber
Generalmajor

Document 1. Page from a STASI report about the Carlos Group.

For our part, consultations about further action will continue with the Cuban comrades and with the KGB of the USSR. The intention is to examine with the Cuban comrades whether a perspective acceptable to members of "Separat" can be offered to them in Latin America.

<u>Enclosure</u>   [signed]   Neiber[3]
                                       Major General

Division 22   Berlin, 28 April 1981

                                                  jä-gl
                                       STRICTLY CONFIDENTIAL!

Report
on the consultations with the security organs of the Hungarian People's Republic with regard to operation "Separat."
    On 24 and 25 April renewed talks were conducted, as agreed, with the Hungarian security organs with regard to operation "Separat."
    Participating on the Hungarian side were:
Comr. Lieut.-Col. VARGA, Head of Division 8 in Main Administration No. 2

    Present on the MfS side were:
Comrade-Colonel DAHL   Head, Division 22
Comrade-Colonel JÄCKEL   Dept. Head, Division 22
Comrade-Major VOIGT   Head, Division 22/8
Comrade-Lieutenant PAUL   Interpreter

    The Hungarian visitor was given accommodation in Object "73" of Division 22, where the consultations were also conducted. His stay as well as his departure to Budapest on 25 April 1981, at 6:15 P.M. passed off without incident.

<u>Main Points of the Consultation</u>
The statements of Comr. Lieut.-Col. VARGA focused on:

    1. Assessment of the present situation in the group "Separat."
    2. Handing over of the documentation as well as explaining the attack carried out by group "Separat" against Radio "Free Europe."
    3. Information provided about measures planned by the Hungarian security organs against group "Separat."

Add to 1:

Continued surveillance and observation of group "Separat" resulted in no essentially new findings.

Some information was, however, obtained. This made possible a more precise evaluation of the group. The essential facts [obtained] are these:

At a meeting of leading members of group "Separat" a new evaluation of the socialist states was made. With the exception of the USSR, negative attitudes were expressed with regard to every individual state.

During a conversation within the group, the head of "Separat" stated, it is his assumption that his activities are being observed by and known to all socialist countries. He assumes that there is also coordination in this respect between the socialist states. He commissioned members of the group to acquire, whenever they had contacts with GDR, information about this cooperation, particularly of that between the GDR and the HPR (Hungarian People's Republic).

The group "Separat" has received several assignments from the Romanian secret service. (Of these) the ones known are

The killing of 5 Romanian families living in exile. In realization of this assignment letter bomb attacks were made on 5 February 1981 in Paris against Romanians in exile.

Attack against the Romanian Department of Radio "Free Europe." Partly realised on 21 February 1981.

In return for these activities, leading members of the group were received by the head of the Romanian secret service, and help with arms, diplomatic passports, etc., was promised or given.

A member of the group "Separat," BELLINI, Giorgio, cover name "Roberto," has been imprisoned in the FRG [Federal Republic of (West) Germany].

According to the findings of the HPR, he had been informed about the preparation and execution of the attack against "Radio Free Europe." Should he reveal what he knows, great dangers would follow—for the socialist states as well.

Add to 2:

By way of extensive reconnaissance measures, it was possible to determine that group "Separat" had, beginning with approx. September 1980, had an assignment from the Romanian secret service to break into the Romanian Department of Radio "Free Europe" and subsequently to blow it up.

The date was set for 14 February 1981. The documents obtained and observation of the group's activities prove that "Heinrich Schneider," the leading member of the group, prepared the action and obviously also participated in it.

Although the attack was not carried out as envisaged, the head of "Separat" travelled to Romania, where he was praised for the action at the highest level of the secret service.

The documentation handed over proves these findings. It was also given to the security services of the USSR and the CSSR [Czechoslovak Socialist Republic].

Add to 3:

These new findings of the security organs of the HPR have confirmed the necessity of introducing, in coordination with the fraternal organs, step-by-step and differentiated measures against the group "Separat." For this reason a relevant proposal was worked out which was confirmed by the minister of the interior of the HPR. Comr. János KÁDÁR also agreed with the conceptual framework for further steps to be taken vis-à-vis the group "Separat."

The aim of the measures should be:

to end the permanent stay of group "Separat" in the HPR, and not to permit an alternative place of residence [for the group] in another socialist country.

to provoke no confrontation with group "Separat," and also to rule out the creation of any difficulties with the states standing behind the group, such as Libya, Syria, VDRJ [Yemen], etc.

Conceptions with regard to practical procedure:

In the first half of May the head of group "Separat" will be summoned to the MfI [Ministry of the Interior] of the HPR for a discussion. On that occasion it will be disclosed to him that due to

violations of the law committed by him and members of his group in the HPR, and

certain activities of the adversary, such as Interpol and Western secret services, against his group,

permanent stay in the HPR and other socialist states is no longer possible.

He will be allowed to re-export his materials stored in Budapest.

The setting of dates with regard to leaving the HPR will be handled liberally (a period of 2–4 months).

However, his permanent residence permit in the HPR will be withdrawn. Transit through the HPR and short stays will continue to be permitted.

The discussion will be conducted in such a way that it should come to no confrontation and that he should accept the measures on political grounds.

Parallel with the discussion with "Separat," other measures of control and observation will be introduced, to prevent the continued importation of arms into the HPR,

to make the group realise that it is under uninterrupted surveillance in the HPR,

and to ensure precise customs controls on entering and leaving [the country].

The fraternal organs will be informed about the discussion conducted and about the reaction of "Separat."

So far, the security organs of the CSSR have agreed with the conceptions of the HPR with regard to procedures vis-à-vis group "Separat." A general agreement of the KGB of the USSR is also in hand. The agreement of the Bulgarian security organs is going to be obtained on 27 April 1981. It has therefore been requested by Comr. Lieut.-Col. VARGA that the MfS also agree to the planned procedure.

The Hungarian comrades, in agreement with the KGB of the USSR, consider multilateral consultation at the deputy ministerial level no longer necessary. What is important, initially, is to put the measures against the group into action and ascertain [its] first reactions.

The representative of the Cuban security organs in Budapest is also to be informed about the measures taken.

Since there are certain communication difficulties with the Cuban security organs with regard to group "Separat" and [since] the Hungarian comrades have no acceptable proposal for the future permanent place of residence of the group "Separat," Comr. Lieut.-Col. VARGA asked that it should be checked out with the Cuban security organs whether they are still prepared to provide the group "Separat" with a new field of activities in Latin America. He asked the MfS to continue consultations in this direction with the Cuban security organs.

The material handed over by the Hungarian comrades includes copies of original documents secured in the course of a conspirative [clandestine] search of the Budapest apartment of the group "Separat." They prove without doubt the participation of the group in the attack against Radio "Free Europe" in Munich, and in attacks against Romanian émigrés in Western Europe. The handwritten remarks on the plan of action are in the hand of "Heinrich Schneider."

Comrade Colonel DAHL expressed thanks to Comr. Lieut.-Col. VARGA for the documentation handed over and the information conveyed. Information was handed over concerning:

planned activities of the group "Separat" in Western Europe,

connections of the group "Separat" with the hijacking of the Pakistani passenger aircraft,

surveillance of the [group's] activities in Budapest.

With regard to the conceptions of the Hungarian security organs concerning concrete measures against "Separat," the following basic policy was determined in accordance with the views we have held throughout:

any move is to be avoided that could result in the defection of the group to the enemy camp,

a confrontation with the group is to be avoided in order to exclude reactions of defiance,

acceptable varieties of a solution are to be sought to make it possible for the group to have a secure place of residence; but such a solution would also have to offer the security organs a certain measure of control [over the group],

the practice of granting transit and short stay facilities to leading members of the group in the socialist countries is to be continued.

Appendix B
A Selection of Policy
Guidances, 1984–1985

Notes of this kind were circulated, over my signature, to all or only selected members of the editorial staff, as the occasion required. They were meant to set the tone for thinking at Radio Free Europe and were of an advisory rather than a mandatory character. They were available as background reading to the editorial staff of Radio Liberty, too.

ON LANGUAGE AND CONTEXT

3 February 1984

Communicating with audiences under Communist regimes harbors two principal dangers: one "contextual" another "semantic"; the two are closely related.

The first danger is that of adopting, wittingly or unwittingly, the philosophical framework in which Marxist-Leninist governments and the media under their control operate. We do not, as a radio station offering alternative views of history and society, accept or tacitly condone that intellectual context. Indeed, it is one of our tasks to show why that context is fraudulent, and how Leninism has, millennial promises notwithstanding (or, as some argue, precisely because millennial promises have been made), led one country after another down the road of economic disaster, barbarism and the destruction of civil society. We know, for example, that Marxist-Leninist regimes do not like dealing analytically with national and religious issues because these do not fit in with their categories. That is one good reason why we raise them and keep them on our agenda.

Placing our challenge outside the framework of Marxism-Leninism is, however, not enough. We must be equally prepared to question the practical application of Marxism-Leninism on its own terms. This requires an imaginative leap from a free into an intellectually closed society. It is a leap not always easy to make but indispensable to our all-round effectiveness.

For example: We demonstrate that a necessary link exists between Lenin's revolutionary rhetoric and genocide in Cambodia—a line as self-evident as that between Hitler's early harangues against the Jews and their extermination. We then reason that wherever Leninism continues to be practised as the governing principle of the state and society, there can be no guarantee against a "return to Cambodia" in one of its many possible forms. Leninism provides no institutional assurance that the dictatorship of the proletariat will not—as Rosa Luxemburg foresaw—turn into the dictatorship of the Party *over* the proletariat. The promise of universal liberty ends up in the universal denial of liberty.

By a similar token, we take issue with the notion of "socialist legality" in the following manner: We do, of course, realize that Marxism-Leninism represents a repulsive morality—indeed an amorality—which we reject. Suppose, however, for the sake of argument that Marxism-Leninism *is* what it claims to be, a humanistic social program for the emancipation of Man and the improvement of his material condition, the attainment of which will exact certain sacrifices. The question is: What sacrifices and who is to make them? How does the legitimization of torture under Stalin accord with the humanistic vision? Or the execution of children aged 13 and 14? Or the show-trials of the Old Bolsheviks? Or the legalized murder of Kostov, Rajk and Slansky? Or the abuse of dissidents in psychiatric prisons under Brezhnev and Andropov? Or the 60 million unrehabilitated dead the Soviet system has so far claimed in its attempt to change human nature? Clearly, we infer, the idea of "socialist legality" is a meaningless phrase even within the terms of the ideology and bears no resemblance to the Rule of Law as it is understood in civilized societies.

Our reasoning will thus lead us to conclude that the most unacceptable aspect of Marxism-Leninism is not its poor, distorted, "Russian" application, but the character of the system itself. It uses human beings as chattels, as a means toward a Utopian end. It tries to purchase the felicity of mankind somewhere "out-there" at the price of making individual men and women poor, wretched and miserable here and now. It destroys lives and human happiness on the strength of a promissory note that has never been honored and never can be.

To be able to proceed in this manner assumes, however, that we command as a radio station a fair knowledge of Communist party history and ideology and know how to apply it. While we undoubtedly had this knowledge in the 1950s and 1960s, we seem to have lost much of it, and lost interest in it, since the mid-1970s. It is essential that we recapture or re-sharpen this important tool in our workshop.

I readily acknowledge that a significant minority of observers of the Soviet scene tend to argue that ideology is dead in Soviet society as a politically motivating force and that we need not pay much attention to its study. Let me recall that Christian monarchs of the Middle Ages seldom acted on the precepts of their faith; yet no historian worth his salt would attempt to interpret their rule without a thorough grounding in dogma and Church history.

To understand what Chernenko or Husak might do next, we must study what their predecessors did in the past and why they did it. As students of Communist affairs we operate in the manner of the Abominable Snowman: we walk backwards but our footprints point forwards.

My answer to our first problem, therefore, will be a dual one: Work *outside* the Marxist-Leninist intellectual context, but be sure that you are well enough versed in Marxism-Leninism to tackle the problems raised by it, if and when these arise, with self-confidence and credibility.

What I am saying is that we should be able to cover the entire spectrum of Soviet and East European questioning. We must be able to appeal to the sentiments of that vast majority of our audiences that will have no truck with the system; but we must also be able to carry conviction with that vital minority that runs the system or silently cooperates with it out of a sense of inertia or self-interest, half hoping that some of the system's superficially reassuring moral claims may one day turn out to be true and that it will be consequently let off the hook, and half hoping that the whole nightmare will somehow go away. There is an area of uncertainty here that we should be able to exploit. But we can only do so effectively if we have the "Problematik" in our bones and share the predicaments of that vital minority.

Our semantic problem is allied to the problem of intellectual context but articulates it more poignantly. I will not now rehearse the arguments we have all used and read *ad nauseam* upon the advent of the year 1984. It will suffice to remind ourselves that he who adopts his opponent's vocabulary implicitly concedes a piece of his opponent's argument and makes a unilateral concession.

If, for example, we concede by the careless use of words that members of the Supreme Soviet are "parliamentarians," we underwrite a lie. Whenever we say that a Czechoslovak "Trade Union delegation" arrived in a Western capital to negotiate with Western Trade Unionists, we underwrite another lie. Whenever we say that the Soviet-style communist system in Eastern Europe is "socialist," we underwrite a third and an especially damaging one, because this particular claim also administers an insult to the free and parliamentary variety of socialism such as Mitterrand's in France or the SPD's in Germany.

At the same time we live in the real world. Rightly or wrongly, the USSR and the East European communist countries have long been recognized as *de facto* governments by the Western powers. We have diplomatic relations with them. Our leaders visit their capitals. It would be senseless to insist that a body of men whom Western news-agency reports grace with the designation "the Bulgarian government" are no more than Moscow's satraps, although they are, in fact, little more than just that. But while reason and common sense dictate that we recognize the facts of international life, our mission as a radio station, speaking as we are for those millions of listeners who cannot speak freely for themselves, demands that we question the *moral* legitimacy of the East European regimes. The choice of our terminology must reflect that moral questioning.

How do we make the right choices? We make them by having, as a prerequisite, an absolutely clear image in our own minds of the corrosion of words and corruption of ideas in Communist usage. If the correct use of words is, as it is, a precondition of the mental health of our audiences, then the preservation of that mental health is, partly at least, in our own hands.

For practical men in a hurry, all this may sound tedious, academic, and even pedantic. Yet I must ask you to go back to first principles every time you write an article or edit a manuscript and ask yourselves whether the names given to things in the Soviet Union and Eastern Europe are not a sure clue to the fraud perpetrated by the Soviet system in the name of democracy and socialism. To what extent do we talk sense when we speak of the "Polish United Workers' Party," seeing that it is neither "Polish," nor is it "of the workers," much less "united" or a "party"? Could Alice have dreamt up a more bizarre Wonderland?

Please bear in mind that it is one of the objectives of the Soviet system to hijack the language and erase certain notions not only from our vocabulary but from our thinking too. It calls "democratic" what is palpably totalitarian; "free" what is coercive; "national" what is Moscow-centric; "popular" what is oligarchic; "socialist" what is tyrannical; "peaceful" what is warlike. It deploys misrepresentation as a legitimate tool of state-craft and is contemptuous of those who do not act likewise.

Two examples. It has been recently reported of Oleg Bitov (*Sunday Telegraph* 29.1.84) that "he first tried composing (his revelations) in Russian, but found the lifelong habit of censorship so deeply ingrained that he was unable to express the truth and had to turn to English instead." By a similar token, Adam Michnik writes: "I believe that the dispute about language is the central dispute of Polish intellectual life of the last 25 years. It is about our ability . . . to name things by their real names. In that (35-year) period the great majority of our people has lost that ability because of the language that has been imposed on them" (*Literary Letters*, No. 4). All of which endorses Solzhenitsyn's observation: "This universal, obligatory force-feeding with lies is now the most agonizing aspect of existence in our country—worse than all our material miseries, worse than any lack of civil liberties" (*Letter to the Soviet Leaders*, p. 46).

But might it, then, not be objected that the perverted use of language has by now got so firm a grip on our audiences that we dare not name things by their real names lest we render ourselves unintelligible? Will they understand what we mean if we say what we mean?

The Orwellian prophecy has, so far at least, not materialized (although we had glimpses of it in the Chinese Cultural Revolution and Cambodia under the Khmer Rouge). True, language in the communist countries is perverted and under continuous attack. True, the naming of certain things has become difficult. True, human survival has put a premium on self-censorship.

But Czechs, Poles, and Hungarians do not talk "Newspeak." The wholesale lobotomy of the national mind has not taken place and is (as we know from the study of brain-washing and menticide) unlikely to take place in our time. *Our* task is the immediate one of counteracting the manipulation and debasement of words and ideas as they are practised by the Soviet system and sometimes, alas, unwittingly by ourselves, too.

What, then, is to be done?

1. Make sure in your writings and translations that your own language is not hijacked.

2. Please remember that news agency reporters are busy men who will use names and employ phrases as given them at source. You are free and indeed required to correct or explain these so far as you do not tamper with substance.

3. Please remember that journalists and research-men and women often suffer from a *déformation professionnelle* in that their preoccupation with Communist literature tends to lure them (if only for the sake of brevity and convenience) into the tacit acceptance of Soviet usage. We must be vigilant that our own research coinage is genuine and we give no quarter to counterfeit money.

4. Remember that undue preoccupation with certain topics can itself aid and abet the Soviet attempt to corrupt our perceptions. An unbalanced flow of comments on economic topics, for example, tends to confirm the Marxist contention that materialism is indeed *the* motivating force of society and history. We do not fight materialism with materialism.

Undue airtime devoted to the fortunes of Western Communist parties may imply the suggestion that our preferred alternative to Soviet rule is an improved (e.g. Eurocommunist) form of Communism, rather than no Communism.

5. Western media-reporting even at its most even-handed tends to emphasize our own shortcomings and disasters. We get no comparable accounts of Soviet and East European shortcomings and disaster, although they exist in plenty. Please make sure that in the resulting imbalance we are

not painted blacker than we are, confirming the Soviet contention that the Western world is, indeed, permanently teetering on the edge of collapse.

6. Please remember that an implied part of our task is a cultural mission: the mission to maintain standards. The right to serious thought is a human right, too. We stand for what is rich in reflection and experience. We discourage what is thin, meretricious and ephemeral.

Try to preserve the dignity of the spoken word and the purity of your native language. Sovietism is undermining both. Do not curry favor with your audiences by vulgarizing what is serious or sacred. Do not mock the values thoughtful men cherish, either on our side or that of our opponents. Not everything that is new is worthy of our attention; nor is everything that is of Western provenance.

7. Please do not permit the Soviet mode of questioning to define the framework of your answers. Do not rely on Communist statistics as your main source of economic information. Unfettered by communist ideology and the physical pressures of communist society, you are your own man. Speak a free man's language.

VARIETIES OF CRISES

5 June 1984

The specter of a war-like crisis that is now so freely conjured up by the Soviet leaders and some (though not all) of their clients in Eastern Europe represents a new turn in Soviet policy. It has been variously called the hedgehog-syndrome, the siege-mentality, the fortress-Russia complex or, more generally, the self-isolation of the USSR in a fit of pique, cluelessness and frustration.

That all three factors exist and account for the great sound and fury that daily reach us from Moscow need not be doubted. What we can and must doubt and cast doubt upon in our articulations is that the world is on the verge of universal disaster. There has been no tangible deterioration in East-West relations except in the sense that the Soviets have said so. That, of course, can itself add a psychological dimension to world-tension. Indeed, it has done so in the eyes of the more gullible in the Soviet population and some of the more faint-hearted in the West.

But it would be an error for us to accept Moscow's self-induced neurosis at face value and add to what (little) real tension has so far been created. Leaders of the US Administration and of Western Europe have repeatedly stated their wish for the resumption of arms control negotiations with Moscow. There is no war-like mood in the Western chancelleries or public opinion. No armies have been mobilized, no war-games mounted, no nuclear warheads readied. The 1983 anti-nuclear campaigns in Western Europe have freely run their course. They won some ground but lost a great deal more. No parliamentary democracy collapsed under the strain. Peace as our supreme good was maintained, the threat of defeat under Soviet intimidation banished. The Western Alliance has survived, even though the strains of 35 years are beginning to tell and call for a rethinking of burden-sharing among its signatories.

There is no real, or, to be precise, no new crisis in East-West relations. The crisis has been continuous since 1945. There is no sudden threat of Armageddon. What we do have is a crisis of the Soviet system and the frustration of Soviet expansionism.

The Kremlin feels hemmed in. In the West it faces NATO. Cruise and Pershing missiles are firmly, albeit defensively, deployed. In the East it faces a hostile China, Sino-American and Sino-Japanese cooperation. In Eastern Europe, Poland is a running sore; Romania is an embarrassment or worse, East Germany a licensed jester that seems to be running away with the script.

Afghanistan has boomeranged back on Soviet propaganda, especially in the Third World. The erstwhile magnetism of Marxism-Leninism has been dealt a fatal blow by our knowledge of the realities of the Soviet system. The Soviet economy is in permanent crisis. It cannot feed its population without capitalist help. The arms' race imposes new and crippling burdens on it. The Kremlin has suffered two succession crises and is led by old men who cannot cope, or cope only with considerable difficulty.

These, then, coupled with the spectacle of a self-confident and economically rising US, are the sources of Soviet introversion and the wild talk about Nazi-America, President Reagan's aggressive intentions, German revanchism and the rest.

The war we are witnessing is the war between Soviet intentions and Soviet capabilities; between what the Soviet leaders used to be able to do and would still like to do, but can do no longer.

It may, of course, be argued that the sudden introversion of a dangerous man may not be a bad thing for the rest of the world. But such introversion runs counter to the Marxist-Leninist credo. It did not last in the past and is unlikely to do so now.

We speak in our broadcasts in the measured tones of self-confidence, economic, military, and spiritual strength. We harbour no millenarian designs on the world. We do not brag or boast.

We do say, however, with President Reagan, that in the last four years the free world has yielded not an inch of territory to Soviet expansionism. The history of our blood-soaked century has taught us that we cannot buy peace by abandoning the means to uphold it.

D DAY REMEMBERED

8 June 1984

As a follow-up to this morning's policy conference, you are advised to pay special attention to those aspects of the various D-day speeches and other articulations that stress the fundamental difference between Hitler's tyranny and the German Federal Republic.

The latter is a pivotal part of the Atlantic Alliance with which the US and the other Western Allies maintain close ties of friendship and solidarity. In our news bulletins and factual reporting we reproduce the observations of Chancellor Helmut Kohl, Secretary of State Alois Mertes and the German press fully and without comment. In our analyses we quote relevant passages from the speeches of President Ronald Reagan, Queen Elizabeth and President François Mitterrand to the effect that what has been remembered on the Normandy beaches is not the defeat of the German people but of a despotic and inhuman system of government.

In his message to Bundespräsident Karl Carstens, M. Mitterrand said: "The 6th of June, reminding as it does all Frenchmen of the beginning of the liberation of their country, also reminds us of a struggle in which so many of your and our people lost their lives in the service of their fatherland in an absurd war between European brothers. Our continent has been injured and divided. It is fortunate that our two peoples are now bound together by a common destiny." In Normandy, M. Mitterrand observed that "the enemy was not Germany, but a Government, system and ideology that held Germany in their grip."

THE DEATH OF BERLINGUER

13 June 1984

Signor Enrico Berlinguer, head of the Italian Communist Party, is being given what amounts to a state funeral. President Pertini praised Berlinguer for "his high moral standards, his clear-sightedness, his political vision, and his consciousness of the public good." He accompanied Berlinguer's body from Padua to Rome in the Presidential plane. Friends and opponents, Christian Democrats as well as Communists, are showing their respect for the dead Communist leader.

What is remarkable about this display of public decency to a public man in a free parliamentary democracy is the stark contrast in which it stands to the fate of opponents of the communist system in the USSR and Eastern Europe.

Traicho Kostov, László Rajk and Rudolf Slansky were shown no such indulgence. Nor were the Agrarian, Social Democratic, Christian Socialist and other opponents of the communist regimes. Nor were Pál Maléter or Imre Nagy—both trapped and then executed under the "liberalizing" Nikita Khrushchev.

WE DO NOT TEACH THEM MARXISM

18 July 1984

In what framework are we to think of the Soviet and East European economies in our programs? Are these "economies" in the narrow sense of the word, or part and parcel of a larger phenomenon that requires a more comprehensive approach? Will they, indeed, respond to the questioning of the economist unaided by the tools of history, culture and ideology?

The Bolshevik revolution, though "economic" in its mythology, was an act of political will. The imposition of Communist rule on the East and Central European countries followed in the wake of the Red Army and was geopolitical in character. The upheavals in East Berlin, Poland, Hungary, Czechoslovakia, and Poland again, though triggered by economic discontent, soon acquired a highly political meaning and were suppressed for power-political and ideological reasons.

In other words, "existing socialism" is a political, military, and ideological phenomenon in the first place and an economic one only in the second. It was the ideological hubris of the Bolsheviks, reinforced by the imperatives of dictatorship, that almost invariably took command in Soviet history, leaving the dismal facts of the economy to take care of themselves as best they might. Bolshevism came first—an industrial proletariat had to be created later to legitimate the revolution. The "consciousness of history," which economic and social factors had failed to implant in the Russian people, had to be injected by a Party led by middle-class intellectuals.

But the paradox has deeper roots. Marxism claims to be a scientific doctrine of economic determinism. If its claim is true and the escalator of history ushers in "socialism" automatically as it were because its time has come, what need is there for violent revolution, a Jacobin party, and the suppression of freedom? *If* determinism, *then* peaceful evolution. *If* revolution, *then* the alleged laws of history are violated and Marx is stood on his head.

One of the great intellectual debates of pre-revolutionary Russia centered precisely on this point: was "social democracy" (as it was then called) to be attained through the slow but inexorable unfolding of history as Marx had predicted (though with uncertain consistency), or by violent revolution as Lenin interpreted the Marxist canon?

The Bolsheviks were in a hurry. History, for them, was too slow and fallible an agent to answer the dilemma. It was Lenin, Stalin and Mao who answered it. The Party seen as an élite of professional revolutionaries; Mao's dictum that "power grows out of the barrel of a gun," and the voluntarism of the Cultural Revolution was their way of saying: "history is what we make it to be." Willpower and coercion were to be the instruments with which—in a supreme paradox—the doctrine of economic and social determinism was foisted upon a reality that could not be trusted to confirm Marx's prediction.

The challenge to us as broadcasters is to be mindful of the political, military and ideological provenance of the Soviet and Soviet-sponsored systems and not to be trapped into "economicizing" what is essentially political. This is a favorite ploy in Eastern Europe. If the problems of Communism can be shown to be overwhelmingly of an economic nature, then the lack of freedom and human rights, the inequities of the one-party state, Soviet occupation and other sensitive issues can be fudged or conveniently forgotten. We must not lend credence to that process. Nor must we lend credence to the findings of those Western observers who prefer not to see the totalitarian and expansionist character of the Soviet system, but insist on describing it as a "modernizing economy."

If, then, Marxism-Leninism is primarily a political, military and ideological phenomenon, we have to deal with it as such. Whilst welcoming economic reform, decentralization and indicative planning to the extent that these provide a better way of satisfying human needs and of modestly enlarging the area of human freedom, we do not see them as providing in their togetherness an alternative and acceptable model of Communism, and we do not offer arguments to make it work better. We do not adopt the limits of discussion set by the East European regimes and do not assimilate their vocabulary. It is not for us to teach them Marxism.

In talking about the failures of the Soviet type of economies we are conscious of five significant facts: (1) that we are a broadcasting station and not an economics seminar; (2) that it is not our task to conduct a dialogue with regime economists; (3) that we are primarily addressing the people, not the government; (4) that the facts of economic life, any modern economic life, are extremely difficult to explain even on the written page, and *a fortiori*, by means of the spoken word; (5) that our economics expertise has to be so utilized as to have an immediate, easily absorbed, personal appeal to the ordinary man's and woman's shopping basket, housing problem and standard of living.

Economics jargon is counter-productive and much to be avoided. Statistical analyses require a degree of numeracy and an attention-span much beyond what we can expect from the ordinary listener. These, too, are to be avoided. We do nothing to sustain the idea that the command economies, reformed or unreformed, offer an alternative model of national housekeeping, yet to be proven right or wrong, and essentially neither better nor worse than our own mixed economies. We do not do so because the testimony of experience tells a different story.

If Soviet history has one lesson to teach us it is surely that wherever the Soviet system has been installed it brought hardship or ruin to the society that adopted or was made to adopt it. Our task is to explain the political and ideological roots of that ruin and to show that freedom, including economic freedom, is not only the most civilized and equitable way of conducting our affairs, but also the one most conducive to prosperity. Not all capitalist societies are free societies—but all free societies are capitalist societies.

REAGAN'S OFFSTAGE QUIP

16 August 1984

President Reagan has uttered two unhappy sentences by way of an offstage joke while testing the microphones at his home near Santa Barbara. "My fellow Americans," he said, "I am pleased to tell you I have just signed legislation which outlaws Russia forever. We will begin bombing in five minutes."

In the US and the other Western democracies many a jocular or ill-informed sentiment is uttered in the heat of discussion or electoral argument. Liberty is a many-colored thing. It is accident-prone.

The question we have to ask is: do those offstage sentences reflect the policy of the US? Do they accord with what the US has actually done since the end of the war?

The Soviet media now depict President Reagan as a man of war. He is said to be hankering after the destruction of the Soviet Union. Soviet cartoons show him as carrying the legacy of Nazi Germany.

A glance at the post-war era, however, disabuses us of this particular vision of history.

The one successful international predator since 1945, and indeed since 1939, has been the Soviet Union. In 1939, in league with Nazi Germany, the USSR partitioned Poland and incorporated large slices of Polish territory and millions of Poles.

Speaking at the Supreme Soviet in October 1939, Mr. Molotov noted with satisfaction, "One blow from the German Army and another from the Soviet Army put an end to this ugly product of Versailles."

As the war went on, Moscow incorporated parts of Finland, Romania and, earlier, Czechoslovakia; it extinguished the independence of Estonia, Latvia and Lithuania; it imposed Communist rule on Romania, Bulgaria, Hungary, Poland and Czechoslovakia; it turned its East German zone of occupation into a puppet state; it tried to bring Yugoslavia and Albania under its suzerainty and made a stab at Greece.

In 1953 the Red Army put down the workers of East Berlin. In 1956 the Red Army suppressed the Hungarian people's revolution. In 1968 it marched on Czechoslovakia. In 1979 it invaded Afghanistan. In 1980 and 1981 the Red Army enveloped Poland in a web of threatening maneuvers culminating in Poland's self-occupation by the troops of General Jaruzelski.

In Korea the Soviet Union supported North Korea's invasion of its southern neighbor. In Vietnam and Cambodia it supplied and supported aggression. Throughout the 1970s the Soviets deployed troops and advisers in Syria, South Yemen, Ethiopia, Mozambique, Angola and other Third World countries either directly or through their Cuban and East German proxies.

Such, in brief, is the Kremlin's record in world affairs since 1939. The Soviet leaders spoke peace but their actions were warlike. They embraced in their rhetoric the Rights of Man but practised the suppression of men and nations. They nailed liberty and fraternity to their masthead but indulged in coercion, intimidation and war.

The leaders of the Western world tend to be less conscious of the needs of international propaganda and less adept at practising it.

As members of open and democratic societies they speak their minds without inhibition, often incautiously, and not always in the best of taste. Such are the uncontrollable ways of freedom and the nature of imperfect leaders in imperfect societies.

But these imperfect leaders are aware or are publicly reminded of their imperfections. They do not claim to have found the philosopher's stone. They do not tell us they are infallible. They do not, therefore, send thousands of Polish officers to be butchered; they do not deport the cream of Baltic intellectuals; they do not reduce Budapest to ruins; they do not tell us that they have a seamless plan for the felicity of all mankind. They are indeed open to error—to the point of indulging in questionable jokes over a disconnected microphone.

Looking at the Soviet record, we are reminded of Adlai Stevenson's observation at the U.N. Security Council on October 23, 1962. "I have often wondered what the world would be like today if the situation at the end of the war had been reversed—if the United States had been ravaged and shattered by war, and if the Soviet Union had emerged intact in exclusive possession of the atomic bomb and overwhelming military and economic might. Would it have followed the same path and devoted itself to realizing the world of the Charter?"

Adlai Stevenson's words are as worth pondering today as they were in

1962. They induce us to ask: what is the true measure of international behavior—an offstage joke of the US President which was, of course, never meant to be translated into reality, or the somber record of Soviet aggression of which proof abounds in all corners of the earth?

FATHER POPIEŁUSZKO

30 October 1984

The murder of Father Jerzy Popiełuszko will be remembered in the annals of martyrdom as an event equal in significance to the sacrifice of Thomas à Becket and Joan of Arc.

Jerzy Popiełuszko paid the ultimate price for having identified the freedom of the Polish people with the faith of which he was an ordained priest. A Pole and a Christian, he was indomitable in the face of provocation. With the power of the word he challenged the power of a secular order that has no moral legitimacy in the eyes of the Polish nation.

Unlike Cardinal Mindszenty or Archbishop Beran, Jerzy Popiełuszko was not a prelate of the Church. His station in the hierarchy was humble. He was a proletarian in a country of proletarians. Like "Solidarity" for which he fought, he came from the ordinary working people and spoke with the voice of the poor and the disadvantaged. Like "Solidarity," he was young and hopeful. As a son of the Church, he was both courageous and meek.

But his meekness as a Christian never appeared to him to call for weakness in the Christian. He resisted evil where he saw evil; and when he spoke up in the defence of freedom, he did so not only because he saw unfreedom as a state of misfortune, but a state of sinfulness.

Jerzy Popiełuszko's life and death are symbols of the spiritual indestructibility of the Polish nation. The solidarity of man with man was his metaphor, and that metaphor is now making history.

GENSCHER DECLINES

21 November 1984

When the dust has settled over the cancellation of Herr Hans-Dietrich Genscher's visit to Poland, one symbol will have impressed itself on the world's imagination with a force it did not have before the cancellation was announced: the grave of the murdered priest Father Jerzy Popiełuszko has become a shrine the world's statesmen cannot ignore.

To those tens of thousands of Poles who file past Popiełuszko's grave at the St Stanislaw Church every day, we now have to add those Western representatives who pay their homage, when visiting Warsaw, to the

martyrdom of the murdered priest—or do not go to Poland if their wish
to visit the grave is denied.

The German Federal Government took a courageous step in expressing
its solidarity with the ordinary Polish man and woman by cancelling Herr
Genscher's visit, even though there were pressing reasons for the visit to
go ahead. The German record of trying to sustain an area of détente within
a strained international framework is well known. So is Germany's long-
standing commitment to peace and understanding with the Polish nation
and government.

The greater, then, the significance of the German decision to let it be
known to the Polish authorities and German public opinion that if a choice
had to be made between satisfying the demands of the Warsaw regime and
those of the Polish people, Bonn knew which way it had to go.

Warsaw's unwisdom of confronting the Federal Government with that
choice is by now obvious. It has put Father Popiełuszko's grave on the map
of the world.

JUMPING SHIP

27 November 1984

Those 400 odd Polish workers who jumped ship in Hamburg, Trave-
münde and Rotterdam last week were not political refugees in the traditional sense. They were, as individuals, not being persecuted for their
faith, or race, or class. Their misfortune was to have been born or sucked
into a society that treats its members as ants in an anthill. Their lives were
lived in the drab monotony of 'socialist construction.' They were alienated
from their nation, their culture and the joy of work.

The men and women who jumped ship also jumped the bread-lines in
Kraków and Wroclaw; they jumped the indignity of having to beg an om-
nipotent state for elementary nourishment in the early hours of a freezing
winter morning; and they jumped the humiliation of being ill in hospitals
without heating or medicine. They jumped the dairy counters that have
no milk for their children, and the benches of the law-courts that dispense
no justice.

Were these, then, really not political refugees? If bread, and milk, and
hope, and the dignity of work are excluded from our notion of politics,
they were not. But politics so defined does scant justice to life under Communist regimes. Marxist-Leninists have taken great pains to tell the world
that the 'bourgeois' notion of human rights is empty of meaning. Human
rights properly understood, they argue, is the right to work, to shelter, to
economic advancement, and health care. It is these that the 'socialist' state
provides for the proletariat.

The Polish Four Hundred—proletarians to a man—thought otherwise, and they voted with their feet to show it. In a restricted Western sense, they are perhaps 'economic' refugees. But when economic deprivation degenerates into hopelessness and grinding poverty it becomes a political problem of the first order, and the men and women who turn their backs on deprivation are political refugees in a sense Karl Marx would have immediately recognized.

It does not, therefore, behove us to say that these 'tourists' defected 'merely' in search of a better life and do not deserve our sympathy. They defected from non-life into life. When they jumped ship they also jumped the whole antiquated dispensation of Marx and Lenin.

CHINA QUESTIONS THE FAITH

10 December 1984

The Chinese move to read Marxism and Leninism out of the economic management of the Communist system (Soviet style) is a fine example of what went by the name of "modern revisionism" not so many years ago, and might do so again.

"Marx passed away 101 years ago," writes *Renmin Ribao*, "some of his visions were the visions of his time. Since then the situation has changed radically. Some of his ideas are not necessarily appropriate. . . . Using some of the theories of Marx and Lenin to define an abundant, rich, modern life can only impede the advance of history."

The importance of these words is hard to exaggerate. They cast doubt on the sacred books and the omniscience of their authors. Can the church stand, dogma denied? Can Marxism and Leninism stand once the rocklike certainties of Marx and Lenin have been called into question?

In some ways the Chinese move is in line with Imre Nagy's 'New Course,' the reforms planned in Prague in 1968, the Yugoslav model of self-management, and the Kádárite dispensation in Hungary. These were attempts to pull the Soviet model of Communist society screaming and struggling into the 20th century. Indeed some of the inspiration for the Chinese reforms comes from these countries. The Chinese, like their mentors in Eastern Europe, have come to recognize that the ways in which Communist societies, Soviet style, manage their economy are those of the age of the steam engine, of teeth pulled with a carpenter's pliers and appendices removed with a barber's razor blade.

The Chinese leaders' move is a pragmatic team's protest against an antiquarianism that has, for more than a century, masqueraded as "science" and brought ruin upon every country that has yet tried to apply it.

Such protests, however, are not easy to put into practice. Men trained to pull teeth with a carpenter's pliers have a vested interest in preserving their craft and their privileges. Previous experiments were quashed as soon as it suited the Party. Restive client states invited Soviet displeasure. Lenin's New Economic Policy was reversed as soon as the Party decided that the time was ripe for a second revolution; Imre Nagy's New Course was quickly buried by a revived orthodoxy; the Prague reforms were nipped in the bud by the arrival of Soviet tanks.

What makes the Chinese experiment different is the thoroughness of the challenge and the openness with which it is stated. "Get rich," the Chinese leaders are now telling their peasants, "and take that old-fashioned bumf in Marx and Lenin with a pinch of capitalist salt."

The challenge is systemic, though the Chinese leaders would never admit that it is. Still more disturbing for the Soviet leaders, the experiment works. Those skilled hands motivated by centuries of the Confucian work-ethic that have turned Hong Kong, Taiwan and Singapore into models of individual thrift and private enterprise, are now beginning to be put to use in a society of 1000 million disciplined men and women.

'Existing socialism' has been weighed and found wanting. It is now attempting to borrow a trick or two from 'existing capitalism.'

Chinese revisionism faces the Kremlin with one crucial question: with their legitimacy weakened and their economic raison d'être thrown to the winds, can Communist societies of the Soviet type survive?

HISTORY IN 1984

5 November 1984

Information is power. No statement more important than this or more pertinent to the concerns of people living under totalitarian regimes can be made in this year of *1984*.

Information corruptly used distorts the truth, wipes out our memory of the past, destroys the meaning of words and undermines our very ability to ask meaningful questions because the framework of authentic thinking itself has been suborned. When all answers are predetermined by the ineluctable "laws" of history, genuine questioning is, at best, an infantile indulgence, at worst a passport to the psychiatric hospital. Faced with the spectacle of an unrelenting ideology, the individual seeks refuge in self-censorship.

Benedetto Croce once noted "all history is contemporary history." The Communist regimes have improved on Croce's observation. "He who controls the past," they say, "controls the future." They found that if your image of the future is based on a myth, you have no choice but to control the past, for the myth cannot be sustained unless the past is so doctored that everything in it points to the prescribed millennium: Luther prefigures Marx; Kossuth prefigures Lenin; Ivan the Terrible prefigures Stalin,

and the entire story of man's life on earth points to its necessary con-
summation in the October Revolution. The human adventure becomes a
mechanical nightmare and the individual a cog in a wheel whose rhythm
and rotation are beyond his control.

The Radio University of the Czechoslovak Service of Radio Free Europe, which I have the privilege to launch today, sets out to offer a corrective to this warped vision of truth and the past. Week after week, distinguished scholars drawn from American and West European universities
will give you the story of the first Czechoslovak Republic from its foundation in 1918 to its destruction in 1938.

Our purpose is not to offer you a counter-story to that provided by official Communist historiography (or historiographies, for the past changes
with the needs of the hour) but a broad spectrum of independent views.
Let what will emerge.

It will then be up to you to judge whether official historiography has
the ring of truth about it—whether it stands up to evidence offered and
examined by scholars whose sole driving force is disinterested intellectual
curiosity and not the service of Marxism-Leninism or the glorification of
some nationalistic vision.

But gathering together the views of independent scholars in these
broadcasts has a further and wider objective. The study of human affairs
ultimately revolves around a core question which is moral. It is one Aris-
totle raised in his *Ethics* in trying to define the characteristics of the Just
Man, and has been with us ever since: "How do I behave towards my neighbour so that I can live at peace with my conscience?"

The independent study of history as an educational process can equip
us with some of the critical and moral qualities with which we can seek
(even though we can never be sure of obtaining) sensible answers to that
basic question. It cannot, of course, provide us with patent medicines. It
cannot give us infallible commands and interdictions. The sort of education history can offer as its end-result is more modest and may be summarised in a single sentence: Education is what survives when what has been
learnt has been forgotten.

The proof of education is not a book, but a man. It is to the formation
of that independent individual that this series of Radio University broadcasts hopes to make a small contribution.

POLISH POLICE IN THE DOCK

31 December 1984

The first two days of the trial of Father Popiełuszko's alleged killers
must have sent a chill down the spines of security policemen throughout the Soviet Union and Eastern Europe. The Torun trial has one simple

message for them: they may, after all, have to answer for their deeds even under the existing Communist system if they are unlucky enough to get caught and the regime wants to make an example of them.

For the four men in the dock have done nothing more culpable than what any security police agent is expected to perform in Kiev, Sofia, Bucharest or Prague in the normal course of his duties. Maltreating or killing the class-enemy, whether "legally," semi-legally or illegally, has never been looked upon as a crime by these men or their masters. Indeed it was, and is, considered to be a mark of loyalty and is rewarded accordingly. Captain Piotrowski, the alleged instigator of the murder of Father Popiełuszko, is a much-decorated security police officer. Lieutenant Pekala and his two colleagues believed that they would be promoted for teaching Popiełuszko a lesson. Men brought up in the spirit of the Cheka and Lenin's "decree on terror" would expect no other treatment.

What has to be explained about this remarkable case is not that Piotrowski ordered Pekala to commit a heinous crime, but that the Jaruzelski regime has summoned the courage to try them in the full glare of Polish and world publicity. No doubt, the General's hope must be that his government will be seen to be acting with fairness and determination along clean military lines, and that this will gain it a measure of acceptance in the eyes of the Polish people. If so, he is taking a grave risk of which he must be aware.

Some Poles may, indeed, give him a certain benefit of the doubt, but many more are likely to ask whether the details revealed about the operations of the security police aren't just the tip of the iceberg—whether many more and even more damaging facts do not remain hidden, and whether the kind of mission these police officers carried out hadn't (as Pekala first confessed) the approval of higher authority. Would there have been a trial if Father Popiełuszko's driver had not got away? If so much is revealed under the force of circumstances, how many more skeletons might there be in the Government's cupboard? And how many people are victims of the *institutional* malfeasance of the Communist system?

The golden rule of dictatorship is never to allow the privileges and immunity of the apparatus of official repression to be eroded, because on this apparatus dictatorial regimes rely for their survival. When the system's linen is washed in public, the dictators themselves have reason to worry. Mussolini, Stalin, Hitler and Mao never made the mistake of allowing this backbone of their rule to be exposed. In no case did they permit members of the security apparatus to be tried or publicly ostracised for over-zealous behaviour. If tried they were, it was for the opposite reason.

General Jaruzelski is, therefore, setting a precedent. If the Torun trial is concluded without untoward incident, and sentences that fit the crime are meted out and put into effect, the General may garner a modicum of popular approval that will leave his regime in a state no worse than it was before Father Popiełuszko's murder—which is not saying very much. But the Polish security apparatus will have been shaken, and so will the security forces throughout eastern Europe and the Soviet Union. If this can happen in Poland, can any policeman, spy or informer be safe?

The nice question to ask is whether Jaruzelski has mounted the trial with or without Moscow's approval. The Politburo and the men running the KGB must surely be aware that the Poles may have opened Pandora's box with consequences that will be bloc-wide.

ENTER MIKHAIL GORBACHEV

12 March 1985

The elevation of Mr. Gorbachev will probably be followed by a more vigorous pursuit of Soviet "peace" propaganda and a more persistent attempt to decouple Western Europe from the United States, and the US Congress from the US Administration, especially on space defense. Mr. Gorbachev will be shown to be a man of "moderation," of pragmatic views untainted by ideology, a man representing a new generation with whom "we can do business." There is, indeed, a view already abroad in some Western capitals that Mr. Gorbachev represents all these things—that Soviet policy will now be governed by the genuinely free choices and personal character of a team of reformed Soviet leaders.

We must be prepared for this fresh turn in our contest with the Soviet system. Speaking from our knowledge of Soviet history, we reflect the view that Soviet expansionism and international militancy flow directly from the nature of the Soviet system and not from the personality, background, education or age of its leaders. Soviet expansionism since World War II shows a steadily rising curve. The aggression against Hungary and the threat of missile deployment in Cuba happened under the de-Stalinizing, "liberal," folksy Mr. Khrushchev. Czechoslovakia, Angola and Afghanistan were given "internationalist help" under the even-tempered, avuncular, and automobile-loving Leonid Brezhnev. Soviet leaders change; the system does not. So far at least, it has shown no ability to change without jeopardizing its chances of survival.

We point out that peace is indivisible. A system that cannot live at peace with its own citizens is unlikely to do so with the outside world. We recognize the legitimacy of the security interests of the Soviet state, but challenge the moral legitimacy of Soviet behaviour both at home and abroad.

Mr. Gorbachev can render quick and persuasive proof of his liberal intentions by removing his troops from Afghanistan, Czechoslovakia and Hungary. He can call a halt to Soviet and Cuban meddling in Central America. He could even help in giving effect to the Yalta Agreement by agreeing, 40 years after the event, to free and democratic elections in Eastern Europe.

The challenge to Mr. Gorbachev is whether he is able and willing to challenge the system that has elevated him.

MOSCOW FUNERAL: A PRIVATE VIEW

14 March 1985

While he was alive, Mr. Konstantin Chernenko made no lasting mark on history. With his funeral, perhaps he did. Who would have thought that 68 years after a revolution which announced the Death of God and denounced the evils of armed imperialism, the General Secretary of the Soviet Communist Party would be laid to rest with the borrowed pomp of Russian Orthodoxy and a military ceremony that would have done Adolf Hitler proud?

The setting, the plot and the actors were a quaint combination of Gothic horror and low comedy. Could Zeffirelli have thought up a more grisly collection than those waxen figures assembled on the top of the Moscow Mausoleum? Under what rubric in the history of Soviet atheism are we to file the spectacle of Chernenko's widow stroking and kissing the dead leader's head in the style of Byzantium? What are we to think of those medal-bearing generals in their outsize hats and cardboard uniforms? Have they stepped out from some provincial operetta, or a Victorian wax-works to bemuse a bored public? Was Mr. Chernenko mocking the dead or the living?

Such were the questions irreverently brought to one observer's mind as he was watching the Kremlin's macabre ceremony. Were the Soviet impresarios aware that they were confirming the outside world's worst suspicions about the real 'feel' of Soviet society? Did they realize that they were rendering hard proof, if such were still needed, that the Soviet system was, indeed, that bizarre mixture of musty decorum, sham religiosity, grim regimentation and totalitarian self-righteousness that the USSR's critics have always said it was? That Sovietism was of and about the 19th century, not our own?

The gruesome tradition of Soviet funerals goes back to Lenin's celebrated entombment. The pomp of his burial, the purple prose of Stalin's Oath of Fealty, and the preservation and permanent display of Lenin's remains infuriated Krupskaya who held strong views about revolutionary ethics.

But the revolutionary ethics of the Soviet system died with Lenin— only the rhetoric, the pomp and the ceremony remain. To these have been added, with the "advance of socialism," the militarism and high orthodoxy of what must strike the Western observer as a profoundly reactionary society.

OPENINGS IN MOSCOW

2 September 1985

A debate about the future course of Soviet relations with Eastern Europe appears to be going on in the Soviet leadership. It centers on the amount of political and economic autonomy the client states are entitled to enjoy within the "socialist camp." The advent of Mr. Gorbachev first fuelled hopes that his widely anticipated "liberalism" would translate into a more permissive attitude towards the members of the glacis. Now we are not sure whether the authentic voice of Moscow is that of the disciplinarians who would have Eastern Europe fitted more rigorously into the Soviet imperial framework, or that of so far unidentified members of the apparat who seem to hold that the small states of Eastern Europe have a legitimate right to pursue their economic and political self-interest on the assumption that these do not clash with (rather might they advance) the interests of the whole community.

The lines are, by now, fairly clearly drawn. One, expressed in *Pravda* on 21 June 1985, urges a heightened sense of political, ideological and economic unity between the USSR and Eastern Europe. It has harsh words to say about the dangers of nationalism and stresses the universal validity of the "inherent general laws" of the socialist system. It allows for no compromise between centralized planning and an enlarged private sector on the argument that any such move would lead to ideological and social destabilization. In foreign affairs it rejects the idea that the client states have a mediating role to play between the USSR and the US.

These are hard-line sentiments entirely in accord with Mr. Gorbachev's observations at Dnepopetrovsk in June 1985 and the speech he had earlier delivered at the Warsaw Pact meeting in April 1985. They are close enough to the Stalinist conception of a centralized super-state to send shivers down the spines of reform-happy Hungarians and wandering Poles. They seem to justify the words of *The Economist:* "the new Soviet leader expects from his allies the same disciplined order he wants to impose on Soviet factories."

A more permissive line was taken in the July 1985 issue of *Kommunist* and less outspokenly by *Novoje Vremja* (August 23, 1985). Oleg Bogomolov and Nikolai Shishlin, speaking presumably for the Soviet establishment, and Károly Németh for the Hungarian, acknowledged the existence of divergent interests and the implicit right of the Communist Parties of the smaller states to pursue them. Economic integration could not be imposed by *fiat.* In a family of equal and sovereign states, wrote Bogomolov, overall economic policies were subject to the voluntary agreement of all. Hungary, said Németh, "is determined to widen mutually advantageous economic, scientific and technological links with the developed capitalist states."

These differences cannot be dismissed as bogus or purely theoretical. They indicate that the Soviet leadership is far from being of one mind about its attitude to Eastern Europe. Nor can we entirely dismiss the idea that the argument is, in reality, not about Eastern Europe at all but a covert way of speaking about the future of *Soviet* society. In either case, one has reason to suspect that Mr. Gorbachev is not, or not yet, as firmly in the saddle as his supporters hope and his critics fear.

Some East European governments have tacitly joined the argument by reprinting, or not reprinting, the contending articulations, or providing their readers with their own summaries. Not surprisingly, Prague and Sofia reproduced *Pravda's* warning of June 21, 1985, while the Poles, Hungarians and Romanians—hoping perhaps that the devil would go away if they did not notice his presence—did not. Bucharest, without directly referring to *Pravda*, reaffirmed its long-standing independent position on the primacy of national interests, while Budapest and the East Germans gave play to the sentiments expressed in *Novoje Vremja* and similar views culled from other Soviet sources. Belgrade, too, showed itself to be sensitive to the incipient schism, siding, as could be expected, with those who see merit in a centrifugal conception of "socialism."

The line-up is spectacularly similar to that which preceded, in 1984, Mr. Honecker's suggested visit, and the cancellation of his visit, to the Federal Republic. The two "tiers" some students of East European affairs then identified continue to exist, even though they cannot be said to represent more than an *ad hoc* community of interests. Yet, they are recurrent enough to alert the Kremlin to the volatility of the whole of Eastern Europe, especially at times of economic hardship and weaknesses at the centre.

So far, the debate about how much independence the Soviet Union should tolerate in Eastern Europe appears to be undecided. Those of the East European Parties and Governments that care to use it have a certain room for maneuvre. Economic self-interest as well as the hope of gaining a greater sense of legitimacy in the eyes of their own people should induce them to argue for a polycentric conception of "socialism" and the maintenance of such economic decentralization and "privatization" as they have so far managed to put in train. Their relative openness and proclivity to act, *sotto voce*, as honest brokers in foreign affairs have served them well. They have gained from détente much more than the Soviet Union. It cannot now be in their interests to fall in with the Soviet drive for a much tighter Comecon and a more closely coordinated foreign policy.

Openness towards the Western world is, indeed, their only hope of escaping from the stringencies of a harsh economic climate. This and a solid record of respecting the freedoms and human rights of their own populations may, in the end, be their best contribution to "socialist construction"

as the young Karl Marx would have conceived it, as well as their passport to acceptance by the civilized world. Everything we know about the
Soviet Union since Stalin goes to show that, even though their sovereignty
is clearly limited, the East European parties and governments have more
leverage in determining their relationship with Moscow than they themselves realize or would care to admit. It is in their national interest to use it.

A GRAVE SITUATION?

23 October 1985

Apropos of our discussions this morning of current Soviet allegations
that the world is facing a "Grave International Situation":

Our answer is that the international situation is no graver than it has
been for a long time and less grave than it has been for some time.

It is the situation of the *Soviet Union* that is grave because America's
great technological lead, represented by the Strategic Defense Initiative,
has once again put the USSR at a hopeless disadvantage. The Soviets must
choose between competing with the U.S. in space or putting their economic house in order. They cannot do both.

For that very reason the international situation may be said to be especially secure—as it was also secure during those first post-war years when
the United States had a monopoly of nuclear weapons but no one lost sleep
lest the U.S. should misuse it.

The Soviet leaders resort to talking about a "Grave International Situation" only when they feel the international balance of power has turned
against them and they need our concessions. It is a fear we do not share.

GORBACHEV'S PROGRAMME IN THE LIGHT OF KHRUSHCHEV'S

29 October 1985

Looking back upon the Soviet Communist Party's 1961 program in the
light of the 1985 document carries one overwhelming message: the Party
has shown itself to be neither prescient nor all-powerful.

The Soviet system's ideological foundation is "scientific communism,"
a discipline that claims to possess the predictive qualities of the natural
sciences. "At every historical stage, the Party, taking guidance from the
theory of Marx, Engels and Lenin, accomplished the tasks scientifically
formulated in its program," says the 1961 Party program.

"Scientific communism" is said to enable the Party to engineer human
beings and the social context in which they will live with clockwork precision. Its mastery is claimed to be the key to the arrival of the fully just,

classless and prosperous society. It makes the future foreseeable and enforceable.

N.S. Khrushchev and his comrades acted on these principles when they put pen to paper and drafted the 1961 Party program.

They predicted:

By the end of a 20-year period "Soviet people will be more prosperous than working people in the developed capitalist countries."
The facts: Soviet people enjoy only a fraction of West European and US living standards.

"The entire population will be able adequately to satisfy its needs in high-quality and varied foodstuffs."
The facts: the population is going short of even low-quality foodstuffs.

"In the course of the first decade an end will be put to the housing shortage in the country."
The facts: 24 years on, the Soviet housing shortage is desperate.

"In the course of the second decade, housing will gradually become rent-free for all citizens."
The truth: Soviet housing has not become rent-free.

"Public transport facilities (tramways, buses, trolley-buses and subways) will become free in the course of the second decade."
The facts: 24 years on, public transportation is not free. Moscow fares have been increased recently.

"At the end of the second decade such public amenities as water, gas and heating will also be free."
The facts: 24 years later none is free.

"The Soviet Union will have the world's shortest and at the same time most productive and most highly-paid working day."
The truth: the Soviet worker is lower-paid than workers in any of the developed "capitalist" countries.

"Within the current ten year period (the USSR) . . . . will exceed the level of US industrial output."
The facts: in 1970 the Soviet Union was way behind US industrial output, especially in the all-important field of advanced technology.

"Within 20 years (the USSR) will leave the present overall volume of US industrial output far behind."
The facts: by 1980–81 the Soviet lag became greater.

"The Party solemnly proclaims: the present generation of Soviet people shall live in Communism!"

The facts: they do not live in Communism. The 1985 Party program mod-estly observes: "The Soviet peoples' . . . hard work opens the stage to de-veloped Socialism."

Everything that could go wrong did go wrong with the 1961 Party pro-gram. "Scientific communism" as the key to a fully rational human envi-ronment has failed the Communist Party and the world communist move-ment. A great and long-suffering people had a ruse foisted on them and are now paying the price. "One-third of mankind is building a new life under the banner of scientific communism," says the 1961 Program. So it does, and we have seen the results—in Ethiopia, for example, where the scientific model has produced widespread starvation.

There is a clear lesson to be drawn from all this. If "scientific commu-nism" has been unable to predict the future of simple things like Soviet shoe-production, how can the Soviet and East European peoples believe Moscow's heady promises about the impending arrival of "Peace, Free-dom, Equality, Fraternity and Happiness"? For that is what Khrushchev's preface to the 1961 program predicted.

Mr. Gorbachev appears to know better. He is not giving quite so many hostages to fortune. Yet the 1985 Party program claims to be heir to Khru-shchev's. Will it fare better than its ill-starred predecessor?

Appendix C
Excerpts from a Radio Free Europe Review, 1956

RFE/Munich
Office of the Political Advisor
5 December 1956

Memorandum

TO: Mr. Condon

FROM: Mr. Griffith

SUBJECT: Policy Review of Voice of Free Hungary Programming, 23 October–23 November 1956.

A rereading of the summaries originally presented at morning policy meetings for these programs makes it clear that <u>the summaries often failed to reflect the content of the program as it was finally written</u> (this is not the case only with programs where policy violation occurred; the summaries during the period under review in many other cases proved to be very inaccurate descriptions of the programs finally produced). In one instance, however, *no* summary of a program where a policy violation occurred was presented in advance, because this program was a press review and under normal circumstances would not have been checked in advance. The normal programming schedule of the desk was disrupted during the revolutionary crisis to a degree not justified, in our opinion, by the exigencies of the situation. Program distinctions tended to become meaningless and writers who would not ordinarily have been permitted to write political commentary apparently did so, at least during the period 23 October to 4 November, with very little supervision by those in charge of the desk. . . .

Of 16 programs which involve distortions of policy or serious failure to employ constructive techniques of policy application, nine were approved by [Viktor] Márjás, three by [László] Béry and five by [János] Ölvedi and one by [László] Feketekúthy (again, none by Andor Gellért). We were not aware at the time that Gellért was not editing and approving scripts before broadcast. As you will recall, Márjás very seldom, and Ölvedi practically never, attended morning policy meetings during most of the period under survey. Márjás's language and hearing difficulties make his attendance at meetings of doubtful value in any case. We had assumed, however, that Gellért would brief his subordinates on the conclusions of morning meetings and on policy guidance given him by us at other occasions during the day. If he did so, his briefing does not appear to have been effective. . . .

[Julián] Borsányi's "Armed Forces Special" #A1 of 27 October violates the letter and spirit of policy in effect at the time. The program gives detailed instructions as to how partisan and Hungarian armed forces should fight. It advises local authorities to secure stores of arms for the use of Freedom Fighters and tells the population to hide Freedom Fighters who become separated from their units. It advises the population to provide food and supplies for Freedom Fighters. The writer tells Hungarians to sabotage ("disconnect") railroad and telephone lines. It fairly clearly implies that foreign aid will be forthcoming if the resistance forces succeed in establishing a "central military command." The program is cast entirely in the form of advice from the outside; there is no reference to information coming from within the country. The program refers to the "Nagy puppet government" and states that Nagy is relying on the support of the Soviet armed forces. Although the writer is too categorical in his phraseology, his attacks on Nagy are in themselves not out of keeping with policy guidance in effect at the time. The program concludes with some rather complex formulations which could be interpreted by listeners as implying help from the outside.

The summary of this program presented at the morning meeting of the day it was broadcast stated:

> Laws and experience of partisan war. Without inciting the participants of civil war, we tell them what are the experiences and techniques of partisan warfare, citing Russian, Yugoslav, etc., experiences. First rule, e.g., is that groups which are fighting dispersed should establish contact with one another and establish a political center, etc., etc.

I considered the program as summarized inappropriate when it was presented at the morning meeting. I pointed out that such a program could be permitted only if it dealt with the topic in purely theoretical terms without any reference to current events in Hungary. Gellért gave assurance that this would be done. This program was approved for broadcast by Béry. There is no evidence that Gellért read it in its completed form.

Borsányi's "Armed Forces Special" #B1 of 28 October gives detailed instructions to Hungarian soldiers on the conduct of partisan warfare. The author states at the beginning of the program that Hungarians must continue to fight vigorously because this will have a great effect on the handling of the Hungarian question by the Security Council of the UN. Without saying so directly, he implies that the UN will give active support to Hungarians if they keep on fighting. The program is over-optimistic in tone. The opening announcement states: "Colonel Bell will tell Hungarian soldiers how ingenious and smart leadership can counterbalance numerical and arms superiority." The conclusion states: "Colonel Bell has told Hungarian soldiers how to obstruct large forces by small ones and by simple means." In the light of subsequent events the program grossly underestimates the ability of the Soviets to move new troops into Hungary. Borsányi implies that the most the Soviets can bring in is about four divisions and that it might take as long as two or three weeks for the Soviets to secure the Danube line if Hungarians fight effectively against them. The program makes a feeble effort at indirect propaganda by recounting a story about how Yugoslav partisans fought against much larger forces of Germans in South Serbia in 1943 and beat them; but the indirectness of this story is completely negated by the obvious comments at the beginning and end of it. This program of Borsányi's constitutes a serious policy violation, for the author in no way makes any effort to demonstrate that he is basing his advice on opinions or even information coming from within the country. Here at its worst is the emigré on the outside, without responsibility or authority, giving detailed advice to the people fighting at home.

The summary of this program presented at the morning policy meeting of the day on which it was written was at the least misleading; it stated only:

> We review the success in November 1943 of the 500 Serb partisans who were able to hold back the 15,000-man German troop near the town of Nish.

The program was approved for broadcast by Ölvedi.

[Gyula] Litteráti's "Armed Forces Special #D1" of 30 October 1956, like the Borsányi programs discussed above, gives detailed military instructions to the population of Hungary, this time on the techniques of anti-tank warfare. Litteráti does not give his advice in quite as direct, categorical a fashion as Borsányi and makes repeated references to Soviet tactics in World War II. The intent of the program is nevertheless completely clear. A case could perhaps be made that this program is theoretically not a policy violation; in its effect, however, it must be considered as such, for the people of Hungary are not only encouraged to fight, but told how. There is a strong strain of over-optimism in the program; the author gives the impression that tanks are really very easy to destroy. The program is very skillfully written, contains little surplus rhetoric and gives on the whole, militarily sound advice. The summary of this program presented at the morning meeting on 30 October stated only:

> We explain the simple partisan means by which it is possible to avoid responsibility in connection with tanks.

Gellért assured me that this program, like others of its type would be written on a purely theoretical basis without specific reference to current events in Hungary. This program was approved for broadcast by Ölvedi; there is no evidence that Gellért read it before broadcast.

Zoltán Thury's "Special Short World Press Review" #1 of 4 November probably constitutes the most serious policy violation of all. At the conclusion of his press review, Thury quotes excerpts from a London *Observer* Washington dispatch of the same day as follows:

> If the Soviet troops really attack Hungary, if our expectations should hold true and Hungarians hold out for three or four days, then the pressure upon the government of the United States to send military help to the Freedom Fighters will become irresistible!

Thury then comments, paraphrasing the *Observer*'s correspondent's words:

> This is what the *Observer* writes in today's number. The paper observes that the American Congress cannot vote for war as long as the presidential elections have not been held. The article then continues: "If the Hungarians can continue to fight until Wednesday, we shall be closer to a world war than at any time since 1939."

Thury's *own* final comment in this program is:

> The reports from London, Paris, the US and other Western reports show that the world's reaction to Hungarian events surpasses every imagination. In the Western capitals a practical manifestation of Western sympathy is expected at any hour.

The tapes of this program have been checked. It was broadcast in exactly the same form as written. The London *Observer* dispatch has been checked word for word. It is true that the normally cautious and realistic *Observer* printed the words Thury quotes (he did not alter them) on its front page. The passage must have been distributed through the Central Newsroom, having been telephoned in from London, since the *Observer* itself does not ordinarily reach Munich until Monday. It has been impossible, however, to track down the original item put out by the Central Newsroom. The fact that the *Observer* printed these words hardly gave Thury authorization to broadcast them to Hungary at a time when Hungarians were likely to be clutching for any straws of hope from the West. This program is undoubtedly the one several Hungarian refugees and correspondents have referred to as "the promise that help would come which RFE broadcast on the weekend of 4 November." The quotations from the *Observer* are bad enough; Thury's own comments are far worse since they clearly represented to the listener the editorial opinion of the VFH [Voice of Free Hungary]. He leads his listeners to believe that military intervention by the West can be expected within a few days. This is contrary to the entire RFE philosophy of broadcasting. To all desks throughout the years we have emphasized over and over again that RFE can never take the responsibility for promising something it cannot deliver. It was agreed with Gellért on 4 November that no promises of hope could be broadcast, that RFE could only attack Kádár and the Soviets for their treachery and give roundups of the reactions of the free world. It was agreed that any free world reactions which indicated promise of more than moral support and action undertaken by the UN General Assembly would be misleading and should not be put on the air.

Thury's press review was approved for broadcast by Ölvedi. There is no evidence that Gellért saw it. . . .

In retrospect it appears to have been a mistake to have permitted the VFH to broadcast any programs on military topics during the revolution. As I recall, these programs were permitted because it was felt by Gellért and ourselves that to broadcast information on the theory of partisan warfare, tank defense techniques and elementary principles of civilian defense in a civil war situation might help save lives during the Revolution and at the least would remind Hungarian listeners to be cautious and avoid sacrificing themselves in foolish gestures of resistance. We were mistaken in assuming that the desk's military writers could write on, or the responsible editors edit, these delicate topics with sufficient cleverness and a proper sense of detachment to keep them theoretical while still offering relevant advice. . . .

. . . The Hungarian Desk was constantly advised both from New York and in Munich to avoid giving the impression that the VFH was trying to direct the Revolution in Hungary. The VFH was likewise constantly advised by us to avoid discussing events in Hungary in too dogmatic terms, but instead to emphasize that our information was incomplete, that the situation was so complex that it could not be judged entirely from the outside. We urged the desk to phrase its own comments as much as possible in terms of lines taken by what seemed to be the more responsible commentaries over the Freedom Stations and the lines taken by the local Revolutionary Councils. Gellért indicated full agreement with this advice and complete understanding of the necessity for it. Program summaries presented at daily meetings generally reflected these principles.

A re-reading of the daily summaries of this period after a reading of the programs themselves often reveals wide disparity between the two. The disparity is more often than not one of tone. While the summaries presented in advance are measured, qualified, logical presentations of arguments and points of view, too many of the programs emerged in final form as bombastic, rhetorical, overly emotional blasts at the Nagy Government or certain members of it. The Freedom Stations were quoted too seldom (in many programs, not at all); little reference was made to the fact that the vfh lacked complete information and therefore was not really entitled to pass final judgment. In short, major mistakes of tone and technique were made in many of these programs; the result was that policy was badly distorted in the final broadcasts. . . .

The next day [26 October 1956] [Imre] Mikes wrote a blast against Nagy and Kádár totally lacking in refinement, subtlety and humility (Mikes "Special Reflector #IV," 26 October 1956); displaying no inclination to admit the differences in the situations faced by the two men, he attacks Nagy for not behaving like Gomulka and states: "Imre Nagy is no solution any more . . . the people backed him, they demanded his return and raised him from the political grave where he was thrown by his Moscow rivals in the eternal fight for power." The writer attacks Nagy for making promises but insisting that the revolution stop before they are implemented. Contradicting himself at the end, he declares "the premier should not make any promises, the people do not need his program now . . . they only need his signature . . . to recall the Soviet Divisions" and in a final frenzied outburst shouts "The last moment was over long ago. It was over when the first martyr of the freedom fight died. Imre Nagy missed the last moment. Yet he still has an opportunity; to follow the will of the people and the nation—away with the Soviets if not away with him for ever!" . . . The program was approved by Béry for broadcast.

The summary of this script presented at the morning meeting gave the impression of a much more moderate approach to the problem. . . .

Another commentary of the same day (Béry: "Special Russia Commentary" (sic) 26 October 56) is less bombastic than Mikes, but indulges in the same kind of unrefined generalizations. It is full of rhetoric and pretends to full knowledge of the Hungarian situation but makes no specific reference to the demands of the Revolutionary Fighters. Béry takes too much of an all-or-nothing position toward Nagy, stating there are only agents in Hungary who obey orders from Moscow. . . . The morning meeting summary gave no indication that it would treat the position of the Nagy Government at all. It seems that Béry must have changed his plan for this commentary after the morning meeting had taken place. . . .

Béry wrote another commentary on 29 October (Béry: "Special Short Commentary #C2," 29 October 1956) which has all the faults of his commentary of 26 October 1956, and displays a perhaps even more pronounced and rather petulant "Nagy-is-no-damned-good" attitude. This commentary, too, is lacking in humility. No reference is made to the fact that we do not have enough information to judge Nagy's position with absolute finality. Béry's commentary could have been highly effective if he had confined himself to summing up the questions about Nagy's position and intentions being asked at that very time by the Freedom Stations and the local National Councils. This commentary was approved by Márjás for broadcast.

The summary of this program presented in advance gives a totally different impression of it—in fact there is very little resemblance between the summary and the program as it was finally written. The reason may be that the summary was prepared by Gellért and the program by Béry without Gellért ever having seen the final product. . . .

[Károly] Szakmáry's "Youth Special #D1," 30 October 1956, contains a feature rare in the programming of the vfh—a reminder at the beginning and at the end of the broadcast that the author is an emigré who feels to some extent ashamed to address people at home because he is not there fighting and does not really know what conditions there are like. This is excellent. But one wishes the writer had had a greater sense of shame, for in the body of the program he does exactly what he says he is ashamed to do. He gives emphatic impassioned advice in a flood of words and rhetoric. He urges fighters not to put down their arms, speaks over-optimistically about the "limited capabilities" of Soviet troops, tells his listeners that the promises of the Nagy Government cannot be taken at face value. The program is chaotically organized. Though it is not a policy violation in terms of the policy in effect at the time, it is a poor application of it. No summary of this program had been presented at the morning meeting in advance of the broadcast. It was approved for broadcast by Márjás. . . .

Borsányi made another crude attack on the Nagy Government in a short glossary on 31 October ("Special Glossary #E2") and two other programs, of those read for this survey, expressed misgivings about Nagy or his associates in milder form ([Emil] Csonka, "Chronological Review of Week's Events #E1," 31 October 1956; [Imre] Vámos, "Special Commentary #E2," 31 October 1956). Mikes's "Reflector #E1" of the same day was one of the most tactless of all of Mikes's poor programs. It is a supercilious polemic with the university youth and the revolutionary army paper *Igazság* on the question of whether Nagy did or did not assent to calling in Soviet troops. For better or for worse, in view of the fact that the revolution was developing, the subject should have been left at that, and we should not have entered into argumentation with the revolutionary forces in Hungary, but instead simply said (as the summary indicated) Radio Budapest reports that Nagy had called them in. Incongruously, at the beginning of this program Mikes states we do not intend to debate and we do not wish to stir up passions. The whole program does just this, except that one suspects such a program may well have stirred up more passions against rfe than against Nagy or any elements in the Revolutionary Forces. Like all of Mikes's programs this one is lavishly adorned with exaggerated phrases and rhetorical flourish. This program was approved for broadcast by Márjás. . . .

Inasmuch as the vfh was in favor of the Hungarian Revolution it was by implication in favor of the Revolution's being carried to a successful conclusion. Policy on the extent to which rfe should indirectly urge Hungarians to continue fighting was never specifically formulated in writing; as the Revolution developed, it became increasingly clear that the best course to follow in judging this difficult question would be to let the Free Radios being heard in increasing volume from within Hungary be our guide. New York and Munich were in complete agreement on this point. As the end of October approached, this subject became increasingly important and was regularly discussed at length at morning policy meetings. It was agreed that programs should point out to listeners that there might be elements of deception in a cease-fire accepted without guarantee that the gains of the Revolution would be preserved and that Hungarians should be warned against attempts by the Communists to infiltrate local Revolutionary Councils. This particular topic was skillfully dealt with in indirect fashion by [Sándor] Kőrösi-Krizsán in his "Special Calling Communists #D1" of 30 October.

As for the general question of continuing the fighting, it was agreed that statements from the Freedom Stations, decisions of the local Revolutionary Councils and confirmed reports from journalists inside Hungary should be reported, summarized and analyzed. Gellért never expressed any disagreement with this approach. In this respect again, however, the desk's principal political commentators were either unaware of this advice (it is difficult to believe that Béry was, since he usually attended morning meetings regularly) or failed to follow it. . . .

A shrill, violent Mikes broadcast ("Special Reflector #C1," 29 October 1956) urged Freedom Fighters not to give up their arms. It did not directly urge them to continue fighting, as such. It lacked any reference to the fact that people in the country might be able to judge this delicate question better than emigrés on the outside and made no reference to the Freedom Stations or other opinion from within the country. This had been specifically advised and agreed upon at the morning meeting when a summary of the program had been presented. The program was approved for broadcast by Márjás.

In addition to the 30 October Litteráti program discussed . . . above, which by implication urged Hungarians to continue fighting, three other programs dealt with this topic directly on the 30th of October. . . . Mikes made a shrill appeal to Hungarians to continue fighting or variously, at different points in the program, merely to retain their arms. (In this, as in many of Mikes's programs, there are so many internal contradictions that it is often impossible to discover one single consistent line; one gets the impression that these programs must often have sounded to listeners as emotional outpourings without any consistent line.) No summary of this program which in any way reflects its contents seems to have been presented at either morning meeting of the days on which it was broadcast. According to the summary for 30 October, Mikes was to have written about the necessity for the Revolutionary Forces to organize their own police forces to replace the AVH and other discredited regime police elements. This would have been a quite acceptable topic, but in retrospect it is clear that no matter what topic he may have written about at this stage, Mikes would have produced a highly emotional program out of keeping with sound broadcasting techniques. Mikes's 30 October program was likewise approved for broadcast by Márjás.

Béry's program of the same day was perhaps worse in its effect than Mikes's for it was much better written from a technical point of view. It clearly encouraged false hopes. Without identifying the source of his information Béry stated flatly that Soviet troops in Hungary were either not fighting or were only fighting half-heartedly. He grossly over-estimated the capabilities of the Hungarian Armed Forces: "With comparatively small losses . . . they can stop for weeks a far greater armed force." Béry declared: "Hungarian soldiers! . . . inactivity is treason!" In the form in which these statements are made, without any reference to supporting opinion from within the country, they constitute a policy violation. No summary of this program was presented in advance. The Political Advisor's Office was not told that it was being written. There is no evidence that Gellért ever approved it, or for that matter even knew of its existence. It also was approved for broadcast by Márjás.

Like Béry, Szakmáry in his Youth Special #D1 exhibits naive and irresponsible over-optimism. He states: "It is evident that a putting down of the weapons based only on the irresponsible promises of Radio Budapest would represent giving up the results achieved so far by the Freedom Fight." As with the Béry program, no summary of the Szakmáry program was ever presented before broadcast.

On 31 October, as far as can be determined from scripts available for this survey, the "don't-stop-fighting" theme seems to be largely absent from VFH programming. It appeared again on 1 November in a Mikes program ("Special Reflector #F1") in what is probably the most emotional of all Mikes's broadcasts during this period. The bad technique, the extreme rhetoric, the violently nationalistic tone of this program must be read (still better, I suppose, listened to) to be believed. As with all these other programs, there is no evidence that Gellért read it before it was broadcast. It was again approved for the air by Márjás.

The summary of this program presented at the 1 November morning meeting is very different from the final product:

There are sporadic signs and reports to the effect that the Stalinist remnants are trying to incite the revolutionary masses to irresponsible interference, thereby frustrating the victory and clean character of their fight for independence. It is this very clean nature of the fight which has brought about the admiration of the entire world experienced in the tremendous amount of assistance, medicines, etc. The arms could not be taken from the insurgents—now they try to take from them their word power, which they will be equally unable to do. . . .

[Tamás] Bogyay, a little known writer on the desk, included some rather peculiar references to Spain in a program which he wrote on 27 October ("Special Historical Report #B1"): "We are reminded of a great war 20 years ago . . . it took place on the Spanish Peninsula, but in part between the same forces which are now facing each other on Hungarian soil. Only in part because the . . . Spanish Civil War was much more than right wing Spaniards fighting against left wing." The meaning of the passage is not entirely clear, but it could be taken to imply that this commentator regarded the Hungarian Revolution as essentially a struggle of the right against the left, or as the Kremlin itself would have it, of fascists against Communists. This is certainly contrary to all RFE's principles. No summary of it was ever presented before broadcast, and a broadcast copy of this program cannot be found in the files; it is possible that it never went on the air; the desk has been unable to tell us whether it did or not.

Miss [Katalin] Hunyadi in a program dealing with the American reaction to Hungarian events on 29 October ("Special Report #C2") describes demonstrations before the UN Building in New York and in Cleveland in such a way as to give the impression that American public opinion will force the UN into action on Hungary. The program goes on to make reference to the fact that in Cleveland "Groups of Hungarians and Americans give their names . . . they want to volunteer to go to Hungary so that they can fight together with the Freedom Fighters." It is no doubt true that people were giving their names to go to Hungary to fight. In the emotional context of this program, however, the subject was handled in such a way that wishful listeners could get the impression that American volunteers would soon be arriving in Hungary to fight against the Soviets. Miss Hunyadi's program was approved for broadcast by Ölvedi. It was never submitted in summary form before broadcast.

A Béry program of 7 November ("Special Commentary #L1") commits a different kind of error, one which is unfortunately characteristic of the spirit of several scripts from the post–4 November period. Béry, obviously tired and depressed at the turn Hungarian events have taken, asks "Is there any sense in this fighting?" He then proceeds to answer the question in purely Western terms by pointing out that the Hungarian tragedy has awakened the West. Never once in the whole program does he make any reference to what is probably the most important aspect of the problem, the fact that the Hungarian Revolution has shaken the Communist system itself to its very roots. The script includes the ridiculous assertion that "the West could have done more for its freedom in Hungary with five divisions than with the 500 it is preparing to set up now." In making this irresponsible, ill-informed statement the author fails to point out to his listeners that any Western intervention in Hungary would have meant an atomic World War III and was for this reason out of the question. Béry misleads his listeners and caters to their delusions instead of informing them realistically.

When Béry's program summary was submitted at the morning meeting, Feketekúthy (in charge of morning meetings after Gellért collapsed) was advised to include reference to the effect of Hungarian events on the Communist movement everywhere, but this advice was not followed. This program was approved for broadcast by Márjás. . . .

The basic problem is not so much that policy was violated as that it was not implemented with imagination, subtlety and cleverness. The incisive, dispassionate analyses of developments in Hungary which Gellért made daily at morning policy meetings are not reflected to the degree we were led to expect they would be (by Gellért himself and by the whole tenor of the morning meetings) in program output. Policy lines which were carefully discussed during these same morning meetings and which Gellért and other members of the desk who were present gave every indication of understanding clearly were frequently applied in crude and unrefined fashion in the programs as they were written. The all-too-frequent failure of program writers to implement policy imaginatively seems to have been merely another facet of their failure to employ effective techniques. It is remarkable that a group of Hungarians, most of whom have been with RFE for more than five years, should have absorbed so little of what has consistently been drummed into them—orally, in guidances, in listening sessions and meetings of many kinds—on radio broadcasting and political warfare techniques. But to the severe test which they faced when the Hungarian Revolution began, the majority of Hungarian editors seem to have neglected to apply most of what they had ostensibly learned of the principles of sound broadcasting and effective political warfare which RFE stands for.

The most crucial failure of all was the failure of leadership within the desk.[1]

Notes

Introduction

1. Program Policy Guidelines from 1976 to 1987, in section 3 of annual reports of the Board for International Broadcasting, Washington, D.C.
2. Ibid.
3. V. I. Lenin, *Polnoe sobranie sochinenii* (Complete works), 5th ed., Moscow, 1970–85, vol. 41, p. 380.
4. Lenin, op. cit., vol. 41, p. 318.
5. Virgil, *Georgics*, II, 490.

Chapter One: Preparations

1. The attempt to identify fully with the people addressed.
2. A full account of this meeting appeared in "Encounter at the Café Dnieper," *The National Interest*, Spring 1992, p. 47.
3. A group of German symbolist poets and scholars, headed by the charismatic Stefan George (1868–1933).
4. Popular Anglo-Hungarian writer of humorous books.
5. I use *man* in this volume in the sense in which Latin *homo*, German *Mensch*, or Hungarian *ember* is gender-inclusive, to refer to either men or women or both.
6. "Whether it is literally true or not, we have a beautiful thing going in Christianity; communism is so much nonsense (*hülyeség*), and repulsively ugly, to boot," my late friend and former university colleague János Pilinszky said to me in 1968. He was at the time an editor of the Catholic journal *Vigilia* and had not yet attained the national fame he was to achieve after his death in 1981.
7. How much and what kind of public and private hardship and conflict is conducive to creativity in culture has been a problem never distant from my mind. Many years ago (in 1964) I discussed it in a long broadcast with Salvador de Madariaga; but we could reach no agreement. I contended that an unrestrictedly open society is not always the best framework for encouraging creative minds to create and others to respond creatively; an irritant, I said, is necessary to persuade the shell to secrete the pearl. Happy love, I argued, has no poetry, whereas suffering and frustration jolt us into articulation. Madariaga (wisely, as I now think) refused to have any of that. He did agree that inner tensions are the seedbed of creativity, but a work of art still needs room for contact with other artistic and intellectual influences, freedom to reach the public, and above all, freedom for the original

creative experience. He did not totally convince me because he was stretching my meaning. Many doctors, he said, have never seen a case of typhoid and would not know how to treat one if they did. According to your theory (he observed) every now and then we ought to have a salutary spread of epidemics so that doctors can learn a little more about how the human being reacts when struck down by a particularly rare disease. This was an extrapolation ad absurdum, but not untypical of many I encountered. See "Cervantes and the Case of Unfreedom," Radio Free Europe, Third Programme Broadcasts, 1964–65, nos. 55–56 (unpublished).

8. Miguel de Unamuno, *The Tragic Sense of Life* (London: Macmillan, 1921).

9. G. R. Urban, *Kinesis and Stasis: A Study in the Attitude of Stefan George and His Circle to the Musical Arts,* "Anglica Germanica" series (The Hague, 1962).

10. Breath, inspiration: "Gib mir den grossen feierlichen hauch / Gib jene glut mir wieder die verjünge," Stefan George, *Der Teppich des Lebens und die Lieder von Traum und Tod mit einem Vorspiel* (Berlin: Bondi, 1921), p. 15.

11. "When Stefan George died in Minusio . . . Stauffenberg with his two brothers and eight other friends of George were at his bedside." Joachim C. Fest, *Hitler* (London: Weidenfeld and Nicolson, 1973), p. 811, n. 7.

12. Stefan George, "Ich bin ein funke nur vom heiligen feuer," "Entrueckung," *Der Siebente Ring* (Berlin: Bondi, 1922), p. 123.

Chapter Two: The Contest of Ideas

1. Interview with Jakub Berman, powerful member of the Polish Politburo (1948–56) with special responsibility for ideology and culture, in Teresa Toranska, *Oni: Stalin's Polish Puppets* (London: Collins-Harvill, 1987), p. 275.

2. The first two epithets appear in Dmitri Volkogonov, *Lenin: Life and Legacy* (London: HarperCollins, 1994), p. xxx. Volkogonov used the word *saint* in a conversation with the author in Moscow in October 1990.

3. See E.U. Commission, Eurobarometer Survey (Brussels: E.U. Commission), 1994.

4. Jeffrey Sachs, former economic adviser to President Yeltsin, in the *International Herald Tribune,* Jan. 24, 1994.

5. I wrote two of our proposals: "A Note on Information Policy," Feb. 1, 1981 (see George R. Urban, *Diplomacy and Disillusion at the Court of Margaret Thatcher* [London: Tauris, 1996], pp. 28–33; and "Case for a Western Information Policy," an unpublished discussion paper, January 1982). We also made verbal representations for the establishment of an advisory agency to follow broadly the pattern of the Foreign Office Information and Research Department, prematurely disbanded in 1977.

6. Members of the original (1981) study group were (Lord) Hugh Thomas of Swynnerton, Leonard Schapiro, Hugh Seton-Watson, Antony Polonsky, Iain Elliot, and I. In 1983 a pamphlet was published, G. R. Urban, ed., *What We Ought to Do About the Soviet Threat* (London: Centre for Policy Studies, 1983). Our second pamphlet appeared in 1986, by which time the group consisted of Lord Thomas, Lord Beloff, the Rev. [later Canon] Michael Bourdeaux, Alan Dashwood, Christopher Donnelly, Iain Elliot, Elie Kedourie, Dominic Lieven, Antony Polonsky, Ian Roberts, and me, with Mary Seton-Watson and Nathalie Brooke as research assistants. The second pamphlet, though jointly written, came out under my name, with a foreword by (Lord) Thomas of Swynnerton: George Urban, *A Case for Coherence: Assumptions and Aims of British Foreign Policy,* Policy Study No. 75 (London: Centre for Policy Studies, 1986).

7. In his foreword to *General Education,* Michael Yudkin, ed. (London: Penguin, 1969), pp. ix–xx.

8. As a senior research associate, School of Politics and International Relations, 1968–70, replacing, after his sudden death, Charles Malamuth, one of Leon Trotsky's former friends and supporters.

9. See *Studies in Comparative Communism: An Interdisciplinary Journal*, Rodger Swearingen and G. R. Urban, eds., July/Oct. 1969, pp. 121–382.

Chapter Three: High Communism

1. "Each Union republic retains the right freely to secede from the USSR," article 73, chapter 8, part 3, *The New Soviet Constitution of 1977*. "Radio Liberty neither supports nor encourages any separatist or secessionist movement and does not raise territorial issues," Policy Guidelines, part 3.

2. Policy Guidelines, part 3.

3. John A. Gronouski. For another discussion of these points see my introduction, G. R. Urban, ed., *End of Empire: The Demise of the Soviet Union* (Washington, D.C.: American University Press, 1993).

4. Such was Radio Free Europe's fear of seeming to touch upon the prospect of any potential disintegration of the Soviet Union that in 1978 the title of a scholarly radio discussion between Hugh Seton-Watson and me was arbitrarily changed by the Radio's management from "The Fall of Multinational Empires in Our Time" to "Nationalism and Multinationalism" and some of our views were doctored. For the original text see G. R. Urban, ed., *Communist Reformation: Nationalism, Internationalism and Change in the World Communist Movement* (London: Temple Smith, 1979), pp. 272–326.

5. Volkogonov, *Lenin*, p. 323.

6. Observations at Politburo meeting, January 7, 1974, quoted by Volkogonov, *Lenin*, p. 323.

Chapter Four: Second Conductors

1. *Public diplomacy* is an American euphemism for propaganda, image building, and the acquisition of goodwill. I use it reluctantly.

2. Harbouring unorthodox opinion was, however, not peculiar to the Central Intelligence Agency. Two decades later, important figures in the KGB played a parallel role under Gorbachev, promoting *glasnost* and *perestroika*. But while the CIA's unorthodoxy hastened the fall of the Soviet opponent, the KGB's led to the disintegration of the very system it had been created to protect.

3. Michael Warner, "Cultural Cold War—Origins of the Congress for Cultural Freedom, 1949–50," *Studies in Intelligence*, U.S. Central Intelligence Agency, vol. 38, no. 5 (1995).

4. For a representative selection of such reports and assessments (from the Soviet Area Audience and Opinion Research Department of Radio Liberty), see "Eye-Witness Accounts from the Soviet Union," in G. R. Urban, *Social and Economic Rights in the Soviet Bloc* (New Brunswick, N.J.: Transaction Books, 1988), pp. 221–241.

5. For an extensive discussion of peaceful coexistence as understood in the East and the West, see G. R. Urban, ed., *Détente* (London: Temple Smith, 1976).

6. For a more detailed discussion of propaganda see my conversation with Vladimir Bukovsky in G. R. Urban, ed., *Can the Soviet System Survive Reform? Seven Colloquies About the State of Soviet Socialism Seven Decades After the Bolshevik Revolution* (London: Pinter, 1989), p. 225.

7. For a penetrating description of the meeting, see Simon Bourgin, "An American Writes from Budapest," in *The Hungarian Revolution*, Melvin J. Lasky, ed. (London: Secker and Warburg, 1957), pp. 29-32.

8. (Lord) John Reith, director general of the BBC (1927-38); advocate of high intellectual standards and moral responsibility in broadcasting.

Chapter Five: Reluctant Americans

1. Jan Novak, former head of the Radio Free Europe Polish Service, in "Poles and Hungarians in 1956," a paper presented at the international conference "Hungary and the World, 1956: The New Archival Evidence," Budapest, Sept. 26-29, 1996.

2. Polish-born British writer on communist affairs; editor of *Survey* magazine.

3. "Where Americans Fear to Tread," *International Herald Tribune*, Nov. 22, 1984.

4. Urban, ed., *Détente*, p. 364.

5. George F. Kennan, *Around the Cragged Hill: A Personal and Political Philosophy* (New York: Norton, 1993), p. 182.

6. A detailed explanation of Radio Liberty's record in dealing with Jewish-Russian and Jewish-Ukrainian issues is contained in Frank Shakespeare's two letters (both dated May 3, 1984) to former senator Charles H. Percy, then chairman of the Senate Foreign Relations Committee.

7. For example, "International Zionism in the Service of Imperialism," *Partiinaya Zhizn'* (Party life), July 14, 1984 ("Zionism extensively uses mass information media at its disposal. . . . Active use is made of Israel Radio, the subversive radio stations *Liberty* and *Free Europe*"); "In the Service of the CIA," APN (Novosti Press Agency), Oct. 3, 1984; "What 'Liberty' and Other 'Voices' Are Singing About," *Pravda Ukrainy*, May 30, 1984; "The Brown 'Canard,'" *Pravda Vostoka*, July 27, 1984; "Unwanted 'Advocates' Rebuffed," *Pravda Vostoka*, Sept. 8, 1984 ("The parasite and hooligan Moshe Abramov beat up an old man in the Samarkand synagogue and was sentenced by the people's court. Well-wishers from abroad, and particularly the well-known slanderer—*Radio Liberty*—defended the hooligan and called him a leader of the Jews"); "Zionists Firmly Rooted in Radio Liberty and the Voice of America Attempt to Whitewash Israeli Crimes in Lebanon," *Sovietskaya Ukraina*, Feb. 6, 1983; "An American-Israeli Deal," Tass/*Pravda*, Feb. 14, 1985 ("*Liberty* and *Free Europe* . . . the subversive U.S. broadcasting stations also cooperate closely with the Voice of Israel, . . . which is the principal mouthpiece of Zionist propaganda").

8. The source of Percy's "trouble" may be tentatively gauged from John Carlin's report "Why America Has Kept Quiet," *Independent on Sunday*, Apr. 21, 1996, p. 17: "The memory remains fresh in Washington of what happened a decade ago to Charles Percy, a Republican senator with a long record of support for the Israeli cause who one day had the temerity to start asking questions about Israeli policy in the West Bank. The American-Israel Public Affairs Committee (Aipac), by far the most powerful foreign policy pressure group in the US capital, swiftly orchestrated a campaign against him. Jewish groups around the country distributed flyers denouncing him as Israel's greatest enemy and poured funds into the campaign of his election rival. Mr Percy lost the election and disappeared from political life."

9. For a detailed discussion of the Soviet side's campaign against the Radios, see Gerhard Wetting, *Broadcasting and Détente: Eastern Policies and Their Implications for East-West Relations* (London: Hurst, 1977), especially pp. 16-38.

10. "Members of the Politburo in Moscow had a greater fear of Radio Liberty than of any other weapon of the USA." Oleg Tumanov, *Geständnisse eines KGB-Agenten* (Berlin: Edition q., 1993), p. 105.

11. Oleg Kalugin with Fen Montaigne, *SpyMaster: My 32 Years in Intelligence and Espionage Against the West* (London: Smith Gryphon, 1994), pp. 194, 196. For Tumanov's version of the same events, see Tumanov, *Geständnisse*, especially pp. 158–167.

12. Kalugin, *SpyMaster*, p. 93. On August 16, 1991, three days before the Moscow coup and the final collapse of the Soviet system, General Kalugin, at a seminar arranged for him at the Munich headquarters of Radio Free Europe/Radio Liberty, gave a similar account of his and the KGB's activities. He said he was visiting the RFE/RL headquarters with "a certain trepidation" because he had spent part of his KGB career trying to infiltrate the building and to put the Radio out of business. He had, he related, "laboured for years" to discredit RFE/RL and was behind the bombing of 1981. See "Ex-KGB General Kalugin Addresses RFE/RL Staffers in Munich," *Shortwaves*, Munich, August 1991, p. 8.

13. Tumanov, *Geständnisse*, p. 315. As a final twist to the Kalugin-Tumanov saga, Tumanov ran an acrimonious campaign against Kalugin during the 1991 elections—and lost overwhelmingly.

14. For Margaret Thatcher's reaction to Reagan's Windsor speech, see Urban, *Diplomacy and Disillusion*, p. 39.

15. If Bailey and I did make that prediction in 1985 (and I rather think we did), then I am inclined to take credit for it. It was interesting that Smith should have felt that our reading of the Soviet scene was "ominous" and "dark." Leaked to Jack Anderson and Joseph Spear, Larry Smith's report was given a dramatic twist in the *Washington Post*, Apr. 20, 1985.

16. On April 2, 1985, in a letter to Congressman Dan A. Mica, Michael Novak subjected Smith's report to a withering page-by-page commentary on behalf of the board of which he was a member.

17. General Accounting Office, Report to the Honorable Claiborne Pell, United States Senate, "Improved Oversight Can Reduce Broadcast Violations at Radio Free Europe/Radio Liberty," Washington, June 24, 1985.

18. Geryld B. Christianson, Senate Committee on Foreign Relations, "New Management at Radio Free Europe/Radio Liberty and the Pell Amendment" (staff report) (Washington, D.C., 1985).

Chapter Six: The Soft Approach to Communism

1. Jan Novak describes his wartime work as a secret courier of the Polish underground between Warsaw and London in *Courier from Warsaw*, foreword by Malcolm Muggeridge (Detroit: Wayne State University Press, 1982). The "retirement" of Jan Novak in May 1976 appears to have been the result of pressure from the State Department, which was in pursuit of détente. After a private conversation in Geneva with Guy Coriden of the U.S. State Department (then American representative for the "Basket Three" negotiations at the CSCE preparatory conference), I wrote to Ralph E. Walter, then director of Radio Free Europe, on February 26, 1975: "[Coriden] said he found himself in the painful position of having to read United States Embassy messages from Warsaw (and to some extent Bucharest) complaining that RFE broadcasts were running counter to United States foreign policy in, for example, not supporting *détente* and in other ways too. He quoted two cases from his personal experience. Both concerned recent Polish broadcasts based (as he claimed) on faulty information. . . . The Polish Department [he observed] must be made to assume its share of responsibility as an independent but American radio station that operates in the American national interest. Guy felt that this could possibly not be achieved without the removal of Jan Novak, and he thought that, in an extreme case, the removal of even twenty to thirty Polish editors might have to be contemplated. . . . Jan Novak's senatorial support had, he said,

298 NOTES TO PAGES 77-97

weakened recently, and therefore the Radio could probably act without worrying too much about this particular inhibition."

2. Policy Guidelines, part 2.

3. Sentenced on December 25, 1989, by an extraordinary military court and executed on the same day, together with his wife Elenei, for genocide, the undermining of the power of the state by organising armed action against the people, destruction of civil property, the subversion of the national economy, unlawful personal enrichment, and other charges.

4. Sentenced to seven years in prison by a Sofia court September 1992, for the embezzlement of public funds. Zhivkov's appeal was rejected by the Bulgarian Supreme Court on January 18, 1994, and the sentence was upheld.

5. See G. R. Urban, ed., *Eurocommunism: Its Roots and Future in Italy and Elsewhere* (London: Temple Smith, 1978), especially my introduction and my talk with Lucio Lombardo Radice, pp. 32–57.

6. The phrase is Edward Gibbon's. He uses it with reference to primitive communism in the early church, *Decline and Fall of the Roman Empire* (London: Dent, 1962), vol. 1, chapter 15, p. 477.

7. For a more detailed discussion, see my introduction (especially pp. xvi–xxiii) in Urban, ed., *End of Empire*.

Chapter Seven: Before the Implosion

1. For example: Agence France Press, the *Baltimore Sun*, United Press International, the *Frankfurter Allgemeine Zeitung*, the *Daily Telegraph*, *Les Nouvelles Littéraires*, the *Times* (London), Associated Press, the *Journal of Commerce*, the *New York Times*, *Economist*, *Der Spiegel*, *Die Presse*, *New Republic*, *Newsweek*, the *Washington Post*, Radio Israel, Deutsche Presse Agentur, *Süddeutsche Zeitung*, *Stuttgarter Zeitung*, *Libération*, *Le Monde*, Reuters, *Die Welt*, *Giornale*, *Handelsblatt*, *La Repubblica*, the *Financial Times*, the *International Herald Tribune*, *Le Figaro*, *Rheinischer Merkur*, *Neue Zürcher Zeitung*, the *Washington Star*, the *Christian Science Monitor*, the *Chicago Tribune*, the *Philadelphia Inquirer*, *L'Unità*, *Le Quotidien de Paris*, and *Le Matin*.

2. Kalugin, *SpyMaster*, p. 196.

3. Information given to Richard H. Cummings, director of security, Radio Free Europe, by the postcommunist Romanian authorities, June 10, 1992.

4. Emil Georgescu was a public prosecutor and later a defence lawyer in Romania. In Munich, in addition to his work at the Radio, he ran a legal practice specialising in immigration cases. He had been a member of the Communist Party. See also Chapter 9.

5. Correspondence between Richard H. Cummings, director of security, Radio Free Europe, and Virgil Magureanu, June 10–July 16, 1992.

6. James Markham's report, Aug. 30, 1984.

7. "Soviet Troops Reported Put on War Footing After Reagan Joke," Reuters, Tokyo, Oct. 1, 1984. The newspaper quoted was *Yomiuri Shimbun*. For my guidance apropos of the Reagan quip, see Appendix B.

8. Vladimir Kusin was listed as agent no. 0212298353, pseudonym Vladimír, in "Kompletni seznam spolupracovniku StB" [Complete list of the collaborators of the State Security Police], by *Necensurovane Noviny* [Uncensored news], no. 15 (Prague), 1992. Also listed in no. 14.

9. Pictures of the ceremony, with Havel, Pell, and Kusin behind microphones, appeared in *Shortwaves*, the Radios' house journal, in May 1990, pp. 1, 4.

10. In October 1984, Otto Pick accepted for employment a Czech journalist who had served as an announcer for Prague Radio in 1974–75, as well as for the external (propaganda) service of Moscow Radio in 1975–79. I had to overrule Pick's decision.

11. Under increasing pressure, however, James Buckley nevertheless gave Kalabiński a short-term contract in the Radio's Washington bureau, and after my retirement, Kalabiński was assigned a permanent post in Washington by Gene Pell. In a memorandum to Buckley (July 12, 1985) I noted:

Kalabiński was an established member of the Polish communist communications élite both as a print and an electronic journalist. For the best part of 20 years he wrote for causes and represented views that were those of the various Communist Party leaderships. His name was widely known in that capacity. In 1974 he received the "Golden Microphone" award. It was handed to him personally by the notorious Maciej Szczepanski, then head of Polish propaganda and a close associate of Gierek.

His expertise as a journalist is not called in question. His moral suitability to serve RFE's stated mission is. Petitions that have reached us from over 30 Polish members of staff show that this feeling is widely held among our Poles. The younger ones argue that they left Poland precisely to get away from the influence of the Kalabińskis. They feel morally offended that they should have to share a microphone with a man so thoroughly compromised.

12. At a Congressional hearing on March 7, 1985, Congressman Lawrence (Larry) Smith questioned some of these changes. He felt they had been made by the director on ideological grounds and were unjustified. The Radio as represented by James L. Buckley and Ben Wattenberg rejected Smith's observations.

13. "I was delighted to hear that you have been named as RFE Director. Please accept my warmest congratulations on your new assignment. I for one know the tremendous importance of the Radios in cutting through the propaganda barrage orchestrated from the East. Please be assured that you will have my full support, as well as that of my colleagues, in your new mission. I look forward to seeing you here in Washington when you next visit our fair city. Shultz" (Oct. 19, 1983).

14. See my account, "A Conversation with Lukács," Encounter, Oct. 1971, pp. 30–36.

15. Arthur Koestler and G. R. Urban, "A Conversation," later published in G. R. Urban, Talking to Eastern Europe (London: Eyre and Spottiswoode, 1964); in the United States, Scaling the Wall (Detroit: Wayne State University Press, 1964). John Strachey, "Lenin in April," ibid.; and "The Challenge of Democracy," the Radio Free Europe keynote lectures for 1963, later published as Encounter pamphlet no. 10 under the same title (London, 1963); Ignazio Silone, Bread Alone? the Radio Free Europe keynote lectures for 1964, later incorporated into Uscita di Sicurezza (Florence: Vallechi, 1965).

16. András Hegedüs, Élet egy eszme árnyékában [Life in the shadow of an idea], an autobiographical interview with Zoltán Zsille (Vienna: Zsille, 1985).

17. G. R. Urban, "The People Are Coming," Encounter, Sept.–Oct. 1985, pp. 16–20.

18. Association of Hungarian University Students, formed in October 1956.

19. Official Communist Party daily paper.

20. Minister of the interior, 1954–56.

21. Official anniversary of Hungary's liberation by Soviet troops in 1945.

22. Hegedüs, Élet egy eszme árnyékában, pp. 256–258.

23. Otto von Habsburg, member of the European Parliament, to G. R. Urban, Feb. 28, 1984.

24. See Otto von Habsburg and G. R. Urban, "A Tale of Two Empires," in Urban, ed., *End of Empire*, p. 154.

25. Urban, ed., *End of Empire*, p. 146.

26. Colin Welch, "A Symposium," *Encounter*, June 1971, p. 9.

Chapter Eight: The National Interest

1. I wrote about this at length in *Diplomacy and Disillusion*.

2. See David B. Funderburk, *Pinstripes and Reds: An American Ambassador Caught Between the State Department and the Romanian Communists, 1981–1985* (Washington: Selous Foundation Press, 1989).

3. Matlock's views appeared to be out of character with the constructive, though still distinctly very cautious, advice he had tendered to the Radio as U.S. ambassador to Czechoslovakia in February 1983. Why he became more accommodating as Ronald Reagan's adviser than he had been in Prague is unclear to me. It may well be that he saw himself as keeping to the middle, compensating for the State Department's soft line when he was serving as ambassador, and balancing the president's hawkish policies when he was serving in the White House.

4. I noted in my diary (April 13, 1985): "[Salgó] has swallowed the Kádár line hook, line and sinker. He wants us to return to the Radio's earlier policies and give the [Kádár] government the benefit of the doubt. He'd like me to go to Hungary to experience the openness of the system. Gene Pell, director of the Voice of America, had recently been there as his [Salgó's] guest. He [Salgó] would arrange the necessary meetings for me too, as he had done for Pell. I thanked him but politely declined."

5. A few days after this discussion, on April 18 and 22, 1985, the electoral nominations in Budapest were so manipulated by the communist authorities that distinguished dissidents such as László Rajk, Jr., and Gáspár Miklós Tamás were prevented from running.

6. Excerpts from "Will the Real George Urban Please Step Forward," *Wall Street Journal, Europe*, July 23, 1985; also in the U.S. edition.

7. State Department minutes of August 1, 1985.

8. On another occasion, however, also in 1985, following a Polish government protest, the State Department publicly repudiated a Radio Free Europe broadcast. This was good for our reputation for independence, but it had a discouraging effect on morale in our Polish Service. The cause of the repudiation was a satire our Poles had quoted from a Polish samizdat journal in which Hitler and Jaruzelski were criticised as men of comparable guilt in Polish history. They were not, of course, but satire does exaggerate.

9. Quoted by Joseph Reaves, in the *Chicago Tribune*, Aug. 11, 1991.

10. Cf. Heiko Flottau, "Politische Nostalgie in Polen," *Süddeutsche Zeitung*, Oct. 2, 1993.

Chapter Nine: Jealousies in the Region

1. In a memorandum to the Radio's samizdat section (May 11, 1984) I listed a rough selection of topics for research and eventual broadcasts: "the common destiny of the East European nations, including the Russian people; the future cooperation of the East European states in freedom; resistance to Soviet/Communist institutions; responses to the presence of Soviet troops; the dangers of Soviet nuclear deployment for Eastern Europe; the Warsaw Pact and the national tradi-

tions of the East European armed forces; Christianity as a focus of national identity; the right to religious education; equality, justice and fair play under the law, *nulla crimen sine lege;* the corruption of jurisdiction under institutions of the Soviet type; parallel society and parallel culture; human rights and human duties; corruption under arbitrary government; penalties of the Soviet economic model; distortions of national history; the corruption of textbooks and what the Poles have done about it; alternatives to state-controlled higher education ('underground universities'); spread of the mentality of Soviet Man and how the Poles have succeeded in limiting it."

2. On June 15, 1992, Najder admitted in a Radio Free Europe interview that he had had contacts with the Polish security police under the communist regime. He added, however, that the meetings had been deliberate attempts to mislead the security authorities. His statement followed reports in the Polish media about a police agent code-named Zapalniczka ("lighter") to whom President (as he then was) Wałęsa had drawn attention. On June 25, 1992, an article by Jerzy Urban appeared in his paper *Nie* under the title "Zdzisław Najder—paid informer." It incorporated facsimiles of three documents. The first, entitled "Statement," was purported to be Najder's acceptance of his role as a secret service informer:

I pledge voluntarily to provide employees of the Security Committee of the Ministry of Internal Affairs with information accessible to me, within the limits of my personal convictions. I pledge also to keep totally secret the content of my talks with employees of the institution above mentioned.

I will sign the statements to be deposited by me under the code name of Zapalniczka.

19 V 58   Zdzisław Najder

The second document, dated October 25, 1959, is a one-line receipt for 1000 zlotys, signed Zapalniczka. The third document defines some of Najder's tasks as an informer (reporting on the Ford Foundation, émigrés in the West, etc.) and explains the routing of such information to the security police. On February 6, 1996, Jerzy Urban was given a one-year suspended prison sentence by a Polish court for having made public these secret documents, but their authenticity was not called into question. The same documents were published in Jan Kowalski, *Zapalniczka* (Warsaw: Iwar Publishing and Information Agency, 1995), pp. 174, 185, and 162, respectively.

3. In September 1987 Pell released Najder under a face-saving formula, after informing me, in my retirement, about his intention. In my "testament" to Pell shortly before my retirement in 1986, I had noted: "Mr. Z. Najder, though a man of ability in the intellectual sphere, is incapable of instilling a united purpose in his staff, or even of keeping the peace. His veracity is open to doubt, his intolerance is pervasive. . . . I recommend the consideration of an alternative leadership." After the Polish changeover Najder returned to Poland and began to play a role, for a short time, in public affairs. In 1990 his sentence was made null and void.

4. Lieutenant General Ion Mihai Pacepa, *Red Horizons* (Washington, D.C.: Regnery Gateway, 1987), pp. 412, 416. Although I have no reason to doubt Pacepa's general testimony, certain elements in it seem to have been written with Western intelligence interests in mind or with the wisdom of hindsight.

5. Ibid., pp. 162–163.

6. On January 15, 1985, A. Russell Poole, the Radios' veteran director of personnel and later vice president for administration, circulated the following memorandum to senior officers:

I spent an hour with Mr. and Mrs. Georgescu yesterday evening at Grosshaden, where Mr. Georgescu is hospitalized. His wife had asked me to come. He was under heavy sedation and scarcely recognized me. Most of the time he was incoherent.

Mrs. Georgescu told me his health had continued to deteriorate and doctors examined and treated him in connection with the injuries he had received in the 1981 knife attack. According to her, it was some time before they discovered lung cancer. She said the disease is spreading rapidly to other parts of the body.

She pointed out this is the third instance of cancer occurring among leading members of the Romanian Service (Director Noel Bernard and Deputy Director Mihai Cismarescu were the others). She asked when would we find out "the reasons" behind this.

This is not the first time someone has expressed a suspicion about the frequency of cancer cases in RFE/RL. It came up several years ago in the Polish area. The late Noel Bernard spoke to me about it.

We have had the radiation level checked in the building—through our company doctor—and have been assured by appropriate authorities that there is no problem.

Today is Georgescu's last day of employment.

7. Kalugin, *SpyMaster,* pp. 181–182.

8. Urban, ed., *End of Empire,* pp. 155–177.

9. In one of my guidances I, too, may have sinned against the spirit of fairness towards the Russian nation. On March 14, 1985, I remembered the ceremony enacted at the funeral of Konstantin Chernenko in language that hurt the sensibilities of some of the staff of Radio Liberty, though not of Radio Free Europe. I expressed my regrets. See Appendix B.

10. The Marquis de Custine, *Journey for Our Time,* originally published in Paris in 1843. George F. Kennan devoted a book-size study to the parallel (*The Marquis de Custine and His "Russia in 1839,"* [New York: Norton]).

11. See especially Richard Pipes, *Russia Under the Old Regime* (New York: Charles Scribner's Sons, 1974).

12. Ilya Ehrenburg, *The German* (Moscow, 1943).

13. For a wide-ranging discussion of these and similar issues, see my broadcast conversation with the late Elie Kedourie, "Nationalism and the Balance of Power," in Urban, ed., *End of Empire,* pp. 101–132.

14. Hungarian broadcasting ceased in October 1993; the Czech and Polish Services were transferred with heavily reduced staffs, to Prague and Warsaw, respectively, and removed from the Radio's corporate umbrella.

15. Recorded in 1983, broadcast in early 1984, published by *Encounter* magazine as "Can We Negotiate with the Russians?" (February 1985), and republished as "Negotiating with the Russians" in Urban, ed., *Can the Soviet System Survive Reform?*

Chapter Ten: Draining the Poison out of the System

1. Kennan, *Around the Cragged Hill,* p. 220.

2. After the fall of communism, many of these men and women, and their counterparts in their home countries, could not find their places in freely elected democratic societies. The moral absolutes of permanent opposition to a dictatorship had to give way to the spirit of compromise, the acceptance of which would

have been out of character with their record and their commitment. In nonpolarised societies, their role, once so noble and important, diminished or disappeared. Cf. Adam Michnik in *Gazeta Wyborcza*, Apr. 6-8, 1996: "The logic of the struggle for freedom against dictatorship and the logic of the struggle for power in a democratic country differ greatly. The first demands courage, dignity, and a bit of fanaticism; the second, professionalism, cleverness, and a good sense of circumstances. This is why people who, under dictatorship, chose moral absolutism usually feel bad in democracy. . . . They worshipped democracy, struggled for it—but they are not comfortable in it. . . . Contempt for executioners and informers turns into contempt for those who have different views."

3. On one occasion during his underground peregrinations, Krizsán apparently had to share a bed with the uninviting Romanian Stalinist politician Anna Pauker. For that, Krizsán later told us, much in his Stalinist past had to be forgiven him. Anna Pauker returned to Romania from Moscow with other Romanian communists in 1944; she became the the de facto leader of the party and later foreign minister. She was purged in 1952.

4. "Soviet strength is in the eye of the beholder," Leszek Kolakowski told me in 1980. "If we look at the internal cohesion and viability of the Soviet system . . . it is at once clear that the Western perception of Soviet strength is in very large measure due to the fact that the Kremlin is in a position to conceal its recurrent disasters from Western eyes and even from those of its own population. The Soviet system has one decisive advantage which despotisms have always enjoyed over democracies: nothing has to be explained, because there is no free discussion—hence the Soviet system may very well succeed in showing a robust complexion to the outside world while inside it is being eaten away by cancer. The Western image of Soviet strength is largely due to the fears and incomprehension of the West." "The Devil in History," in G. R. Urban, ed., *Stalinism: Its Impact on Russia and the World* (London: Temple Smith, 1982), pp. 266-267.

5. In it we put scholars and political thinkers of distinction before our microphones. They included J. F. Brown, Zbigniew Brzezinski, Margarete Buber-Neumann, R. V. Burks, Robert Conquest, Maurice Cranston, Brian Crozier, Petru Dumitriu, Lewis S. Feuer, William E. Griffith, Alfred Grosser, Ronald Hingley, G. F. Hudson, K. A. Jelenski, Leopold Labedz, Richard Löwenthal, Roderick MacFarquhar, Salvador de Madariaga, Michael Oakeshott, Richard Pipes, Bruno Pittermann, Leonard Schapiro, Hugh Seton-Watson, Alfred Sherman, Peter Wiles, Harry T. Willetts, and Donald S. Zagoria. Our Third Programme followed on the heels of a yet earlier initiative, known at the Radio as intellectual cooperation, whereby the College of Europe in Bruges had supplied us with a series of talks and lectures covering a wide range of mainly European topics. Frank Munk, a social scientist from Portland, Oregon, had been in charge of the operation.

6. In a guidance of July 17, 1984.

Chapter Eleven: Misapprehensions

1. "What the Soviets Really Want," *New York Post*, Nov. 19, 1985.

2. *By-line*, Dec. 1995.

3. For a longer discussion of these questions, see my article "The Paradox of Truth-Telling," *Encounter*, Nov. 1989, pp. 31-33.

4. "Western TV—Surrogate for Freedom," *New York Times*, Feb. 7, 1986.

5. Ernst Bloch, *Das Prinzip Hoffnung* (Frankfurt: Suhrkamp, 1985).

Chapter Twelve: Dialogues

1. They were published in the following symposia: G. R. Urban and Michael Glenny, eds., *Can We Survive Our Future? A Symposium*, with Michael Glenny, Arnold J. Toynbee, Philip Rieff, Nigel Despicht, Werner Heisenberg, Jacques Ellul, Erich Jantsch, Louis Armand, Maurice Cranston, Edward Shils, Michael Shanks, Andrew Shonfield, Dennis Gabor, Edward Goldsmith, Herman Kahn, François Bouricaud, Hellmuth Bütow, Maurice Duverger, Théo Lefèvre, James Fawcett, Gunnar Randers, Bernard Cazes, Ossip K. Flechtheim, Brian Aldiss (London: The Bodley Head, 1971); *Toynbee on Toynbee: A Conversation Between Arnold J. Toynbee and G. R. Urban* (New York: Oxford University Press, 1974); Urban, ed., *Détente*, with Bruno Pittermann, Sir William Hayter, François Bondy, Robert F. Byrnes, Claus D. Kernig, Johan Jørgen Holst, Wolf H. Halsti, Richard Pipes, Alfred Grosser, Adam Ulam, George W. Ball, Dean Rusk, Zbigniew Brzezinski, François Duchêne, Leopold Labedz; G. R. Urban, ed., *Hazards of Learning: An International Symposium on the Crisis of the University*, with Seymour Martin Lipset (introduction), Lord James of Rusholme, Donald G. MacRae, Mick Farren, Paul Seabury, Eldon L. Johnson, Richard Löwenthal, Alain Touraine, Max Beloff, Jeanne Hersch, Alexander King, Golo Mann, Richard Hoggart, Lord Ashby (La Salle, Ill.: Open Court, 1977); Urban, ed., *Eurocommunism: Its Roots and Future in Italy and Elsewhere*, with Manuel Azcárate, Lucio Lombardo Radice, Fabio Mussi, Jean Elleinstein, Renzo de Felice, Rosario Romeo, Domenico Settembrini, Altiero Spinelli, Luigi Barzini, Andrei Amalrik, Bartolomeo Sorge, S.J. (London: Temple Smith, 1978); Urban, ed., *Communist Reformation*, with Eduard Goldstücker, Antonin J. Liehm, Zdenek Mlynar, Ota Sik, Manuel Azcárate, Eugene V. Rostow, Claiborne Pell, Jacob D. Beam, Vladimir Maximov, Hugh Seton-Watson (London: Temple Smith, 1979); Urban, ed., *Stalinism*, with Boris Bazhanov, W. Averell Harriman, Theodor Prager, Adam B. Ulam, Robert C. Tucker, Milovan Djilas, Leszek Kolakowski, Roderick MacFarquhar, Bao Ruo-wang, George F. Kennan, Leonard Schapiro; Urban, ed., *Can the Soviet System Survive Reform?* with Max Kampelman, Alexander Zinoviev, Galina Vishnevskaya, Alain Besançon, Vladimir Bukovsky, Giorgio Napolitano, Milovan Djilas; Urban, ed., *End of Empire*, with Sidney Hook, Hugh Trevor-Roper (Lord Dacre), Elie Kedourie, Otto von Habsburg, Adam B. Ulam, Milovan Djilas, Sir Karl Popper.

The first symposium to arise from my work with Radio Free Europe appeared during my 1960-65 stint with the Radio, in 1964, under the title of *Talking to Eastern Europe* in the United Kingdom and as *Scaling the Wall* in the United States. Apart from a dialogue with Arthur Koestler, it consisted of essays and talks by John Strachey, Leonard Schapiro, Lewis S. Feuer, Margarete Buber-Neumann, K. A. Jelenski, Petru Dumitriu, George Mikes, G. R. Urban, Ronald Hingley, Maurice Cranston, J. F. Brown, R. V. Burks, Peter Wiles, Deryck Viney, Arthur E. Adams, and Michael Oakeshott.

2. Perhaps the most dedicated, Frank P. Uhlir of the Czechoslovak Service, died during my tenure, in January 1986. A man of great learning and a patriot, Uhlir transformed my various dialogues into coherent exercises in higher education for his audience. He wrote to me on March 30, 1984: "Starting with your series some fifteen years ago . . . I was more or less automatically pushed from one 'milestone' to another through hundreds of books. Allow me to thank you." I spoke for the Radio at his funeral.

3. My series in 1972-73 on the alienation of labour and workers' codetermination, with the participation of Raymond Aron, Ralf Dahrendorf, Hugh Scanlon,

Ota Sik, Oswald von Nell-Breuning, S.J., George Woodcock, Michel Crozier, Jan Tinbergen, and others.

4. *Toynbee on Toynbee.*

5. Melvin J. Lasky, "The Art of the Interview," *Encounter*, March 1989, pp. 62–63.

6. In Urban, *Stalinism*, pp. 180–245.

7. See Urban, ed., *Eurocommunism.*

8. Elie Kedourie and G. R. Urban, "Nationalism and the Balance of Power," in Urban, ed., *End of Empire*, pp. 118–120.

9. Michel de Montaigne, "Of the Art of Conversing," in *Selected Essays*, Blanchard Bates, ed. (New York: Random House, 1949), p. 412.

10. See Luigi Barzini, "The Italians and the Communist Party," in Urban, ed., *Eurocommunism*, pp. 211–235; "Liberty and its Discontents," *Encounter*, May 1978, pp. 7–24; the latter in German translation "Über die Freiheit, oder Westeuropa am Ufer der Elbe," in George Urban, *Gespräche mit Zeitgenossen*, with a foreword by Melvin J. Lasky (Weinheim, 1982), pp. 135–169.

11. Hugh Trevor-Roper and G. R. Urban, "Arnold Toynbee's Millennium," *Encounter*, June 1957.

12. Hugh Trevor-Roper and G. R. Urban, "Aftermaths of Empire," *Encounter*, Dec. 1989; also in Urban, ed., *End of Empire*, pp. 69–99.

13. In addition to Margaret Thatcher and me, those present were Foreign Secretary Douglas Hurd, Charles Powell (Thatcher's foreign affairs adviser), Hugh Trevor-Roper, Gordon Craig, Fritz Stern, Norman Stone, and Timothy Garton Ash. See my *Diplomacy and Disillusion*, pp. 118–159.

14. Sidney Hook and G. R. Urban, "End of an Era of Political Faiths," in Urban, ed., *End of Empire*, pp. 1–68.

15. A play on the title of Popper's book *The Open Society and Its Enemies* (London: Routledge and Kegan Paul).

16. Karl Popper and G. R. Urban, "The Best World We Have Yet Had," in Urban, ed., *End of Empire*, pp. 201–220.

17. "Communism with an Italian Face?" *Encounter*, May 1977, p. 10.

18. In Urban, ed., *Eurocommunism*, pp. 255–277.

19. Plato, *Gorgias.*

Chapter Thirteen: Companions

1. Melvin J. Lasky, *Utopia and Revolution* (Chicago: Macmillan, 1976).

2. Alexander Solzhenitsyn, *The Gulag Archipelago* (London: Collins and Harvill, 1974); (Count) Nikolai Tolstoy, *Victims of Yalta* (London: Hodder and Stoughton, 1977); (Lord) Nicholas Bethell, *The Last Secret* (London: André Deutsch, 1974).

3. "Christ and the Commissar," in G. R. Urban, ed., *Stalinism*, pp. 198–199.

4. Shortened version of my conversation with Djilas, see Urban, ed., *Stalinism*, pp. 222–224. A fair part of this piece on him appeared in the *Times Literary Supplement.*

5. For the full text of this episode, see Urban, *Stalinism*, pp. 222–224.

6. "Portrait of a Dissenter as a Soviet Man," *Encounter*, Apr.–May 1984; "Why the Soviet System Is Here to Stay," in Urban, ed., *Can the Soviet System Survive Reform?* pp. 45–107.

7. "Why the Soviet System Is Here to Stay," p. 91.

8. Alexander Zinoviev, *The Reality of Communism*, Charles Janson, trans. (Lon-

don: Victor Gollancz, 1984). The quotations appear on pp. 102, 126, 105, 122, and 104.

9. Ibid., pp. 104, 128.

10. Urban, ed., *Can the Soviet System Survive Reform?*, p. 90.

11. Iain Elliot, editor of *Soviet Analyst*, lead writer for the *Times;* later associate director of Radio Liberty, deputy director of the RFE/RL Research Institute, and director of the Britain-Russia Society and of the British-East European Centre; Elizabeth Elliot, deputy head of the BBC Russian Service, member of the board of *Soviet Analyst*, and head of the BBC Ukrainian Service.

12. Urban, ed., *Can the Soviet System Survive Reform?* p. 58.

13. Ibid., pp. 105–107.

14. It would be instructive to know how Zinoviev explains the postcommunist scene. He may very well claim that his theory stands because the Soviet system has never disappeared, and much could be said for that view; or that the system is on its way back, and for that, too, evidence could be mustered.

15. Margaret Thatcher certainly believed that Zinoviev was odd. I noted in my diary (April 27, 1984): "The P[rime] M[inister] attended a Keston College reception for Michael Bourdeaux apropos of his Templeton Award. 'I've read your conversation with Zinoviev,' she said to me, 'and thought the man was a bit confused. He seems to believe that if you could hit upon the right mathematical formula and find powerful enough computers you could both explain and control the Soviet system. Do you believe such a thing is possible? I don't. What is he up to? A very strange phenomenon, don't you think?'"

16. John Strachey, *The Strangled Cry* (London: The Bodley Head, 1962), p. 18. Raymond Aron made a similar point: "Koestler told me himself that, paradoxically enough, *Darkness at Noon* prompted a few conversions to communism—though very few in comparison with the conversions the other way." The quotation is taken from Aron, "A Writer's Greatness," *Encounter*, July–Aug. 1983, p. 10.

17. Arthur Koestler, *Arrow in the Blue* (London: William Collins and Hamish Hamilton, 1954), p. 51.

18. Arthur Koestler, *The Act of Creation* (London: Hutchinson, 1964), p. 263.

19. They appeared in Arthur Koestler, *The Invisible Writing* (New York: Hutchinson, 1954), pp. 176, 178–179. George Mikes told the story of the birth of these translations in *Encounter*, July–Aug. 1983, pp. 36–37.

20. Arthur Koestler, *The Invisible Writing* (New York: Macmillan, 1969), p. 211.

21. Celia Goodman, ed., *Living with Koestler: Mamaine Koestler's Letters, 1945–1951* (New York: St. Martin's, 1985), pp. 1, 118.

22. Koestler, *Arrow in the Blue*, p. 15.

23. Goodman, ed., *Living with Koestler*, p. 118.

24. Cf. George Mikes in *Encounter*, July–Aug. 1983, p. 37.

25. Arthur Koestler, *The Thirteenth Tribe: The Khazar Empire and Its Heritage* (London: Hutchinson, 1976), pp. 100, 172.

26. Hyam Maccoby, in a scathing obituary notice, makes a somewhat similar point about Koestler's attitude towards European Jewry, on grounds, however, with which I do not agree. *Encounter*, Sept.–Oct. 1983, pp. 50–53.

27. This was the first series of Radio Free Europe Keynote Lectures (1963), subsequently published as pamphlet no. 10 under the same title by *Encounter*. It covered ten major broadcasts and ran to forty-five pages. The lectures, Hugh Thomas observed in his biography of Strachey, are "still in demand and used as a text on democracy by undergraduates all over the world." Hugh Thomas, *John Strachey* (London: Eyre Methuen, 1973), p. 293.

28. Strachey, *The Strangled Cry*, p. 12.

29. Cf. "[September 18, 1950]. Dinner in the House of Commons (private room) with the Crossmans. Other guests: John Strachey (now Secretary of State for War), Arthur Schlesinger Jr. and his wife and Raymond Aron. Very lively discussion about the isolationist line of the Labour Government, and of the British in general. John S. [Strachey] and Dick [Crossman] defended this against everybody else; their line is that they'd be delighted to see France, Germany, Italy and Benelux getting together so long as Britain doesn't have to be in, submitting to the authority of shady foreigners and having the welfare state corrupted by immoral inhabitants of non-socialist countries." Goodman, ed., *Living with Koestler*, p. 159.

30. *The Strangled Cry*, p. 12. I quote Strachey from his book, but what he told me that day over lunch was almost identical with the view he had committed to paper.

31. "What makes it nevertheless hard to take this final step is the reflection of the pain it is bound to inflict on my few surviving friends, and above all my wife Cynthia. It is to her that I owe the relative peace and happiness that I enjoyed in the last period of my life—and never before." From "To Whom It May Concern," *Encounter*, July–Aug. 1983, p. 17.

32. (Lord) Thomas of Swynnerton, chairman of the Centre for Policy Studies.

33. Leader of the British Labour Party; see report of his speech at the Labour Party Conference in Brighton, *Daily Telegraph*, Oct. 5, 1983.

34. "Wrapped in the Mantle of History," *Guardian*, Oct. 1, 1983.

35. Enoch Powell, "The Ominous Misunderstanding of Soviet Intentions," *Guardian*, Oct. 10, 1983.

36. Margaret Thatcher, *The Downing Street Years* (London: HarperCollins, 1993), p. 813.

Chapter Fourteen: 1956 Reconsidered

1. George Urban, *The Nineteen Days: A Broadcaster's Account of the Hungarian Revolution* (London: Heinemann, 1957). Some of this book is based on a collection of eyewitness accounts by Hungarian refugees, recorded by members of the Hungarian-language staff of the BBC in November–December 1956 and early 1957 under my supervision. The resulting transcripts ran to 950 pages. Most aspects of the fighting and most parts of the country were covered.

2. The first Soviet intervention, involving Soviet troops already stationed on Hungarian territory, came, formally at least, in response to a call by the Hungarian Stalinist government of Hegedüs on October 23–24, 1956. It ended in a standoff amounting to a short-lived political victory for the revolution. The second intervention was a full-scale invasion from abroad by fresh Soviet forces, on November 4, 1956. These were insinuated by deception; one of the sources of the disinformation was Yuri Andropov, the Soviet ambassador in Budapest, and another Mikhail Suslov and Anastas Mikoyan, who were in Budapest "advising" the Hungarian communists. We learn from KGB general Oleg Kalugin: "Andropov was to make his name by playing a pivotal role in suppressing the Hungarian uprising. During the 1956 revolution, Andropov earned a reputation as a cool leader in a crisis. Especially valuable to the Kremlin were his repeated assertions to the Hungarian leader Imre Nagy that the Soviet troops were, in fact, not pouring into the country but were being withdrawn. It was a total lie, but Andropov was so convincing that—even as Soviet troops were launching a final offensive to crush the rebellion—the Soviet ambassador convinced Nagy that the Red Army was on its way home" (Kalugin, *SpyMaster*, p. 255).

3. On May 13, 1986, William E. Griffith, the 1956 Munich policy adviser, ex-

plained in an interview in Bonn with László Ribánszky, head of the Hungarian Service of Radio Free Europe: "One of the problems we faced was what to do about these broadcasts from the provincial radios, which we could hear, although they could not be heard throughout most of Hungary, because we had better means of listening to their broadcasts. We decided that we would simply broadcast summaries of what they were saying. Now, what they were saying at that time was—I would not say inflammatory, but certainly calling for continued revolutionary activity. On the other hand, it is difficult to see how it would have been if we didn't report what was going on in the country" (Radio Free Europe broadcast, unpublished).

4. John P. C. Matthews in the *Budapest Sun*, Nov. 4-10, 1993.

5. In the judgement of Vámos, with whom I spent time in Budapest examining some of his materials in May 1996, the tape recordings were more likely to have come from German civilian or military monitoring sources than from Radio Free Europe. This would make sense, for the materials handed over for examination to the German government in 1956 are said to have been in the form of scripts, not tape recordings.

6. From a sloganised appeal of October 28, 1956, urging the revolutionaries to take control of the the Ministries of the Interior and Defence. Imre Nagy was prime minister. This, like many other anonymous appeals, was introduced by the first bars of Beethoven's fifth symphony.

7. From Julián Borsányi's letter to Ralph E. Walter, director of Radio Free Europe, Munich, February 13, 1969. Borsányi makes the same point in the émigré journal *Magyar Élet* (Hungarian life), "What Was Behind Colonel Bell's Programmes of 'Incitement'?" Nov. 28, 1981.

8. Urban, *The Nineteen Days*, p. 269.

9. Sándor Márai, *Napló* [Diary] *1945-1957*, entry for November 22, 1956, quoting an eyewitness (Washington: Vörösváry Publishing Co., 1958), p. 311.

10. James A. Michener, *The Bridge at Andau* (New York, 1957), pp. 250-253.

11. One of these, issued by William E. Griffith, at 1500 on October 31, 1956, warned against accepting a Finnish type of solution and pointed to Cardinal Mindszenty as having the prestige necessary to lead the nation.

12. "With no less joy have we learnt that our beloved sons, cardinals of the Holy Roman Church, Stefan Wyszynski . . . and József Mindszenty . . . who had been expelled from their sees, are acknowledged to be innocent men, unjustly accused of crime, and as such have been restored to their positions of honour and responsibility and welcomed in triumph by rejoicing multitudes" ("Laetamur admodum," *Acta Apostolicae Sedis* 48 [1956], pp. 745-748).

13. From Miklós Lázár's report from Madison Square Garden, New York, "ten days before the American presidential elections," October 27, 1956 [emotional, shrill delivery].

14. "Report of Mikoyan and Suslov to the CPSU Central Committee, Budapest, October 25, 1956," A "Jelcin dosszié" [The Yeltsin file] (Budapest, 1993), p. 51.

15. András Hegedüs, *Élet egy eszme árnyékában*, pp. 262-263. Yuri Andropov, the Soviet ambassador, forwarded the letter to the Soviet government only on October 28, 1956:

Budapest, October 28, 1956.
In code
Top Secret
Not to be copied
Sent from Budapest. Urgent

I hereby forward a letter from the Hungarian Government
to
The Council of Ministers of the Soviet Socialist Republics
Moscow:
On behalf of the Council of Ministers of the People's Republic of Hungary, I appeal to the government of the Soviet Union to send Soviet troops in order to put an end to the riots that have broken out in Budapest, to restore order as soon as possible and to guarantee the conditions for peaceful and creative work.
October 24, 1956
Budapest
Prime Minister of the People's Republic of Hungary
András Hegedüs.
28.X.56 [October 28, 1956] Andropov

Andropov Report, October 28, 1956, Cold War International History Project, *Bulletin* no. 5 (Washington, D.C.), Spring 1995, pp. 30-31.
    16. "Mikoyan-Suslov Report," Oct. 27, 1956, *Bulletin* no. 5, pp. 29-30.
    17. V. N. Malin's handwritten notes on meetings of the Soviet leadership, *Döntés a Kremlben, 1956: A szovjet pártelnökség vitái Magyarországról* [Decision at the Kremlin, 1956: Debates of the Soviet Party Presidium on Hungary], Vjacseszlav Szereda and Rainer M. János, eds. (Budapest, 1996), p. 37. The Old Bolsheviks' assessments are quoted from pp. 70-72.
    18. For evidence of Imre Nagy's enlistment and activities as NKVD agent "Volodya" and the circumstances in which former KGB chairman V. Kriuchkov brought these facts to Gorbachev's attention on the day of Imre Nagy's reburial in Budapest as a national hero (June 16, 1989), see "Report on Agent 'Volodya': Russian Documents on Imre Nagy," *Bulletin* no. 5, pp. 36-37. For inspired speculation about the extent to which Nagy's work as an informer was responsible for the repression of fellow communists under Stalin's terror, see Rainer M. János, *Nagy Imre:* Politikai életrajz [Political biography], vol. 1, *1896-1953* (Budapest: Institute for the Study of the 1956 Revolution, 1993), pp. 199-212. At his trial in June 1958, Nagy himself stated that during World War II he had been an NKVD officer. See Dér Ferenc, *Nagy Imre, Egy magyar miniszterelnök* [A Hungarian prime minister] (Pécs: Regie, 1993), pp. 21-22. Also, Pavel Sudoplatov and Anatoly Sudoplatov report (*Special Tasks: The Memoirs of an Unwanted Witness—A Soviet SpyMaster* [London: Little, Brown, 1994], p. 367): "Since the 1930s Nagy had been a full-time NKVD agent, code-named Volodya, whose services were considered highly valuable."
    19. The magnitude of the insurgents' success can be gauged from Marshal Zhukov and Marshal Sokolovsky's joint report to the Soviet leadership on October 24, 1956, giving a detailed rundown of Soviet forces deployed for the suppression of "unrest" in Budapest on the night of October 23, 1956 (Malin, *Döntés a Kremlben, 1956,* pp. 171-172):

> We have put a total of five Soviet divisions on a state of the highest alert . . . :

manpower strength	31,000
tanks and self-propelled guns	1,130
artillery pieces and mortars	615
anti-aircraft batteries	185
armoured personnel carriers	380
other vehicles	3,930

> At the same time we put on the highest alert one fighter division and one fighter-bomber division out of our air forces stationed Hungary, as well as one fighter

division and one fighter-bomber division in the Carpathian Military District—a total of 159 fighter aircraft and 122 bombers. . . . The Special Rifle Division, having entered Budapest between 2:00 and 4:00 hours local time, has taken the city's most important objectives and is continuing the restoration of order. . . .
October 24, 1956
G. Zhukov
V. Sokolovsky

It is worth noting that these forces were comparable to the entire armoured strength of the British army in 1978 (900 tanks, 252 self-propelled guns), and superior (at least in numerical terms) to the armoured strength of the British army in 1996 (541 tanks, 179 self-propelled guns). The fresh Soviet forces deployed against Hungary on November 4, 1956, were still more powerful.

The total number of Soviet troops deployed in Hungary during the revolution and its aftermath was 7,349 officers and 51,472 men. Soviet casualties were given as 669 killed, 1,540 wounded, 51 missing. Hungarian civil casualties resulting from the fighting between October 23 and December 31, 1956, were 2,652 killed, 19,226 wounded.

Number of convictions by various courts under the Kádár government between November 4, 1956, and April 1, 1958: 14,378.

Number of executions in the same period: 229. Of these, 31.8 percent were aged fifteen to twenty-four; 42.8 percent, twenty-five to thirty-four; 17.5 percent, thirty-five to forty-four (*1956 Kézikönyve: Megtorlás és Emlékezés* [Handbook for 1956: Reprisals and remembrance], András B. Hegedüs, chief editor; Peter Kende, ed. (Budapest, 1996), pp. 301–307. The Soviet military figures are taken from the Archive of the Politburo of the CPSU.

20. Robert T. Holt, *Radio Free Europe* (Minneapolis: University of Minnesota Press, 1958), p. 167.

21. Gomulka's speech at the eighth session of the Central Committee of the Polish United Workers' Party, *Szabad Nép*.

22. Malin, *Döntés a Kremlben, 1956*, 165–169.

23. William E. Griffith, "RFE and the Hungarian Revolution and the Polish October," conference paper at the international conference "Hungary and the World, 1956: The New Archival Evidence," Budapest, Sept. 26–29, 1996.

24. Veljko Mićunović, *Moscow Diary* (London: Chatto and Windus, 1980), pp. 141, 134.

25. *Manchester Guardian*, Nov. 2, 1956.

26. I use the word *quisling* advisedly. Kádár's warning words to the Soviet leaders at the November 2 and November 3, 1956, enlarged sessions of the Soviet Presidium in Moscow may surprise the historian. Kádár was about to stab his country in the back, but he was doing so with a troubled conscience. That cannot, however, change the fact that on November 4, 1956, having deserted Imre Nagy's national government, of which he had been a member, he returned to Hungary at the head of a Soviet-appointed group and then proceeded to suppress the national uprising, sending more than two hundred of the revolution's leading participants, including his friend Imre Nagy and his associates, to the gallows. What is the proof of the dichotomy in Kádár's thinking?

The so-called Malin documents which came to light in 1995 (published in Budapest as *Döntés a Kremlben, 1956*, in 1996) show us (if the accuracy of these handwritten skeleton notes can be trusted) a János Kádár trying to fight off the spectre of being reduced to the status of a Soviet puppet, while at the same time committing himself loyally to the Soviet view that what was happening under Nagy in

Hungary was, in the final analysis, a counterrevolution which had to be put down by the Red Army.

On November 2, 1956, Kádár assured the Soviet Presidium that "the insurgents . . . were workers . . . they [merely] wanted to remove the Rákosi clique. . . . We didn't at first see that; we declared [the whole thing] to be a counterrevolution, thus turning the people against us. [But] they didn't feel themselves to be counterrevolutionaries. . . . No one wanted a counterrevolution." Kádár then told the Soviet leaders that, as a member of Imre Nagy's government, he, too, had voted for the declaration of Hungary's neutrality (pp. 75, 79).

On November 3, Kádár was once again trying to overcome his dilemma and soothe his conscience. He reminded the Soviet Presidium that Hungarian "national feelings had been insulted," that the Hungarian people "did not want to destroy the people's democratic system," that "the withdrawal of Soviet troops from Hungary was very important," that "any strengthening of military relations between us [Hungary and the Soviet Union] will weaken us politically," and that the new government "must not become a puppet government . . . it needs for its activities the support of the workers" (pp. 89–90).

In one and the same breath, however, he stressed that "communists are being murdered [in Hungary]. The counterrevolutionaries are the murderers, and Nagy is providing them with cover. The government is powerless to put them down. What is to be done? A socialist country must never be surrendered to the counterrevolution. We agree with you [the Soviet leaders] that the right thing to do is to form a revolutionary government" (pp. 89–90).

Thus the schizoid attitude that was to suffuse Kádár's long rule—an increasingly permissive, anti-Stalinist communism at home on the one hand, and unswerving allegiance to the Soviet Union on the other—had its origins at these dramatic meetings of the Soviet Presidium. The November 3 meeting of the Soviet Presidium ended the day's business with the appointment of Kádár as Hungarian prime minister and the naming of other members of the new Hungarian government.

János Kádár's betrayal is clear. As a leading member (minister of state) of Imre Nagy's government, which was facing a life-threatening confrontation with the Soviet superpower, Kádár defected to the enemy camp in the government's and the Hungarian nation's hour of need (late November 1, 1956), returning from there at the head of Soviet forces three days later as the Soviet Union's appointed agent. None of the concessions he made in subsequent years—having first settled scores with the leaders of the uprising—can change or atone for the fact that on November 4, 1956, János Kádár was indeed a quisling.

That Kádár owed his appointment to the Soviet leaders, and no one else, is unmistakeably clear from Khrushchev's own account of the circumstances in which the choice was made. Talking to the Polish Communist leaders headed by Gomulka in May 1957, Khrushchev recalled: "The following day [November 3, 1956] . . . Tito personally took us to the port [of Brioni]. . . . We said farewell, we kissed each other. Well then—we took action. . . . I arrived [in Moscow] by air with Malenkov at three or four in the afternoon. Kádár as well. Bulganin called from Sofia, at the time he did not know Kádár. . . . They [sic—Khrushchev and Bulganin] discussed who was to be the premier. They decided on Kádár. When they asked the Hungarians, they all said Kádár, although at first they thought [Ferenc] Münnich or Kádár. And that's how we formed the [Hungarian] government in Moscow. At 4:15 [November 4], Zhukov began to act."

"Notes of talks carried out on May 24 and 25 [1957] between the Party-State PPR [Polish People's Republic] Delegation and the Party-State USSR Delegation," document no. 17 in *The Hidden History of Hungary, 1956: A Compendium of Declassi-*

fied Documents, Csaba Békés, Malcolm Byrne, and Christian F. Ostermann, eds. (Budapest: Institute for the History of the 1956 Hungarian Revolution; Washington: National Security Archive, 1996), n.p.

János M. Rainer, one of the foremost analysts of the 1956 Hungarian Revolution, describes Kádár's selection by the Soviet leaders in the following words: "This [Khrushchev's] thinking about the personality of the future leader of a country which was, after all, at least formally sovereign . . . reminds one of those [imperial] crown councils at which the governor of some second-rate colony was chosen" (Döntés a Kremlben, 1956, p. 142).

27. N. S. Khrushchev, Khrushchev Remembers, with an introduction, commentary, and notes by Edward Crankshaw (London: Sphere Books, 1971), p. 381. On October 31, when the Soviet Presidium finally decided to invade Hungary, Khrushchev couched his proposal for the invasion in these words:

> The [our earlier] evaluation should be revised; the [our] troops should not be withdrawn from Hungary and Budapest; we should take the initiative in restoring order in Hungary.
> If we withdrew from Hungary, this would encourage the American, English, and French imperialists.
> They would regard this as [a sign of] our weakness and go over onto the offensive.
> [Our withdrawal] would demonstrate the weakness of our positions.
> In that case our party would not understand us.
> We would be handing them [the imperialists] Hungary in addition to Egypt.
> We have no other choice (notes from the CPSU C.C. Presidium session, October 31, 1956, compiled by V. N. Malin, published in Döntés a Kremlben, p. 62).

28. Mićunović, Moscow Diary, p. 133.

29. Zoltán Benkő, "Szabad Európa Rádió, 1956 október 24–november 3," Valóság [Reality], 1993, no. 5 (Budapest), p. 83.

30. Report of International Research Associates, "Hungary and the 1956 Uprising," pp. 3–4, quoted in Urban, The Nineteen Days, p. 269.

31. Interview in CIA–Weapon in the Cold War, BBC/Bavarian Radio Television documentary, part 1, 1992.

32. General Béla Király, Honvédségből Néphadsereg (Paris–New Brunswick: Edition Magyar Füzetek [Hungarian letters], 1986), pp. 283, 292.

33. Kálmán Mikszáth, "Az öreg diktátor" [The old dictator], in Töviskés látogatóban [Töviskés on a visit] (Budapest: Franklin, n.d.), p. 171.

34. On May 22, 1997, Radio Free Europe pledged to provide the Hungarian National Széchenyi Library with copies of about five thousand audiotapes, some six kilometers of microfilm, and about seven hundred thousand pages of programme scripts. According to a Radio Free Europe statement, these materials contain copies of everything that was preserved at the Radio from the 1951–93 period. On June 6, 1997, A. Ross Johnson, consellor to RFE/RL, noted, "This is far from a complete record. . . . The tape collection is very partial."

35. Senator Feingold may have been unaware that the vast majority of Russians and Central and East Europeans have no command of English and cannot therefore make sense of the transmissions of CNN. Nor can they expect CNN to provide continuous expert information about their internal affairs.

Appendix A

1. Erich Mielke, minister for state security.
2. I.e., opposite number or authority.
3. Major General Gerhard Neiber, deputy minister for state security.

Appendix C

1. Document no. 16, *The Hidden History of Hungary, 1956*, Békés, Byrne, and Ostermann, eds. Reprinted by permission.

Index

Acheson, Dean, 209–210
Adenauer, Konrad, 214
Ady, Endre, 22, 199
Albania, 7, 133–135
Aliulis, Pater Vaclovas, 109
Andrejevs, Georgs, 109
Andropov, Yuri, 230, 307
Antall, József, 108
anticommunism, 64, 71, 81–82
anti-Semitism, 65–66, 68–70, 71
arms control, 6
Aron, Raymond, 306, 307
Austria, lessons from, 150–151
Aytay, Miklós, 221

Bailey, George, 6, 66, 70, 75, 89, 95–96,
    139, 153, 156, 158
Balkans, 133–135, 242, 243. *See also*
    Yugoslavia
Baltic states, 108–109, 185
Barzini, Luigi, 172
Bavaria, 82, 83–87
BBC, 2, 27–28, 46, 53–58, 86–87, 211–212,
    227, 231
    George Urban and, 17, 20, 54–58, 86,
    211–212
Belgrade agreements, 242
Beloff, Lord, 294
Berkes, Ross, 81–82
Berlin, Isaiah, 33
Berlinguer, Enrico, funeral of, 263–264
Berman, Jakub, 26
Bernard, Noel, 56, 127
Berton, Peter, 35
Béry, László, 217, 218, 222, 224, 281, 282,
    286–291 *passim*

Bethell, Nicholas, 183
Bialer, Seweryn, 222
Binder, David, 90
Bitov, Oleg, 259
B'Nai Brith, 66
Board for International Broadcasting
    (BIB), 38, 59, 71–72, 74
Bogomolov, Oleg, 276
Bogyay, Tamás, 290
Borkenau, Franz, 49
Borsányi, Julián ("Colonel Bell"), 217,
    218–219, 224, 282–283, 287
Bosnia, 244
Bourdeaux, Rev. Michael, 294
brainwashing, 40
Brandt, Willy, 67
Brazauskas, Algirdas, 163
Brezhnev, Leonid, 43, 77, 274
Britain, social and political shortcomings
    of, 15–16, 17, 22–23, 54, 82–83, 86–87,
    114, 179, 205, 209–210
Brooke, Nathalie, 294
Brown, James F., 165, 167, 303
Brzezinski, Zbigniew, 32, 135, 303
Buber-Neumann, Margarete, 47, 303
Buchanan, Patrick, 90, 91
Buckley, James, 70, 74, 89, 101, 107, 139,
    153, 154–157, 299
Bujak, Zbigniew, 147
Bukovsky, Vladimir, 90
Bulganin, Nikolai A., 225
Burks, Richard V., 34, 47, 303
Burnham, James, 49
businessmen, Western, 37

Café Dnieper, Kiev, meeting at, 14–15